In India, the land of *netas* and *babus*, reality seems almost surreal, like the dream that took Alice through Wonderland.

T.S.R. Subramanian's book is anecdotal, combining wit with irony. It incisively pieces together the gradual decay in public administration in post-British India. The growing subservience of the bureaucracy to the political system unravels step by step. A self-serving elite is formed that is preoccupied with its vested interests. The entire administration, its infrastructure and its development programmes become the terrain for serving the personal and political interests of the *neta* and *babu*. The voice of the common man in India goes unheard. The poor continue to remain in poverty. The humour and crispness of the narrative barely conceal this underlying theme which is the central focus of the book: it is not a memoir, nor gossip chatter.

TSR bases his book on his rich repertoire of experience and a prodigious memory for detail. The book documents, through a personal narrative, forty years of politics and bureaucracy. However, as a portrayal essentially of the human condition, it has timeless value with universal appeal.

The book starts with the young officer in idyllic field postings in Uttar Pradesh. He gradually learns the ropes before moving into the corridors of the Secretariat in Lucknow, and then Delhi. The transition from the lilting and unhurried pace of rural India to the rough and tumble of central administration is seamlessly developed. The narrative has a comprehensive sweep, including anecdotes and analysis covering agriculture and rural development, industrial policy, the license Raj and privatisation; India's trade, trade policy and GATT; the Emergency and rule of law; public policy and administrative reforms.

A retired IAS officer from Uttar Pradesh cadre, T.S.R. Subramanian had his primary education in Thanjavur, Tamil Nadu and college education in Kolkata, West Bengal. He then obtained a Diploma from the Imperial College of Science in London, and later a Masters degree from Harvard University. He joined the IAS in 1961. After working in a series of field assignments, he moved into posts in the state secretariat at Lucknow and had stints in the Commerce and Textile Ministries of the Government of India at New Delhi. He was chief secretary of U.P. in the period immediately after Babri Masjid. He rose to the post of Cabinet secretary in Government of India, the highest civil service position in the government, and worked under three prime ministers in this capacity. He also worked for five years as senior adviser in the International Trade Centre, Geneva, a U.N. organisation. Currently, he spends much of his time on the golf course.

JOURNEYS THROUGH
BABUDOM AND *NETALAND*

Governance in India

T.S.R. SUBRAMANIAN

RUPA

Published by
Rupa Publications India Pvt. Ltd 2004
7/16, Ansari Road, Daryaganj
New Delhi 110002

Sales centres:
Allahabad Bengaluru Chennai
Hyderabad Jaipur Kathmandu
Kolkata Mumbai

ISBN: 978-81-291-0587-5

10 9 8 7 6 5 4 3 2

The moral right of the author has been asserted.

Printed at Rekha Printers Pvt. Ltd., New Delhi

Dedicated to
Lalitha, Bharti, Shankar and Amy

Dedicated to

Jalabhai, Bhanu, Shabnam and Amy

CONTENTS

ACKNOWLEDGEMENTS

I would like to thank S Ganesh and Kamala Ganesh for editing the book.

PREFACE

I WALK DOWN THE LUSH GREEN FAIRWAY, THE dew crunching under my feet, seeing the first rays of the sun. The therapeutic green of the golf course brings me peace and solace. My mind wanders back in time to memories of the past. It goes back sixty years. I am standing on the lawns in front of my primary school building in Thanjavur town. The national flag proudly flutters in the morning breeze. The day is 15th August. I can hear my principal as he proudly proclaims, "You are now free. Your future is now in your hands. The good Lord will give you, the children of this country, what is your due. A glorious future lies ahead."

My mind wanders again. I recall the scene of my interview for the Indian Administrative Service (IAS) examination, at the Dholpur house in New Delhi. I had just arrived from London to appear for this interview. One of the board members asked me as to why I wanted to join the administrative service, when I was already set on a future abroad in the field of science. My answer came naturally, spontaneously: "I want to have a chance to serve the people of India." As I walk down the greens now, I look back and try to recall how the board members took this simple response. I had given a matter of fact reply, not an uncommon one those days. There was a natural acceptance of what was said. And today after retirement, while sitting in the IAS interview board, I would sometimes put this same question back to the candidates. But never would I get the same reply that I gave then. If someone were to talk of a desire to serve the public, it would sound hollow, contrived. A board member or two might even conceal a smirk on his face.

In the heyday of the national movement, Subramanya Bharati, patriot and Tamil poet, had imagined the future independent India: "Even if only one of our 30 crore population suffers from want, we will destroy the whole world," he wrote. As of recent count, there were at least thirty crore poor in India. If we were to redeem Bharati's pledge today, one would have to destroy the entire solar system, not just the earth.

In August 2002, I undertook a railway journey from Delhi to Chennai and back. It was my first train journey in a long time; in the later years of my civil service career I had got used to hopping in and out of places by air. Cutting across the heart of India, the train passed through a number of states – Delhi, Haryana, Uttar Pradesh, Madhya Pradesh, Maharashtra, Andhra Pradesh and Tamil Nadu. It was monsoon time. As I looked out of my air-conditioned compartment I could see people wading in ankle or knee deep water. There was a slum area close to every railway station, big or small. Large tracts of railway property were occupied and densely packed with people. In ramshackle mud housing with leaking tarpaulin, or tin covers, hundreds of thousands of people were eking out an existence, euphemistically called 'living below the poverty line'. I could not imagine how they survived disease, how the sick members could revive from illness, how the children could get the most basic of education. I doubt if this sight would have been very much different if had I taken some other route.

Later, at a party, when I was enjoying a drink on the luxurious lawns of a farmhouse in Delhi, I talked about the scenes I saw to a senior railway board member; I also jokingly chided him for not protecting railway property. He seemed greatly distressed by what I described, and was upset that I was subjected to these unseemly sights. He asked me, in full earnest, "But you did not have to see all that; why did you not draw the curtains on the windows? Were they not functioning?"

The bottom third of our population is invisible when the curtains are drawn, counted out in all calculations: it does not exist in India for all practical purposes. All the policy initiatives and developmental actions are taken by the top half of the population, for their own benefit; and all the moves are driven by the group interests of the major players: the politicians, bureaucrats, businessmen, professionals and the judiciary. There is an unspoken conspiracy that India belongs exclusively to this ruling class, with the middle classes being the beneficiaries of the leftovers;

and the poorest one-third left behind. This is the post independence dharma of India.

I came to this realisation about our invisible population gradually and cumulatively in the course of thirty-seven years in the IAS. I have spent many years of my career in Uttar Pradesh, from the most backward districts to the secretariat in Lucknow and public sector corporations in Kanpur. I served as chief secretary of Uttar Pradesh and this gave me a vantage view of the working of the entire state administration. My stint as Cabinet secretary in the Central Government likewise, gave me insights into the hub of national policy making and implementation, the pulls and pressures, the dynamics. I have also had postings in Madras, Delhi and in a United Nations organisation in Geneva. My early perceptions on what motivates the actions of the ruling classes have been reinforced in each and every posting.

The system has deteriorated from what it was when I joined. This perception is only partly explained by my own growth from a young, enthusiastic and a somewhat naïve probationer to an experienced bureaucrat who got to see the underside of government and participate in its inner workings. At entry point, one can still see enthusiasm and sincerity, but somewhere along the line, the system nudges young officers onto a different track. Whether at all I managed to escape this trap, or fell prisoner so long as I was in the thick of service, the reader can best judge. It is a question that is put to me from time to time.

Not that everything was lily white when I joined. One could see some colonial remnants in attitudes and practices that did exist, but there was none of the total cynicism with which the system is manipulated. I might have been impressionable in those younger days but I do carry the impression that there were then a much larger number of outstanding personalities – both bureaucrats and politicians – dedicated to the values of good administration and government. I saw senior officers then acting with autonomy and gumption, not bowing down to their political masters – or afraid of their juniors. But the tide has turned, the balance has shifted, and what we now have are the remnants of a system whose innards have crumbled.

If an explanation must be found for the present rot, it can be argued that the success and efficiency of the British system of administration was in the context of a colonial state and a subject people, outside the democratic framework. Our society had its primordial loyalties to family, caste, clan or faith and furthermore, the ground reality was that of a deeply hierarchical society with skewed distribution of wealth and privileges. This was an inheritance from many centuries. The kinds of checks and balances and accountability needed to anchor a modern administration within a democratic framework were just not in place after Independence. So, in this view, the developments in the fifty-five years since Independence are simply an inevitable unfolding of an inherent structural weakness. But such analysis can become an endless and arid zone of debate, secondary to the sheer immediacy of the quiet drama that is being enacted in India.

Be that as it may, the tale that I tell here is a straightforward one of the various posts and assignments that I held, the people, places and events that made a deep impression on me. Not all the anecdotes convey a message. It is also a tale of human foibles and heroism, the beauty of the Uttar Pradesh country side, the texture of life there and in the corridors of the secretariat, and the delights of travel be it Ranikhet or Firenze. Leaving these interludes aside, the drift of events, and the trend of changes, as I look back, is unmistakable. It is a tale of betrayal of the people of India.

The sometimes flippant tone of my narration is a response to the ludicrous, indeed tragicomic, texture of governance in India: the casual way in which events are dealt with by those who have defining power over the everyday lives of millions of ordinary people. It is an idiom to express my sense of sadness.

1 MORADABAD: FIRST POST

*The lantern was swaying rhythmically with the dim
light and looming shadows making bizarre patterns.
I saw a large spider moving just a few feet away from
my right foot.*

*The experienced old man told me: "Never commit
your position in writing". It was a lesson I chose to
ignore in my own career.*

I REACHED MORADABAD TOWN IN UTTAR
Pradesh, in the middle of the rainy season of 1962. It was the first assignment
of my career. Till that time I had never had any contact whatsoever with
the government apparatus. This was also my first foray into the 'Hindi
belt'. Not having seen till then a real life tehsildar, indeed not even having
heard of the institution of district magistrate till the stint at the training
academy in Mussoorie, I was a little apprehensive about what awaited me
in rural India. In the event, my entry was fairly smooth and pleasant. I was
received in the household of the collector of the district, S V S Juneja, with
his command that I should stay in his bungalow for the first few months.

Indeed, it was an old custom that the British joint magistrates arriving
fresh from Oxford or Cambridge, needed to be 'broken in' before being
exposed directly to the wilderness of India – hence the time-honoured
system of spending the initial two or three months living in the household
of the collector. This was an excellent arrangement. The young entrant
could absorb the sights and experiences in a cushioned environment, till
he got over the bewilderment of the small-town ambience, and the realities
of local administration. This provided for a gentle entry period. Years later,

when I went to Ghazipur as collector, I continued the practice. The two joint magistrates who were posted under me in successive years spent their first few months in the collector's house and got the first taste of their field postings from there. Alas, I understand this custom is no longer in vogue.

Moradabad seemed very far from the training academy at Mussoorie located barely a hundred miles away. Here, I had spent the past year, carefree in the company of young fellow probationers, in a semi-academic atmosphere. I had spent the year previous to that in London as a student in the Imperial College of Science and Technology, working for my Diploma, a halfway house to a doctorate in applied mechanics. Professor Scorer, my tutor, had been aghast at my desire to disappear into the rural wilderness of India, abandoning the pristine beauty of investigating large perturbances in air-flow in the atmosphere. He was so distressed by this thought that he had offered me a fellowship to continue my research. An annual expense paid holiday to India was an additional inducement for me to stay on. His final words when I bid him goodbye were, "I am taking over my new position as Professor at Ann Arbor, Michigan, and here is my address. You can join me there any time. All you have to do is to send me a telegram as to when you are arriving in Ann Arbor, and reach there without waiting for a reply. This offer is valid for two years from today." Before going to London, I had spent the previous eight years as a student in Calcutta where I completed my MSc in Mathematics.

As I ventured about exploring the collectorate compound, Moradabad also looked very far from South Kensington and Esplanade. I would sit in as a spectator at the collector's *mulaqadi* – a daily ritual lasting for an hour after breakfast, in the collector's official chambers attached to his residence. During this hour, anyone could come to await a brief meeting with the collector himself. All kinds of people from the town and countryside – farmers, doctors, petty politicians, informers – would come in one by one to spend a few seconds, or a minute or two, or if their spiel was interesting enough, even five or ten minutes. They would recount their woes, ask for assistance, give information, or merely squeal on a fellow human being – stabbing colleagues in the back was a popular sport then, as it is now. The entire goings-on in the district would reach the collector's ears one way or the other. Much of the information received was heavily spiced or disguised with spin by the sycophants or the supplicants – each ingratiating visitor had an ulterior motive; but at the end of all the interminable gossip and intrigue, a picture of people and events would emerge. There were naturally some patterns to these visits. One sycophant, when asked why he had come, would say, "I have come for your *darshan*"; to which an exasperated collector would reply briskly, "O.K., you have had *darshan*; you can go now." By whatever name this practice was called, I found out later that most successful field administrators followed it. They would set apart a generous slice of the day just to meet people and listen to what they had to say.

Within a week of my arrival, the collector went on a monsoon inspection visit of the tehsil at Thakurdwara, located twenty-five miles away from Moradabad town. I went along. We reached there at dusk, for the night halt at the local inspection house. This was a small bungalow with three large bedrooms, each with an attached bathroom cum toilet, one of which was allotted to me. Electric power did not reach Thakurdwara those days – there were no ceiling fans. Each bedroom and bathroom had a six feet by two piece of heavy dark cloth hanging vertically from the ceiling, with control ropes leading outside the room. The *punkahwala*, a peon who was located out of sight, would slowly sway back and forth with the rope, thus rustling the *punkah* to generate movement of the air. There was a 'Petromax' lamp in the bedroom and a kerosene lantern in the bathroom, which was furnished with a wooden portable commode, as running water had not yet reached Thakurdwara. I wonder if it has by now. Soon after we reached the guesthouse, the collector had a brief discussion with the tehsildar. After a leisurely cup of tea in the porch, we retired to our respective rooms, to get ready for dinner.

It was late in the evening, as I sat on the seat in the toilet. The lantern which was set a little farther away, was slightly unstable on its perch and was swaying rhythmically, with the dim light and looming shadows making bizarre patterns. These created an eerie sight in the stillness of the late evening, in the jungle like surroundings. Suddenly, I saw a large spider seemingly with hundreds of legs, moving not far away from my right foot. In the shadow of the swaying light, it had a frightening effect on me. For a few moments, I was genuinely scared. It was all in the mind, but the loneliness of the atmosphere and the presence of the tarantula so close to my immobile foot suddenly gave me the shivers. I asked myself, "What the hell am I doing here, in this remote area, which does not even have electricity, in the company of spiders and ghosts. I am through with all this; next week I am on my way to Ann Arbor in far away Michigan." I instantly forgot the tarantula and was already composing a telegram to Dr Scorer in my mind.

Next evening, when I returned to Moradabad, I went to the local post office and telephoned my father at Calcutta, to tell him that enough of this wilderness. I was returning to Calcutta the next day; I would leave for the USA, as soon as I got my visa. I had then, as always, underestimated my father's understanding of events and people. He did not interrupt me, and told me that if this was what I really wanted to do, he would help me make my travel plans. But he also said that as a personal favour, could I give it a try for three more months? After that, at any time I chose, I could make my way to USA. In his subtle way, he had given me sound advice, advocating a little time for allowing my thoughts to settle. Looking back at the Thakurdwara inspection house, if someone were to now offer me a holiday in a place like that in the wilds, with nothing to disturb one's sleep except the odd tarantula and a few ghosts, I would grab the chance.

The next evening at 5'o clock, as we were preparing to leave for Moradabad, Juneja asked the tehsildar for the bill for the expenses, and added that every item should be included. That is how, as we sat in the collector's pick up, after he had paid for the food for both of us at Thakurdwara, including one dinner, one breakfast, one lunch – in all a princely sum of Rs.14 – we saw the first item in the bill "One cock: Rs.5/-". That was the deliciously cooked chicken curry we had the previous evening.

For the first two months, I was the understudy of a sub divisional magistrate, a fine old gentleman by the name of Tandon. Nearing the end of his long career of thirty-odd years, he had risen to the post of a sub divisional officer by unstinted hard work and merit, with a bit of luck thrown in. He started his career in the early 1930s as a lowly patwari – a village level functionary whose primary job it was to maintain the land records of the seasonal crops sown in each field, as well as the ownership details, over an area of four or five villages. Tandon had many stories to tell. His memories went back to young British magistrates who would, whip in hand, gallop from village to village surveying the fields and verifying the authenticity and correctness of the entries in the patwari's registers; the whip would be used on an errant patwari or naib-tehsildar's back, much as on a slightly disobedient horse. Instructions were that I should spend all the time after breakfast with the sub divisional officer, go wherever he went and observe whatever he did, including sitting in his court to watch the proceedings – the sub divisional officer who had revenue and executive functions, also functioned as the sub divisional magistrate.

My first lessons in administration were learnt from Tandon. I was to remember him time and again during my career. One evening, we were returning after a field visit. It was already 11 pm by the time we were back in town, and there was no time for dinner. As we entered the town, Tandon drove straight to the petrol station and filled up his tank, even though it was more than a quarter full. Then, as he returned home, he meticulously reversed the car in his garage, before entering the house. When I asked him why these chores could not wait till the next morning, his answer was that a field officer should always be ready to leave at a moment's notice, as he could get news of some event at any time of day or night, requiring his immediate departure: he should not be delayed by unnecessary preparation time. Then, he added the following to conclude the lesson: It is imperative that one promptly reaches the site of an incident, be it a riot or a major accident or a natural disaster. It does not really matter what one does there; what matters is to be able to say later that one reached the spot immediately!

A further lesson was given to me by Tandon during that time: "Never commit your position in writing at any stage, unless it is absolutely essential. Do not sign any paper unnecessarily. Keep your options and opinions open at all times." Evidently he had followed this advice meticulously and with success. So, after all, government servants have been following this approach for decades. Even then, the police sub inspector would not maintain his General Diary up to date, only to fill it in much later, in a manner that was dictated by circumstances. This was one piece of advice though, that I chose to ignore in my own career. It got me the reputation of an effective and efficient officer; but then on more than one occasion it also landed me in serious trouble. Each time I would remember what Tandon had advised.

I had my first experience with a commission of enquiry during my Moradabad days, and this was also my first lesson about the survival instinct of government servants. There was a minor clash in the town and the district magistrate accompanied by the superintendent of police rushed to the spot, supported by a posse of policemen. In their judgement, the situation warranted action and some force had been used. The matter would ordinarily have been forgotten, but some influential people were present in the mêlée, including a few legislators who kicked up a ruckus. The government promptly ordered a judicial enquiry. Over the next month, I could see the careful preparations made by the local administration in advance of the inquiry. The paper work was created meticulously, new witnesses were discovered and coached, with much generation of 'authentic' information. All these ensured that there was no way in which any fault could be pinned on the local administration. To them, it did not so much matter what happened on the ground, so long as the authorities could establish that they were physically present at the place of the event and careful 'preparations' for an inquiry were done.

Some time within a month of my arrival, I was assigned to 'Mohurrum duty' at a large village called Aghwanpur, about fifteen miles from Moradabad. Mohurrum is an annual festival, essentially of the Shias, to commemorate an ancient event in the Muslim calendar. Tall, multicoloured and highly decorated structures of wood or bamboo called *tazias* are taken in a procession to the *karbala*, usually located just outside the town. At this time, tension often builds up between the Shia and Sunni sects, and sometimes Hindu-Muslim issues flare up. It also provides a field-day for anti-social elements to create disturbances and incite violence. The administration is on high alert in a large number of towns in Uttar Pradesh, where there has been a history of tension or communal clashes on Mohurrum.

Apparently, there had been some trouble at Aghwanpur the previous year and the district magistrate asked me to be present there on Mohurrum.

On the specified day, I reached Aghwanpur with my orderly in the morning, driving my own car as I did not have an official vehicle allotted to me. I was received by a tehsil official who asked me to stay in a room in the primary school building in the village, which was to be my base during this assignment. Some time in the afternoon, the senior most police officer, a young deputy superintendent of police assigned for Mohurrum duty called on me, and assured me that he had surveyed the scene and made the necessary enquiries, and that he anticipated no trouble or violence. However, some tension in the village arose upon the delay of *tazias* reaching the *karbala* that evening. Around 9 pm, there was a large mêlée in the centre of the village, not far from my base, with different groups charging at each other and making war like noises. I was not fully briefed as to what my role was to be, but the police officer was competent enough. He took charge, shouted a few instructions, and then some policemen swiftly came on the scene wielding *lathis* and the mob was rapidly dispersed. Around 11 pm, news came to us that the *tazias* had finally been taken to the *karbala*; the flash point was over. I settled down to rest in my room, but it was very uncomfortable with the mosquitoes allowing no sleep. Around 1 am, I decided to return to Moradabad, as indeed there was nothing more to do in the village.

There was no police escort or jeep available, and in a foolhardy move, I started in my small Fiat car on the journey back to Moradabad, accompanied only by my unarmed orderly. Soon after we reached the highway, when we were still about ten miles away from the town, I had to slow down the car as I saw a large obstruction in the middle of the road, just as we were entering a culvert. As I was about to stop, Ashfaq, my orderly, shouted to me to charge ahead fast. I gunned the motor, precariously manoeuvered the car in a narrow gap at the edge of the obstruction and hurtled past the culvert; just catching a glimpse of eight or ten people armed with sticks emerging from the shadows of the roadside under the culvert, and shouting at the top of their voices. They were local dacoits and it was indeed a providential escape. This incident taught me the lesson not to travel at night on rural roads without escort.

The festival of Holi, which marks the transition from winter to spring, was another occasion when communal tensions would get whipped up. Moradabad town had a reputation of being communally sensitive. The entire available police and the magistracy would be deployed on Holi duty, on the day of the festival. The celebration of Holi by the policemen themselves would take place two days later. Thus, at the police lines, there would be a rowdy and high-spirited celebration of Holi, with *bhang* flowing freely. Sarabjit Singh, a young magistrate from the Provincial Civil Service, with his recently married wife was a neighbour in our officer's colony. He was large and rotund, and had a jovial disposition. At the Police Line celebrations, Sarabjit was a popular target for the policemen, who would, in fun, dunk him in the water pond and give him unending glasses of *thandai*, laced liberally with *bhang*. Sarabjit was carried physically to his house at the end of the celebrations one afternoon; and he took a full ten days to recover from the overdose of *bhang*. Most of the following week, he was lying inert in his bed but occasionally would come to life in 'lucid' spells. He could be seen wearing just a lungi, working at a large plate containing a mountainous quantity of cooked rice and *dal*. Lost to the world, he would recite in free verse his own compositions in Bhojpuri, a language known for its richness and musicality. Sarabjit's continuous outpouring of free verse and lilting poetry was indeed a compelling sight, and those who knew, said the compositions were exquisite. The news of this impromptu composer spread rapidly and by the time Sarabjit regained normalcy, the number of daily visitors to hear him had swelled. Sarabjit later shared some technical information with me; he explained to me the difference between a heavy dose of whiskey and *bhang* – the first gets your head spinning round and round, while the latter makes the head go up and down. Alas, Sarabjit died not too many years later while still in service, and I lost a good friend.

Those days, the separation of the executive and judicial functions was still some years away and each executive magistrate had to act as presiding officer in the court room to try Special Act cases. The cases were mostly petty in nature, relating to violations of the Gambling Act, Opium Act, Essential Commodities Act and some others. For an administrator, presiding over a court case is excellent training. One can see that two versions of the same incident are presented, the facts are disputed; and even if agreed, the same fact is interpreted from diametrically opposite perspectives and arguments from different positions are presented. Thus, one quickly learns that there are two possible views in a given situation. This trains one to be receptive to different interpretations and not *ab initio* jump to a conclusion on any matter. Also, interacting with judges and lawyers gave insights into the functioning of the legal system in actual practice. I enjoyed this phase of the work immensely, as also the chatter relating to court work emanating from the six benches that functioned simultaneously in the Collectorate compound.

There was the case of an additional judge, reputed to have a fine mind, whose judgements were well written and impeccable. It was generally anticipated that he would rise to become a judge of the high court. The story that made the rounds was that prior to the conclusion of the arguments in each civil case, the representatives of the opposing lawyers, would meet the Peshkar – court clerk – and hand over to him a prescribed amount of money, commensurate with the nature and complexity of the case. On judgement day, a few minutes prior to the delivery of the verdict, the losing lawyer would be refunded his entire payment; the judgement would be on merits, impartial and well argued! No one I knew had tested out the extent of deviation from absolute impartiality if one of the parties' representatives had not settled the matter first with the peshkar!

Another executive magistrate called Fanthome was a legendary figure. For one, he was known to be eccentric. He not only had a reputation for honesty; he was simple, direct and unorthodox in his methods. In one of the Opium Act cases in his court, the prosecution alleged that the accused was wandering suspiciously in the night and when challenged by the sub inspector from a distance of about ten yards, he ran away, and was overtaken by the policeman, who on a search found the illicit opium in his shirt pocket. Now the accused was poor and could not afford a lawyer, and defended his own case. The sub inspector, who said he had caught him, was an overweight middle-aged man, with a sizeable potbelly, who had on oath rendered the evidence about the chase and the search. When asked if he had anything to say on his own behalf, the accused said, "Your Honour, just look at this policeman and look at me; see how fat he is. Is there any way he can catch me? How can you believe him?" Fanthome was impressed with this line of logic. He asked the accused to stand at the door of the court and asked the sub inspector to stand ten yards behind him and said that as he gave a signal, the policeman may start the chase. He warned the accused that if he was caught, he would go to jail for six months; but if he ran faster, he need not return to the courtroom! The chase started and the accused sprinted out of sight, as the bulky policeman was still wheezing up to the door. Such was the stuff on which Fanthome had built a reputation for unorthodox methods.

As a magistrate, I came in contact with Raj Bahadur Pande, a senior criminal lawyer of the district, whom I got to know very well. Pande had a brilliant quick-silver mind with an acute insight into the processes of criminal law administration and ready repartee. He was also an excellent raconteur. When only thirty-five years old he was offered a judgeship at the Allahabad high court; he would surely have made it to head the Supreme Court in Delhi in the normal course of time. However, Pande refused the offer on the grounds that the salary of a high court judge was not enough to meet his life style! There was a party at his house every evening and he would invite whomever he met during the day for dinner at his house. He would insist that every bottle of scotch that was opened must be consumed the same night. He would be sozzled every night; but was all business early the next morning. All his clients were defendants in major crimes; for all the dacoits in the region, he was 'vakil saheb'. Each morning, he would meet his clients to obtain the facts and by merely punching holes in the process of investigation, or on the conduct of prosecution, he would secure a 'not guilty' verdict – mainly relying on his ability to discredit the prosecution from proving cases 'beyond reasonable doubt'.

Every Friday late afternoon, Pande with his family would leave in his big Dodge car for Nainital, where he would spend the weekend in an inebriated condition, to return to court work on Monday morning. The three-hour drive to Nainital passed through dense forests infested with dacoits; and it was uncommon for a car to drive through that area after dusk without police escort. Indeed, or so the story went, Pande would on occasion be accosted by gun toting bandits who did not recognise the car. When they would open the car door and see the occupant, they would tear off their facemasks, reverentially salute 'vakil saheb' and apologise profusely for bothering him. After all, even if the assailants were not already his clients, they might have to turn to him at some stage for protection.

After staying for three months in the collector's home, I moved into a small apartment. My father had sent a domestic servant, a cousin of the cook at my father's home in Calcutta, to help me. Bhuvaneshwar Jha hailed from the Mithila region in north Bihar. He bought the groceries, did the cooking and managed the house. Those days, I would not come home for lunch and would return from the day's work around seven in the evening. As part of my training curriculum, I had also been allotted the work of cinema magistrate. I was to oversee the work of the entertainment tax inspector, whose job was to see to the correct collection of entertainment tax in the movie halls of the district and to check if the taxes were properly credited to the government account. One day, I realised I had totally neglected this work; and decided to do a test check in some of the movie halls in Moradabad town. Accompanied by my orderly, I went to one of the cinema halls around 4 pm, then showing a matinee film. I checked the registers, did a rough head-count in the various classes of the hall of the people present and was generally satisfied that there was nothing amiss. I also verified that the owners had the vouchers showing the deposit in the bank relating to the payment of the tax collections into the government account. This done, I moved on to the next cinema hall, not far away. As I entered, I was effusively received by the manager. He told me that my brother was already there, watching the movie and I could join him. Puzzled, I walked up to the premium balcony area, where I found Bhuvaneshwar Jha sitting on a sofa, legs resting stretched out on a stool, with a small table by his side supporting a plate of samosas, sweets and tea. A beatific smile on his face, he was enjoying the scene of the hero pursuing the heroine on the silver screen. Then as he saw me, he shot up from his chair, and toppling the plate of samosas to the floor, sprinted away. It was the theatre manager's turn to be puzzled. He gave me the information that 'my brother' came to watch the movie at least twice a week for the matinee show, and enquired why he left in a hurry! I looked around the other cinema halls in the vicinity, and discovered how the magistrate's 'brother' spent every working day afternoon. Naturally, on returning home that evening, I fired Bhuvana, relieving him of his work in my household, and also depriving him of free entry to the movie halls of Moradabad.

One day I went on an inspection of a sugar factory in Bilari. I used the official pick-up jeep, with its hooded frontage and semi-covered back portion. The driver and I sat in the front cabin, with my office clerk and orderly sitting in the rear cabin. The inspection, to check compliance with the excise regulations, lasted a few hours. I was a bit foggy about the procedures for verification, but it was a learning experience to familiarise myself with the books that were used for calculating the amount of tax payable on past production, and to see if that was duly accounted for. After the inspection, I returned to the jeep, escorted by the factory manager, and got into the cabin. As I sat in the cabin, something made me look into the back of the vehicle and to my surprise I saw two fifty kilo bags of sugar. New to this work, I was a little puzzled, and I asked the driver how the bags came there. The manager of the sugar factory with a simpering smile intervened to say that this was the normal courtesy, and the way for the factory to thank its visitors! One of the bags was for me, and the other for sharing by the staff. I got the two bags out of the vehicle, back into the factory; warned my assistants and orderly that I did not want to see this kind of thing to happen again. So this was part of the training, to learn that at every visit of an inspector to a factory or cinema hall or any other place, it was expected that the owners should express their 'gratitude' for the visit.

That winter I had occasion to see my first election campaign as an administrator, from close quarters. Bye-election to the seat of a member of parliament (MP) was being held – the contestants were Hafiz Mohammed Ibrahim, the then Union minister for railways and Acharya J B Kripalani. Hafizji was quite old by then and looked feeble. Every three or four days, he would come by train from Delhi, arriving around 9 pm, would meet the party workers and after his campaign work would return to Delhi the next evening. Since the visit was technically an official one by a Union minister, a small reception committee consisting of the city magistrate and three or four others would receive him at the railway station every time he came. The reception committee would stand in front of the railway saloon coach on arrival and would be formally introduced one by one to him by name. This happened at least ten or twelve times in the period preceding the elections, with the same ceremony being repeated; each time Hafizji would not recognise the city magistrate and one had to go through the same routine; he was indeed old by that time.

I was told that Acharya Kripalani was an old frail man. The local joke was that whoever won the bye-election, there would have to be a new bye-election within six months. But it was not quite so. In the event, Acharya Kripalani won the elections; Hafiz Mohammed Ibrahim lost the election. Within three months, Hafizji was no more, but Kripalani continued as MP and as a political figure at least for ten more years. Power is the best medicine!

Should one desist from jumping too early to conclusions about an officer and his style of working? Or about anyone for that matter! In this context, I recall the visit of Mutsaddi Lal, of the Indian Civil Service (ICS), who was the then commissioner in Bareilly Division. He had come for his annual winter inspection of the district planning and development office in Moradabad. Virendra Dayal was then the district planning officer. The commissioner's visit was scheduled for three days, a full-fledged detailed inspection. I had been told to be on duty for the next three days, attached to the commissioner.

The nature of duties had not been specified to me, but still the work given came as a pleasant surprise. On the appointed morning, the commissioner arrived at the Public Works Department (PWD) inspection house, and after a formal ceremonial welcome, moved half an hour later to the residence of the superintendent engineer of the PWD. At 10.30 am, I found myself in the company of the commissioner, the superintendent engineer, and his wife, and the four of us sat at the bridge table. Sharp at 12.15 the first gin was served, the second gin about twenty minutes thereafter, and by 1'o clock we got up for lunch. The commissioner adjourned for a short nap thereafter, and at 3 pm the same group reassembled at the bridge table. At 4 pm, tea and snacks were served and at 6 pm the table was dissolved. This was the routine for all the three days, followed by an official dinner one evening at the collector's house and on another evening at the district judge's home. The third day, the bridge session finished a little earlier, as the commissioner returned to his guest house, where he was met by the planning officer, who had spent the previous three days working on the draft of the inspection report of his own office, relieving the commissioner from this burden too. The commissioner glanced through the draft report and mentioned to the district planning officer that the draft could have praised the planning office a little more than it actually did! He dictated a few sentences to his assistant to remedy the defect and then sat in his car for the return journey to Bareilly. That was how the detailed and exhaustive 'inspection' of the district planning office, as well as the evaluation of the work of the district planning officer was done by the commissioner. This was in 1962, and this encounter left me bemused.

Ten years later, in 1972, Mutsaddi Lal the commissioner, had become the chief secretary at Lucknow and I was posted in the chief secretary's branch as a joint secretary. I came in close touch with him. I may have given an impression that Mutsaddi Lal was casual in his methods. However, I found him taking hard and difficult positions as chief secretary, in defending individuals or events, or supporting certain points of view in his dealings with the then chief minister, Kamalapathi Tripathi – an obstinate man, prone to whims, who played favourites. Lal would frequently take firm positions in extremely trying and difficult circumstances. One day, he invited me to his house for a drink, and after discussing some official matters, recalled his visit to Moradabad ten years earlier to inspect the work of the district planning office. Without being apologetic, he told me that he had already a clear picture of the work of the district planning officer, before he came to Moradabad that time. He wanted to give a signal to the district planning officer about the confidence he had in the latter's work; hence the procedure adopted. Indeed, if the commissioner had had some doubts about the work of the planning office, he would have conducted the inspection in a different way. Lal added that in his view, this was the best way to extract the maximum enthusiasm and interest from the district planning officer.

Sometimes I wonder whether the planning department itself had little to do or was it that the commissioners responsible for planning had little to do? One day, I accompanied Virendra Dayal, who was officiating as collector of Moradabad at that time, to Bareilly to attend the divisional planning committee meeting. All the district collectors, district planning officers and the local officers dealing with development matters participated in this meeting. We left for Bareilly at 8.30 am to attend the meeting scheduled at 10. The drive normally took about one and a quarter hours, but at Clutterbuckgunj, on the outskirts of Bareilly, the jeep had a flat and we were delayed by some twenty minutes. We arrived at the meeting hall a few minutes late. It looked as if the meeting had not started. The head table was empty and the twenty or so participants were outside, laughing and chatting, seated on chairs in the main hall. The then officiating commissioner was I D N Sahi who was appropriately nicknamed "I Do Nothing" Sahi. After about ten minutes; Dayal asked, "When is the meeting starting?" There was laughter all around. We gathered that the commissioner had opened the meeting and stated that he had no comments to make and that he hoped that everything was going satisfactorily; everyone immediately agreed that everything was going as well as possible. Thereupon, the commissioner concluded the meeting, since there was no further business to transact. So much for planning and development!

That I managed to get through my interview for entry into the IAS, following the written examination was a bit of a chance. Professor Ganguli, who was then the vice chancellor of the Delhi University was on the panel. He had been a professor of mathematics, and finding so to say a kin, naturally asked a series of questions on pure mathematics. I recall his asking me about "Fermat's last theorem" – which in 1961 had not yet been "proven". He also asked me what "Riemann hypothesis" was. I promptly replied that I was innocent of any information on these, at which Ganguly muttered, "I am afraid Science's gain will be Administration's loss"! But then K M Panikkar, who was a member of my interview board stepped in to ask more relevant questions. He looked at my name and asked, "Does the name Ramana, have anything to do with the Maharishi at Tiruvannamalai". I replied, "Indeed, it does, I was named after him". I also added perhaps cheekily that, "In fact, today happens to be his birthday". Menon persisted: "Do you think that is auspicious?" and I promptly replied, "I will tell you when the results are out!" It carried the day.

In his interview, K S Ramakrishnan, a batch mate who left the service prematurely, was asked as to how administrative bottlenecks occurred. He replied with the telling one-liner, "My experience with bottles indicates that the bottlenecks are always at the top." It took me nearly forty years to truly understand the validity of this simple statement.

2 RANIKHET: FIELD POSTING IN THE QUEEN OF THE HILLS

*The sub divisional magistrate had to be heralded in
by an orderly in ceremonial dress to get the respect of
the villagers.*

*"Yes, Sucheta, go and take the police salute: they
cannot catch thieves but they salute well."*

ONE DAY IN THE AUTUMN OF 1963, I RECEIVED
an order posting me as sub-divisional magistrate of Ranikhet. People I
asked knew vaguely that Ranikhet was up north in the Himalayas, but
had no idea about the exact route to take. I found out that from the rail
head at Kathgodam where the plains end, Ranikhet in the Himalayan
foothills is a fifty mile run through mountain roads. It was a salubrious,
picturesque place for an assignment, at a height of about 6,000 ft. We
were ensconced in a bungalow with a breathtaking view of the Nanda
Devi – Nanga Parbat – Hathi Parbat ranges. Located on top of a small
hill, the house was cosy and convenient, with a fireplace in each room.
Ranikhet had a large number of nice little bungalows each with its own
steep driveway leading right up to the door of the house. It was an idyllic
place for a posting early in one's career. In earlier days, the wives and
families of the British officers would migrate there for the summer season,
leaving their husbands behind in the heat of the plains. A neatly maintained
cantonment town, it is also the headquarters of the Kumaon regiment. I
read recently of a move to protect Ranikhet town as a heritage area, and
would go along with that.

People can be petty and pompous even in idyllic surroundings. Within a week of my arrival, I went to make a courtesy call on a distinguished judge of the Allahabad High Court, who was on vacation, staying at the nearby forest rest house. He was booked at the best suite in the forest rest house for a week and thereafter for the next three weeks, he was to stay at the nearby bungalow of the Mahant, or religious head, of Gorakhpur. I met the judge, and after the usual courtesies, he told me that the Mahant had asked him to stay in the east wing of his bungalow, which was currently occupied by a Burman. He asked me if I could meet Burman, the head of the Indian Standards Institution (ISI) who was also vacationing in Ranikhet, and request him to vacate the east wing for him. I duly met Burman, who in a friendly manner said that the Mahant had asked him to stay in his bungalow, without specifying the wing. Since he had arrived earlier, he would prefer to continue to stay in the east wing. However, if Mr Justice so desired, he could make a personal request to Burman to move to the west wing and he would gladly oblige. I duly conveyed Burman's message to the distinguished judge who flew into a rage. He said, "I am a Justice of the high court and I am not going to beg before a government official." He ordered me to get Burman vacated from the east wing. I politely told him that this was a private matter and that I had already done enough, and could not continue to function as an intermediary. The next day, Mr Justice called for me and told me bluntly, "You have the police under your charge; use them effectively. Check his car license, find a reason to harass and to hound him, to teach him a lesson." This, from a custodian of the Indian Constitution and an interpreter of the laws of the nation! I quietly eased my way out and had nothing more to do on the subject. I learnt later that the judge had actually moved into the west wing, thus enhancing my respect for the ISI.

Ranikhet was a fairly large sub division but those days had only one road cutting through the entire mountain area. There were a number of inspection houses of the forest department dotted all over the sub division, some in remote corners. When I happened to visit Ranikhet later in the 1980s, I noticed that a large number of new roads had sprung up, that crisscrossed the sub division. I travelled through the rural areas of the sub division, and though there was improved road access to the villages, I did not perceive any significant improvement in living standards. Commercial horticulture or tourism had not developed in any meaningful way as was perhaps the hope when the roads were conceived. I was told that the new roads had merely helped the organised and illegal decimation of the forest areas, with the transport of the timber made easier through these new road links.

Very soon after my arrival in Ranikhet and again about one year later, the post of district magistrate of Almora became vacant, due to the transfer of the respective incumbents. So for about one and a half months each, I had the special opportunity of acting as collector of the Almora district. I could well have been the youngest person to hold a district charge, in the history of Uttar Pradesh, or for that matter anywhere in India. This gave me an opportunity to tour the district extensively, which at that time covered a large territory: the district has since then bifurcated into two. I recall my visits to Champavat and Lohaghat lying close to our borders with Nepal and not too far from the borders with Tibet. I discovered to my amazement that Swami Vivekananda had spent some time at Champavat, where there is still a serenely beautiful Ramakrishna mission ashram run by dedicated monks. Perhaps the pooja season influx of Bengali tourists to the UP hill stations was inspired by Vivekananda's sojourns in the UP hills. Even more astonishing, Adi Shankara had visited those parts and travelled there extensively centuries back. At Pathal Bhuvaneshwari near Verinag, there is a breathtaking network of caves, where as in many other places in the Himalayas, Shankara had established and consecrated a shivling that continues to be under worship.

During the time when I first officiated as district magistrate, Ranikhet had the privilege of the visit of H C Gupta of the ICS, who was the administrative member of the Board of Revenue, based at Allahabad. The board was the highest body in UP to rule on, and to pronounce *diktats* on all revenue matters. It was held in high esteem by such young officers as myself then. As the senior most members of the service were sent there as its members to adorn the board, the board sahib was worshipped only next to the good Lord Himself. So, it was an important occasion for such an exalted figure to honour us with his presence. Alas, much later when I acquired seniority in the UP service, I could see that the board was a toothless tiger, a convenient berth to lodge senior officers who were incapable of taking on any responsibility. Gupta was to spend a full ten days on duty in the salubrious environs of Ranikhet. I had not yet learnt my lesson: not to be over-zealous about visits by dignitaries. I sent a flurry of telegrams to his assistant at Allahabad, asking for the details of the field visits and engagements that had to be arranged for the inspection visit by the member board. I did not get any satisfactory reply – there was a curt message, asking me to arrange a meeting of all gazetted officers posted in the district to meet the board sahib on the day after his arrival. When I telephoned the assistant about the agenda for the meeting as also whether I should invite those officers who were in far-flung inaccessible places in the district, I was told that all officers, without exception, were to be called and the member would conduct the meeting. I did not realise then that the assistant had probably not checked with his boss before giving these instructions.

All the eighty or so gazetted officers posted in the district, belonging to different departments were asked to assemble on the appointed day, sharp at 9.30 am, in a location near the guest house where the board sahib was to stay. Many of them had travelled by foot, and by road, for more than two days, to participate in the conference. At 9.30 am, I called on the board member and asked him whether he would meet the officers in small groups in the office room in his suite, say department-wise or in any other way. Gupta asked me to line up the officers, single file, in a parade inspection formation – we soon had eighty civilian officers standing shoulder to shoulder on the lawns of the Forest Rest House.

Promptly at 11'o clock, H C Gupta met the first officer in the line, the senior-most sub divisional officer in the district and pleasantly asked him, how he was and if he had any problem. The officer said that a number of clarifications and interpretations of the Kumaon Tenancy Act and Rules were awaited from the board, and this delayed the disposal of the land dispute cases. Thereupon, the member board clarified in a helpful tone that the interpretations of the UP Zamindari Abolition Act were comprehensive and available in book form, and that the sub divisional officer should refer to them. The officer pointed out that the UP Zamindari Act was not applicable to the hill areas of Kumaon and Garhwal, where the Kumaon Land Tenancy Act and Rules only were relevant, and that despite repeated reminders, the clarifications were not forthcoming. The board sahib suddenly flared up and chided the officer, "If I have to do everything from Allahabad, I don't need officers in every district; why are you all there? You must deal with pending government work effectively and efficiently; I am very surprised at this incompetence."

With this admonition, and having so resolved the doubts of the sub divisional officer, he moved to the next person on the line, the civil surgeon of the district and asked him whether he had any problems. Naturally, the civil surgeon had no problems and no comments to offer. Over the next twenty minutes, Gupta walked through the assembled line of officers, asking each one of them if they had any doubts or problems. Not one officer expressed any doubt or question or comment or need for any clarification – apparently everything was in perfect apple-pie order! Thereupon, the board member, having satisfied himself that the district administration was performing satisfactorily, dismissed the meeting; and that was that. When I asked him about further meetings and engagements for the next ten days, he told me that he was concentrating on the study of some important files and that he would call for me when required. The next time I was required to meet him was to see him off on the appointed date!

Ranikhet was a large sprawling sub division with unspoilt, simple mountain folk inhabiting the area. On the only road which went through the sub division, where I would take my old Fiat car, one could go to Dwarahat where a cluster of ancient temples are located, and to Choukhutia. Elsewhere, for places off the road, I had to walk the undulating mountain terrain, sometimes alternating between steep climbs and then going down hill. The orderly of the sub divisional magistrate wore a ceremonial dress, white in summer and black in winter, with an impressive headgear. In fact, he represented the authority of government to the simple folk of the area. If the sub divisional magistrate were to enter a village alone, he would have been totally ignored – he had to be heralded in by the orderly in the ceremonial dress to get the respect of the village.

I recall many field inspection trips in the deep interiors of Ranikhet, much of it heavily forested, amidst scattered villages. The inspections would mainly include verification of the progress of drinking water schemes, checks on whether wheat and sugar rations were reaching the remote areas, monitoring visits to primary schools, local enquiries regarding the working of government dispensaries, including the attendance of the doctor in-charge. The visits would also cover examination on the field of pending disputes and those regarding land and grazing rights. For land-dispute cases pending in the court of the sub divisional magistrate, adequate notice to appear would be given to the parties and their lawyers – thus, it was not uncommon for groups of litigants and their lawyers to be in the entourage of the sub divisional magistrate.

Sometimes the inspection trip would start as early as 6 am and would continue till 6 pm without break. A mile or so before the destination, the orderlies – Bhairav Datt or Bhola Datt – would sprint ahead, and keep warm water ready, with a liberal sprinkling of salt, to bathe and massage the master's feet – a practice, no doubt from the British era. There were a number of forest rest houses dotted across the sub division in picturesque spots with a wonderful view. These basically consisted of one bedroom and an attached room. I was once stranded in a remote rest house in the midst of heavy snowfall, which made trekking treacherous and impossible. I spent all of four days and nights in that cozy spot, with a log fire going, perusing with delight the old, indeed ancient, issues of the *Illustrated London News*, and other reading material belonging to the 1930s and '40s. The custom, those days, was that any visitor who finished a book or a magazine should leave it behind in the guesthouse; he was free to take away any half-finished reading material. I do not know how the local attendants rustled up enough material for food. I recall having hot meals, delicious though simple. This remote guesthouse had hardly been used for years as I could see from the guest register. Almost every morning, as one looked out of the windows of the inspection house, one could see fresh pugmarks of leopards or other wild animals, which had come to sniff the food or for the warmth of the cottage. How much would I now give for a holiday like that again!

We would spend our time talking about life in the hills. Bhairav, my orderly, once told me the story of driving alongside with one of my predecessors, Anadi Segal, who took the road from Ranikhet to Dwarahat in his car. As one descends towards Dwarahat to reach the valley, there are a series of hairpin bends on the road. Suddenly Anadi lost control; the car teetered to the edge and toppled down the hillside, making sideways somersaults. It skipped two levels of road and settled down, fully upright, on the road at a lower level, with its front facing towards Dwarahat. Anadi got out of the car, shook himself to see if he was all in one piece and inquired about the welfare of Bhairav. When he found all in proper order, he quickly regained his composure. He told Bhairav that they had lost some time, but saved some driving distance, and then they drove on. I recently had the pleasant surprise of a reunion with Bhairav Datt, now a sprightly young man of over ninety years, who bounded up the stairs to my apartment to alternatively prostrate before me and hug me with affection.

Ranikhet would get a stream of visitors. C B Gupta, who was the then Member of Legislative Assembly (MLA) representing the area would visit Ranikhet from Lucknow once every three months. Gupta had earlier been the chief minister of Uttar Pradesh and would again be the chief minister in later years. A canny politician of the old school, his primary interest, indeed obsession, was the development of the state and the advancement of the people. He represented the generation of stalwarts like B C Roy and Kamaraj, a vanishing tribe. The first time I had met him he told me that I should visit a village called Manila, located atop a nearby hill, with a wonderful view of the mountain range. Gupta fancied that Manila had the potential to be developed as a tourist resort. I assured him that I would visit Manila, as indeed I intended to. When during a conversation on his next visit, he asked if I had visited Manila, I replied, "Not yet; but soon will." Again with other things to do, I could not go to Manila. After Gupta's third visit, I made up my mind not to visit Manila, even though I had gone on inspection to villages very close to it. It was a false sense of pride. Though it was in my own sub-division, just because the local MLA prompted me, I decided not to go. So it became a sort of joke between Gupta and myself. Every time he would ask me whether I had visited Manila, each time I would reply, "not yet, but I intend to". Gupta would have surely got to know about my extensive travels in the interiors and realised that I was too stubborn to follow his advice on any matter relating to the sub division. But I am sure he did not hold this against me.

On one occasion, the chief minister, Sucheta Kripalani had come to Ranikhet, accompanied by Acharya J B Kripalani, then a MP. I was then officiating as collector of the district, and so was in attendance during the visit of the chief minister. They were staying in the forest rest house overlooking the Himalayan range and had spent two quiet days there. Their scheduled departure was at 8 am one morning. As I reached the guesthouse at about 7.45 am to greet the chief minister, I found Sucheta and her husband standing outside the guesthouse, admiring the view. After about ten minutes, her staff officer moved up to her to tell her that it was time to leave. Further reminders were to no avail, and finally, the staff officer went up to her and said peremptorily, "The guard is ready for you to take the salute." I recall overhearing Acharya Kripalani, in his inimitable drawl, telling his wife in Hindi, "Yes, Sucheta, go and take the police salute; they cannot catch any thieves but they salute very well!" It took me many years in service to understand fully the prescience of that cryptic remark.

My first lesson on the effectiveness of Indian scientific research began at Ranikhet. The Directorate of Fruit Utilisation was located in Ranikhet. It was supposed to be a research institution for horticulture products, and was also designed to be a key agency for catalysing the development of fruit belts in the Kumaon/Garhwal region on a commercial scale. Dr Srivastava, a horticulture scientist, or so it was claimed, headed it. Indeed, he could well have been a scientist early in his career; but as I could see he had evolved into an administrator whose only expertise was the knack of pleasing politicians. Srivastava had discovered that it was enough to state to all and sundry, in seminars and symposia the avowed need for developing fruit belts in the hill region – it was not necessary to do anything concrete in this regard; indeed, he may have found that was counterproductive. He would keep politicians and senior bureaucrats happy, by frequently sending them gift parcels of the fruit of the season, three or four times a year, from the produce of the Ranikhet farms and gardens.

The main work of the two vans of the Fruit Utilisation Directorate was to ply from Ranikhet to Lucknow supplying crates of seasonal fruits to key persons. The sub divisional magistrate in Ranikhet rated one crate of apricot and pears in April, two kilos of delicious cherries in May and two instalments of apples in July and August. I am sure a graded system, based on Srivastava's perception of hierarchical importance had been carefully worked out. Srivastava himself would probably deliver the crates to the more important targets, and use the opportunity to brief them about the pioneering work being done! This practice met with success – he was hailed in all quarters as a model of success.

Much closer as I was to his field of activity, I could see through his game. So, looking back now, as early as in the '60s, substance was not recognised as of any consequence – so long as the decision makers were kept under the illusion that something was happening. This is what can now be called targetted marketing, government style. It is much easier to flatter the powers that be than please the citizens. Thus, in advertising the family planning programmes all over the country, the implementers have discovered that reaching the real beneficiary, the public – is a very difficult task. However, if they could reach the people that count in the government and the elite and sensitise them that major efforts were being made, that was enough. It is thus, that we hear pleasing Hindi jingles on *saksharata* or the need for a small family or for a new vasectomy technique after the English news broadcast on the radio. As an avid listener of the radio, I have not heard these messages repeated during the Hindi language broadcasts or on television or after the Hindi news or indeed anywhere else. These important messages, extolling the virtues of a small family are exclusively designed to educate the listeners of the English news on radio! Our programme implementers have known the immense value of targetted marketing, way before it was recognised as a technique in the advertisement industry.

Dr and Mrs Bose were my neighbors in Ranikhet. Dr Bose was a scientist in the Directorate of Fruit Utilization. A warm and friendly couple, they were close family friends to successive sub divisional magistrates of the time. Dr Bose had, in his own way, put local fruit to good use. His expertise was in producing wine from a local berry called *kafal*, and he would give us a bottle or two every quarter, as a personal gift. Of course, the production of this wine was illicit; no matter, it was excellent company in front of the fireplace during the cold evenings of Ranikhet.

Talking of spirits, I had several good friends from among the junior army officers posted in the cantonment. I recall going to Captain Dr Bhaduri's residence, for a farewell drink when I was posted out of Ranikhet – apart from myself, Bhaduri and his assistant surgeon were present. In time honoured tradition, Bhaduri brought out the drinks and without verifying our preferences, I was served Scotch, Bhaduri poured himself Indian whiskey and his assistant was served rum. The hierarchy was established and there was a tacit acceptance.

My relationship with the senior brass was more formal. Colonel Sinha was the crusty station commander at Ranikhet, which was the headquarters of the Kumaon regiment. Like most army officers, he had a chip on his shoulder that the country at large, and civilian officials in particular, did not recognise their importance. His remedy was to act pompous and churlishly over-sensitive. While dealing with civil service officers, Sinha was constantly holding on to his turf. A slightly uneasy relationship, but it never turned bitter. I would invite Colonel Sinha to all the official civilian functions and he would reciprocate by inviting me to some. But he would carefully omit me from the Dussehra celebrations, when there was a ceremonial slaying of buffaloes in the regimental headquarters.

My stay in Ranikhet gave me further insights into the functioning of the judicial system in our country. The wife of a local army officer, had been attacked by her domestic servant. Col Cariappa was from Coorg, and had brought the boy servant from his native area. For whatever reason, the Coorgi boy had one day lost his balance and repeatedly stabbed Mrs Cariappa with a sharp kitchen knife, when Col Cariappa was away on tour. She was rushed to hospital and close to death for a while, but made a complete recovery in course of time. The Coorgi boy, who could not speak English or Hindi, was taken into custody but the interrogation could not proceed. He was brought before me by the police. I could converse with the boy in Tamil, as he was fairly well conversant in that language. He broke down before me and made a full and complete confession. I recorded his confession in my capacity as a magistrate, in Tamil and added an English translation, in my own handwriting, each four pages long. I then read the confession over to him, mentioning that it would be used against him in trial. The sobbing boy admitted to stabbing her repeatedly without specific provocation. The confession in Tamil and in English language, bearing my signatures in each page and his fingerprints were duly sealed and taken over by the investigators. I had forgotten the incident till two years later when I got a summons from the sessions court in Ranikhet to come and give evidence in this case and to attest to the authenticity of the confession. I duly came to Ranikhet and after being sworn in as a witness, recorded my statement, recounting the facts and attesting to the confession recorded by me in my capacity as a magistrate. The lawyer of the accused did not cross-examine me nor did he have any points to raise about the validity of the confession. So about six months later I was absolutely astonished to learn that the boy had been acquitted for want of evidence. Even if Mrs Cariappa was not willing to give evidence, as was probably the case since it may have involved reviving unpleasant memories, surely there was enough evidence against the boy. To this day, I cannot believe how the case resulted in acquittal. So mysterious and unpredictable are the ways of our judicial system.

Another episode during that visit to Ranikhet disturbed me greatly. Outside the courtroom I happened to meet the president of the Ranikhet Bar Association. He greeted me most effusively and praised me saying that all the members of the Bar Association thought that I was the best sub divisional magistrate they had come across in many years. He then invited me to be the chief guest at a dinner to be hostèd by the Bar Association. I was most delighted at the high praise showered on me but expressed regret that I could not avail of their kind invitation, as I was leaving for Ghazipur that afternoon. I was flattered to be called the best sub divisional magistrate they had come across and questioned him guardedly as to why they thought so. I really thought that the bar members were recognising my sincere work in court.

I need to explain the nature of my court work. In the course of my court work at Ranikhet, there was a backlog of more than 1,500 cases, mostly relating to petty land disputes under the Kumaon Tenancy Act and Rules. Most pending applications related to the Nayabad Rules, in which farmers had sought the court's approval for alienation of their land and for its sale. The local land rules discouraged the sale of the land, as it led to fragmentation; frequently the sale was due to indebtedness and the need to repay loans. The other set of cases related to grazing rights – disputes between two villages or a village and a farmer relating to whether a piece of land was public grazing land or private. Most of the cases were simple and straightforward. I would carefully hear both parties and their lawyers, try to ascertain the truth from the litigants of both parties and come to a conclusion. I gave my findings in a relatively short, speaking order, mostly written in my own hand. I did not encourage any postponements. Each time a new date had to be given, I would personally fix the date, ascertain the convenience of both parties, including their lawyers, mentioning to them specifically that no further postponement would be granted and read out the next date to the parties. I would then ask them to repeat that date to insure that they understood properly. But then, I would generally see with amusement that the litigants would wait till my departure. They would then ascertain again the date from the court clerk. At that point, presumably, a token of appreciation would change hands. Trust the court clerk not to mischievously alter the date fixed by the magistrate! At the end of my tenure, most of these simple cases had been disposed of and there was a near clean state. I thought that the Bar Association chairman was expressing satisfaction at the speedy disposal of so many pending cases; probably in the way the old British joint magistrates administered justice, accurately and swiftly, without fear or favour, and even-handedly. It was thus, that I asked the Bar Association chairman as to why the lawyers in Ranikhet rated me so highly.

His answer astounded me, and brought me down to reality. He sounded earnest enough when he said, "Sir, your judgements were so short and to the point that we could take every one of them on a revision petition to the higher court in Almora, which has reopened all these cases for fresh hearing. You have indeed contributed so much for the income of the lawyer community in Ranikhet, that we are so grateful." I was close to tears of frustration and anger when I heard this. The lawyer had no concern for justice. It dawned on me for the first time that in India the judicial system is meant for the benefit of lawyers, the judiciary, the prosecutors, the investigators and the police. The litigants, the citizens of the country are bit players and are of no consequence. I was to see the same pattern repeated in every other walk of life in India, where the interest of citizens is involved – the schools are meant for the teachers and the school administrators – not the students; the hospitals are meant for the doctors and the nurses – not for the patients; the airlines are meant for the employees and the government users – not for the passengers.

I left Ranikhet in mid-1965. It was then a very peaceful area with hardly any crime. In fact, the police looked after only the Almora and Ranikhet towns. In the rural areas, the patwaris combined their land revenue powers with police functions. I learnt much later that around 1968, there was an altercation between two families in one of the villages of Ranikhet sub division. Unlike in the plains of Uttar Pradesh, there was no strong caste identity in the hill region – the different castes – Brahmins, Thakurs and the scheduled castes and others lived in harmony with no tensions between them. It so happened that in this village all the families belonged either to the Thakur community or were scheduled castes. A scheduled caste family, due to a territorial dispute blocked a marriage procession of a Thakur family. The enraged Thakur group attacked the scheduled caste family, and some people including two children were killed in the assault. Such tragic disputes between the castes were unusual in that part of the world. I was informed that the next day the chief minister of Uttar Pradesh and the Union home minister both landed up in that area, to display their sorrow. So far so good – but then they promised special courts to try the accused for a speedy judicial verdict. Then they peeled off in their helicopters and forgot all about it. Now, the established process for creating special courts is complicated – it requires approval from many authorities, including the higher judiciary to conclude the process. Apparently, no one had the time, patience or energy to follow through on the promises made, and establish the special courts. As usual, the criminal case lingered on for many years. I do not know what happened there, but one thing is certain – the local people of that area who used to be simple, genuine folk had lost all faith in the pronouncements of the politicians from Delhi or Lucknow. The patwari, who was king of the region, lost his position overnight. The sub divisional magistrate whose word was law had been marginalised. For every little incident in the district, there would now be a call for the Union minister or the chief minister to visit.

This passion for the higher-ups to descend on the scene immediately has been at a heavy cost to administrative efficiency. It has become important for the politician to arrive on the scene to make promises, and that is the end of the matter. No matter that the local administration would be crippled and rendered impotent. Cornwallis, who had set the standards for sound administration, would have shed tears if he had learnt that the state chief minister and the Union home minister had visited the scene of a tragedy in a rural area of Ranikhet the very next day after the incident.

3 GHAZIPUR-ON-GANGA: A YOUNG COLLECTOR'S DIARY

The Ganga would overflow its bank and rise flush with the rear entrance to our drawing room. It was but an easy passage for the snakes that inhabited the banks of the river to cross over to the comfort of the collector's house.

"Sir, in those days tehsildars behaved as collectors. Today, collectors think and behave like tehsildars and they are treated like tehsildars."

WHEN I GOT MY ORDERS POSTING ME TO Ghazipur as collector and district magistrate, in the summer of 1965, I made enquiries at Ranikhet where I was then posted about the exact location of Ghazipur and how to get there. Most people had not even heard of the place. The few, who had, vaguely knew that it was somewhere in east UP. The advice I got was that I should proceed to Lucknow, the state capital and make enquiries there. At Lucknow itself, most people knew that Ghazipur was somewhere close to Varanasi and I was advised to go and make enquiries there. In fact, Ghazipur is one of the easternmost districts of UP, bordering Bihar. In an underdeveloped state such as UP, it was considered a 'least developed area'. Ghazipur itself was a small, somnolent and peaceful town, with a population of 40,000. Ghazipur district had a population of about twelve lacs, spread over six tehsils (sub divisions). Most of the district was alongside the north bank of the river Ganga; but the southernmost tehsil, Zamania, was south of the river. The nearest road bridge across the Ganga was at Varanasi, forty-five miles away, due west. Access to Zamania, during most of the year, was through a pontoon bridge at Ghazipur town and during the monsoon months through ferry.

We landed at Ghazipur and proceeded to the collector's residence. It was a sprawling old bungalow, with large rooms and high ceilings. The house was located right next to the river, in a compound stretching over ten acres. The drawing room and the attached dining hall were immense, though in decrepit condition. The wooden flooring in the hall had seen better times. The British must have hosted many an evening there exclusively for the benefit of the white sahibs. During the rainy season from July to October, the Ganga would overflow its banks and submerge the garden behind our house and rise flush with the rear entrance to our drawing room. It was but an easy passage for the snakes that inhabited the banks of the river, to cross over to the warmth and comfort of the collector's house. It was thus, that during our two years residence there, we must have found and killed at least twenty snakes inside the house, including in the bedrooms and living rooms. In fact, there was a snake living in the crevices of the wall in our kitchen, and despite attempts to poke it out from time to time, it survived our full tenure in that house.

The day after arrival at Ghazipur, the young collector set off to make the first formal call on the divisional commissioner, who was located at Varanasi. Bhagwant Singh adorned that post at that time and he was the chief representative of government in the division, which covered Ghazipur and four other districts. My appointment was at 10 o' clock. At 8:30 in the morning, I was in the official jeep, with the driver Sirajuddin at the wheel and an orderly sitting in the back seat. The forty-five mile drive to the commissioner's house from the Ghazipur collector's house usually took an hour and a quarter. When in a hurry, I have covered it in a little more than one hour. The other day – thirty years later – I covered the same route and the journey took me more than three hours, along rutted streets with large potholes, with shops and residences encroaching on the highway and village bazaars restricting traffic to a crawl in a single lane. So much for progress in road transportation between 1965 and 1995!

To come back to that May morning, we left the collector's house and shortly hit the highway. Sirajuddin accelerated and we quickly reached a speed of over 110 kilometers per hour. The vehicle was bobbing up and down like a rubber ball. I turned to Siraj and told him to go a bit slower. Siraj obeyed his master's command and immediately decelerated to a new cruising speed of about twenty km. "This is a little slow, Siraj," I again admonished, "we can go a little faster". Siraj accelerated and soon started cruising again at 110. I again suggested to Siraj that he was a little fast and perhaps could slow down; suddenly the car sharply decelerated again.

Sirajuddin was a dark, swarthy man with an impressive 6'2" frame and a flowing beard, which fell well below his chest. His looks were those of a sullen executioner in the court of a Turkish sultan from the middle ages. Although I was not a good judge then in relating a person's age to his appearance, I guessed that Siraj was somewhere around seventy years old. The retirement age in UP at that time was fifty-five years. I guessed that Sirajuddin, in the official records would probably have been shown as being in his mid fifties. It was a common practice to understate one's age, sometimes by as much as fifteen years while applying for government jobs. In fact I even know of colleagues in the IAS from UP who had understated their age by a sizeable margin.

On that journey, it became clear that Siraj was playing games with his young master. He must have seen collectors of yore, from the British days and was having a little fun with the latest specimen to take that chair in Ghazipur. Summoning up all my courage and hiding my trepidation, I barked at Siraj, "STOP this vehicle, NOW." When the vehicle stopped, I ordered him to get out and sit on the passenger's seat and I moved to the driving wheel. I started the vehicle, and drove it for two or three miles at about a speed of eighty. I then stopped the vehicle and asked him to take over and that was that. I still wonder what would have happened if Siraj had refused to stop the vehicle. After all, the government rule states that only the official driver shall be authorised to drive the vehicle, except in an emergency. But Siraj did not stretch the point that far. When you go to a district, a number of new challenges would be thrown at you. Every interest group would try to test your will power and assess how you cope. This was my first test as a district collector.

Before I went to Ghazipur, I had called on the chief secretary, Uttar Pradesh at Lucknow. K K Dass of the I C S was a sprightly gentleman, looking younger than his years. Dass offered me a cigarette in his chambers, gave me a cup of tea and along with it some advice. He told me "It is O.K. if you sleep with *gramsevikas* – but do it discreetly! However, under any circumstances, if you fail to maintain law and order, I will finish you off. Ghazipur is a backward and difficult district, but you have a chance to make a useful contribution." More than what he said, what impressed me was the amount of time he gave me, and the attention he devoted to me. His injunction was "Every time you come to Lucknow, you must make it a point to see me, even if it is just for one minute. I will find the time for you, if you can". He was true to his word. On each of my visits to Lucknow, on an average once in three months, he would devote at least five minutes to me, offer me a cigarette even if there was no time for a cup of tea and ask pointed questions about local political trends, the crop situation and other administrative minutae. His standing instruction to his personal secretary, Ratan, was that whenever an officer came from outside Lucknow, he should be fitted in for a meeting, however brief.

Compare this with the present day. Senior officials at headquarters run like headless chickens from meeting to meeting, with no time to spare for anything else. When I was chief secretary in Lucknow and later as Cabinet secretary, I tried to follow the lesson taught to me by Dass, to meet as many visitors as possible. This gave me an excellent overview of the progress of various schemes and an insight into the trends and events in the field. I had occasion to remember his injunction regarding law and order at least twice. Years later, in 1992, when I took over as chief secretary in riot-torn UP, immediately after the demolition of the Babri Masjid, I telephoned the district magistrates and gave them the same message though not the first part. I remembered him again in 2002, in post-Godhra Gujarat, when the chief secretary failed to convey this strong message to his field functionaries, with tragic results.

Life in rural districts like Ghazipur in the 1960s continued to retain some of the quaint features of an earlier era of civil service, not without its charm. Yet, one could already discern early signs of the deterioration that was, in later decades, to erode the bureaucracy and in fact, the entire polity. My recollections of Ghazipur are shot through with incidents and events of both kinds.

The standard practice was to have two inspections in each tehsil, every year; once during the monsoons and again in winter. In Saidpur, I used to meet Saxena, the tehsildar. An impressive and able officer, he commanded respect in his beat. I used to consult him occasionally. Unlike most people of his tribe, who were sycophantic, fawning and spineless before superiors – while being aggressive, nasty and rude before the common citizens – Saxena was self-assured, spoke frankly without compromise, but without being disrespectful. In some context, he once mentioned to me that he had worked under a number of officers from the British days, including white and brown ICS officers; *en passant*, he mentioned that I was a "born" officer – the highest form of praise for him. I considered carefully whether this was subtle flattery – and naturally – came to the conclusion that he was speaking his mind. One evening in the winter of 1966, I went to Saidpur to attend a party given by Saxena's staff; at the time of his retirement. I was sitting next to him, eating mushy boiled sweet and stale over-spiced samosas, drinking lukewarm muddy tea and listening to his subordinates effusively praising him. Saxena was rendering a near-tearful response. On these occasions, the custom is that nobody senior to the retiree gives a formal speech – his tribute is to be confined to presentation of a bouquet of flowers. During these proceedings, I asked him, "You have now been in service for about forty years – you have seen many changes in administration; what important change has taken place?" Saxena took a moment to think about the question and his answer was, "Sir, in those days, tehsildars thought and behaved like collectors and were treated like collectors – today collectors think and behave as tehsildars – and are treated as tehsildars." This was in 1966. I just cannot imagine what comparison Saxena would have come up with today, had he continued on in service.

Late in September 1965, the president of the District Municipal Board, Ahmed Hassan Khan Warsi came to me, and mentioned that as per tradition a small public meeting would be held on the 2nd of October, the birth-date of Mahatma Gandhi, at the office of the Municipal Board in the town. He invited me for the occasion. The meeting was scheduled at 10 am and I joined two or three other speakers on the raised podium, waiting for the crowd to gather. Even by 10.15 am nobody had come, and in fact only one person was sitting in the hall. I suggested to Warsi, "Only one person is sitting there. Why don't you say a few words and then we will wind up the meeting?" Warsi gently told me that the gentleman was a board employee and was waiting to fold up the durries at the conclusion of the meeting! So much for Mahatma Gandhi and his memory.

His Holiness the Shankaracharya of Sringeri visited Ghazipur on my invitation. The Sringeri pontiff represents in an unbroken lineage the heritage of Adi Shankara. When I learnt that Sri Abhinava Vidhyatheertha was camping in Gorakhpur while on tour in north India, I went there to request him to make a detour and spend a couple of days at Ghazipur. He consented. Many administrative details had to be worked out, as his entourage included two busloads of attendants and assistants, as well as a large number of idols for the daily pooja, which was meticulously and ceremonially performed by him. I vacated most of my house for the Shankaracharya and kept only a small portion in a corner for my own use. The officers' club, which was also located right next to the river, was vacated for the accommodation of his entourage. I remember vividly that I had gone to visit the officers' club as it was being whitewashed, and seeing an immense snake, at least fifteen feet long, slowly crossing the road. Apparently its abode in a crevice between the rafters in the ceiling of the card room where we used to play bridge most evenings was disturbed by all the activity! I was worried about the arrangements for the daily pooja and other requirements and shared my concern with Shahbuddin, the tehsildar of the area. Shahbuddin was a short, middle-aged man, sporting a flowing dark beard, which reached his knees. He told me, "Sir, just do not worry, leave all arrangements to me". When I gently hinted to him that his presence in the sacred pooja space would raise eyebrows, he said, "Just don't worry, sir. Everything will go like clockwork". He was true to his word. Flowers, fruits, milk were in abundance and the arrangements were perfect. Just prior to his departure, the Shankaracharya expressed satisfaction at the arrangements, and wanted to meet the person who was responsible. I hesitated, concerned that the knowledge that a Muslim was associated with the pooja arrangements would not meet with his approval. But on his insistence, Shahbuddin was produced before him. His Holiness blessed him gracefully, gave him a coconut and expressed appreciation at the arrangements; the tehsildar bowed and accepted the coconut.

After the departure of the Shankaracharya, I asked Shahbuddin how much I owed him for the provisions, flowers and other arrangements. He said I owed nothing at all, as all these were contributed by various people for the visit of His Holiness, and added, "You should take this as my humble contribution, because a great sage came over here and we had the good fortune to do something for his pooja." For me, this incident captures the flavour of Hindu-Muslim relations in eastern Uttar Pradesh in the '60s. These have since been politicised and the waters muddied by politicians for gathering votes.

There was an opium factory in Ghazipur town, built during the British days. It was designed to centralise the processing of the controlled poppy cultivation in eastern Uttar Pradesh. A gentleman called Asthana belonging to the customs service was in charge of the factory at that time. I subsequently learnt that he was an important member of the Anand Marg, not that this is of any relevance. I visited the opium factory a couple of times. Asthana would escort me and on one occasion, he took me on a detailed guided tour of the factory. As we went to one side of the factory, we could see a channel to carry the effluents away, through the neighbouring fields to the river. The effluents contained traces of opium. I saw a large number of monkeys next to the channel, some of them standing by, and some drinking the effluent water. I asked Asthana about the monkeys. He told me that he had studied the psychology of the monkeys that came to drink water and said that they were also much like human beings. Some monkeys would come and sniff at the water and not drink it and then turn away while a few would sip once, and would not return. Some would drink for a couple of days and then run away and some others would drink for a couple of days and then come back after a week or so to drink again. Some would drink once and then get hooked. They then could not leave the channel and would stay there till their end, eschewing all food, and drinking only the opium-flavoured water. He pointed at a few gaunt looking monkeys and said that these monkeys would never leave the vicinity of the channel and that he could predict to the day when each monkey would die.

Sometime in the 1940s, there was a collector called Mason in Ghazipur district. I am not sure if it is the same Mason who authored the book *The Men who Ruled India*. It is said that Mason introduced cricket to Ghazipur. But it died out in a few years. However, it had caught on to some extent in Mohamadabad, a tehsil town, about twenty-five miles from Ghazipur where a prolific zamindar family, with the surname of Ansari had retained the cricket tradition.

I come across an inspector in the electricity department called Siddiqui who was interested in cricket. With his help, I established 'nets' in a portion of the grounds in the collector's compound. We procured the bats, balls and other kit. I had spoken to the principal of the local high school, and we got about thirty young volunteers in the age group of thirteen to sixteen to start playing in the nets. Most of the boys had never heard of cricket; perhaps none had even seen a cricket game being played. Cricket on television was not available those days. We had to start from scratch with the basic demonstration of batting, bowling and fielding, all of which were new concepts to these children. In the course of a month or so, some of the boys had picked up the basic elements of the game. Some had the potential to become reasonably good batsmen and some others good bowlers, with a fairly decent line and length. A short list of twenty regulars was established, for net practice everyday. The collector had the privilege of batting and then returning to work, leaving the nets in the charge of Siddiqui. In about a year's time, the basic elements of the game had been established. In fact, we organised and played a few local matches in Ghazipur, and also took the team to tour a couple of nearby district towns. In the spring and summer of 1966, the group had intensive practice for the following winter. I had organised an elaborate schedule of cricket matches regularly over every weekend in Ghazipur and every other nearby town, including Varanasi, which boasted of a university team. We even got the season's schedule of fixtures printed! The rise in performance of the Ghazipur team was quite remarkable. We won a number of matches, as the boys gained experience. At least five centuries were scored by Ghazipurians, of which two were by the collector. I recall a match that we played in early 1967 against the Varanasi district team, which included six university and two state level players – a two innings match over three days. It was a close affair. The Varanasi team won on the third day with invaluable help from the local umpires. I then lost track of the team but later learnt that six of our players had played university level cricket at Gorakhpur and Lucknow Universities and one had even made it to the state team.

With the above experiment to go by, I was quite convinced that the enormous talent available in the rural areas could be channelised merely by giving decent playing facilities and providing regular equipment to the young boys and girls, for their abilities to surface. Most schools do not provide basic playing facilities and the limited amounts earmarked for equipment gets filched somewhere along the way. All that the children require in order to flourish and bloom is the basic opportunity to play. Any sports development programme in India has to be organised at the grassroots level, by provision of basic sports facilities and material. The bulk of expenditure and organisation is currently focused on construction of large stadia and provision of facilities at the highest level. While these are essential, the primary need is to have sustained organisation of basic facilities at the grassroot level and in rural areas. Our sports development programmes have failed because we have not organised the first step correctly. This failure on the sports front is also symbolic of a larger tragedy, encompassing the full spectrum of Indian talents and abilities. Endowed with excellent human resources, it is the lack of provision of basic opportunities for education, skill development and general exposure that has throttled the average Indian.

There were two elections held during my tenure in Ghazipur. One of them was the election to the state assembly in 1966. The main contestants were the Congress party and the Communist Party. The latter was gaining a strong foothold in the district. I recall a visit by C B Gupta to Ghazipur, campaigning for the Congress party. A Congress wave was sweeping the state, and he was tipped to be the next chief minister. I had known Gupta well from my previous posting at Ranikhet, from where he was the sitting MLA. One morning I got a call from the local circuit house. Gupta was on the line. In his gravelly voice, he asked me how I was and said he wanted to see me. Could I drop in and have a cup of tea with him? I certainly did not want to go and meet him at the circuit house, particularly during election time; the visit would be noticed and could affect my reputation for impartiality. Never mind that he would most likely become the chief minister within a month or so, and I could find myself on his wrong side. I told him very politely that I was not feeling well and that I could not travel to the circuit house. Could he come and see me and have a cup of tea? The shrewd old fox that he was, he told me, "I will talk to you tomorrow morning, let us see if you are feeling better by then." The next day morning, his call came promptly at 7'o clock. He started the conversation with, "I presume you are still not feeling well." I laughingly replied, "Yes. As long as you are in town, I will not be well enough to travel to the circuit house." You could banter with him, so long he understood that you were doing your job well. Anyway, Gupta told me on the phone, "This Sarjoo Pandey, the Communist leader needs to be watched carefully. He is full of tricks; don't let him get away with it." I told Gupta that I would ensure that a proper atmosphere was maintained and that nobody would get away with anything unfair.

Soon the elections rolled in. The returning officer was one Bishnoi, a competent provincial civil service officer. We had to mobilise the resources from all government departments, particularly to provide the presiding officers and other officials in the polling booths. For this purpose, I had called a meeting of all district departmental chiefs asking them to provide the personnel, even at some inconvenience to the departments, for the smooth conduct of the elections. All responded but for one superintending engineer in charge of the irrigation department who was un-cooperative. Bishnoi had tried to convince him to cooperate and when he failed, I asked him to assign the superintending engineer himself to be posted as presiding officer, in a remote polling booth in a sensitive area with a history of violence. Normally, as a courtesy, executive engineers and superintending engineers are not assigned direct polling duties, but I had to make a point in this case. The moment he heard about it, the superintending engineer lost his cool. He stormed in to see me and protested agitatedly, threatening to talk to Lucknow to get the orders changed. I stood firm and told him that severe action would be taken against him under the legal provisions for the conduct of the election, and insisted that he should proceed to his duty. When he found he had no choice, he offered full cooperation from his department. I ensured that a substitute was provided, and the intransigent engineer was allowed to return only after he had reached his post and spent a few hours at the assigned spot. In times of major activity, I have always found stragglers. An unflinching approach is required to ensure that nobody gets out of line.

During this election, there was an interesting episode during the counting phase for the Ghazipur/Sadar (city) seat, one of the six seats being contested. The counting was organised in a large *shamiana* abutting the Collectorate building, with the usual complement of counting tables, counting personnel, supervisory personnel, Petromax lights and provision at each table for seating of observers representing the candidates. The race was neck and neck between the Congress candidate Krishnanand Rai and the Communist party candidate whose name I forget. Counting had started at 8'o clock in the morning and even by 6 pm, when three quarters of the votes had been counted, no discernible trend was visible. Those days, ballot papers from all polling stations in a constituency were not mixed, as is the practice now, and so trends could be misleading. Sometime late in the evening, Rai charged agitatedly into my room and complained about large scale malpractices both at the time of polling two days earlier, and at the time of counting currently going on. Apparently, he found that he was trailing and thought he should take preemptive action. I asked him to explain what his specific allegations were. At that moment, some of his followers rushed into the room and whispered to him that he was currently leading and that he should withdraw his objections. Rai now told me that he was fully satisfied and that he had no complaints. Prudently, I held him back and asked him to record his views down in writing. In his excitement to get back to the counting arena, he signed a short note that stated that he was fully satisfied with the election process both at the time of polling and during the counting phase, and had no complaints. Within fifteen minutes, the communist candidate rushed into my room complaining that major malpractices were going on in the counting tables and demanding that the counting be stopped immediately and all papers be sealed till an enquiry was conducted. I asked him to calm down and specifically point out what the irregularities were. Now, his supporters trooped in and loudly whispered to him that he was leading and was likely to win. So, this candidate also told me that he no longer had any objections. I quickly pulled out the draft ready for him and he also signed gladly to signify his "full satisfaction" with the election process.

At the end of the seesaw counting which went on till about 10 pm it then appeared that the communist candidate had won the seat by twenty-eight votes. But at the head table, there was one column in the master tally sheet still to be filled in and that related to the postal ballots, mainly from the personnel of the defence services. The counting of the postal ballots had been earlier concluded, but the results had not yet been posted on the master sheet. Lo and behold, there were additional twenty-nine votes for the Congress candidate. This meant that Rai was winning the assembly seat by exactly one vote. I asked the presiding officer to recheck the numbers three or four times. Already the communist camp had left to celebrate the victory on the streets of the town, not knowing of this development. It was now midnight. Before making the final announcement and inviting objections prior to the formal announcement, I alerted the superintendent of police to make extra deployment of forces all over town. The few straggling representatives of the communist candidate raised objections and wanted a recount prior to the announcement of results. The presiding officer rejected this since the candidate had just recently declared in writing his full satisfaction with the process. At 3'o clock in the morning, the final result was declared. It was all fair and square and the Congress had won. Subsequently, the communist candidate had filed an election petition asking for a recount. As it happened, the election petition became infructuous, as the assembly got dissolved within about a year, due to a split in the Congress party. I believe this has been the only instance till date in India's rich election history, of a candidate winning by just one vote.

I witnessed a parliamentary election too. As district magistrate, I was the returning officer. The two main contestants were Vishvanath Singh Gahmari of Congress and Sarjoo Pandey of the Communist Party. Gahmari had represented the Zamania parliamentary constituency continuously from the first elections held after India became a republic. A tall, distinguished-looking man in his early seventies, he came from village Gahmar in Zamania tehsil. Gahmari was a relatively well known political figure, even though probably a backbencher in Delhi. Sarjoo Pandey was the major force behind the growing communist movement in eastern UP and he had a very active cadre of workers to mobilise support in the rural areas. He too was a sitting MP at that time from the adjacent Saidpur constituency. However, due to a delimitation exercise, which reserved the respective areas for contest only by scheduled castes, these two leading figures shifted base and came into direct conflict in the newly created Ghazipur constituency. The election campaign was hard fought and with both Gahmari and Pandey working and travelling at a furious pace throughout the constituency. Despite some tension, the polling took place peacefully. The counting, as usual, was done in a *shamiana* abutting the collector's office. Till about 10 pm, as the counting proceeded into the late evening, Gahmari and Pandey were neck and neck. I was sitting in my large chambers adjoining my office, and Gahmari and Pandey each with their followers were with me in the room, getting periodical updates. The race was close. Suddenly in the last leg, the results started turning in favour of Sarjoo Pandey and by 11 pm it became certain that Pandey had won the seat. Gahmari was to be no more an MP. Suddenly in that half an hour, I could see a change taking place in him, right in front of my eyes. From a youngish looking man with poise, serenity and dignity, he transformed into an ashen faced, haggard, shaken old man. His grey hair seemed to turn snowy-white and suddenly he looked puny.

This matches with the description of Emperor Dashrath or Priam, the Greek king, who changed their appearance in a flash to become haggard old men. It was an experience seeing this change come over this old man. I learnt that he died soon thereafter. I believe that if he had won that day, he would have vigorously contested the next election five years later!

Ghazipur was one of the four 'least developed districts in UP', identified as a 'Patel Commission District', designated for special assistance development schemes. Special incentives for promoting small scale industries had been announced in these districts. Thus, the district magistrate was also designated as joint director (Industries), within the jurisdiction of the district. The days were hectic, visiting the various development blocks in the villages and overseeing the programmes. Some of us in the district bureaucracy considered ourselves as 'agents of change' and worked with a missionary zeal for rural development – though perhaps with little to show for it at the end. In that period, many kinds of subsidies to farmers – for crop loans, digging wells, drought protection – and subsidies to artisans and weavers were made available. But misuse of subsidies by persons who were not the intended beneficiaries was becoming increasingly common. Combined with growing politicisation of the district administration and with skewed policy priorities, this seriously undermined the stated goal of development of rural areas.

I recall that when I took up my assignment in Ghazipur in 1965, there were only a total of nine tubewells in the entire district. They were mainly in the properties of large and rich landholders – in general, the concept of pump-set irrigation was unknown. The boring equipment for installing pumpsets and tubewells was scarce. Also electricity was not available in most parts. Diesel sets had not come fully into vogue. I undertook with great vigour a pumpset programme coupled with a rural electrification programme. The water table in Ghazipur district was quite high and water could be struck at a fairly small depth below ground level. I arranged for the procurement of boring equipment, and for the purchase and installation of pump sets and small tube wells. By the time I left the district in 1967, more than 3000 tubewells had been installed and were functioning. A demand for pumpsets had been created and the programme was well launched. As I shall recount in a later chapter, tubewells are the suitable medium for irrigation in east UP, and not large irrigation canals. For a variety of reasons, irrigation policy in UP has become skewed with the major accent on canal irrigation, to the neglect of private pump sets.

Talking of wells, we used to have frequent visits by M A Quereshi, an ICS officer, probably from the 1941 batch. He was then holding the newly created post of agriculture production commissioner (APC), a post I was to hold much later. Quereshi belonged to a place called Ballia, and to reach there from Varanasi, one had to pass through Ghazipur. This was the reason why Quereshi used to make frequent inspection visits to Ghazipur to oversee various government programmes. One of the fads of that time was a rural programme funded by the Centre, christened the 'million wells programme'. The idea was to encourage the farmers to dig *kuccha* storage wells in large numbers, supported by a hefty subsidy. It is obvious that such a programme with huge potential for abuse, would elicit great interest, with wells being dug repeatedly in the same spot, and the subsidy being claimed each time. Once I was travelling near Ghazipur on the Ballia Road just prior to the visit of Quereshi; I saw a large number of red flags on either side of the road, as if there were hundreds of golf holes abutting the highway. When I asked my planning officer what these signified, he told me that the commissioner had given instructions that a red flag should be mounted on each freshly dug *kuccha* well. He liked to see these flags wherever he travelled by car, as a reminder of the 'success' of the million wells programme. When I remonstrated that there was no well at all wherever I had checked personally, I was told, "It doesn't matter; Quereshi Sahib never gets off the car between Varanasi and Ballia." So much for field inspections!

I discovered that the postures that politicians strike are often for narrow ends. I recall an encounter with Raj Narain, the firebrand MP, who had taken on the likes of Indira Gandhi, and whose name is enshrined in important constitutional cases that date to the Emergency years. His histrionics were to make him a legendary figure. He had been invited to a divisional planning committee meeting in Varanasi. Soon enough he was on his feet, bare feet that is. His sandals were in hand and he was violently thumping the table complaining about malpractices. Bhagwant Singh, the commissioner, leaped out of his chair and with his massive frame pinned down Raj Narain, out-shouting him. We were first petrified, and then amused by this spectacle. The malpractice he referred to had to do with the alignment of a new highway that was being constructed. The commissioner wanted to constitute a committee chaired by me, but I had the presence of mind to duck out of it. The superintending engineer who looked into the matter, later told me that all Raj Narain wanted was a minor change in the alignment of the road to accommodate a crony. An overseer was asked to resolve the issue; he did this with a flick of the wrist on the drawings. I heard later that Raj Narain had expressed satisfaction with the planning and development works in the division.

There was more than one occasion to recount, with Bhagwant Singh present. I recall that during the severe drought of 1966 – the sown kharif crops had withered, and drinking water was scarce for man and beast – Bhagwant Singh invited all the collectors to Varanasi at the time of the visit of A L Dias, the then Union food secretary. Dias had reached Varanasi the previous day and had visited some badly affected pockets in the adjoining districts. The next morning, the five collectors of the division met for breakfast at the commissioner's house at 7 am, to briefly explain the situation to him. Dias was to take the 9.15 am flight to Patna where an important meeting had been organised to discuss the Bihar drought, at which the Union finance minister and finance secretary were also to be present. It was a tight day for Dias, as he and the others had to then take an afternoon flight from Patna to Delhi, to be in time for a Cabinet meeting scheduled for the same evening. This would be presided over by the prime minister, who was scheduled to leave for Moscow immediately thereafter. In those days, unlike in current times, there was no provision for the Government of India to come to the financial aid of states for providing relief for natural disaster. The Central Cabinet was about to launch such a scheme, and to announce a major package of 'natural disaster relief' financial assistance to the two states, the first time the Centre was to do so.

As the working breakfast concluded in the commissioner's house, Bhagwant Singh who was lost in his own world invited Dias to his garden. He showed him with great pride the new compost pit system that he had pioneered and also exhibited the new Yanmar hand-driven tractor that he had introduced in the region. I could see Dias getting fidgety about his flight. He mentioned this to the commissioner who airily dismissed any thought of urgency, called for his special assistant and ordered, "Khan, telephone the airport and tell them that a VVIP is with me; the plane should not take off without him." After the details of compost pit and the Yanmar tractor were sufficiently expounded we left for Varanasi airport in two cars – the big Dodge with Dias and Singh going ahead and the five collectors packed into the Ambassador behind. The imported car quickly accelerated, leaving the Ambassador behind. As our car reached the entrance of the large airport compound, we simultaneously saw two things happening: the commissioner's Dodge car was emerging from the OUT gate of the airport and the plane to Patna was taking off in the background – it just could not have had Dias on board! I could well imagine the scene within the Dodge car. As we re-entered the drawing room of the commissioner's house, we could see Singh and Dias sitting in the far corner as we sidled into the room alongside the walls, to find our chairs in that large room. There was pin-drop silence. Apparently, Dias had just spoken on the phone to the chief secretary of Bihar. Raman, the chief secretary, came on line shortly thereafter and said that he was sending the Bihar state plane to Varanasi to pick up Dias. He was awaiting clearance from DGCA, Delhi and this was expected shortly. The Patna meeting had been rescheduled for later, and thereafter the heavyweight contingent could still get back to Delhi in time for the Cabinet meeting. This relieved the atmosphere somewhat. The commissioner suggested to Dias that he might like to go to Circuit House to have a beer while he awaited the Bihar state plane. Dias gruffly refused, got up and told the commissioner that he would prefer to go to the airport and await the arrival of the plane from Patna. I suspect this was the inside story as to how Uttar Pradesh got a very poor share of the drought relief that was announced by the Centre in 1966!

These days, it is common practice for nearly every state to declare a 'natural disaster' at the slightest pretext – there is a 'drought' or 'flood' or 'severe winter', one or the other in every state, nearly every year, to attract money from the Government of India for disaster relief. This has now become part of the political process, with the ease and quantum of finances released dictated by the political complexion of each state. This provides easy access to quick-disbursement money, with greater opportunity for fraudulent use than usual, greasing the political machinery at the district and local level, with the connivance of the departmental staff. Everyone in India except the long suffering local resident, loves a 'natural disaster' – the political leaders are delighted to have an excuse for diverting attention from the lack of governance; their images flashed all over the papers and TV, with their noses pressed against the helicopter windows. The same images can be used again and again, year after year, and need not vary. Of late, political leaders have found such helicopter visits provide a good respite from their headquarters pressures – some even catch up with their file and paper work at this time. The media loves natural disasters, as it makes for good copy and the scenes are photogenic and poignant, if dismal. The local level politicians and officials are thrilled by this windfall supplement to their income. The only person who does not like it is the common man. After all, the system is designed to serve the interest of all the groups, except the ordinary citizen.

In Ghazipur, I also saw for the first time how public money was wasted in the name of development and why programmes have failed in much of rural India, despite countless crores of rupees that have been spent. I was ex-officio the chairman of the Board of the District Cooperative Bank of Ghazipur district. The primary purpose of the bank was to provide crop loans, at concessional interest rates to farmers of the district to procure inputs – seeds, fertilisers, pesticides – the loan being repayable at the end of the crop season. There was a large subsidy element in the interest rate at which the loan was supposed to be given to the farmers. However, unscrupulous members of the Bank's board had evolved a mechanism to corner a large proportion of the concessional funds. They would then funnel the loans in their personal capacity to the farmers at market interest rates or higher; and pocket the substantial subsidy element. The repayment of the short term loan would be through fresh allocation from the next cycle of input loans. This racket would ensure that the favoured directors and their cronies could divert much of the subsidised loans for their personal benefit, and the programme's intended beneficiary was kept out of the subsidy loop. The then registrar of the Co-operative Society asked me to suggest some names for the board of directors of the bank. After a search, I identified five or six people, well reputed local citizens, most of them professionals with high integrity. I also telephoned my friend and service batchmate J P Singh at Lucknow, who was then with the Cooperative Department, to tell him that I had done the selection with great care, after enquiry. When the actual board was announced by the government a fortnight later, imagine my surprise not to find a single one of my nominees in the list. The board, as constituted by the government, consisted entirely of known local scoundrels and petty politicians. The chairman of the board was greatly distressed. An angry letter was shot off to the Registrar, Co-operative Societies, questioning the credentials of those included in the board and firmly indicating that I would not preside or participate in any of the meetings of the body; today such a letter would have drawn a reprimand from the government. In any case, I stuck to my decision for the remaining period of my tenure in Ghazipur. The politicians at the state headquarters had already learnt that the business end of any development finance flow can be well controlled by packing the management with unscrupulous political cronies – the development effort was already doomed from the beginning.

The other episode relates to the distribution of marketing subsidies to a number of handloom societies at the end of the fiscal year, sometime in the last week of March 1966. I received an amount of rupees fifty-three lakhs, an astronomical sum those days, for distribution to thirty-seven co-operative societies, which had claimed the subsidies under a scheme where the government provided cash incentives to cover marketing expenses, to promote the labour intensive handloom sector. The office of the Directorate of Industries at Kanpur told me that the money had to be distributed to these production and marketing societies before 31st March. All the paper work had been done to identify the authenticity of these societies and to scrutinise the vouchers. Instead of straightaway disbursing the amount to the listed societies, I organised six parties, headed by senior officers, to visit the societies and report to me about their genuineness, before disbursement. The teams fanned out the next morning and came back late in the evening to report to me the actual position on the field. Not one single agency out of the thirty-seven listed production and marketing units was in actual existence at the address indicated. Other particulars given in the application were found to be fraudulent; the subsidy was not eligible to be distributed. I promptly returned the money to the director, handlooms at Kanpur with a scathing letter, including the reports of the inspection teams, and asking for enquiries against the local officers of the department of industries who had authenticated the claims. I also suggested a review of the entire procedures, to plug the loopholes in this programme. I awaited an adulatory message for exposing the fraud. Instead, I received a brusque telephone call bemoaning the fact that the funds allocated for this purpose could not be utilised within time, due to frivolous objections raised by me!

The field realities and procedures for distribution of cash subsidies and incentives have resulted in diversion of large amounts from the development budget, to political lackeys, unprincipled middlemen and unscrupulous lower level government functionaries, with connivance at worst or negligence at best by senior level field supervisory personnel. Such diversion of funds encompasses every conceivable field department. In a nutshell, these systematic leakages have ensured that the development assistance does not reach the targeted beneficiary in rural areas.

The fairly sanguine acceptance of leakage from public funds as legitimate source of income came home to me sharply when my wife and I attended the wedding of the daughter of the executive engineer in the public works department in Ghazipur district. As is usual on these occasions, there was a separation of the sexes, and my wife was closeted with the other women in another room. As we were returning home, she told me that one or the other of the women would walk up to Mrs Garg, the mother of the bride and ask her about the salary of the prospective son-in-law, who was an assistant engineer in the same public works department. Indeed, there is no delicacy in Indian society in asking these exceedingly private questions, in a public manner. Anyway, the answer was *invariably* that his salary was rupees three hundred plus two per cent. My wife was puzzled; in all her innocence, she asked me what that two per cent meant. I mention this, to indicate that already by the early '60s, a regular siphoning of the amount allocated for public works was becoming systematised. If an assistant engineer was entitled to two per cent we can imagine the percentages due to the two or three levels in the hierarchy below him and to those who were his superiors. In the engineering departments, it became a regular practice for public funds to be drained off for the benefit of the implementers. This does not include the amount claimed by the local politicians, as well as the margins that the contractor had to reserve for himself. The system had allowed these to become part of normal functioning, again illustrating the fact that public works were not meant for the benefit of the public. They were mainly designed to line the pockets of the implementers and the intermediaries and politicians. All this has now become common knowledge in India. It is noteworthy that in March 2003, Mayawati has openly talked of the cuts received by the legislators, in the implementation of rural developmental schemes. No wonder that the demand for much greater funds to be placed at the direct disposal of MPs and MLAs has gained ground. No wonder also that across party lines, nobody wants a discussion on these embarrassing matters in any public forum.

Somewhere near Ghazipur town can be seen a decrepit non-descript old monument, commemorating the final resting place of Lord Cornwallis – his 'Final Settlement' as it were. Cornwallis, though he may have 'lost the Empire' in America, was a brilliant administrator, who was the second governor general of India. He was on his 'Permanent Settlement' campaign, which he personally supervised, and was proceeding westward from Calcutta when he died. He was buried in Ghazipur. In essence, Cornwallis had, through the concept of the permanent settlement made the process of management of land tenure and collection of land revenue easy to administer for the British government.

The land tenure and land revenue systems in India that were established during the Mughal period endured for a long time. The two types of records – the record of rights (*khatauni*) and the record of seasonal sowing (*khasra*) were created by the Mughals, and administered – verified and re-verified physically every year – by field functionaries. These records documented the permanent right holders of particular plots, and mapped all the plots of the village, the tillers of each plot and the crops sown each season. The Cornwallis method was to reestablish these facts, group the plots under a local zamindar with whom the tenants were permanently settled and create the system of levying the annual land tax through the zamindars. The task of the detailed management of the crops and land revenue as well as the welfare of the ryots was left in the hands of the zamindars. The collectors and the commissioners were the agents of the British Empire, who, as their names imply, would ensure the regular collection of land revenues into the coffers of the empire. However, the collector and commissioner were to be paid a regular fixed monthly salary, rather than a percentage of their collection. This was the grand design envisaged by Cornwallis and implemented in large parts of north India. In the entire area of Bengal and Bihar, Cornwallis had personally supervised the process of permanent settlement. It was only after Independence, in the '50s, that the zamindars who were considered as intermediaries were abolished, and the land vested directly with the tenants who became the owners of the land. The reforms of zamindari abolition were not well implemented in Bihar where feudal landlords managed to continue – in fact, right up to the present – with their private armies to ensure their permanency. The land related turmoil in the whole of Bihar can be traced to the half-baked implementation of zamindari reforms in that state. In Bengal, the reforms, at least on the land tenure side, were effectively implemented, and the permanent settlement was fully undone. In Uttar Pradesh, Cornwallis had just entered the eastern most area and the permanent settlement had not proceeded far. After the abolition of the zamindari system in UP, the next real reform was the consolidation of land holdings, implemented between the 1960s and '80s. The idea was to consolidate the fragmented land holdings of each family or individual, to increase productivity. While the administrative process was reasonably well implemented in general, the upper castes benefited enormously through this process – the system was heavily loaded in their favour in the procedure for evaluating fertility and consolidating the scattered holdings. Those days, Mandal and the other forms of caste-based politics were not as intense as they are today.

The basic village records, the *khasra* and *khatauni*, known by different names in various parts of India, were in the custody of the patwari or the lekhpal, the lowest level revenue department functionaries, also known by different names in different states. A hierarchy of revenue officials did the supervision of this work: the kanungo, the naib tehsildar and the tehsildar who reported to the sub divisional officer. The *khasra* and *khatauni* were vital documents to the peasantry as they reflected ownership rights, tenancy, changes due to land transfer and succession. These records were maintained at village level with counterpart information stored at tehsil level. The proper and accurate maintenance of these records was a key function of local government. These records served a dual purpose – from the government's point of view, they were used to compute its due share of revenue in the form of land tax; from the point of view of the peasant, the document's importance lay in establishing ownership and tenancy rights. Under the British administration, great care was taken to ensure the proper maintenance of these records. A major part of the administration's efforts was to maintain the accuracy of these documents through field visits and inspections; a system of strong rewards and ruthless punishments was in place to ensure that the field functionaries performed their duties with diligence and care. After independence, the importance of these records progressively declined, because land revenue became insignificant, relative to other direct and indirect taxes.

However, the importance of these documents from the point of view of the rural citizenry did not diminish – it became even more important over time to establish ownership and tenancy rights, especially for obtaining loans, and in the context of land litigation. Ironically, the attention of the government machinery to these documents sharply declined, and with many other duties thrust on the district collector and the sub divisional officer, there was hardly any supervision of the maintenance of records at the village and the tehsil levels. The drastic reduction, and in some states the populist measures to 'abolish' land revenues, spelt the death knell for maintenance of land records with any degree of accuracy. The net result was the total license granted to low level revenue functionaries. In the absence of effective supervision and fear of punishment, these became gold mines for them. The peasantry came under the stranglehold of the patwari, lekhpal, and tehsildar, whose increasing clout was not contained in any manner. On the other hand, the problem was compounded with a conspiratorial nexus between lower level revenue functionaries and petty local politicians, to swindle the peasantry. Mischievous entries in the revenue documents increasingly became common. For each application for a crop loan or a land development loan, requiring mortgage of land, it became the norm to get the records amended by a heavy payment of graft. In those days, the 'partal' or regular field inspection was an essential part of the work of collectors and the sub-district officers. As a collector in the '60s, I would set apart one full month in winter for field verification of the accuracy of village level land records, including night halts in camps in remote villages, and surprise inspections. Errant patwaris or naib-tehsildars were summarily suspended. During monsoon tehsil inspections, the accuracy of tehsil records, and their concordance with field records were scrupulously verified and errant officials punished. After the '80s, this critical aspect of the collector's work has been effectively discontinued, with disastrous consequences for the rural citizenry. The net result has been a dramatic increase in land related litigation in rural areas in the Hindi belt; thus, in much of India, especially in the north, nearly every peasant family could be found engaged in litigation relating to land. The improper, unsupervised and mischievous maintenance of land records has resulted in untold misery to Indian peasants. The cases drag on endlessly till finally, in sheer exhaustion, and with the efflux of time, the case dies and the land comes into the possession of the local political thug, with the connivance of the local functionary. This is one very important aspect of rural dynamics, which has not received adequate attention from any quarter.

When I was Cabinet secretary much later, I took an interest in the subject of computerisation of land records. I allocated funds for experiments in two states, for computerising the land records, devising a system for maintaining land records and leading to drawing of village maps on the computer. Task forces were established, and given multi-disciplinary technology assistance. The chief secretaries of the concerned states gave full cooperation and the Government of India underwrote the entire expenses. I thought that after successful trials in a few districts of the two states, a nationwide programme could be launched. I found to my horror, at the time of the first review, that the trials had utterly failed to take off. The local officials in the concerned districts, from the tehsildar downwards were totally un-cooperative; naturally because the computerisation would knock out the perennial source of income they had so far enjoyed. The political echelons in the state were either unwilling or unable to enforce full cooperation. The software teams, who were camping in the concerned districts to accomplish the tasks were thwarted from moving forward. As is usual in these matters, by the time we understood the issues and remedial action could be initiated, I moved away from that post. I have not followed up what happened after that.

The other significant contribution of Cornwallis, which has left a lasting impression, is the creation of the Indian administrative structure. The establishment of the institution of the collector and the commissioner and the creation of field machinery with the objectives of maintaining peace, law and order as well as collection of revenue were brilliantly achieved. These institutions served the intended purpose for at least a century and half with efficiency and were generally even handed. One would be astonished to hear that the salary scales fixed for a commissioner and collector were so high that there was no need to change them for many decades. For the first half of the twentieth century, the collector was in the same income bracket as the top five or six people in the district. He had a legitimate income on par with the richest landlord or most highly eminent lawyer. He had no reason at all to bow or to bend before anyone else. On the contrary, armed as he was with formidable powers, he commanded high respect. Everyone in the district looked up to him for guidance. The failure of independent India to re-conceive and drastically restructure its administrative apparatus, to bring it in tune with the newly perceived tasks of a sovereign republic within a democratic framework has been a policy failure of the highest magnitude. If Cornwallis had reappeared in the 1950s to create a new 'permanent management' or 'permanent development' structure for India, we would perhaps not be in the mess that we are in today! Sardar Patel, the iron man, had the right instincts and the right vision to build a new steel frame; alas, he did not live long enough. The others just did not have the imagination or the tenacity.

4 LEATHER EXPORT COUNCIL, MADRAS: RELAXED INTERLUDE

Suddenly, the train started out of Siena station and I shouted out once again at the juice vendor, who gave me a beatific smile, kissed my 5000 Lira note and waved an energetic good-bye.

No exporter would go anywhere near an Indian mission abroad: the feeling was that they would not get any help and they could get into some difficulty.

IN THE SUMMER OF 1968, I WAS POSTED IN Madras, as the city was then called, as secretary, Leather Export Promotion Council. I soon found out that the Commerce Ministry had sponsored two separate councils with overlapping functions, one in Madras, and the other in Kanpur. The Madras based council was supposed to deal with semi-tanned hides and skins, but in fact, its members were also engaged in exports of finished leather and leather goods. Curiously enough, the Kanpur based council for Finished Leather and Leather Goods also had under its purview the export of 'wet blue', a semi-tanned leather.

These were not just the contradictions the two institutions bristled with. With the two rival councils at loggerheads all the time there was a cleavage among the leather exporters. This was not by chance, but one more of those clever moves by the bureaucrats and politicians at Udyog Bhawan, the seat of the Commerce Ministry. By keeping the industry divided, it was possible to retain control and supremacy over the industry players. I was to see later – illustrative of the games played by Udyog

Bhawan – similar conflict situations brought about in the textiles and the chemicals sectors, again aimed at creating divisions within the industry. A modern day version of divide and rule, one could say.

I was the first government official to be ever seconded to any export promotion council in India. Since then, one by one, practically every such council has had government officials posted as chief executive. I do not know if this is a good move, but then a bureaucrat at least gets to see the perspective from the other side of the table. Here I was on the other side, representing the traders' interest to the government – a process that gave me an insight into the working of trade, industry and the economy at large. I interpreted my assignment to have three components. The first, was to promote the interests of the leather export community. The second, was to use my position as a government officer to carry credibility and bring the problems of the trading community before the government for redressal. And the third, was to act as the eyes and ears of government in pursuing sound policies.

During the three years I was with the council I would, at least twice a year travel abroad, to organise the council's exhibits in fairs and exhibitions in various countries. There would be the *Semaine du Cuir* at the *Porte de Versailles* in Paris every September; and preceding that the *Campionario di Firenze* in Italy; a leather exposition at Earl's Court in London in May and a leather exposition at Atlantic city near New York in October. I had to plan the participation of the council at these events, arrange appropriate space in a vantage position, collect the exhibits from the members and have them displayed attractively, arrange adequate publicity and reach potential customers. Just imagine getting semi-tanned hides and skins displayed artistically!

Apart from the feverish activity associated with preparations for the fairs and exhibitions, and arranging monthly meetings of the executive committee and compiling and circulating relevant paper clippings to the members, there was not much to do on a day-to-day basis in the council. Much of the work was routine and could be done quite well by my assistants. There were periodical visits from the government top brass, and special meetings had to be arranged on these occasions. The visit by a ministry official from Delhi was an important event and could not be ignored. The less important the visitor the more the bother, but I suppose this is consistent with the general scheme of things. Thus, the secretary to the Commerce Ministry, during his occasional visit would spend half-an-hour or so with us and then go on to other engagements. However, the junior-most official from the ministry would give us a headache. Keeping him pleased was vital for the ministry's grant-in-aid to flow into the council. Thus, for this official's visit, cars would be arranged to take him and sometimes his family for entertainment visits, shopping, as also on pilgrimage to nearby shrines. Appropriate gifts would be identified and purchased; the entire staff would then celebrate with a *badakhana*, after the visitation was over and successful, and we had seen the back of the visitor.

Many of the leading leather exporters from Madras were self-made entrepreneurs. The business was highly speculative, and fortunes were made and then lost, in short periods. Till about the time of independence, the entire export of East India tanned leathers and skins, essentially dried semi-tanned leather was to the United Kingdom where the leather was finished and processed and then distributed in Europe and USA, by a tribe of canny British factors. Exports from India were on consignment basis to the London importers, who in a speculative market retained windfall profits as they came, while passing on losses to the Indian exporters. One of the pioneers in the Madras trade was Jamal Mohammad, a leader in the leather trade, who operated in the 1940s and '50s. He was largely responsible for shifting the trade from consignment basis to a fixed price contract basis. He died a pauper, as did many others in the Madras leather industry before and after him.

Nagappan Chettiar ushered the next major revolution in the late 1950s and early '60s. Nagappan's achievement was in breaking the monopoly of the London importers and establishing direct export linkages with the European continent, USA and later with Japan and the Far East. He also led the shift to finished leather and leather goods, backed by sizeable investments. Nagappan had studied only up to the fifth class. Apart from Tamil, he knew no other language; but gradually got to understand spoken English and could later attempt a broken form of speech in that language.

Yet, twice a year Nagappan would visit Europe and USA to develop new contacts, book orders and follow up on business. I could understand that money talks its own language.

Nagappan was the chairman of the Leather Export Promotion Council in Madras during much of the time when I was posted there. A towering and well-respected figure, he had an acute, sharp mind. I have met hundreds of people in the political, bureaucratic, judicial, academic and business fields during my career, but found Nagappan's mind to be closest to what could be described as a genius. He was the undisputed leader of the leather industry in India at that time. I only wish that one could have had a person like him as the Union minister in any economic field – with his understanding, feel, uprightness and sensitivity, he would have left his mark on any sector he touched.

However, typical of the Madras leather industry of those days, he died a broken man. This was sometime in the mid-'70s, not long after I left the council. It all came about due to his pride and unshakeable faith in his own ability and judgement. Apparently, he had sent goods on a consignment basis to a leather factory in Germany that went bankrupt and could not pay him. Even though Nagappan was well insured through the Export Credit Guarantee Corporation, he did not intimate this event to the Reserve Bank of India (RBI), as it would have been a slur on his ability to judge the reliability and credit-worthiness of the German company. Indeed, he took over the management of the German company, hoping to utilise his own leather stocks, but failed in the attempt. In short order, the RBI came down heavily on him, probably assisted in this process by some of his many enemies in the trade. His passport was impounded, his ability to travel was denied; thus eliminating whatever chances he had of retrieving the situation. Even if he were not covered by insurance, he could easily have absorbed the losses. But his pride and faith in his infallibility did him in.

In the autumn of 1969, my wife who is a vegetarian, accompanied me on the circuit to Europe and USA. Nagappan was also a vegetarian. His grasp of European languages was worse than his English. Besides, in those days, waiters and chefs did not understand what vegetarianism was. I recall that Nagappan would invite us for dinner. In restaurants in Germany, Spain, and France he would give precise, explicit and comprehensive instructions. He would explain which vegetables to use and how they were to be prepared, how the rice was to be cooked, and that no lard be used. Then we would get very tasty vegetarian food, even better than that at the best Indian restaurants. He was a gracious host. Every year on the 30th January, at the beginning of the India Leather Fair at Madras, Nagappan would throw a party, a sit down meal for more than 2000 guests, on the sprawling lawns of his Sterling Road bungalow. The guests used to look forward to the deliciously cooked full partridges. At parties held at his house, the guests would be served tea and cold drinks out on the lawns. Those days there was prohibition in Madras, and so select guests were invited to a room inside, where Indian whiskey was served; and then some ten or twelve very special guests would be invited to an inner chamber, where Scotch was served. The special guests in the room would generally include the local joint chief controller of Imports and Exports, chairman of the local Port Trust, and the representative of the Directorate General of Trade and Development (DGTD).

During those three years, I had many occasions to travel abroad, most of the time in the company of Indian leather exporters. During these visits, I noticed time and again that no exporter would go anywhere near an Indian embassy or consulate office. They would steer clear as the feeling was that they would not get any help or benefit; but may in some form or the other get into difficulties. The fears of the exporters were not without basis, as I myself found out.

Some time in late January 1970, the Government of India suddenly slapped an export duty of ten per cent on semi-tanned leather, prior to the annual budget. The export duty came into immediate effect, to cover all exports after 1st February. The background was that the international demand for semi-tanned leather was high at that time and the government wanted to mop up part of the windfall-profits. Now, many export contracts from Madras had been entered into in the previous few months, at prices far lower than the current prices. So, the new duty would be an added burden on the exporters. The same evening that we heard about the announcement of the export duty, Nagappan decided to renegotiate all the pending contracts on behalf of the Madras exporters with the Leather Importers Factors' Merchants Association (LIFMA), based in London. The two of us took the overnight flight from Madras to Bombay, took a morning connection and arrived in London. Late in the evening, I called on our commercial counsellor at the Indian High Commission and explained the difficulties we were facing and invited him to the meeting with the LIFMA authorities, fixed for 9 am, the next morning at LIFMA's office. I thought our embassy would assist us in our negotiations. I still had much to learn.

Next morning the counsellor was not in sight, but the meeting started promptly at 9 am. It then concluded in ten minutes time. Nagappan, in his inimitable English told LIFMA that in the past when prices crashed, the London importers cancelled their contracts, citing an obscure clause in the standard LIFMA contract form relating to *force majeure*. Nagappan mentioned to them that this was also a *force majeure* situation. He asked the British importers to bear the entire ten per cent of the sudden duty imposed by the Government of India. If not, he in turn would have no option but to advice the Madras exporters to cancel all pending contracts, under the same clause and allow re-negotiations to take place at current prices. There was only a moment's silence. The president of LIFMA looked at his committee members, turned to us and stated that the importers would bear the ten per cent increase. The matter was fully settled to our satisfaction.

The commercial counsellor from the High Commission then turned up half-an-hour late just as we were having tea. I explained to him that the negotiations were fully settled and that the British importers had agreed to bear the entire brunt of the duty. Thereupon, the counsellor chose to address the gathering. He lamented on the tendency of Indian exporters to renege on their contracts, and lectured on the need for Indian exporters to stick to their contract terms in all circumstances. He went further and openly advised Nagappan and the Madras exporters to fulfill all the pending contracts, bearing the full burden of the export duty, since it was imposed by the

Indian government on exporters and was not intended to penalise the importers! There was a stunned silence. The British importers had amazement written over their faces. Nagappan and I did not know where to look.

As the air cleared, we politely persuaded the counsellor to get back to his mission, to attend to his other important engagements. Then the LIFMA authorities resumed the negotiations, which were already once closed. Nagappan at the outset stated that in deference to the Indian High Commission's wishes, exporters would bear ten percent of the duty burden, with the remaining ninety per cent to be borne by the British importers. This concession was a windfall bonus to the importers, brought about by the Indian Embassy's intervention. The meeting terminated immediately thereafter. I could now get the picture as to why the Indian exporters would not get to within ten miles of any Indian mission abroad, unless they were compelled to do so for some passport or other visa requirements.

Another episode put my pretensions and me in place, and also showed the scant interest overseas missions have for our business interests. During one of my visits to Delhi, the then Commerce Secretary K B Lal had asked me to give a detailed report, based on a personal investigation, on how the 'switch-trade' worked. He wanted the report within a month or so, as the annual negotiations with the USSR authorities were to be held in November of that year and he needed some ammunition. In switch trade, the goods consigned to the USSR were in fact being diverted to Europe. The shipment of Indian leather would be invoiced to some Russian port say, Odessa, with trans-shipment at a European point, say Rijeka. The original shipment and other documents would have been prepared against a Russian importer. However, the consignment would be offloaded in Rijeka, with the connivance of the Russian importer and the raw materials diverted to Italy for processing. Whereas the transaction on record was under the terms of the Rouble-Rupee barter agreement, the actual payment by the Italian consignee would be in US dollars or pound sterling, which carried a premium against the prevailing Rouble-Rupee rate. The margin would be split between the Indian exporter, the proforma Russian importer and the Italian consignee – the loser would be the Indian system – at the expense of India's foreign exchange earnings in free currency. Even though this scrutiny was technically disloyal to the leather export community that I represented, I made a thorough investigation, collected data, and suggested a number of steps to drastically reduce the level of switch trade in semi-tanned leather.

I put together most of my findings when I was in Florence for the annual fair that year in early September. Between the Florence fair and the Paris fair in late September, there was a week's gap, which I spent in Berne, Switzerland with an old friend. At Berne, I met the commercial counsellor and explained to him that I had an important report to send to the commerce secretary and asked if he could give me the assistance of a stenographer for half a day to prepare the report, to be sent by the Secret bag to Delhi. Even after identifying myself as on deputation from the government's service, the counsellor looked at me disdainfully and told me, "We are not here to cater to the needs of every itinerant Indian businessman; the Embassy's services are not available to every Tom, Dick and Harry." I then met the first secretary and explained my need. He was even more hostile and asked me to leave and not waste his time. Finally, my friend's wife kindly took a half-day off from her work and typed the report for me, which I dispatched by airmail to the commerce secretary from the local post office. Much later, when I met the commerce secretary, he thanked me profusely and told me that the material was of immense help in the Russian trade negotiations, and based on the report he was able to get many changes made, not only relating to leather but also for other commodities. So much for the help provided by our missions in furthering India's business interests.

On this theme of lack of interest by our missions in economic matters, I can relate a number of stories and incidents. I recall that in 1969, at the Florence fair, India was the specially highlighted country. With the help of Air India and other Indian organisations, India Day was celebrated with a cultural show and other events. The chief guest at the inauguration of the fair was the Indian economic ambassador at Brussels. The ambassador, with his family, attended the inaugural function at the appointed time, which took all of ten minutes, and then disappeared to view the Duomo,

Michelangelo's David and Cellini's Perseus. He was not available to meet Indian leather exporters or talk to them about their problems or even try and understand how he could be of help to Indian exporters from his exalted position in Brussels.

One cannot blame these people really for their stupor. During the 1970s and '80s, the Indian missions abroad had no orientation whatsoever for commercial work. One notes, *en passant*, that very senior Indian foreign service officials of the rank of additional secretary or secretary are posted as consul generals in places such as Houston or Chicago. Similarly, one finds senior officers lobbying to get postings as ambassadors to such places as Berne, or Lisbon or Oslo – where apart from some protocol functions and a few social engagements, one cannot find anything significant to do. Noting that the quality of life in these places is quite good and there are excellent golf courses within striking distance, one can speculate as to how these officers spend their time. The minds of people, engaged in work of no responsibility or significance, cannot but go rusty. I believe that there is a greater awareness on economic work in our embassies in recent times. However, with better tele-communications, direct business-to-business contacts are much easier today – in any case, one hardly ever used the Indian missions to develop commercial or economic contacts.

I did once find an Indian mission helpful. This was in Paris, where at the annual September leather fair, I used to go and collect a crate of champagne and a crate of other spirits, for use in our pavilion at the fair, paid for by the council at concessional embassy prices. At the end of the first year's fair, four or five champagne bottles were left over. I met the director of the fair and his assistant on the concluding day and presented them with a couple of bottles each. This worked like magic – for the next year, we got an offer for a much larger floor space for our pavilion, at a better and more prominent location – something we had been asking for in vain for a number of years. Who says our missions do no useful work?

If Indian missions did not take trade visitors from India seriously, neither did foreign governments pay much heed to our visits. Perhaps the two are linked, or perhaps not. When I was in the Commerce Ministry, I accompanied V P Singh who was the commerce minister at that time to Washington. The Indian embassy arranged a reception in his honour. More than 200 guests were present. But practically all were employees from the Indian mission, with a few Indian staff members of the World Bank and the International Monetary Fund (IMF). No senior government functionaries from the US or senators or legislators or even business leaders were to be seen. The only Americans present were three ladies who monopolised the conversation with the visiting Indian minister. I soon discovered that they were junior staff members of the U S Chamber of Commerce attached to the Chapter that deals with India and other South Asian countries. I had to rescue the minister from this chatter and advise him to conclude the evening quickly.

We need to compare and contrast this with the routine parties hosted by foreign missions in India, which attract Indian ministers and senior bureaucrats in droves, in a parched condition. During foreign visits as head of the Indian delegation, or when accompanying ministers, I found that our access to senior levels in the host government was quite limited. We were fobbed off with meetings with inconsequential junior officials. Contrast this with the readiness and eagerness with which our senior officials and ministers receive even very junior visitors; and the access we have allowed to Delhi-based foreign ambassadors into the various Bhawans in Delhi. There used to be a joke that the ease of access for foreign diplomats was inversely proportional to the seniority levels in Indian officialdom. Thus, it was easiest to meet the Indian minister, a little more difficult to call on the secretary, while the joint secretary would not readily grant a meeting. When in the Commerce Ministry, I discovered that a U S Ambassador had separately met the minister, secretary, joint secretary, deputy secretary and a section officer, all on the same day, and all meetings fixed at short notice – apparently, he had better access within our system than we ourselves had.

Indian officials abroad are not taken seriously for one more reason. One repeated theme I picked up all over the world from friends and well-wishers, both Indian and foreigners, was the Indian missions' preoccupation with Kashmir. Apparently, the instructions to our embassies are to project the Indian position on the Kashmir issue, and convince the international community of the validity of the Indian stand. Accordingly, an Indian embassy official, at the first given opportunity, talks about the correctness of India's stance and the absurdity of Pakistan's position. This happens day in and day out, even in places which do not know of the existence of Pakistan or have heard of Kashmir only as woollen pullover material. Thus, in Lima and in Buenos Aires and in Ottawa, in Prague, and of course at Geneva, and New York, and in countless other places, local government officials and other diplomats on the cocktail circuit shun Indian mission staffers, and turn the other way before they are cornered. They know that the Indian is waiting to raise the topic on the absurdity of Pakistan's position. The obsession with which we have flogged this theme in season and out, here, there and elsewhere, has been counterproductive. It is almost as if our missions and consulates abroad have been established exclusively for propagating the – without doubt flawless – Indian position on Pakistan. Other than the Pakistan theme, there is so much to talk and project positively about India.

Indian officials can behave in the strangest of ways when they are abroad. Meyyappan, who also wore the hat of president of the London Tamil Sangam, told me of the visit of a minister from Tamil Nadu, during the 1970s, to London. Meyyappan had been Nagappan's chief representative in London, looking after his European operations. Years after I left the Leather Council, during one of my visits to London I had dinner with Meyyappan and we were chatting away. As the tale went, M the minister, was a tubby balding man, with his girth about the same as his height. He was using the Dorchester Hotel as his base during a visit to Europe. Meyyappan recalled driving him to nearby places in London, for sightseeing. On a visit to Cambridge one day well before lunchtime, M already had a few drinks under his belt. As he was walking on the bridge across the Cam, he would accost the students passing by, girls in particular, with the question: "Do you know that I am an important minister of a state which is larger than your country?" The girls would initially get startled, and then burst into giggles on hearing this rotund figure describe himself. It was thus that M spent his time, based in the Dorchester. In between, he went for three days to Paris and returned to the Dorchester for a few more days.

One day, he just returned to India without informing the hotel and leaving behind an unpaid bill of about £17,000, a significant amount even by today's standards. He must have lived well in the Dorchester and entertained lavishly – £100 bottles of red wine or a £300 bottle of Armagnac is not too uncommon in certain places in London. That is how, as Meyyappan told me, the Indian high commissioner in London, T N Kaul, received a letter from the Dorchester, and I am quoting as closely as I can:

"*Excellency,*

The Dorchester has had the privilege of hosting Mr.M, who, we understand, is a senior member of the administration in a state in India. He stayed with us from ...... to ......in our Suite no...... He left the hotel on ...... without any intimation to us. His hotel bill, to cover all his expenses was ...... £ ... which remained unpaid on his departure.

The Dorchester has a proud history of over 250 years. We have had kings and emperors, dictators and despots, prime ministers, and political leaders, business tycoons and billionaires, whom we have had the privilege of having as our guests over the period. During their stay with us, some of them from time to time suffered misfortunes like loss of kingdom, expulsion from the country, collapse of administration, or crash of the stock market. Some of them had become exiles or paupers during their stay with us. Many of them had asked for time to pay their bills and in some instances, when they were unable to meet their expenses, we had waived the amounts. However no guest has so far departed clandestinely without informing us. Since this is the first occasion of a departure without intimation, the visit of Mr.M has been of special significance to us.

We are bringing the above to your notice, not to request you to settle the bill or reimburse the amount, but to keep you informed of this special event in our history. We have already written off the amount of the bill.

Yours truly, "

Meyyappan told me that on receipt of this letter, the High Commission promptly paid the entire dues to Dorchester and High Commissioner Kaul sent the original letter to Prime Minister Indira Gandhi for her to use in an appropriate manner in the politics of the day. Later, I had asked my old friend, Rajgopal, who was then special assistant to the Union home minister in Delhi to verify its authenticity – he told me that the story was substantially true!

In the leather industry, I came across research that was irrelevant to business needs. The Central Leather Research Institute (CLRI), one of the forty or so national laboratories was located also in Madras. It had a number of competent scientists and technicians, many of whom were abreast with the latest trends, with work experience in foreign laboratories. One would normally have expected CLRI to have a high level of interaction at least with the Madras leather industry, if not across the Indian leather industry. Astonishingly, there was absolutely no working level interaction. The scientists with their research programmes, and the director with his own agenda did not cross the path of the leather industry. Once or twice a year, at industry conferences or seminars, some of the scientists would read papers on one aspect or the other. The director would be formally present on the occasion and the interaction would end there. While the leather exporters would take advice from foreign experts and sometimes invite them to come as their resident experts, a CLRI scientist was neither invited, nor even allowed entry into any factory. The CLRI did no industry-sponsored research on the needs of the leather exporters, and none of the factories had any contact with CLRI's research.

At that time, the director of CLRI was Dr Nayudamma who later rose to the position of the director general of the CSIR, the governing body that administered all the national laboratories. Presumably, this reward must have been due to his major contribution to the leather industry in India; and the record number of technical papers produced by his institute. No one in the leather industry read these papers. In conferences, inaugural functions and other important business occasions, Dr Nayudamma would be invited and placed prominently on the podium. He would refuse to deliver a speech on the grounds that he had nothing significant to say, which of course was absolutely true! Presumably, this was a well thought out strategy to impress all and sundry that he was a man of action and not given to mere words. He rose to become a scientist of national eminence in India, with the reputation of being in the vanguard of science. Perhaps, under his guidance, all the national laboratories in India would have produced even more scientific papers, with little or no interaction with their respective industries. He at least built his own career with great success, never mind his contribution to science.

I was to see this total lack of relationship between research and industry repeatedly in my career. The Silk Research Institute (CSTRI) in Mysore had very little interaction with the silk industry. As I have mentioned elsewhere, the large number of national and state level agricultural universities and research institutes had their own research programmes and agenda, tuned to the academic needs of the scientists and researchers, with no relationship to the needs of the farming community. Research papers meant for academic advancement were copiously produced, to obtain overseas recognition, and sometimes to get assignments abroad. The diverging interests of the national research laboratories and the respective industries could probably be traced to their ties with different parent ministries in Delhi but this can be only a part of the explanation. Whatever be the reason, Indian scientists in national agencies, do little for Indian industry, and that is such a waste.

This can be contrasted with the close relationship between educational and research establishments with industry in other countries. When I was with the International Trade Centre in Geneva much later, I could observe the relationship between academia and industry, though my observations were limited to the business schools in Europe and the US. I found that in the US, every professor had a direct hand in guiding a student's research, which was sponsored by local business, on topics related to their day-to-day problems. Practically every professor was encouraged to spend half his time collaborating with local industry, while ensuring that his teaching responsibilities were not neglected. In fact, the professor would encourage his students to participate in his own research projects, giving them a feel for live, practical issues. In the United Kingdom, I found the situation somewhere half way between USA and the Indian practice; academia had considerable involvement with relevant industry issues, though much less in scope and extent than in the USA.

If poor grassroots interaction between science and industry is one failure of the system, another is the poor treatment meted out to Indian scientists in their home country. We are unable to recognise merit when handed on a platter and our system is designed to promote mediocrity and sham. I recall the case of an Indian scientist who was treated badly on his return to the job he had left behind in India. The same person was then welcomed back when he returned to the job he had left in the USA. During one of my autumn visits to Paris, taking the Pacific route back, I spent three days in Chicago with my brother's friend, Dr Krishna Moorthy, who was working with General Foods. Ten years earlier he had worked in India as a scientist in the Central Food Technology Research Institute (CFTRI), a national food research laboratory in Mysore. He then found an opening with General Foods, known the world over for their Kraft cheese. Krishna Moorthy joined their research lab, near Chicago, and had risen to a position of eminence in the fats and oils field in the US. He was later named to the Presidential Advisory Council on edible oils under the Reagan administration.

I was staying at Krishna Moorthy's house, along with his wife and two lovely children, a boy aged six years and a ten year old girl. Early one morning, we were just preparing to load my bag in the car, with Krishna Moorthy scheduled to drop me at the airport, on his way to work. I saw Mrs.Krishna Moorthy starting to sob. She was crying out aloud, saying she wanted to return that very day to India and would not spend one more day in America, the godforsaken country! In tears, she came to me, with Krishna Moorthy and the two children watching helplessly, caught hold of my arms and beseeched me not to leave her behind; that she would not let go of my arms till we reached India. One can visualize the scene. I was young those days and this young lady was practically hugging me and begging not to let go of her. I was distressed and embarrassed to get into the middle of this domestic crisis in the house of my hosts. The scene continued; Krishna Moorthy promised to take her to India without delay and to settle down in India and only then her tantrum exhausted itself. As we left the house, she was sobbing quietly in a corner, homesick for India.

My next contact with the Krishna Moorthys was more than ten years later, when I was based in Delhi. They were on a holiday and I had arranged for their accommodation in Delhi and provided a car to take them to Mathura and Agra. Over dinner at my home one evening, I asked Krishna Moorthy how he had been over the past few years. Apparently, he did keep his promise to go back to India. He returned to the CFTRI in Mysore and asked for an assignment. The CFTRI, he said, cared a fig for his experience in the laboratories of General Foods in the US, the expertise he had and the honours he had garnered in that field. The maximum they would do was to let him join them as a junior scientist and treat his absence as '*dies non*' – this paltry concession would be a waiver of the maximum age limit for recruitment to the lowest level, in view of his qualifications! Krishna Moorthy had offered to work for them without pay if given an adequately challenging assignment, all to no avail; after all, CFTRI was a national laboratory that had its own aims and objectives and recruitment of world class talent falling in their lap was not one of these. Krishna Moorthy had tried out Mysore and Bangalore for one year, and disgusted, returned to the US where he was welcomed back with open arms by the US company, which made him an additional director on their board. As for Mrs. Krishna Moorthy, now she had absolute contempt for everything Indian – she found the taxi drivers insolent, the beggars at Mathura obdurately intrusive, the Chennai weather humid and uncomfortable, Delhi polluted and unbearable. After every sentence, she would regularly refer to conditions "back home in the USA" and told me that when they would next leave the US for a holiday, they planned to go only to Europe and did not intend returning to India.

Krishna Moorthy had changed too. During my brief stay in Chicago ten years earlier, when he had asked me what I wanted to do, I asked to attend a baseball game – I had never seen one before. My host was reluctant as he had no interest in baseball and had not seen a game even on television – not to mention seeing one in a stadium. On my insistence, he accompanied me to the Cubs Stadium – it was a double-header that day between the Chicago Cubs and the Cincinnati Reds. The match started on a sunny, warm day. I enjoyed the game but could see Krishna Moorthy become increasingly uneasy as he did not even know the basics of the game. At the end of the first game, he urged that we leave; I insisted on staying on for the second game. Towards 4'o clock, as we were well into the second game, a cool wind started and within half-an-hour, the temperature dropped sharply. While we had some warm clothes with us, they were not enough to deal with the wind-chill factor. With chattering teeth, Krishna Moorthy would nudge me, proposing immediate departure – I would tell him, just one more innings, please! This went on till the match was over, and we got to the warmth of the car and drove home. Ten years later when I met Krishna Moorthy, he said that after the shivering introduction to baseball that October day, he had become a card-carrying member and a loyal fan of the Chicago Cubs. He had a season ticket for the Cubs Stadium, and would travel to see the Cubs in away matches, as many times as possible every year. The transformation was complete.

Rafael Thanjan, a junior official in the Director General of Trade and Developmen was a very important individual for the members of the Madras Leather Export Council. No industrial unit could be started or a unit expanded or machinery imported or technology negotiated, even in the private sector, without the prior approval of DGTD. Indeed, it was an absurd situation that all industrial units had to turn to DGTD for every major decision. The DGTD also had a role in initiation of policy changes including the structure of the import and excise duties. The Leather Development Council was a body constituted under the aegis of the DGTD, chaired by a senior official of DGTD, with membership from the leather exporters, financing institutions and some public representatives. It was charged with responsibility for debating the various improvements relating to the technical and commercial side of the leather industry and its exports. Thanjan, the development officer in DGTD for the leather sector was the member secretary of the council, which met once every quarter at different venues in India.

One of the members seconded by the government to the council was Raj Bhoj, who had earlier been a nominated member of the Rajya Sabha. Raj Bhoj was a political gadfly of sorts, who had in his younger days, been a private secretary to Jagjivan Ram, the noted Congress leader, who had held important positions in the Congress government. Apparently, he had conferred Raj Bhoj with the 'Gold Pass', which entitled the latter to travel by first class anywhere in India for free – it was a privilege granted by the railway minister to a few, on his discretion. Thanjan, as the secretary to the Development Council, had to approve the travel claims of the participants at meetings, particularly the non-officials. Non-official members of the council were entitled to travel by air and claim reimbursement based on proper certification of actual expenditure incurred. Thanjan told us this story over a drink in Nagappan's house. A Development Council meeting was held in Bombay, and Raj Bhoj had travelled in the same first class coach as Thanjan, both on their outward journey from Delhi to Bombay, and on the return leg from Bombay to Delhi. Raj Bhoj would display his gold pass with a flourish. Bhoj's travel claim for participation at the meeting had included the amount of the Delhi – Bombay – Delhi airfare. This, when he had not even spent any money for the train travel! There was also the certification appended in the claim form, with Raj Bhoj certifying that he actually had spent the money for the purpose for which it was claimed and certifying the mode of travel. Thanjan said, "Though I knew that the claim was false, I did not want to get into any political trouble. So I quietly cleared the bill, without any fuss." I was aghast at this astounding story. Thanjan had failed to discharge his duty as a drawing and disbursing officer and besides this made him an accomplice and an accessory after the fact. Without saying so, I chided him as to how his conscience would allow him to do what he did. He told me that it was much better that he turned the other way, and ignored any knowledge of the falsity of the claim – after all Raj Bhoj was a politician, who could get him into trouble by getting a false inquiry initiated against him. This story exemplifies the malaise in our system, a micro instance of the tragedy of the failure of governance in India.

At the same Bombay meeting, there was a dinner hosted at the Taj hotel, with the participation of members of the Leather Development

Council and a number of Bombay-based leather exporters and industrialists. Prohibition was in force in Bombay at that time. However, liquor was flowing freely at the dinner and the leather exporters were guzzling whiskey happily. I saw the most remarkable sight of Raj Bhoj in a state of roaring drunkenness; he was literally rolling on the floor, from wall to wall, making uncouth noises. For the first time, I had come across the real meaning of 'rolling' and 'roaring' drunk.

At another meeting of the Leather Development Council held in Srinagar in 1970, Raj Bhoj announced to us that he was a candidate for the forthcoming elections to the post of president of India. He jokingly extended an invitation to all of us, saying that the next meeting of the Council would be held in the Rashtrapati Bhawan. Actually, he did not do too badly coming in third in the polling, with a substantial number of votes. Sometimes I wonder what would have happened if he actually had been elected as the president of India: But then we have seen stranger things happening in India. I am sure he would have persuaded the External Affairs Ministry to serve alcoholic drinks at official receptions in the Rashtrapati Bhawan. I have been to countless dinners and receptions at the Rashtrapati Bhawan, all very staid, dull affairs. Surely a couple of drinks would have livened up the proceedings in situations where we currently drink toasts British style, sipping orange juice.

When I was in the commerce ministry, we would host a number of official parties for foreign delegations, to reciprocate the hospitality we received from them abroad. The rules did not permit serving of alcoholic beverage in ministry parties. The technique used was to arrange the dinner in a hall in one of the five star hotels. By a strange coincidence, one of the public sector organisations under the ministry would invite the very same guests for cocktails, in the same hotel, on the same day and it would be in an adjoining hall. As a further coincidence, there would be no partition between the cocktail room and the dining area; and surprisingly the cocktails would end just as the dinner started. These strange manoeuvres would be arranged, so that the ministry could follow the letter of the rules. After all, we could tell the people of India that alcoholic beverages are not served at official parties. This will be no more a lie than any number of devious answers to more substantive questions, trotted out by the ministry for informing the parliament and the public. No matter if the public sector agency had nothing whatsoever to do with the visiting delegation, except to pick up the cocktail bill. After all, what are these agencies meant for, except to help the ministry in its time of need.

I am sure an obliging External Affairs Ministry would have found some similar solution to help out 'President' Raj Bhoj. The government ministries are resourceful in such matters. I want to leave this theme, imagining a scene of Raj Bhoj rolling back and forth on the floor of the main Rashtrapati Bhawan reception hall! Though such a thing has never happened before, we cannot underestimate what government functionaries are capable of doing.

The assignment with the Leather Council gave me plenty of spare time; I needed activity to work off my excess nervous energy and I took to playing cards in the evenings. On many evenings, including on working days, I used to play gin rummy at a local club, starting early in the evening and going on till late at night, occasionally even spilling over into the morning. The game was absurdly interesting, rivetting, and possessive, with an addictive quality bringing me on to the table day-after-day. The three to four tables were set in a large covered hall, with open sides to allow the breeze, more or less shaped like an airport hangar. Here, I again saw a demonstration of 'roaring and rolling' drunkenness. At that time Madras was also under prohibition. On and off, a salesman of agricultural pumps would come there late in the evening to get drunk. He would carefully rescue his half-bottle from inside the recesses of his dress, lug it into the shadows in the slats between the two tennis courts nearby, and out of sight of anybody, proceed to enjoy his drink. Around 10 pm, he would then emerge back to the hall, and after a while the fireworks would start. He would roll up and down the hall, shrieking to high heaven. After a brief look at this spectacle, the card players would blank out the scene, and concentrate on the important work at hand. Around midnight, our pump salesman would exhaust himself, and in a puddle he had made, proceed to sleep and snore explosively for the rest of the night. The club authorities were indeed tolerant to permit recurrence of such an obnoxious event every now and then, and during prohibition days. The reader may well wonder why I would go regularly to a joint like that. I wonder too.

My travels made me realise that people are quite much the same wherever they may be. In every country I have visited there was something to remember. In Italy, I learnt very early to 'watch out.' It is a delightful country with cheerful citizens who are all the time bubbly and effusive. But one has to take extra care while interacting with the denizens of this great country, which led the European renaissance. In 1969, while travelling for the Earl's Court exhibition in May, I stopped over for a day in Italy in preparation for the Florence fair that was to follow in September. One evening I arrived in Rome, and while checking out the next morning, I cashed the necessary travellers cheques, to pay my hotel bill in lira. I recall that I got an exchange rate of 1498 lira for one pound sterling. I then went to the Banco Di Roma to cash a pound bank draft, for a much larger amount. The cashier at the bank counter was very helpful, and started counting the money in lira for delivery to me. As I glanced at the delivery slip, I found that he had applied a rate of 1452 lira. I had expected a better rate for the draft compared to the travellers cheques, and immediately told the cashier that I had got 1498 lira that morning at the hotel for my traveller cheques. He nodded understandingly, snatched the transaction slip from my hand, tore it up, redid the calculation in the machine, handed me the new slip at the exchange rate of 1498 lira, counted and handed out the money and dismissed me! If I had mentioned to him a figure of 1520 or even 1600, I wonder what would have happened. Was I too hasty in mentioning the number 1498 only as the exchange rate? I really do not know how the bank's books were managed using such a 'flexible' exchange rate, which changed from minute to minute; or perhaps the cashier was playing his own games with his bank.

After this, I took the fast train from Rome to Florence. It was morning rush hour and even the first class compartment was jam packed, with people standing in the corridors. At Siena, where the train stopped briefly, I leaned out to the platform, to the soft drink vendor and bought a bottle of Arancata Amara – probably costing 150 or 200 lira. I handed over a 5000 lira note and asked for change; the vendor nodded but was seemingly very busy with other passengers who were purchasing drinks, in the hot summer weather. As I would shout to the vendor for change, he would nod at me courteously, start to count the change, and then interrupt the process to again service other customers. Suddenly the train started leaving out of Siena station; and as I shouted at the vendor once again, he gave me a most cordial smile, kissed my 5000 lira note and waved an energetic good bye – he was wishing me *bon voyage*.

Though the duties cannot be called as heavy, I learnt a great deal during that assignment. Working in an environment so different from what a government servant is used to, enabled me to understand better what makes the economy tick. During those three years, I had made a series of recommendations, which formed the substance of the report of the Sitaramayya Committee. I argued for merger of the two councils, so that there would be only one body covering the entire leather sector. I recommended phasing out semi-tanned leather exports, through disincentives, and then further progressively discouraging the export of finished leather, by providing incentives for manufacture and export of leather goods. I also delineated the detailed methodology, by which these were to be achieved. In the event, most of the recommendations have actually been implemented, though more slowly than they ought to have been.

So, those were the duties associated with my post, interspersed with spells of little to do, the rigours and tribulations of five-star travel in India, and travels spanning three-months every year to wonderful places in Europe, USA, and the Far East – onerous indeed. I immensely enjoyed this assignment. However, only much later, in fact really only after my retirement, did I actually understand the relationship between effort put in and rewards received in the course of public service. Here I was in this posting, with plenty of time to play cards, and travel abroad and generally enjoy myself. At the end of the day, I had, within the system, become an expert in foreign trade, paving the way for my postings to the Commerce Ministry and later to the ITC in Geneva. The law of administration that governed the situation, but which I did not recognise then, runs as follow: "Effort put in and rewards received are inversely related". I found the law applied to each of my postings. In the Geneva posting, I had to put in the least effort, and this was the most rewarding. I had worked some sixteen to eighteen hour days on the postings in the Small Industries Corporation, the assignments at Lucknow immediately after my return from Harvard, and the spell as Cabinet secretary. At the end of these assignments, I was slapped with enquiries: trivial, absurd and unconscionable. But enquiries they were – pesky, irritable and a nuisance. I failed to realise what every sensible public servant knows backwards: that he should do the minimum work, if any, required to sail through without disaster. Was I the idiot? But then, on balance there was the recompense that I enjoyed every moment of the work. Can those who take the soft options say the same?

5 KANPUR: PORTFOLIOS IN INDUSTRY AND EXPORTS

I found that the letters to New York, Ottawa and Frankfurt were in dark brown government envelopes, with glue spilling all over, and with addresses written in Devnagiri script. I opened a few and discovered that the letters were written in chaste Sanskritised Hindi.

The relevant export documents were shown to the inspector, at his residence, along with an envelope containing cash computed at fifty paise for each pair of shoes exported. The inspector never once felt the need to even look at the export consignment.

ON COMPLETION OF MY ASSIGNMENT WITH the Leather Council in Madras, I moved back to Lucknow in UP in 1971 and then held, until 1979, a series of postings in Kanpur shuffling to and fro all the time between stints in Lucknow and a study break at Harvard. The Kanpur phase, in a manner, concluded my field postings, and I was to move on after this mainly into secretariat jobs in Lucknow and Delhi, again with a sizeable break in Geneva. In Kanpur my postings were in UP Small Industries Corporation, then with the newly formed Export Corporation, and finally as director of Industries.

Until Noida, just across the river from Delhi, overtook it in recent times, Kanpur was the major industrial town in Uttar Pradesh. A number of industries, mainly in the textiles, engineering and leather sectors had flourished in this town in the pre-independence era. So, a number of state-run organisations such as the state Small Industries Corporation operated out of Kanpur. In the 1960s, Kanpur started losing its pre-eminence as an industrial centre. Big houses in Kanpur such as the BIC group of industries were on the decline and besides, there was a general lack of impetus for industrialisation in UP, which also affected the Kanpur industry.

I was posted as the managing director of the Uttar Pradesh Small Industries Corporation. One of the main functions of the corporation was to supply iron and steel, coal and other controlled raw materials to registered small scale units for their own use. It would obtain the allocated quota of steel from the concerned central authorities, transport and store the steel at its twelve warehouses and distribute it to the registered small scale units. This was a complicated activity, run fairly efficiently and on commercial lines. The practice was that the director of Industries would provide the lists of small industries eligible for allotment of raw material, and the corporation would do the actual distribution. During the period I was there, A K Sharma, the director of Industries jettisoned the established procedure and started ad hoc distribution of iron and steel for an immediate consideration. After some time, even the formality of verifying whether a particular unit was registered or not, or was eligible for allotment or not was dispensed with. The director started issuing allotments at random, distributing his favours freely. Thus, for example, a newspaper reporter for his services rendered, would get ad hoc allotment of two tons of steel. That piece of paper would be worth Rs 3000. Touts and *dalals* opened their temporary offices inside the directorate compound. They would buy all these ad hoc allocations or permits, pay the premium in cash to the permit holders after getting their discharge on the reverse, consolidate the permits for truck size or even rake size quantities, and draw the steel for sale in the open market at a premium. These permits had turned into negotiable instruments! The director doubtless, had political blessings for these brazen activities. There were rumours that a close relative of the chief minister had registered a large number of bogus units, near Varanasi, with Sharma's active connivance.

As the custodian of the small industries quota, I took up the matter with the director, pleading difficulty in management of the stocks, and in having to cope with the losses to the corporation. I suggested that the director might keep for himself a small quota of five per cent of the state's allocation, for discretionary allotment, and hand over the rest for planned distribution of the quota steel. But he would have none of it. Matters came to a head. I complained to the Industries secretary, who was chairman of the board, that I could not be held responsible for the commercial functioning of the corporation in these circumstances. This made me the director's personal enemy. He started a newspaper campaign. Everyday, in one newspaper or the other, there would be a write-up against the mal-administration and bungling in the Small Industries Corporation. The campaign continued for some months. There were no personal allegations against me; but the impression was created that the corporation was a den of corruption. Exactly the opposite was true, as the origin of the problem was in the director's office.

As luck would have it, Sharma was transferred abruptly from his post, I believe against the wishes of the chief minister, but on orders from Delhi. It seems somebody had complained to Indira Gandhi about the corruption in the Directorate of Industry in Kanpur. Some people thought I was behind this manoeuvre and that I was not as innocent as I looked! In the event, a CBI enquiry was held against Sharma and a case of corruption was established. Three years later, when I was the secretary in the Appointments Department at Lucknow, I was surprised one morning to see Sharma come into my office early, at 8.30 am. He looked gaunt and wasted and could not dare to meet my eye. He told me that corruption charges against him had been finalised by the CBI. A chargesheet was being filed in the court. It was being sent to the state government for the formality of its approval. Could I kindly save him by referring the matter to the Legal Remembrancer of the state government and thus, delay the process. In the normal course, I would have taken the paper straight to the chief minister, obtained his approval and sent the state's concurrence to the Government of India the very next day. I do not know why I obliged Sharma, despite the anguish and mental agony he had caused me. I did refer the matter to the Legal Remembrancer, thus, giving Sharma breathing space. Much later I understood that the case had been filed in the court, and sometime later that Sharma was no more.

Sometime after Sharma's departure, a new minister for Small Industries, who was not familiar with the industry sector came in. I was told that in his previous department, there were a large number of government employees and the minister had established a regular system for obtaining a steady income, by meeting requests related to transfers and postings. However, in the Small Industries Department, he was initially at a loss to know his source of income. He was soon told of the technique followed by A K Sharma, which he immediately adopted, and soon a well-regulated system was established in his office, this time inside the secretariat in Lucknow. Thus, a visitor could walk in, deposit the 'fees' with one clerk, meet another clerk in the next room to obtain a permit for steel and leave the room. It was a neat operation. I mention this because it was common knowledge that nearly every minister found his own devices to extract money from the customers of that department. But, this was done discreetly and usually from the minister's residence. A neat assembly line like set-up run from the minister's office was certainly unusual.

A business based on raw material shortages had been created, engaging people in unproductive activities and generating large amounts of black money. Small industries were thus established only on paper, in order to be eligible to draw iron and steel from the small industries quota, to sell in the open market, at a premium. It was not uncommon for one small scale unit to obtain six or seven separate functionality certificates, showing different ownership and marginally different registration addresses, in order to claim many times its requirement of iron and steel or coal. Small industry was not the business of the small industrialist – his main business was cornering scarce raw material, for a profit. The inspectors of the industry department became rich people, mainly by colluding in furnishing false certificates on the existence of these units. Periodic checks were conducted by the Industry Directorate to flush out the false units. However, in the prevailing political atmosphere where the lower functionaries were steeped in systemic corruption, such campaigns produced only token results. An honest joint director of industry who verified capacities with undue diligence was soon transferred out. The aggrieved 'industrialists' could find shortcuts to reach the minister concerned and then the officer would be accused with the slogan of being anti-industry and shunted out. I recall that Rajat Kumar, a young, able and upright IAS officer was posted as joint director. He personally checked the credentials of a number of units and cancelled the registration certificates of bogus units. Some assailants entered the youngster's house one evening, and stabbed him in open view of visitors. He survived after many anxious days in the hospital. It was not surprising that soon thereafter he resigned from the services, to look for a career elsewhere.

It was an era of shortages, thanks to a cumbersome industrial licensing system. The DGTD in Delhi was the licence recommending authority. It was not easy for a medium or even for a large industry to run this gauntlet and set up or even expand manufacturing capacity. Elaborate and time consuming investigations were part of the procedure for licensing industrial units. This inhibited new industry. Only a handful of industrial houses in India had the savvy and the contacts in Delhi to 'influence' the power centers and obtain licenses for manufacture of basic raw materials. Technology transfer from abroad was also restricted, creating a further bottleneck. It was as if the objective was the creation of hurdles rather than industrial products. And, to protect the industries that had obtained licences, a tariff wall on imports had been built. Naturally, this led to a serious shortage of raw materials of all sorts. Iron and steel was in permanent short supply, as were other basic items like soda ash, cement, basic chemicals and polyester. Any basic building block required by the processing industry was in short supply. Those days, one ton of steel products – of bars or rounds or plates or sheets – would carry a premium of between Rs.1500 to Rs.2000 per ton. In other words, the market price for one ton of these items would be approximately double the basic controlled price fixed by the government. The government took upon itself not only to fix the issue prices of the iron and steel manufactured by the government run plants; it also fixed the issue price of other manufacturers of steel such as the Tatas. Not only that, the government controlled the distribution channels for the steel. Similarly, there was an acute shortage of coking coal for industrial uses. There was no reason why this should be so, since India has abundant coal resources. Between the shortages created by the collieries and the hurdles of railway transportation, coal and coke were in short supply, even in areas in Uttar Pradesh that were well connected by railways to the collieries nearby. I wonder what the situation would have been in more distant places.

All this was not an accidental or casual occurrence. Those days the manufacture of basic industrial raw materials in India was in the hands of a few identifiable industrial houses, whose interest was to block imports and create a permanent aura of shortages, which would result in premium prices and windfall profits. This was achieved by a close and illicit nexus at the highest political levels. There was too, the complicity of senior bureaucracy, whose sense of pomp and self-importance was inflated by the deferential attitude of the big industry leaders. I am reasonably sure that there was some kind of a grand conspiracy to maintain a tight leash on availability of basic raw material items and to create an atmosphere of shortages and frequent price-hikes. The origins of black money in India – to feed the political machinery, as also to line the pockets of industrialists – had its roots in the manufacturing sector of industry.

Any policy maker could have seen that the prime need for economic development of India, with the quality of its human resources, was to make available raw material, intermediates and components at international prices. Had this been done, Indian products would be unbeatable in world markets. This is true of the textiles, electronics, light engineering, leather, pharmaceutical and countless other fields. Had such a policy been initiated in the 1950s and the '60s, India would have been a great economic power by now, instead of sliding into an also-ran position. This distortion in our policy framework – that we were 180° opposite to where we should have been – is a testimony to the vested interests that have controlled our economy and our society. It was possible for Japanese steel makers, and later the Koreans, to convert Indian ore into iron and steel, and sell it back to India at half the ruling Indian prices – and ironically, this needed, and got a 120% import duty wall to protect the domestic steel industry. To boot, the Japanese could invest in a 300 mile railway line from Koraput, pay for the mining costs, pay for the development of the port on the east coast, and take the ore 3000 miles, to bring back the steel to sell it at half the Indian price! Can policy making get any more weird? The prime beneficiaries of this policy were the public sector steel units and Tatas, with the cost borne by millions of small manufacturers of light engineering products – and the Indian consumer. As we can see, if we look around, such distortion is not peculiar to industry alone.

As part of their annual exercise, the Public Undertakings Committee of the state legislature that year took up the work of the Small Industries Corporation for examination. During the daylong meeting, the thirty or so legislators present went on a diatribe against the corporation. The theme was corruption in the corporation. They would not let me get a word in edgeways to explain the work that was being done or to throw light on the issues they raised. It is not improbable that the then Director of Industries A K Sharma, and his cronies had briefed the committee members, and fed them with the earlier press coverage. The chairman of the corporation, P K Kaul, who was also the state industries secretary was also not allowed to speak. Kaul, who was later Cabinet secretary in the Government of India, and then ambassador to USA, was a no-nonsense officer with an uncanny ability to get things dône. At the end of the discussion, Kaul managed to get a word in. He said that he knew the work of the managing director personally and had full confidence in him. The MD had not been allowed to explain the multifarious activities of the corporation of which steel distribution was only one part. Kaul added that if it was the unanimous view of the committee, let them make a recommendation to wind up the corporation.

This was my first detailed contact with a committee of the legislature. I then understood for the first time that most legislators had no interest in facts; they were easily enticed by anyone, to take any point of view. I was to come into contact with committees of elected representatives in Uttar Pradesh and in Delhi many more times, in different *avatars*. I had not found serious reasons to change my view that the examination by a committee of the legislature on any matter is a farce; it is yet another trapping that our democracy has fostered, a game legislators play.

The corporation, at that time, had advertised for the recruitment of a civil engineer, to help supervise the construction of industrial sheds, in industrial estates that were being sponsored by the corporation. Those pre-golfing days I used to be a relatively late riser in the mornings. About one month prior to the actual date of interviews and selection, the minister for small industries began waking me up with a phone call, invariably at 6.30 in the morning, to remind me that his candidate had to be selected. It was annoying to be woken up with this message almost every morning, for about four weeks. I had told the minister a couple of times that I would do my best – where was the need to remind me everyday? The morning calls would still persist. In deference to the minister's wishes, I had made the mistake of including his nominee in the shortlist for the interview without having gone through his CV. So, he had been invited for the interview.

I had an inflexible rule throughout my career, that on recruitment and promotion matters, I would proceed by the merits of the matter, and not be guided by recommendations or intervention from any quarter. The effect of an unworthy selection would persist for thirty-five years, and so it would be a disservice to the system to depart from merits. In accordance with this principle, I had not even mentioned to the members of the interview committee about the keen interest shown by the minister in a particular candidate. I had mentally made a note that if the minister's nominee was fairly competent and would find a place even at the second rank, I would create one more post to accommodate him.

In the event, during the interviews which went on till late evening, the minister's nominee was nowhere in the picture. In fact, he was ranked tenth, dead last. The experience required was in construction of industrial sheds, structures above ground level. The poor boy's work experience was in the mining field, below the ground level. Early the next morning, as anticipated, the minister's call came at 6.30, optimistically enquiring about confirmation of the selection of his nominee. I haltingly explained to him why the boy could not be selected. Half way through my explanation, there was a loud grunt, an angry exclamation, and the sharp comment that he was asking for my immediate transfer, and the phone was banged down to abruptly end the conversation. I told my wife at breakfast that we might brace ourselves for an early move. Luckily, the minister did not carry enough clout in the system to get me transferred out. For the next few months, his relationship with me was frosty, and he was looking for every chance to do me down or humiliate me. This event happened in 1973. I wonder if today any officer can dare go against the wishes of a minister expressed so explicitly and persistently.

On the subject of recruitment, I should refer to the dismissal of a senior official of the corporation that happened during that period. I took the view that Vinay, who had earlier been recruited from the open market for a senior executive position in the corporation, was not effective. I had spoken to him a number of times but he would not pay heed. One day, I mentioned to the board that since I was not satisfied with Vinay's performance, could the board meet him and have a chat with him and form its own views? Kaul, who was the chairman, would have none of it. He said that the MD was the chief executive and was fully responsible for the corporation's activities and had full authority over all the employees, however senior. This threw the ball back to me. I spoke again to Vinay and mentioned to him guardedly that the board was not satisfied with his work. Would he pull up his socks? Three months later, when I found no improvement, I raised the issue at a board meeting, and proposed that his services be terminated forthwith. The board agreed instantly. The same day, three months' pay in lieu of three months' notice was given to Vinay and he was asked to leave the corporation. Now Vinay was the son of a legislator, which probably explained why he had been selected in the first place.

He sent objections and appeals to all quarters and sent a petition to the chief minister, alleging wrongful dismissal. The matter was taken up in the Assembly. After a few days, I received a letter from the industries secretary, enclosing a petition by Vinay claiming wrongful dismissal, and asking for re-appointment to the corporation, *inter-alia* alleging that I was prejudiced because the MD could not bear to have an official in the corporation drawing a salary higher than his. I was a little annoyed at being asked to explain my conduct, despite the matter having been discussed in the Board in detail. Anyway, I sent a detailed reply, meeting every point raised. To my surprise, this was the last I heard on the subject. About a year later, I had occasion to see the relevant file in the secretariat. Based on my reply, Kaul had prepared a detailed note analysing the subject. He had clarified that he was a party to the decision and that if the chief minister was satisfied, the matter should be closed once and for all. I found from the file that the chief minister had concurred. Subsequently, on the number of petitions that had come from various quarters to Kaul, he had cryptically recorded that the matter had been carefully examined and that the chief minister had agreed; and there was no need to do anything further. Though the file had become voluminous, mainly due to the representations received, no further examination was done nor was the matter reopened.

I mention this episode to contrast the handling of the matter with the present day scenario, and to highlight Kaul's effective and neat disposal of the matter. He closed the issue, not allowing it to linger on. Today, it would be unusual for an MD to propose and carry through the abrupt termination of the services of a senior staff member. It would also be unusual for the board to agree – it would prevaricate, procrastinate, and have the matter repeatedly examined. And at the government level, no secretary would have the courage to take full responsibility and firmly shut the case. Again, political pressures from different quarters would not allow the matter to rest; and sooner or later, an order would come to reinstate the employee, thus humiliating the MD and disturbing the ethos of the corporation.

After the stint with small industry, I was asked to take over as the managing director of the Uttar Pradesh Export Corporation. This was a refreshing change from small industry. H N Bahuguna was the chief minister at that time, and he could have been looking for ways to create openings for employment in the state. He saw potential for stimulation of UP's excellent handicrafts through the export route. The corporation had been in existence for a few years. But as I took over the assignment, I found to my consternation that the export corporation did not even have an office or any employees. It functioned in Kanpur out of the residence of its chairman, a senior government official. I was asked to sit in the office portion of his residence which accommodation I flatly refused. Over the next month, I hired office premises, recruited a few key staff either from outside or on deputation from other departments and set about conceiving the outfit's work programme.

I had asked our office manager to send a letter to potential contacts overseas, our own missions abroad, and concerned government offices in India, about the functioning of the export corporation, advising that I had taken over as the managing director. Walking past the mail dispatch section one day, I came upon a bunch of envelopes ready for post. I found all of them in the thick dark brown government envelopes, with glue spilling all over, and with all the envelopes carrying addresses in Hindi. Since I could not decipher the destination, I asked for clarification and discovered that the destinations were places such as New York, Ottawa and Frankfurt – written in the Devnagiri script, with the Hindi pronunciation of the destinations following the imagination of the scribes! I slit open a couple of envelopes and discovered that the letters to all the foreign addressees were written in chaste Hindi. There was not a slim chance that these letters would have gone past the Kanpur post office, not to mention reaching their destination. When I asked for an explanation, the answer was simplicity itself: the office assistant and the dispatch clerk showed me the order issued by UP government, which categorically decreed that all official correspondence emanating from government offices, including state corporations, should invariably be in Hindi, in the Devnagiri script. The assistant pointed out to me censoriously that the government order did not have any exception clause for letters addressed to foreigners and foreign destinations. He hinted that he did not want to be hauled up for transgression of government instructions! I tore up the letters and envelopes, dictated the letter afresh in English, and in the initial months personally supervised the dispatch of all communications, prepared in the Queen's language, in flagrant violation of the UP government's standing instructions.

Having sorted out the language hassle, it was on to business. It was not clear whether the corporation should be a purely commercial agency, using government funds for embarking on export business in competition with private exporters, or a development organisation, providing infrastructure, technical and other assistance including training to exporters. The latter model would allow the corporation to work in cooperation and not in conflict with manufacturers and exporters. A third model would be a bit of both – to work, both in competition with exporters, and also in collaboration with some manufacturers, sometimes enabling them to become exporters. I prepared a policy paper mentioning the three alternatives, detailing the pros and cons, outlined the financial implications and asked my board for guidance. Very soon the paper went up to the government for its view. I found that nobody had any views on the subject, nobody had thought the issues through, and nobody even cared. The government felt it was fashionable to have an export corporation and it would be in the interest of the public to promote exports and that was it. It was left entirely to my own devices and it was up to me to decide which way to proceed. Which was just as well.

Those were interesting days. I had to chart out a path for the corporation to take, create a road map, and conceive of the resources and input requirements as well as the likely outputs in the short and medium run. I was not quite sure that I was equipped with the necessary experience to do this but this can hardly hold back a government officer. The managing director willy-nilly jumped into the fray. Four areas of operation were initially identified for export promotion – hand knotted carpets from Bhadohi and Mirzapur, carved wood from Saharanpur, brassware from Moradabad and chikan work of Lucknow. All these were traditional handicrafts of Uttar Pradesh, in the hands of petty manufacturers and traders who did not have the required organisation or resources to expand their activity.

But for the brassware operation, all others became fairly successful in the short run and a base was laid not only for expanding the corporation's activities but also for improving the overall condition and generation of employment at these centers. A wood seasoning plant was established at Saharanpur to provide seasoned wood, which would prevent warping after the carving. This, coupled with injection of new designs and some marketing efforts, started yielding new export contracts and in new markets. The Lucknow chikan work, which was basically a household activity, was re-organised. Arrangements were made for supply of basic textiles, threads and accessories from a central point. Sewing machines were supplied. A central standardisation and inspection procedure was drawn up. Warehousing was arranged so that stocks could build up, to execute bulk orders. These measures helped bring the household industry in Lucknow on to a more organised footing with potential for growth, at the same time, retaining its identity as a household craft. The hand knotted carpet industry had a base in Bhadohi that dates back to the Mughal days, commencing with the settlement of groups of weavers brought in from Iran. It had an old tradition but marketing contacts were weak and the local organisation not well established. Thus, the weavers, under the supervision of a master weaver would weave the carpets and hawk them at the best price available to middlemen or traders, who resold them to exporters. Central agencies such as the All India Handicrafts Board and the Handloom and Handicraft Export Corporation had some operations in that area, though these were not very effective. I could fortunately locate and hire an excellent local official, Anwarul Hasan, who knew the carpet industry intimately and was able to organise the export corporation's work in that area on a sound, though limited footing. These led to tie-ups with master weavers. A number of business contacts were established, and regular supply lines were assured to a number of European importers, to start with in Germany. The corporation's relationship with existing carpet traders in Bhadohi-Mirzapur was initially antagonistic and we had to survive an anxious period, which passed off. The carpet wing of the export corporation was getting set to fly.

One major innovation I introduced was to expand the manufacturing base by imparting training in weaving of carpets in the Bhadohi-Mirzapur area. The corporation experimented with a new formula that became successful. This was to create training programmes in collaboration with existing manufacturers and exporters. The scheme was drawn up in a manner that would attract interest of all concerned groups, the businessmen, the locals and the government. Perhaps it was this balancing of interests that helped make the project succeed. I do not now recall the wording of the scheme as it was drawn up, but the outline was as follows:

i. *The cost of training would be shared equally by the corporation and the businessmen.*

ii. *Stipend to the trainees and payment to the master weaver would be defrayed by the corporation.*

iii. *The businessmen would provide the premises and supply raw material, mainly wool – and have the right to retain the products made by the trainees.*

iv. *New and better looms would be provided on loan by the corporation for use by the trainees.*

v. *Primary schooling would be provided to the trainees, for a minimum of three hours a day, in collaboration with the Education Department with costs defrayed by the corporation.*

vi. *The businessmen undertake to absorb at least half the number of the trainees at the end of the completion of training.*

vii. *The corporation would provide free looms and working capital for trainees who showed the interest and potential to branch out on their own.*

This became a popular programme. All the elements had fallen into place. The trainees found gainful employment after the three months training period and the associated businessmen found the proposition profitable. The local community was happy that the children were learning new skills. I found many communities asking for such centres in their area. I could draw funds from the All India Handicrafts Board in the Central Government, and from the state government for opening new centres. We branched out into non-traditional locations. For instance, in collaboration with the Indian Tobacco Company in Shahjahanpur, a large number of centres were opened in an area where carpet weaving was unknown. Many years later, after my retirement, I drove through Shahjahanpur and was thrilled to find a fairly well established and thriving carpet weaving industry. Centres were also opened in Agra. The corporation's forays provided a fillip to carpet exports, and added to employment. At the end of the day, I could see that a well thought out scheme, properly implemented, can indeed work even if limited resources were available.

We had a visit by a high-powered purchase team from the Hudson Bay Company of Canada, buyers for a department store chain. The Trade

Development Authority, an outfit under the Commerce Ministry had invited the three-member team. This was part of an effort to push Indian products in the Canadian market. On this visit to UP, their interest was primarily in handicrafts, especially carpets, brassware, Agra stonework, and woodcarvings. Chief Minister H N Bahuguna, dynamic that he was, saw the visit as an opportunity for promoting UP handicrafts. He called me to say that the state plane would be at my disposal and asked that the visiting Canadian team be taken around. I escorted the three-member team to Bhadohi, Saharanpur, Moradabad and Agra in those two days and organised a special display of exhibits at these places. The state plane used was a Fokker Friendship, a Dutch six-seater aircraft. The Canadian team called it the 'small fokker' and had no end of fun on the punned variant of the plane's make. One member of the Canadian team had apparently been an air force pilot in his younger days, during the Second World War period. However, he had not sat on the controls of a plane since that time. The pilot of the UP aircraft was a dare devil, in the best traditions of the state's airline menagerie. He took to heart the chief minister's injunction that the visiting Canadian team should be given royal treatment and obliged the Canadian ex-pilot by asking him to sit in the co-pilot's seat. This went on for one or two flights and then the ex-pilot expressed a desire to take the controls. The pilot must have obliged him, since, to the horror of the other two Canadians and myself, the plane started lurching in the approach before landing in the runway at Varanasi. We had a jerky, bouncy landing with the plane veering in all directions, giving us the fright of our lives. The leader of the Canadian group, who was one of the passengers, flatly refused to get on board for the subsequent flight, if the ex-pilot was given access to the cockpit!

At Moradabad, while the Canadians were most welcome, the private brassware manufacturers refused to permit my entry into their factories, as the export corporation was a competitor – the existing manufacturers and exporters were well entrenched, and inimical to the corporation. I found this a humiliating experience, after having earlier been the master of all that I surveyed in that district, from the vantage position of a senior magistrate! At the end of the two-day UP *darshan*, the Canadian team liked many of the products but no commitment or orders would result. The Canadians told me that they were reluctant to do business with a government organisation. I understand they developed business relations subsequently with some private exporters. At least the spadework done by the corporation was not a total waste.

By and by, the corporation went into the export of shoes from Agra. Groups of tiny shoe making units were formed, sometimes each member having only one or two machines. The group would be provided with samples, helped with quality checks, provided technical support, and supplied with components. The corporation would put together the produce of the various groups to fulfill an export order. This is essentially what many private exporters did. I sought and obtained a token portion of the bulk orders obtained by the State Trading Corporation of India (STC), for supply of shoes to USSR. Prem Seth, father of Vikram Seth the Indian novelist, who was the director in STC, grudgingly gave us a tiny segment of the Russian order expecting that we would fall flat on our face. However, so satisfied was he with the feedback he received from Russia, that he started directing larger portions of the order for execution by the export corporation. This became a major segment of the corporation's work and we had to develop some additional groups to meet these requirements.

The Russians had their own inspectors to check the products ready for shipment. I found the Russians no different from Indians at least in one respect. Their inspection methods were quite cursory and depended primarily on the way they were looked after. The looking after included liquor and other forms of entertainment involving the oldest profession. And for the exporter those days, there was also the compulsory pre-shipment inspection by the Export Inspection Agency (EIA), a Government of India body. The body was charged with the duty of physical inspection of all goods meant for export; ostensibly to protect export quality. The actual procedure followed by the agency in Agra in the case of shoes was simple and elegant. The relevant export documents were shown to the inspector, at his residence, accompanied by an envelope containing cash, computed at fifty paise for each pair of shoes to be exported. Never once during those two years that I observed, would the inspector ever have the need to physically look at the export consignment. A proxy look at the envelope was sufficient for giving his stamp of approval! I was told that some intrepid but foolish exporters had taken the consignment of export shoes to his residence, but without the envelope. Even without having a look, the consignment was declared to be defective. It did not comply with the established export inspection procedures.

The export corporation, also a government agency, had some difficulty in meeting the under-the-table-fees of the EIA, as well as the more substantive needs of the Russian inspectors. We found a method. As the back-to-back Letter of Credit (LC) was opened with the STC, there were concurrent instructions to the bank that when the LC was encashed, a certain percentage of the amount would automatically be debited from the corporation's account. This would then be credited to a special 'group welfare' account operated by representatives of the manufacturing group. This amount was to be used by them specifically for the welfare of the EIA employees and the Russian inspectors. Much later, when I was in the commerce ministry, I pushed hard and successfully to eliminate compulsory pre-shipment inspection in cases when the foreign importer undertakes on his own, to arrange the inspection. As the next logical step, the pre-inspection procedure was altogether eliminated for all products.

Towards the end of my stay in the Export Corporation, Kaul, the industry secretary suggested that we should conduct an export potential survey of UP's handicrafts, and that the Indian Institute of Foreign Trade IIFT would be a suitable agency to prepare the report. The findings would come in handy when soliciting resources from the state's finances, as well as from other sources. I readily agreed with the need for a document listing the products and the promotional steps that required to be taken. However, in my enthusiasm, I said there was no need to waste money by inviting an outside agency. I had detailed information on the various products at my fingertips, and just needed to take fifteen days off to prepare a comprehensive report – in any case, the outside agency would have to depend mainly on the corporation for the relevant data. Kaul chided me for my naïvete. He told me that a report prepared by the IIFT would be an authentic document, which could be waved at the finance department, and among the legislators. Never mind if it substantially contained the data given by the managing director and reflected his views. A report prepared by the MD would have no value whatever even if it said the same thing. His words were that, "It does not matter what view is expressed so long as the right person expresses it!"

In retrospect, I took many risks in expanding the commercial activities of UP Export Corporation and got away unscathed. If I had taken those risks as a private entrepreneur, and if they succeeded as they did, I could probably have turned into a successful businessman. However, it was providential that I did not make any slip, or meet with any ill-luck. The system would have pilloried me and thrown me to the wolves. The average government servant is on deputation to a commercial agency for a short time and this is too brief a period to take risks or to identify oneself with the success of the venture. That is the surest route to inviting a departmental inquiry and ruining one's career. The government servant takes a safe 'no risks - few rewards' path. It is not in the nature of government servants to take risks – that is an entrepreneurial quality, which rewards well when successful, or punishes failure. For the entrepreneur, a business is a lifetime activity.

Two decades later, when I was the textile secretary in the Government of India, the issue of child labour was much debated – it was prominently discussed in the US as well as in European centers in the context of abuse of human rights in India, Pakistan and elsewhere. With my personal experience of working in the poorest parts of India, I knew that young children were looking for any kind of meaningful training and gainful employment. It is a tragedy of our planning process that along with a primary education, children in the rural areas do not have access to any vocational training, which will lead to gainful occupation. With the massive illiteracy that pervades much of India, especially in the Hindi belt, families in rural areas can barely eke out a basic existence. They cannot afford the marginal cost of sending children to school, despite the process of the actual schooling being free. They cannot forego the marginal gain that comes out of the child's alternate occupation, however insignificant it may be. Denial of employment to children, on the grounds of child labour, is a major imposition on the child and on his/ her family. This is not to say that these are grounds for defending child labour. But how can one object unless an alternative way is found to provide vocational training combined with primary education. Some of the groups in the US or Europe, so vociferous in declaiming against child labour, in the name of child abuse and human rights, might well have a vested interest. Thus, we may find hidden support for any move to ban or inhibit the import of hand knotted carpets emanating from manufacturers of machine knotted carpets in Europe. Some groups have also sprung up in India against child labour and it became fashionable to mount an agitation in this regard. Without ascribing motives, one wishes these protestors realise that they should not deprive these children of their only means of life-time occupation, with no alternative in sight.

On the last day of May in 1975, I was surprised to hear from the department of Personnel in the Government of India that I had been selected for the Mason Fellowship at Harvard University. This was a one-year mid-service programme leading up to a Masters in Public Administration. The course was to commence in early September at Harvard but there was a ten-week preparation at Colorado University commencing on the 8th of June. I was peremptorily asked to report at Boulder in Colorado that day, just a week ahead. There is a background to this.

During one of my routine visits to Lucknow from Kanpur in the previous year, I heard in the corridors about the Mason programme, but was also told that it was too late to apply for inclusion in the nominations for that year. On an impulse, I called on the chief secretary, who promptly lifted the phone and gave a direction to the personnel secretary at Lucknow to have my candidature forwarded by telex to the personnel ministry in Delhi. I forgot all about it till December that year, when I received a call to be present at a selection interview at Delhi sometime in the middle of January 1975. The interview was to be conducted by one Prof Guissinger from Harvard, along with U C Agarwal, the Establishment Officer, a key functionary of the Personnel Department." There was only one vacancy for the fellowship. There were ten candidates for the interview and I was called in last at around 1 pm. Only Prof Guissinger was present; Agarwal had left after interviewing the previous nine candidates, as the day had been declared a holiday due to the death of an important dignitary. Guissinger now on his own, conscientiously spent all of forty-five minutes with me and appeared favourably disposed at the end. But as I could see from the confusion he was exhibiting, he was evidently in some sort of a dilemma. Professors, after all, are more transparent than civil servants and can barely hide their thoughts. Anyway the interview ended, and I returned to my headquarters. Sometime in February, I learnt that S Ramakrishnan had been selected and I was not; that was that and the matter was closed for me. And then, suddenly towards the end of May I was intrigued to get the message to proceed to USA.

I discovered later how this had come about. Apparently Agarwal had indicated his preference for S Ramakrishnan, an officer working directly under him in the ministry as the first choice. He must have made up his mind well in advance of the interviews, in the classic government mould of having the minutes of a meeting finalised well before a meeting even begins. There is an irony too: a personnel officer pushing his own assistant forward, but that is a small abuse. Before decamping from the scene, Agarwal had extracted a promise from Guissinger that Ramakrishnan would be the selected candidate, and now Guissinger's conscience was demanding that I be placed at No.1. He resolved this dilemma by placing Ramakrishnan first to fulfill his promise, and myself after that to satisfy his conscience. Here started a comedy of errors.

It so happened that one of the other candidates was anxious to be selected. He had asked a MP who was visiting Harvard, to check out on his chances for selection. The MP had taken the trouble of visiting the administrative offices of Mason Fellowship, and was shown the recommendations made by Prof Guissinger. The report, in the first para mentioned the name of Subramanian Ramakrishnan to be selected for the fellowship – Ramakrishnan's first name happened to be the same as my surname. And in the next section, the report listed the other candidates in order of merit, in case more fellowships opened up for the course. So, in that second list my name, again a Subramanian, was placed at No.1 and the name of Mehta was placed at No.2. The MP did not take into account the coincidence involving Ramakrishnan's first name and my surname. He wrongly presumed that in both lists the same person was at the head. And so, he promptly conveyed to Mehta, mistakenly, that he was the first candidate in the waiting list in case a new fellowship opened up. Evidently, Mehta then pulled wires in Delhi with various funding agencies and finally persuaded United Nations Development Progravence (UNDP) to sponsor one more fellowship for the same course. The Personnel Department promptly sent the message to Harvard indicating the availability of one more fellowship, asking for the name of the first person in the waiting list for acceptance in the course; confidently assuming that Mehta's name would be sponsored from Harvard. They were surprised when Harvard sent the offer to me – Ramakrishnan later told me about the look of astonishment on the face of Agarwal, his secretary, when he received the message from Harvard, mentioning my name. Apparently, Agarwal, not being present at the interview when I came in last, did not even know of my existence and besides, he had worked actively for Mehta's inclusion. That was how I got the invitation for the one year-programme at Harvard! There are quite some Subramanians around, and I will recount later how a similar mix up of names had me on the mat.

I was sponsored by the state government, as an observer for the Election Commission in the Azamgarh bye-election. This was the first election to Parliament after the Congress was totally wiped out of the Hindi belt following the Emergency. This was for the first time that an election observer was appointed. Since then, we have graduated to a situation where large numbers of observers are deputed to each constituency. In the event Mohsina Kidwai of the Congress won, presaging the storming back to power of

Indira Gandhi. The excesses of her rule were forgotten within two years. Public memory is short indeed. The public only saw the ineptitude, bungling and misrule of the Janata Dal in the previous two years. The Azamgarh elections were conducted in the peak of summer when, under the broiling sun, the temperature often reached 120°F in the open. On polling day, I was in my jeep, with my armed escort, criss-crossing the constituency, and visiting polling stations, to observe if the proceedings were smooth. At mid-day, I stopped the vehicle on a side road, under a tree, to have my sandwich lunch, which I had brought along.

In the far distance, I could see through my binoculars a field where a peasant clad only in his loincloth, was tending to the land in preparation for the planting, in advance of the approaching monsoon rain. I soon also saw his young wife, carrying a small basket containing his meal, accompanied by her two children. From a distance, I could observe the children bounding ahead to embrace him as they approached him. I also could see the affectionate greeting that the woman gave him, in a loving yet dignified manner, without even coming close to touching him. I could sense a certain restful peace in that rural scene, under the fierce mid-day sun in one of the most backward parts of India, among rustic folk who lived barely above subsistence level. I looked at this sight, contemplating the tranquility that the good Lord had bestowed on those who are content with the most elementary things. I thought of the politicians and the bureaucrats and the industrialists and the professionals who extract from such people the last bit of juice for their own luxury and their own narrow ends. Had the man not heard of the election or if he had, could he not perhaps spare the time to further democracy? He was immersed in his own simple routine with its minimal needs. His fortitude and inner strength are what have prevented a bloody revolution in India, despite the deprivation and exploitation of the class he represents.

6 LUCKNOW: IN THE CORRIDORS OF THE SECRETARIAT

As we approached the main building of the inspection bungalow, we saw a crowd gathered there. With garlands and bouquets they rushed towards our car. I could see a large smile break out on his face – he temporarily forgot that it was a secret mission. And then one person from the crowd shouted, "This is not him – This is not the irrigation minister." The crowd turned back.

The collector, in the annual entry, had a gushing full-page celebration of the personality of his probationer, a prospective son-in-law. The report concluded with the prediction, "he will go far". His commissioner, on review, recorded his own telling view cryptically: "the farther the better!"

ON COMPLETION OF MY FIELD ASSIGNMENT with the Leather Council in Madras in 1971, for the first time in my career the secretariat corridors beckoned me. I was back in Uttar Pradesh spending the first few months as joint secretary in the chief secretary's branch at Lucknow and then in the appointments department before moving to Kanpur. Then, in 1976 after my return from Harvard, again back in the state secretariat in Lucknow, I had my first taste of the Emergency.

I returned from Harvard in the middle of 1976, and was then posted in the secretariat at Lucknow, as special secretary appointments in the personnel department. N D Tewari was then the chief minister. That was in the thick of the Emergency during the prime ministership of Indira Gandhi when Sanjay Gandhi was ruling the roost in Delhi. He had a free hand to pursue with vigour the programmes of his choice, no matter that he neither had practical experience of affairs of state nor any insight into administrative matters. No doubt, his youthful enthusiasm was exuberant, but he launched himself like a misguided missile. N D Tewari was in close touch with him and would be in Delhi every two days to confer. Not for nothing was he nicknamed New Delhi Tewari. Sanjay was being groomed to be the next person in formal authority at Delhi and in anticipation, N D Tewari would be regularly at his feet.

At that time, T N Dhar, who functioned as secretary to N D Tewari, found the going so hot, that he managed to peel off for a three-month course somewhere in the United Kingdom. He got me installed in his place as secretary to the chief minister for this period, presumably because of my reputation for hard work and sincerity, or perhaps since he thought I was the only person around who would not manoeuvre to stick on to the seat even after his return. At any rate, during the height of the Emergency period, I had a ringside seat for about four months to see how the state was administered.

Each time Tewari returned from Delhi after a Sanjay *darshan*, he would carry with him a large sheaf of representations and applications from various quarters given to him by Sanjay Gandhi who, in turn, would have received them from political intermediaries or cronies. Sometimes more than a hundred in number, these covered requests, complaints, allegations, or reports of irregular activities, asking for some favour or some action from the government. One of my tasks was to get my office to tabulate these applications, send them to the concerned district magistrates for immediate enquiry, obtain a factual report and insist on remedial action where called for. Every time the chief minister would go to Delhi, he would carry an updated version of action taken on previous complaints and applications. Apparently, the effort of a proper enquiry in each case, irrespective of whether the remedial action sought was taken or not, kept Sanjay Gandhi satisfied. To be fair to the chief minister, he never even once applied pressure on me to get this or that done. By the same token, when these applications were dispatched to the district magistrates for being looked into, I never applied any pressure or made any request for a specific action to be taken. I merely insisted that a factual report should come promptly and any appropriate remedial action, as considered fit should be undertaken.

In general, the grievance redressal mechanism in state and Central governments is notoriously weak, slow and ineffective. The grievance redressal system ought to have been a routine function of the district administrative apparatus as well as the various departments of the state government. At least with the Sanjay Gandhi method, the complaints got a prompt hearing, whatever the result. Only the utter failure of the normal systems and the non-existence of a *bona fide* machinery had led to the creation of this special channel during the Emergency. Out of thousands of petitions passing through the chief minister's office during those four months, I found that in about seventy-five per cent of cases no action was called for nor was any action possible and so these were reported accordingly. In about twenty per cent of the cases, the complaints and allegations were found to be true and some remedial action could be undertaken; and the remaining were frivolous or preposterous, not deserving a second look. So it can be grudgingly admitted that this mechanism had its uses, perhaps one of the milder amongst the despotic actions of that time.

One of Sanjay Gandhi's obsessions was the family planning campaign undertaken by him. There is no doubt that the most basic of India's problems relates to its large population and its high growth rate. Sanjay Gandhi rightly saw this as a primary issue to tackle. But his methods were draconian. Every state was given a large family planning 'target' to fulfill by one method or the other. Male sterilisation or vasectomy was the preferred mode and the UP authorities were not worried whether the operation was conducted voluntarily or otherwise. Targets had to be met. The programme as undertaken was one dimensional, focusing on vasectomy and ignoring the socio-cultural realities of a population consisting of different ethnic backgrounds in a democratic setup. Coincidentally, one of the courses I had just taken at Harvard related to the socio-economic bases of population growth, and dealt with the correlation between population growth on one hand and female literacy, medical and health facilities, and economic development on the other. I personally found the programme as implemented in UP to be unimaginative, brutal, and not rooted on sound economic principles. I had a ring-side view again of the operations of the state machinery in implementing the massive task given to it by a person in Delhi, who was not even in an official position. Everyday, lists would be compiled of vasectomy operations undertaken on males and 'loops' fitted on the female population, districtwise – analysed against the daily, weekly, and monthly targets and brought up for review personally by the chief minister every day. These compilations were apparently reviewed in Delhi since we would periodically receive Sanjay Gandhi's comments, expressing appreciation here, or disapproval there; and occasionally demanding transfer of one district magistrate or other for poor performance.

I recall one incident to typify the kind of actions undertaken. An over-zealous local district magistrate had ordered that every bus crossing Muzaffarnagar, a town on the Delhi – Dehradun highway, be stopped at the bus stand and males aged between twenty and seventy be forcibly taken to an adjacent temporary medical camp, where a team of doctors awaited them for compulsory vasectomy. No matter whether the person was married or unmarried; had children or no children – no matter even if he had already undergone one or more sterilisation operations! Each male, able bodied or otherwise, was subjected to this process. As the word spread, terror stricken passengers would avoid that route and buses would go empty past the town. This process was repeated in a number of places, though I must add, not with such brutality or callousness.

In many rural parts of UP, during the winter of that year, in shivering low temperatures, mobile medical teams with armed escort, would descend on remote villages and scour the outlying areas to locate males who would fulfill the district quota. This created so much tension in the rural areas that there were reports of the males fleeing villages on hearing a rumour about an impending visit of the medical team, and then staying in the bulrushes in the wild open for three or four days, in wet or shivering near-zero temperatures, returning to their homes only after they felt secure enough. Many such stories were verified and found to be true. The Congress party paid the price for this callousness, with its utter rout in the following year's election, when astonishingly it could not secure even a single seat in the Hindi belt. But, equally astonishing, in the general elections held two years after this rout, the Congress party of Indira Gandhi stormed back to power. Such is public memory indeed as the politicians have well understood.

The Muslims in UP were particularly agitated with the family planning programme and the way it was being implemented. They saw a deep-rooted consipiracy to reduce the Muslim population in the country. Mullahs and masjids became the centre of opposition to the programme and contributed to the growth of resentment amongst Muslims. The word spread that family planning was contrary to Islamic laws and did not have the sanction of Islamic traditions – it was un-Islamic for a Muslim to undergo vasectomy. On their part, the Government of India and the state government were anxious to get Muslim religious leaders of the state to endorse the programme, and clarify that vasectomy was not un-Islamic. So, efforts were made to get Muslim religious leaders to issue *fatwas* proclaiming the legitimacy of family planning.

One such major religious leader whose *fatwa* was eagerly sought was Ali Miyan who lived in his ashram-like abode on the Sai River in district Rae Bareli. His *fatwa* would have an enormous role not only in influencing the Muslim community in west UP but also in parts of Rajasthan, Madhya Pradesh and Delhi. The Central Government made efforts to obtain Ali Miyan's *fatwa*. Late one night, I was told that Mohammad Yunus, a person in close proximity to the prime minister of India, was visiting Lucknow and would travel to Rae Bareli, located fifty miles away from Lucknow, on a confidential mission. Would I meet him next morning at the Lucknow railway station and escort him to Ali Miyan in Rae Bareli district? The chief minister himself was not aware of the details of the confidential mission and one of the reasons I was deputed was to keep an eye on Mohammad Yunus's activities, to see what he was up to. I met Yunus at the railway station. He was accompanied by a gentleman who was not introduced to me. We sat in the large, imported car that was waiting and proceeded to Rae Bareli. I did not know the purpose of the visit, nor indeed even of the existence of Ali Miyan. On the way, Yunus asked me whether I knew that the mission was confidential and told me that no one should be informed of it. I affirmed, truthfully adding that I myself knew nothing of the mission and there was no question of anyone else being informed by me. Once we reached Rae Bareli town, neither Yunus nor I knew where to proceed and so I decided that we might as well go to the main inspection house.

As we approached the main building of the inspection bungalow, we saw a crowd of about sixty people gathered there with garlands and bouquets who rushed towards our car. I could see a large smile break out on the face of Yunus – he temporarily forgot that it was a secret mission – and as a politician he was pleased to see the large reception committee. As he got out of the car, sticking his neck out to be garlanded, one person from the crowd shouted, "This is not him – This is not the irrigation minister." The group melted away, leaving Yunus with one foot in the car and one on the ground, with his neck sticking out. He turned to me furiously – "This is a secret mission; and now they will know that I have been here." I tried to assuage his feelings, factually stating that nobody had recognised him, which probably irritated him even more. Meanwhile, we espied the jeep sent by the district magistrate, with a junior officer, who told me that he had come to escort the party to Ali Miyan's residence.

We got into the jeep and then proceeded through a winding country road, with the district magistrate joining us on the way. After a few miles, we came up to the cottage where Ali Miyan lived, on the banks of the Sai River, next to a small mosque with an adjoining minaret. Ali Miyan was an elderly man, simply clad, with a gentle, serene face. He seemed to be totally at peace with himself and fitted well in that rural setting next to the river – he looked like a *rishi* of our *Puranas*. He received the four of us and welcomed us inside the cottage. Yunus turned to me and to the district magistrate and gruffly asked us to wait outside and walked in with Ali Miyan. I could see a flicker of embarrassment on Ali Miyan's face – he promptly returned, personally carrying two rattan chairs, and set those down, requesting the two of us to sit down, not leaving us till we were seated and comfortable. He soon reappeared, carrying cups of tea. The discussions between Mohammad Yunus, and his side-kick, with Ali Miyan went on for about an hour and a half. We could not hear the detailed conversation, but the drone of Yunus' voice could be heard now and then raised to a pitch, with the word *fatwa* mentioned. We could barely catch the occasional murmured responses of Ali Miyan.

It was about 11'o clock in the morning, in late August towards the end of the monsoon season. The nearby pond was full and a number of boys and girls were ecstatically romping in the water, sharing the pond with the buffaloes. Villagers in the cottages nearby were going about their normal business, unmindful of the weighty message brought by Yunus from Delhi. It was an idyllic scene, quintessential rural India, reflecting the serenity and repose of Ali Miyan himself.

At last the three of them came out – one look at Yunus' face showed that he had failed. But he was still making one last ditch effort. He was inviting Ali Miyan to Delhi, and I could distinctly hear the word Bharat Ratna mentioned. Ali Miyan remained composed, and said gently that he had no plans to visit Delhi in the near future. He moved towards us, gravely apologised for not having taken care of us properly, and then said good-bye to us all. As we returned to the inspection bungalow to change from the jeep into our car, and during the two-hour drive to Lucknow, not a word was spoken by anybody. I left Yunus at the residence of one of his friends; from where he presumably went to the railway station later that evening. That was the story of the *fatwa* that was not.

When we met Ali Miyan at Rae Bareli, he had only recently returned after spending two years in Cairo University, where he was a professor of Islamic Studies. I came across Ali Miyan more than fifteen years later in 1993-94 when I was chief secretary in Uttar Pradesh. I must have met him then a couple of times, briefly. He did not recognise me from the 1975 visit, nor did I remind him of Mohammad Yunus. By that time, alas, Ali Miyan seemed to have been sucked into the Muslim politics of the state in some manner and seemed to have lost that serenity and poise – and innocence. But my vivid memory of him is that of a saintly person as he was in 1975, and of that wonderful rural scene of tranquility and beauty that I enjoyed for a few hours in his ashram.

I recall that during this period, early one morning around 5'o clock, I was woken up with an urgent summons to reach the chief minister's residence. As I rushed there, an assembly was gathering around the chief minister. Present were, the chief secretary, the secretary of the home department, the director general of police and the staff officer to DGP. Soon to join the gathering was Samiuddin, on contract as the 'advisor, secular affairs' to the state government. Samiuddin, a tubby old man, with a completely bald head and a thick beard, was a recently retired government official. His current designation was a euphemism for his allotted work, which was to handle the Muslim backlash, especially in the context of the reluctance of the Muslim community to have anything to do with the family planning programme.

There was a crisis at the time of the meeting in one of the outlying police stations in Meerut District, close to the Bulandshahr border. About twenty policemen had taken refuge in the police outpost. They were totally surrounded by a large mob, consisting mostly of Muslims, wielding menacing weapons and shouting virulent slogans. The commissioner of the division, who was camping at an adjoining inspection house came on the line, to give his update on the situation. The mob had gathered, vowing vengeance against the police personnel for some alleged misdeed, almost certainly relating to some excess in the course of a family planning camp. The commissioner described the mob as firing country made guns into the police station, where the hapless policemen had taken refuge. Some of us sitting next to the chief minister could hear the pitched voice of the commissioner describing the scene and could also clearly discern the sound of the gunfire – the firing by the mob as well as the return fire by the encircled policemen. The commissioner was asking for reinforcements and support from headquarters. As soon as the phone call ended, the chief minister asked the chief secretary for advice on what immediate steps to take.

The compulsive need for a favourable *fatwa* had reached ludicrous levels. So, we suddenly heard Samiuddin, the secular advisor, piping up, "We need a *fatwa* immediately; I need to go to Cairo to get a *fatwa*". Normally N D Tewari, the chief minister was a genial, cheerful man, who never utters a harsh word against anyone, tolerant of a lot of trash and balderdash. However, for once I saw him in a temper, as he barked at Samiuddin, "You should have got the *fatwa* earlier; you may get the *fatwa* later. Meerut is now burning; the immediate problem now is to stop the violence and to prevent its spreading to other districts. You just shut up." After this uncharacteristic outburst, which demolished Samiuddin's Cairo visit plan, I found him curled into a bow, wrapping himself around his beard as he actually started sobbing quietly. For some reason, he was overcome with emotion. We had to rush reinforcements from nearby places, alert the district magistrates in cities close to Meerut and other sensitive areas to take precautionary steps, mobilise the para-miltary forces, and alert the army. As we left the room to give the necessary orders, I caught a glimpse of Samiuddin slumped in a chair in a corner, still whimpering. I could hear him muttering to himself the following words, "I need to go to Cairo; I will get the *fatwa*; I will also stop over in Mecca for Haj; I will also take *Begum* for the Haj …!" And I was not the only witness to this scene, lest the reader think this is over-dramatised.

During the Emergency, I saw at close quarters the operation of the Maintenance of Internal Security Act (MISA) and also of Conservation of Foreign Exchange and Prevention of Smuggling Activities Act (COFEPOSA), a related act covering economic offences. This is relevant to the current national debate on the subsequent Prevention of Terrorism Ordinance (POTO). Are such provisions essential to cope with terrorism, and would they not be abused? At any rate, what I saw was abuse of the provisions of law. One of my tasks everyday, as secretary to chief minister, was to confirm the detention of a number of new victims of these acts, by affixing my signature at the end of a long string of signatures. The seal to affirm my signature would read "For and on Behalf of The Chief Minister". This was based on a local executive order issued by the chief minister delegating the powers to his secretary, so that he would not need to sign each document himself. Everyday about thirty or forty such files on detentions would come up for approval by the chief minister, duly signed by the DGP, secretary in the home department and the chief secretary. Typically, the file would contain a two or three page note by the local police authorities stating the cause for the detention, followed by a series of notings and approvals at the district level affirming the facts mentioned in the first note, and attesting to the danger posed to internal security by the person concerned.

There would also be a single master list for each day, listing the file identification number for each of those victims whose detention was brought up to the chief minister for his one signature for the day, as a token of having read and applied his mind, without having to go to the trouble of signing each case file separately. Nobody was bothered about the merits of each case, whether the detention was necessary or not. The only concern was that the hierarchical signatures should be affixed before the mandated fifteen days – and the legal procedural requirements should be fulfilled. The merits of the case were not just irrelevant: they were to be ignored. This was the procedure enforced in the chief minister's office when I took over. I must add, that for the first couple of days I did not do anything to upset the apple cart. When I had mentioned my misgivings to the chief minister about the need for greater scrutiny, he had said that such detentions were necessary to create an 'atmosphere'. He himself was taking final responsibility and that we need not interfere with the established official process.

I attended a meeting of the board convened by the chief secretary to review the detentions. I got a notice one morning from the chief secretary's office about a meeting in his room at noon that day, to review the cases of detainees. I believe that the Supreme Court had at some stage ordered that each detention under these Acts would have to be ratified by the chief minister personally within fifteen days and also that the cases of each detainee must compulsorily be reviewed at least every six months, for continuation of the detention, failing which, the detainee would have to be automatically released. These were supposed to be the safeguards against arbitrary detention by the executive, particularly at the lower levels of administration. As is well known, the Indian genius can, and does, manifest itself to circumvent all procedures and safeguards.

I got to see how the Supreme Court's instructions were complied with. The meeting promptly began at noon. The members of the Review Committee assembled around an oblong table, with the chief secretary at the head followed by the secretary to the home department, the director general of police, his assistant, and myself as representative of the chief minister. I discovered that we had all of 4,000 detention cases for review during that meeting. Broadsheets had been compiled with large documents glued together, of a size that was in vogue at the time of the earliest computer print-outs. Each page had about a hundred names listed in serial order, shown district-wise, and mentioning in brief the details such as date of detention, offence for which detained, whether and when the case had been reviewed and with a 'Remarks' column. At the time when computers were not available for use in government, it was an amazing piece of work, compiling and updating so much information periodically and presenting it in a compact form. There were forty or fifty such pages in a sheaf placed before each member of the review board.

The chief secretary briskly started the meeting saying that we had a lot of work to do before lunch. He got on to page no.1 and asked a rhetorical question, "Any comments?" and after pausing just a moment, said, "We confirm; next page" and moved on. Before I could catch my breath, we had moved to page six. At serial No.495, was a petty ration shopkeeper in a remote village, whose alleged offence was that he had given misleading information on the price of food grains chalked on the notice board in front of the shop. For this offence, he had already been held in detention for more than nine months, and his case had been 'reviewed' once. Apparently, the local authorities in their wisdom still saw him as a major threat to the internal security of the country and so in public interest it was necessary to continue his detention.

I looked at this case, stopped the chief secretary in mid-track before he went on to the next page, and stuttered, "Sir, look at this case. He has already spent nine months in detention. In all probability the original offence, even had it reached conviction stage would have got him a token fine or at worst a minor prison sentence under the Essential Commodities Act. Has he not gone through enough?" The chief secretary gave me a withering look; and reminded me that I was representing the chief minister in the Board and asked me whether I had consulted the chief minister about the position to be taken by his representative in the review Board.

When I replied, "No Sir," he asked me to consult the chief minister before raising such frivolous issues again. That shut me up. The meeting proceeded smoothly thereafter with no heckling or disturbance of any sort. As required by the Supreme Court, the Board had 'carefully' – to use standard government parlance – reviewed about 4,000 cases of detainees all in the course of an hour. I noticed that the offence in most of the cases was not too dissimilar to that of the petty shopkeeper I had intervened for. Incredible as it may sound, at the end of the review process, the continuance of detention of every single one of these cases was found to be proper, legitimate and in public interest. The Board did not feel the need to do even a token review of just a few cases as a pretence that there had been application of mind. In those days, even a fig-leaf was not required as cover.

Of the 8,000 or so MISA/COFEPOSA detainees in UP during the 'Emergency', some would undeniably have been justified and appropriate. However, local officials and politicians took advantage of the draconian laws, aided by mindless neglect of safeguards in Lucknow, to do down a local petty trader, a citizen who refused to give a bribe or do a favour, perhaps a political opponent, or a local scoundrel. This was a collective miscarriage of justice on an unprecedented scale.

Sometime after the Emergency, MISA/COFEPOSA was revoked. But again, sometime in the 1980s, the Terrorism and Anti-Dacoit Act (TADA) was enacted, giving the state the powers of detention without trial. When I reviewed this matter much later as chief secretary during 1993-94, perhaps the total number of TADA detentions in Uttar Pradesh was around 900. There were not as many cases as compared with the use earlier of MISA/ COFEPOSA. Again while some of the detentions were justified, most represented miscarriage of justice giving a handle to local authorities for the oppression of the citizens. I had intervened strongly then, arranging for a case-by-case review of the detainees; and as a result of this process, many were released. Despite the efforts put in, I am still left with the impression that the system was highly unfair, with a large number of unfortunate victims.

While some potential terrorism can indeed be contained through detention measures, the potential for abuse by the law enforcement machinery is very much a reality, as experience shows. I am not suggesting a soft approach against terrorists, or even petty criminals. On the contrary, our present approach to violations of the law is too mild, tolerant, flabby, non-punitive, ineffective and effete. What I am objecting to is that when mindless procedural authority is handed over to petty local officialdom, citizens are harassed. Those detained are mostly innocent, and all the while the criminals go scot-free. The rule of law is, in fact, circumvented.

After my four-month stint as secretary to chief minister, I was delighted to see my predecessor T N Dhar again so that he could resume his assignment. The work hours had been long. I believe Dhar was a bit surprised that he could resume his post without any effort on my side to hold on to the assignment. This left both of us happy, and I resumed my work as in-charge of the appointments department.

One evening around 5 pm that winter, T N Dhar, the secretary to Chief Minister Tewari, telephoned me from Delhi and said that the chief minister had decided to replace the current chief secretary and that Kripa Narain Srivastava, the then agricultural production commissioner should take over as chief secretary the same evening. Dhar said he was conveying to me the chief minister's verbal orders for implementation. Apparently, Sanjay Gandhi had just dictated the instruction to the chief minister. I understood later from the grapevine that Col Anand, the father-in-law of Sanjay Gandhi, was garrison commander in Goa at the time when Srivastava was posted as chief secretary there, and this was almost certainly the circuit utilised for eliciting this *firman* from Sanjay Gandhi. Be that as it may, Dhar told me over the phone that it was the chief minister's explicit direction that the change over must take place the same evening.

On that very day, the then chief secretary, Mahmood Butt was on his way back from Nairobi, where he had gone ostensibly to drum up support from the Indian community in Kenya to invest in Uttar Pradesh. Whatever one may make of his excuse to visit Kenya – and presumably the dialogue with the Indian community took place in the course of a safari – the chief secretary was to land in Delhi at ten that night. He was to come by the morning flight the next day from Delhi to Lucknow, reaching at 8 am, I asked Dhar what the hurry was; and that Dhar might send Tewari's order in writing, to reach the following morning; when the change over could take place. Those days, the use of facsimile machines had not come into vogue. Dhar was exasperated by my lack of understanding. He told me that the chief minister's order should be implemented immediately, presumably timed to take place before Mahmood Butt returned. The implication was that Butt would resort to his own political manoeuvres, given the slightest opportunity and hence the need to preempt this. I bluntly told Dhar that formal orders of UP government would be issued only after the receipt of written orders of the chief minister, under his signature. I also explained that if in the course of the next couple of hours, the chief minister changed his mind, as politicians are wont to do, then where would we be? I was a bit wary of getting involved in these tangles and perhaps a bit too careful. Dhar was exasperated, and said I was being unduly difficult. After much remonstration and discussion, we agreed that Dhar would obtain the chief minister's written orders to replace Mahmood Butt as chief secretary and that Srivastava should take over that very day. He would then read out the orders to me and reproduce the content by telex. Formal orders for the take over by Srivastava were issued after this procedure was followed.

I had, on my own, suggested to Srivastava that he might perhaps like to wait overnight to meet Butt early in the morning, before actually taking over. In the event, within a minute of getting hold of his orders, Srivastava had physically barged into the chief secretary's room and had assumed his seat there. He was graceless enough to rifle the drawers of the main table of the chief secretary, emptying the contents into two or three large satchels for delivery to Butt's residence that night. I checked that evening with the UP resident commissioner in Delhi whether Butt was being received at the airport. The resident commissioner mentioned that since the chief minister was in town, a junior officer would go to the airport to meet him. I implored him, and he agreed, to go to the airport personally and gently break the news of the changes to Butt. That was just a saving grace to the unholy and deplorable way in which the take over of this high office took place that day. I also recall that about a year and a half later, when I was no longer in Lucknow, Srivastava had himself to suffer the ignominy of summary ejection from his position and in similar circumstances, was asked to hand over to his successor.

After the election at the conclusion of the Emergency, the Congress party was totally routed in north India, amazingly unable to procure even one seat in the Hindi belt. There was a change of guard in UP, with a non-Congress coalition government taking over after the 1977 elections. Kripa Narayan Srivastava who was appointed as chief secretary by the erstwhile Congress regime, was flexible enough to remain in the good books of the new government. He had used his persuasive skills with Ram Naresh Yadav, the new chief minister who was a very inexperienced, simple and gullible man.

With a new government of a totally different complexion in place, the order of the day was to condemn all Emergency excesses. Turn-coats galore surfaced in the administration. Officers who were enthusiastic henchmen of the erstwhile Emergency administration, suddenly wore the garb of implacable opposition and contempt for the emergency excesses. The very same persons became the loyal slaves of the new dispensation. Who said that civil servants are rigid and inflexible? When their own interests are involved, they can put a chameleon to shame. It was thus that Srivastava continued as chief secretary, the prime mover in the new dispensation.

I did maintain excellent personal relations with the chief secretary. However, late in 1977, when I was posted in Lucknow as the appointments secretary, I fell into his bad books since I was not able to oblige him in a particular matter, details of which I would rather not mention. Suddenly, he became inimical and got me transferred back as the managing director of the Export Corporation, a post I had held two years earlier. One evening, as I was at my desk, my section officer, with a long face broke the news to me. Within fifteen minutes, I signed my handing over charge certificate and asked for a meeting with the chief secretary, to take leave of him. I met him, and as he understood that I had handed over charge, he was taken aback. He expected me to come and cringe before him, and ask to remain in the same post. I did ask though that as it was the mid-session of schooling of my children, could I, instead of going to Kanpur, get any posting in Lucknow till the year's schooling session concluded? His response was cynically logical, "How many times have you told me that IAS officers are not like tehsildars; their personal convenience is of no significance when government work is involved." At this, I promptly withdrew my request.

Srivastava's anger against me did not subside with my banishment. After a month or so, I was astonished to read in the newspapers that a major enquiry had commenced against me for committing 'Emergency excesses'. In the local press, this was headline news. The front page box story read "Senior IAS Officer caught for Emergency excesses". I had no clue as to what had hit me. After a few days of anxiety and frantic enquiries, I came to understand that the government was considering a departmental enquiry against me for suppressing, while I was in the Appointments Department, a file alleging Emergency excesses against another IAS officer. The facts in the Kafkaesque scenario were as follows. In the month of December 1975, when I was at Harvard, two journalists in Bareilly town had allegedly been tortured in the main city police station, under the supervision of the sub-inspector. The alleged torture included pulling out of the nails of the journalists by the sub inspector; and at that time the district magistrate of Bareilly was also said to be present. Apparently, the issue had been raised in the parliament in Delhi and in the state assembly a number of times. The Central Government and the state government had replied many times in the parliament and assembly respectively, that they had enquired into the matter and that there was no truth in the allegations. Subsequently, a Bharatiya Janata Party (BJP) MP had written a letter reiterating the charges to the home minister of India. The letter found its way to the inspector general of police in UP who asked the deputy inspector general of police (DIG) to personally conduct an inquiry. The DIG had come to the conclusion that the said torture did not take place, and gave a clean chit to the sub inspector of Bareilly police station. His enquiry report reached the desk of the UP home secretary, who sent it down for processing to his department. As it came down to the section officer in the home department, he noted that there was no case against the police official concerned and no action need be taken. However, since the allegation mentioned that the district magistrate, an IAS officer was present, would the appointments department also look into it? This was typical of the 'examination' of any matter in a government department – no one ever wants to take the responsibility of the closing of a file. In the appointments department, the under secretary noted the facts I had mentioned above and suggested on file that we may also call for the comments of the commissioner of Bareilly division. Somehow, I had overlooked the advice given to me by Tandon, my first mentor when I joined service, and that was never to express firm views in writing. I had, on the contrary, noted as follows:

> "A high level enquiry has been conducted; the Home Department has reached the conclusion that no offence had been committed by the police officer concerned; no irregularity has been established; what is the point in prolonging the matter by asking for the Commissioner's comments. Besides, a number of times both in the Parliament and in the State Assembly, Government have stated that no torture was done and there can be no charges laid. We may return the file to the Home Department, with the comment that under the circumstances, there is no need to examine the role of the District Magistrate of Bareilly."

This was written sometime in late 1976, on an incident alleged to have taken place in 1975 when I was in Harvard. No charges were ever laid against the sub inspector or the district magistrate, or anyone else, for the alleged torture. As a matter of fact, many thousands of excesses of various sorts were indeed perpetrated by the bureaucracy in UP. In the entire state, not one official from any department, IAS or police or other, was charged with any Emergency excess! I was the only person in the system who had perpetrated an Emergency excess! I had the unique distinction of being the subject of an enquiry on a charge for an event that took place when I was

12,000 miles away. Such is the viciousness the government can display. And such is the ability, not just of politicians, but even of government servants to harass and hound those who cross their path.

Naturally the enquiry against me could not proceed – there was nothing to enquire into, no basis to frame any charge and no credible way to even appoint an enquiry officer. Nothing could be done except to hide the file, and in the supercharged atmosphere of those days, hold me up as a perpetrator of excesses. For public consumption, it was said that an enquiry was proceeding. That was how the issue came up when the promotion committee met, for considering the selections to the super-time scale, which takes one to commissioner's rank. I believe the chief secretary told the committee, "There are serious charges against Subramanian of committing Emergency excesses; he cannot be promoted." It is to the discredit of the committee members that none asked for the charges to be spelt out and for a formal statement to be placed by the department before the committee. In the atmosphere of the day, everyone was terrified when the words "Emergency excess", were used. So pusillanimous are our senior bureaucrats. That is how I was, for a while, overlooked for the super-time scale.

My junior batchmate J C Pant, to his credit, refused his own promotion on the ground that I had been wrongly denied promotion, and declared that he would await his turn only after my case was cleared. While I appreciated Pant's gesture, I told him not to be foolish and get involved in what was essentially a vendetta against me. The state's vigilance and Criminal Investigation Department (CID) apparatus were set in motion to locate something concrete to incriminate me. I understood, through my own sources that plainclothes teams had gone to places of my previous postings, including Moradabad, Ranikhet, Ghazipur and Kanpur, to sniff out anything adverse, however tiny, so that the book could be thrown at me. All I can say is that I was very lucky that no real or imagined evidence was found, or could be concocted with a modicum of credibility.

But the tide turned. In course of time, by the summer of 1978, Srivastava vacated his post as chief secretary. The new chief secretary, D K Bhattacharya sent word for me the very next day after he took over. He must have had his hands full, but yet he spared two hours of his time.

He asked me to tell him everything I knew about the matter. When I finished, he took out my file from his cupboard and told me that my version tallied fully with the facts before him. He asked me to stay on in his office room and disappeared for about half an hour. Apparently, he had gone elsewhere, wrote a note on the subject with his own hand, gone up to the chief minister, to obtain his approval and returned back to his room, to tell me, "I am totally satisfied that you have been unfairly targetted by the system. This matter is now closed. You will receive orders today of your promotion to the higher rank, with retrospective effect from the date on which it was due. You may go back now to Kanpur, and treat this matter as closed. If you sue the government for malpractice on the facts of the matter, you may win the case and claim damages. However, I would advise you to forget this episode, and take this matter totally out of your mind. After all, we receive so much undeserved goodness in our lives, we should also be ready for undeserved brick bats." Within fifteen days, I got my orders posting me as the director of Industries, a post seen as prestigious at that time. This was mainly to send a signal that I had been restored in the government's eyes. Bhattacharya, as a further token of the government's faith in me, made me a formal observer at the Lok Sabha elections at Azamgarh in the summer of 1978. When one refers to people like K N Srivastava, one also needs to speak of the likes of Bhattacharya, who adorned the system.

Later, I had occasion to meet Ram Naresh Yadav who had been earlier the chief minister, and who was now the deputy chief minister, due to a political change. He invited me to his residence, took me to a private portion of his house, and in a dignified manner, said, "Many of us are new to politics and are easily fooled by clever civil servants. Without intending to do so, we commit many mistakes, and frequently harm others. It is fortunate that in some cases, we are able to reverse the damage and do a redressal. I want you to promise me that every time you come to Lucknow from Kanpur, you should not leave without meeting me, however busy I may be. Even if I am inside a Cabinet meeting, I want you to send me a slip, so that I can come out and we can meet even for a few seconds. I have since made detailed enquiries about you. I wish to say that we are proud to have an officer like you working for the state government." Gracious words, from a simple man, and I was touched to hear his words of healing for the unfair treatment meted to me.

That was an occasion for me to think about the uses of Article 311 of the Constitution, which provides protection to government servants against arbitrary action without due process. Till I was at the short end of the stick, I had hitherto held the view that Article 311 provided an umbrella and cover for lazy, inefficient, and corrupt civil servants who cannot be got rid of easily. However, the authors of our Constitution had the foresight to envisage that vicious and self-seeking civil servants could as well be arbitrary in their dealings with their own officials.

I frequently came across false and spurious cases mounted against innocent civil servants by vengeful superiors or politicians. It is so easy to start a vigilance enquiry on flimsy and politically motivated grounds. Once the wheels are set in motion, nobody will take the interest to close the enquiry. The targetted officer becomes tainted, is held up in public contempt and his career prospects get blighted. Even when it leads nowhere, serious damage is already done when the enquiry commences. For a variety of reasons, these false allegations have been on the increase. In most instances, the investigating agency well knows that the allegations are false, and politically motivated. Unable to proceed, it is also unable to close the case. And the system revels in keeping an officer in limbo.

The malaise has now spread even to the central investigating agencies, which hitherto had a spotless reputation for probity. The practice of mounting false cases, even by hitherto uncorrupted central agencies on political grounds, is very much on the increase. This has the potential to destroy the system. In the past, when one heard that the Central Bureau of Investigation (CBI) was enquiring against a particular person, the presumption was that he must be guilty. Today, one suspects if it is a false charge, knowingly pursued by the agency with an ulterior motive. It is ironic that this is the situation, when a large number of senior public servants who are steeped in corruption go free. Once upon a time, we knew who were the corrupt ones, and could identify them. Today, we may be hard put to certify, with absolute confidence the honest ones. It is tragic that in such times the number of false and framed cases is on the increase.

When I was later the chief secretary in UP, I had set up a group to review pending vigilance cases. I gave clear instructions that those cases which were pending for more than one year, of which there were many, should be completed within fifteen days and then the officer should either be exonerated or charge sheeted. I wonder if this could be working today. Perhaps, the review group must have collapsed under its own weight.

I had planned to visit Badrinath and Kedarnath with my family in the summer of 1977, and elaborate preparations had been made for our departure from Lucknow one day at 5 am. Just before our departure, the Tewari government was asked to resign by Indira Gandhi and a spell of President's Rule was ushered in, preparatory to elections in the state some ten weeks away. Chenna Reddy, governor at that time, took charge of the administration. The job of the governor and his aides is normally fairly cushy and comfortable, attached with pomp and pageantry – but not so when President's Rule is imposed, especially with elections close by. So, Chenna Reddy now needed an administrative secretary. The day previous to our departure, at 9 pm, I got urgent summons from the governor's house, asking me to meet him. When I saw him around 10 pm that night, he told me that I was to take charge as his administrative secretary with immediate effect and to return the next morning by 7 am to start work. It was not quite the ideal first encounter with a boss. I remonstrated with him my inability to do so, since I had already fixed the pilgrimage to Badrinath and Kedarnath. I said that I would take over after a week, on my return from the hills. Reddy would have none of it, and peremptorily asked me to take over the assignment forthwith. This was my first brush with the man and his style. Against my better judgement, I complied. Much later, events that landed me in personal difficulty made me feel that the cancellation of that pilgrimage had perhaps been inauspicious for me.

After a five minute introductory meeting on the first morning, when the governor briefed me on his working methods, I was left to tackle the tasks of the office. Later that evening, when he called for me about a particular paper, which he found not to his satisfaction, he flared up and gave me a volley of abuse, using intemperate language. I immediately flung that file back on his desk, and flared back saying that I did not want the assignment that was thrust on me. I was not used to being shouted at and that I was walking out immediately and would he find another administrative secretary of his choice? As I stomped out of the room, Chenna Reddy quickly followed me, invited me back, apologised to me profusely and asked me to forget the incident. Reddy, with his mercurial temperament, would flare up and use foul language with a number of officials and others. However, he never again raised his voice with me and was sweetness itself so far as I was concerned for the length of the President's Rule, and for all the time I knew him subsequently. By the second round, following the earlier spat over the pilgrimage, we had things worked out.

Chenna Reddy was larger than life. He had large appetites, not only in relation to his food intake, but also in other directions. As for food, his daily breakfast would consist really of three full breakfasts – starting with cornflakes and eggs and toast, proceeding to parathas and vegetables and jalebi, concluding with idlis and dosa and vadas and washed down with cups of filter coffee. His lunches and dinners were similarly elaborate; comprehensively catholic. He would partake in sequence, composite meals in western, north Indian and south Indian cuisine. One can only imagine his other appetites. He obviously had an extraordinary metabolism to digest all this intake, since he maintained a trim figure, without the slightest trace of a paunch. Every morning he would have a two-hour horse riding session at the police lines, trotting, cantering and galloping, but even this would not explain how he could burn off the extraordinary amount of calories that he consumed. I once recall that he wanted to suspend the collector of Mathura district. The charge was that the idlis served at the governor's breakfast when he was touring the district, were stony and ice-cold! The poor collector had not even known what was being served for H.E.'s breakfast. I had to intervene on behalf of the offender, and the governor finally let him off with a volley of abuse.

In the privacy of his chambers where I had free access, I would frequently see him holding hands on a late evening, with visitors of the fairer sex. While he was generally discreet in this regard, he was brazenly open in the presence of the insiders of his office staff and so what I write is first hand.

Back at work, Chenna Reddy was a strong administrator with clarity of thought and clearly blessed with high acumen. He would cut through complex issues after just a moment's examination and get to the fundamentals. He was also very methodical and purposeful. He would maintain a daily diary listing the things to be accomplished that day; the tasks that had been accomplished would be struck off and the remaining ones carried on to the diary of the next day or on to a separate weekly diary that he would elaborately prepare in his own hand. There was also a monthly diary in two parts, the major policy matters to be tackled in the month, as well as the administrative tasks to be completed. And if this were not enough, he also had an annual diary, which he never opened in front of me. I used to wonder if perhaps he had one grand diary of things to accomplish in his whole life; and perchance yet another for his future *janmas*! Be that as it may, he had fixed ideas on the things to be accomplished, and pursued each in meticulous detail, till completion.

I will give an instance of the single-minded way that he pursued the tasks that he assigned himself – though this particular one had a dubious intent. About a fortnight before the President's Rule period was scheduled to end, he asked me to speak to the medical secretary, Ghulam Hussain to expedite the processing of a file to elevate a particular lady doctor to the rank of professor at the government's medical college. After a few days, he asked me – doubtless from his diary notes – why the file had not come up to him for approval and whether I had spoken to the medical secretary. I enquired of Ghulam Hussain, who told me that he was examining the matter and mentioned informally that there was no merit in that case and that the requirement of the governor for her promotion was based on not just medical services rendered to the public. He hinted that I need not take too much interest in the matter. I had to hurriedly tell Hussain, in case he had any doubts in the matter, that I myself had no interest in the case and

I was merely passing on the query of the governor. As the file did not come to the governor for another few days, I was asked to peremptorily inform the medical secretary to send the file to the governor immediately for his perusal. By this time, there was a week or so left of the President's Rule. When the file still did not come, I was directed to send urgent summons to Hussain to appear personally before the governor. I was present at the meeting that evening. It was the most comprehensive and fierce attack by a politician on a senior bureaucrat that I have seen. The governor used strong but not intemperate language, and laced with unassailable administrative logic.

He said, "Mr. Ghulam Hussain, do you think you own these files? You are a government servant and have the full right to express your opinion on any file, and that is all the right you have. Attack the proposal as much as you want, with all the vigour at your command, using all the facts that you can collect and invoking any arguments that you can imagine. But, you have no right to hold up a file, as you are not the owner. I own the file as the administrative governor of the state. I have the right to ask for it; and whether I agree with you or overrule you, you have to implement it. It will be insubordination of the highest order to hide the file under your sleeves. I know what you are thinking – President's Rule will end in five more days and that if you could hold on, you can defeat the proposal; but remember that you are not the government – you are only a cog in the wheel. I am the government; and I demand that the file should come to my desk by 6 tomorrow evening. You may write anything you like on that file or you can even send it blank without an opinion. Now you may please go and obey my instructions." Ghulam Hussain, a respectable old man of great dignity listened impassively, and at the end of the blast, he tried to explain the weaknesses in the proposal to elevate the fair lady to the post of professor. Chenna Ready cut him short, "I have not called you to discuss the case with you; I have called you to order you to send the file to me. You have hitherto disobeyed the directions I have given, conveyed to you by my secretary. This meeting is over – you can get out."

The words were harsh indeed but highlighted one important administrative truth namely, that bureaucrats in the secretariat do not own the files. They are merely temporary custodians, who have the right to express their views without fear or favour and to advise freely and dispassionately. As directed by the governor, the file was received at 6 pm the next day. To his eternal credit, Hussain had strongly attacked the proposal in a six-page note, mentioning all the facts. He raised valid, credible and irrefutable arguments why it would not be proper to elevate the lady to professorship. He had also shown the file to the finance secretary, who added arguments from the finance perspective, as to why the proposal should not be implemented. Hussain had added his further comment that it would be an atrocious precedent and bring chaos to the management of the faculty in the various universities. Chenna Reddy asked me to read Ghulam Hussain's notes in full; he himself was not adept at reading Hindi though he understood spoken Hindi perfectly well. After hearing the full note, Chenna Reddy mentioned to me his thought that Ghulam Hussain was a man of substance and guts. He then asked me to prepare a draft speaking order, overruling the department's objection, and approving the elevation of the lady doctor. I remonstrated, saying that there was no case at all for promoting her, that the arguments of Hussain were unassailable and that there was no way any credible order could be issued to overrule the department's recorded view. Reddy said that what he needed was a government order, not a credible order. He was well aware that there was no case; and he merely wanted my advice as the Devil's Advocate to find ways to punch holes in the department's case and then to approve the promotion. He did not want any inputs for helping him make up his mind. All he asked for was some secretarial assistance, in preparing a half page draft order demolishing the departmental arguments and have it put up to him for his signature. I complied, adding in the forwarding note I prepared that these were not my views, but merely represented the thinking of the governor. That same day, the professorship was approved; and as a demonstration of his knowledge of bureaucratic ways, he added a few sentences that the order should be delivered to the concerned college authorities by 11 am the next day, that the lady doctor actually should take over by 5 pm that day, and that by 7 pm the compliance should be reported to him. He is no more now, but his diary would probably have the entry.

Ruthless and arbitrary as he was, and draconian as his methods were, Chenna Reddy at least expressed his needs openly and explicitly, not afraid of putting down his views in writing and not afraid of contrary views written by others. Many politicians in power have been even more whimsical, demanding and unreasonable in their desires, wanting unconscionable approvals for a monetary consideration, without the courage to express their views openly. Unlike Chenna Reddy, they resort to subterfuge, carefully identify and select pliant, spineless, colluding bureaucrats and elevate them to key positions. And obliging officials are ever so ready to play ball, anticipating the needs of their political masters, sparing them from even the need to make a wish-list.

I recall a meeting of the governor's council, a forum where the decisions taken by the governor were formalised and rubber-stamped on behalf of the government, corresponding under President's Rule to the state Cabinet. The members of the council were generally retired bureaucrats, toothless, grateful to have a whiff again of active administration, however fleetingly, and unwilling to risk their fragile position by speaking up strongly on any matter which would annoy the powers that be. The three sets of governor's councils that I had come across during my career were very similar and equally effete, and in all cases, the retired officials being just thankful for the perks and privileges that they enjoyed, however temporarily. One member even told me that he enjoyed the red light and siren on his car, the armed escort vehicle, and his extensive tours; which all brought back to him the memories of his days of active service.

The item under discussion that day was to consider proposals for approval of new pay scales to the engineers of the irrigation department, and to confer on them better emoluments. There had earlier been an agitation by the engineers followed by the appointment of a committee, which had proposed the pay revision now under consideration by the governor's council. The sponsor of the item was Aggarwal, a chief engineer, who was then functioning as secretary to the irrigation department, in tune with the government's policy to have senior technical personnel occupying positions as secretary to government. As soon as Aggarwal walked in and took his chair, the governor asked for a discussion on the item. Aggarwal briefly presented the proposal, and asked for approval. The finance secretary strongly opposed it on a number of grounds. The governor said that under these circumstances, the pay increase would not be approved. Thereupon, resigned to his failure, Aggarwal got up from his chair and was leaving the Cabinet room. As he approached the exit door, Reddy shouted at him, "Mr Aggarwal, come back." Aggarwal returned, and was preparing to sit down in the chair he had just vacated. Reddy said, "I did not ask you to sit down. What kind of a secretary are you? You have come here today before this council to argue the case on behalf of thousands of engineers who are anxiously waiting outside, and all over the state, for the outcome of this meeting on a matter vital to their career and interests. You don't press their case, seriously argue their case, or disagree with the finance secretary on his points; and when I give a decision, you meekly submit; without arguing the matter. You just give up and leave. How are you fit to represent your staff; you are not a leader of men, and so how can one have trust on you or give you his loyalty?" Thereupon Aggarwal, tried to argue the case again, saying how important it was that the pay revision should be accepted. He was again rudely cut short by the governor, "You got your chance and have utterly failed; you can go now."

I suspect that whatever the strength of Aggarwal's case, Reddy was not likely to have approved the pay revision, during the brief period of President's Rule and would have left the difficult decision to the next popular government; unless of course there were other circumstances involving the personal interest of the governor! Aggarwal probably knew this too, which is why he did not put up a fight. Be that as it may, Reddy seized the opportunity to deliver a homily on the principles of administration.

It was a grinding, gruelling period of about ten weeks as administrative secretary to the governor, during which time again I had a ringside view of every department of the state government, and the pressures and pulls that constitute decision-making. At the end of the period, Chenna Reddy asked me to prepare a draft of a 'special entry' to be approved by him to be placed on my personal file by him. I replied that this was unethical, and asked him if he would write what he wanted and not even show the matter to me. Again Reddy told me that he merely wanted secretarial assistance – I was not to help him in making up his mind. I prepared a draft for his approval; Reddy looked at it and told me that I was far too modest. He called his personal assistant and dictated three more lines effusively praising me; and after signing the order, sent it off to the appointments department to be placed on my personal file. He also invited me for dinner at his residence on the last day of President's Rule, when I had one more occasion to see how he enjoyed life to the full. I used to meet Reddy on and off thereafter and even once much later in Chennai when he was the governor of Tamil Nadu. He would always be very friendly and cordial.

Much earlier, I was in Lucknow for a while, in 1971, before moving to the Kanpur postings. In the secretariat, I had looked after the personnel and appointments departments as well as the general administration branch, working much of the time under the direct supervision of the chief secretary. Personnel is one of the departments – finance being the other – which has tentacles into the working of every department, and provides an overview of the entire administration. It is a time-honoured principle that those who control the finance and personnel functions have a strong grip on the entire administration. I was fresh from the field and new to the Lucknow beat. I energetically took up a study of the deployment of the Indian IAS and PCS (Provincial Civil Service) officers in the various segments of UP administration. The jobs were identified in different categories. One was the general administration, covering district magistrates, commissioners and others. The second was industrial administration covering assignments in the industrial sector in the field, in the secretariat and in public sector units. Data was obtained on the deployment of officers over the previous five years. I discovered that thirty-five per cent of the officers were deployed in the industrial sectors. Uttar Pradesh hardly had any industries to boast of and this was a sector that was not critical to the state's economy. On the other hand, less than five per cent of the officers were assigned to agriculture and allied sectors, an area vital for the state's economy. And it was surprising that only seven per cent of the officers were deployed in the important social sectors such as education, health and public welfare. The state's administrative apparatus had unconsciously diverted the administrative resources of the state to the glamour, privilege and perks attached to the assignments in the various industrial sectors; not taking into account the relative insignificance of these segments of activity to the welfare of the citizens of the state. This is not to say that placement of more IAS and PCS officers in these sectors would have led to generation of greater agricultural production or diversification in the agricultural sector; nor that more officers in the social sectors would have led to better indices for human resources development in the state. Probably, it could even have been the other way around! The study, however, did point towards the skewed mindset of the administration, and need for rethinking the priority assigned by the state administration to the various sectors. I felt that a massive re-deployment of officers was necessary, to correct this imbalance.

I submitted a detailed report of my conclusions to the chief secretary, and the chief minister. When the note went to the then chief minister, Kamalapati Tripathi, he wrote in his own hand in Hindi, in his nearly indecipherable scroll, "I congratulate the joint secretary for an excellent analysis. I agree with his conclusions and the recommendations deserve to be implemented. However, the joint secretary needs to be reminded forcefully that Hindi is the official language of the state; use of Hindi in official work is not only obligatory but use of any other language would be treated as indiscipline." He had concluded with a sting in the tail. The message was clear. Indiscipline, and not initiative, was the core of the matter. The matter was promptly forgotten and consigned to the archives in the caverns of the secretariat building. A mention of the problem and a declaration of intention to solve it is adequate action; nothing concrete ever needs to be done. Very soon thereafter, in a manner, my study findings were indeed acted upon. I was posted to Kanpur in the Small Industries Corporation! I have already covered this murky phase in the previous chapter.

In the Personnel Department, I had the opportunity to see many 'Character Rolls', which embody the annual assessment of the work of each senior officer, and are key documents that affect his career advancement. These dated as far back as the 1930s. Nearly all the entries written at that time by the British officers, on the work of junior officers, were in explicit language, highlighting sharply the salient positive and negative aspects of the personality of the officer reported upon, his intellectual abilities, attitude, and interest taken in work. The language was direct, blunt and succinct; and reading a half-page assessment gave one a pen-portrait of the officer's personality and abilities. Some of those junior officers had now become my senior colleagues. I had the occasion to see the annual entries given by their British bosses, dating back from their time of joining. I already had a mental picture of each senior officer; based on hearsay and personal knowledge. The British had, even during the first three or four years of the young officer's service, identified and recorded clearly his personality traits and characteristics. The match was uncanny. The reporting officers could, with an unerring eye, size up the personality of the young probationer, summed up over a half page. Quite amazing, that the images were valid even after a period of thirty years.

I could then see for the same officers, the entries given by the Indian bosses, in the post-Independence era. These were quite a contrast, blandly positive in their assessment, effusive, and generally wishy-washy. A reading of this shallow version would not at all present a true portrait that captured the person. An element of hypocrisy, cronyism and lack of objectivity had already crept in into the higher bureaucracy's thinking by that time. Officers were circumspect in recording their views on their subordinates, and would readily and gushingly outline the positive features, while ignoring the negative aspects. If the officer reported upon was the son or son-in-law or nephew of a senior ICS officer, the report would be a paean of unalloyed praise and flowery approbation – not matching with the real personality of the officer that I knew. Perhaps the writer was guarding against the chance that the ICS officer would get to see the report. I still recall a collector's gushing full-page celebration of the personality of his probationer, a prospective son-in-law. The report concluded with the prediction, "he will go far". His commissioner, on review, recorded his own telling view cryptically: "The farther the better!"

I saw much the same later on, as personnel secretary in Uttar Pradesh, then as chief secretary in the state, and again as Cabinet secretary at the Centre. I had occasion to peruse hundreds of confidential reports on officers from across the country, written in the 1970s, '80s and '90s. Three clear trends emerged. Firstly, all senior officers in the later decades became effusive in their praise of their juniors. Practically all the officers reported upon were placed in the 'Outstanding' category. Even when the reporting officer did not think well of his junior as a reading would make evident, the categorisation would still be 'Outstanding'. The only conclusion that can be drawn is that the senior officers had progressively lost their independent judgement. Secondly, in general, they were afraid to state their views bluntly. Indeed, some seniors had become scared of their very juniors, and it showed in the annual remarks they wrote. Such a fear of subordinates stemmed from many factors such as potential for exposing the weakness of superiors, carrying tales against the superior's interests and finally, intervention by courts in the process of promotion. It is not uncommon to hear about junior officers showing their annoyance at adverse or lukewarm entries, taking their bosses to court, fixing them through a whispering campaign or by incriminating them in departmental enquiries. Thirdly, the resort to intimidation of senior officers by subjecting them to crippling departmental enquiries, on frivolous or malicious or even patently false grounds had taken its toll. Senior officers had started playing safe in general and recording namby-pamby annual remarks was only one more symptom of this malaise.

Thus, a typical entry that would read: "Work and conduct satisfactory; he discharged his functions reasonably well. On the whole, many of his targets could be generally stated to have been met – category: Outstanding". A translation of this entry is that the reporting officer found the work of his subordinate awful, most of the targets were not met; but he had, in the interest of conformity and safety, categorised him as Outstanding. The entry-giving officer was never pulled up for his hypocrisy. Promotion assessment committees, given the task of evaluating character rolls and recommending promotional panels, very well know of this lacunae. So, they can, if they wish, form their own judgement by going through annual reports, and reading the minds of the reporting and reviewing officers, not just going by the overall rating. However, many committees do not take the time and effort to assess the real import of each entry and to re-categorise the 'Outstanding' into an appropriate lower category. It is also at the back of their minds that if the reported officer were to take the committee to court, alleging *mala fide*, many courts would go only by the wording of the categorisation, without reading the mind of the officer giving the entry. The complex issues relating to annual evaluation need to be re-visited, and a revised method, taking into account current field realities, needs to be in position.

There was a time when committees set up to evaluate annual remarks and to recommend promotion panels, used to function with independence and integrity. There were some norms, which were in vogue till quite recently at the Centre for promotion to the level of joint secretary, with only half the number making it, and the rest being casualties. Again, from the level of joint secretary to additional secretary and then to secretary, the attrition rate would be fifty per cent at each stage. Thus, in an IAS batch of some eighty officers, less than ten would make it as secretary. If this exercise is done with impartiality and objectivity, only the best can reach the top. After all, the promotion process should keep public interest in view; not serve as a charity to the officer, or to equitably cater to the interest of every officer, or to pander to the interests of politicians. If officers are selected with care, there will be greater competition for real performance, and senior officers will also retain the respect of the public. There has been deterioration in this regard in the past few years, notably in the very recent past. Interference by ministers, and also from the Prime Minister's Office (PMO) has wreaked havoc in the empanelment process. Non-empanelled officers have invariably located dubious political sources to get reconsidered for empanelment. Respect for the procedure for empanelment has been the casualty. Over time, officers have started considering it easier and expedient to find political routes for obtaining a promotion, rather than go through the difficult route of hard work and merit. Incalculable harm has been done to the empanelment system, by diluting the processes and allowing political interference in sacrosanct territories. Both as chief secretary in Uttar Pradesh, and later as Cabinet secretary, I fought hard, generally successfully, to keep political interference out of the selection process. The pressures were enormous as the stakes were high, but as it became known that the established processes and procedures were inviolable, the pressure dropped dramatically.

7 TOURISM IN UTTAR PRADESH

*The S bend on the Jamuna river is the magnificent
site of hundreds of Shiva temples. Each temple had
tinkling bells strung together from the ceiling. There
was a light breeze and the notes produced by
thousands of ringing bells had an ethereal quality.*

*Rather than the kind of sleazy developments now
being mooted, perhaps it might even be better if these
ancient monuments, decrepit as they might be, were
just left alone to themselves and their history.*

MY POSTINGS IN UTTAR PRADESH WERE IN
varied locations: Ranikhet in the Himalayas, the somnolent Ghazipur on
the banks of the Ganga, the hustle and bustle of small town Moradabad
and big cities such as Lucknow and Kanpur. I have travelled across the
length and breadth of this vast state. UP has many wonderful spots of
natural beauty to visit and places of religious, and historical interest. There
are also many wildlife and bird sanctuaries. If only more attention were
paid to developing the tourism infrastructure, the state has the potential to
become a major tourist destination.

One of my favourite destinations was Agra, and not really for the Taj
Mahal. My first visit to the Taj was in 1961 as a probationer in the service,
during *Bharat Darshan*, the 'see-India' tour. In subsequent years, though I
visited Agra often, I did not go to the Taj except for one long look at this
glorious monument on a full moon night, when it shimmered like a dream
palace. Another place of wonder near Agra is the Fatehpur Sikri palace
built by Emperor Akbar. With proper furnishing and props, the palace

could be developed as a major tourist centre in its own right, rivalling the Taj, or the Versailles Palace. In current times, one sees that efforts are on to in fact, commercialise these areas involving real estate deals and entertainment malls. However, this is not the kind of development that will attract tourists from abroad. What is needed is good infrastructure for simple decent food, stay and safe travel without disturbing the ambience of these historic sites. Rather than the kind of sleazy developments now being mooted, perhaps it might even be better if these ancient monuments, decrepit as they might be, were just left alone to themselves and their history.

I would visit Agra every year, usually during the winter. The visit would include a night's stay at the Bharatpur bird sanctuary. In the 1970s, it used to be a glorious spot with an amazing congregation of different species of birds. Of late, I have been told that the number of birds visiting Bharatpur has significantly diminished. This has happened for several reasons, including water shortages and the inexorable encroachment by settlers. I had once organised a visit to the bird sanctuary by G Engblom, then the director general of the International Trade Centre in Geneva, an organisation I later worked for. Engblom, who had earlier worked as foreign secretary for the Swedish government, had thought of India as a hot country where the ambient temperature was always high. He was not adequately prepared with woollens for his 5 am field visit in Bharatpur to watch the birds. He explained later to me how his teeth were chattering and he was shivering in the jeep. He said that even in Sweden, he had never at any time felt so cold as he had that day in Bharatpur.

In the course of my work, I had developed a keen interest in the Agra area for its leather, glass, stoneware, handicraft and carpet weaving industries. I have always enjoyed visiting these clusters even when I had no specific purpose for the visit. This also gave me an opportunity to reminisce about some previous involvement in the state's traditional industry. Another regular place of call for me was Firozabad with its glass-blowing industry. The glass blowing industry had its own peculiar organisation and the artisans displayed remarkable skills in making exquisite glassware. But then, the workers worked for a pittance in hazardous conditions at close to furnace temperatures, inhaling harmful gases and chemicals that shortened their life span drastically. It is a pity that this industry could not be modernised, on the lines of Venetian glassware or Delft ceramics, which have become world class centres blending traditional skills with modern technology and safe practices.

During one visit to Agra, I had planned to visit Bah Tehsil and nearby areas to see the handicrafts there. In particular, not too far from Bah, there is a town called Jalesar where tiny bronze bells are manufactured. When strung together and hung out in the open, they tinkle musically with the breeze. I was talking about my planned visit with Arvind Varma, the then district magistrate at Agra. He exclaimed, "Don't you know how dangerous that place is," adding that he would have to escort me himself. So we went to Bah Tehsil about fifty miles from Agra. We stopped at a magnificent crocodile farm *en route*. The forest department was rearing different species of crocodiles and alligators in a segment of the Jamuna river. In the picturesque surroundings we would get close enough on a small motor boat for a sixteen feet alligator to leap at us, and miss us by just by a couple of feet, or so it seemed at that time. Was this the danger that led the district magistrate to accompany me?

We went on to Bateshwar, where the Jamuna river takes a lazy 'S' shaped curve. On the north side of the river is Uttar Pradesh and on the south side is the state of Madhya Pradesh. Near that place the three great rivers – Ganga, Jamuna and Chambal – all flow eastward parallel within fifteen miles of each other. The famous Chambal ravines, the operating base for many dacoits are located not far from that area. The 'S' bend on the Jamuna is the magnificent site of hundreds of temples, dedicated to Lord Shiva. Some temples are tiny and some relatively large. In later years, whenever I traversed that area by helicopter, or by the state plane, I would request the pilot to come down close enough for yet another look at this superb group of temples, a sight that gave me greater pleasure than a similar aerial view of the Taj. It was a special sight to see the array of temples right on the banks of the river as it curves back and forth. Each temple had its tinkling bells strung together, hanging down from the ceiling. At the time we were there, there was a light breeze and the notes produced by the swaying of thousands of bells had an ethereal quality.

Arvind explained the significance of these temples and the bells. This part of Agra district was home to many dacoit groups and their families. Each time a robber-band embarked on one of their routine exploits for loot or pillage, they would come and pray in front of their favorite deity for a successful 'mission'. On their safe return, in gratitude for the blessings received from the Lord, they would hang yet one more string of bells. If the exploit were a more daring one, then a small new temple would be erected. What were the deeds it took, I wondered, to have the larger temples built. The icon of Lord Shiva would be established in the shrine, followed by a *badakhana* – a large public feast on the big green meadow abutting the temples. It was on this particular meadow many years back, that a large number of dacoits laid down their arms and 'surrendered' before Vinobha Bhave.

On my return, I narrated the details of this thrilling visit to my mother. She expressed her concern saying, "Why do you risk going to these dangerous dacoit-infested places?" I replied, only in half-jest, "Are these dacoits more dangerous than the IAS officers of India?" Strangely enough, the village Kalyanpur, a well-known Brahmin village, is right next to the green meadow in Bateshwar where the dacoits converged. Perhaps the dacoits required the services of the Brahmins to expiate their sins. Kalyanpur village has provided a number of famous state and national politicians, including the present prime minister, Atal Bihari Vajpayee. The dividing line between public service and disservice is indeed thin.

The state went about reforming the bandits, with some success. No useful occupation was available to the bandits, and the ravines also provided an ideal hiding place for fugitives. The terrain allowed for no cultivation. The substance of the government's scheme was to flatten out the ravines and make it cultivable by provision of lift irrigation. This would induce the local residents to change over from banditry to become land lubbers. I had something to do with overall supervision of this activity for a period. The 'Ravine Reclamation Programme', funded by some international agencies was undertaken in the 1980s and '90s in these parts. By some freak chance, this was one programme that was successful, and the money was reasonably well spent. But perhaps this was no accident.

The dacoits were straightforward no-nonsense folk, used to shooting straight. They were unused to the devious ways of local officials. They might have found the leakage of funds through conspiratorial arrangements below their dignity and refrained from such a form of banditry. I recall at least two visits to the reclaimed area and meeting the dacoits-turned-farmers who were indeed hospitable. The delicious taste of freshly harvested chickpeas toasted on a open-pan right on the field still lingers in my mouth!

Not far away runs the Agra-Kanpur segment of the Grand Trunk Road (GTR) from Calcutta to Delhi. This road traces its origin to Sher Shah who had laid it nearly five hundred years ago. The stretch of land between the Ganga and Jamuna near the highway was home to the Thuggees, bands of robber tribes who extracted tributes from passers-by and were not afraid to kill or maim at the slightest provocation. I recall once reaching Etah town on the GTR around 9 pm. Kanpur was only 130 miles away and I wanted to drive on. Bulaki, my driver, who came from nearby areas, was a gentle person, efficient, polite and obedient. However, even he flatly refused to drive me on the next stretch of the GTR from Etah to Kannauj. I discovered later that on that stretch of road, nobody drove alone at night though it was a national highway. Incidentally, Mulayam Singh Yadav had his origins from among these districts and these were the environs in which he grew up.

Arvind Varma, the district magistrate in Agra, recounted this incident to me during one of my visits. He was asked by the then speaker of the Indian Parliament to personally attend to the visiting speaker of the Australian Parliament and his wife, who were making a one-day trip to Agra to see the Taj. Arvind went to the airport to receive the incoming flight, took his official car right on to the tarmac, went up the ramp as the door of the incoming flight opened. He thought he had identified the Australian speaker and his wife sitting in the first row. He proceeded to garland them and they were escorted in the official car from the tarmac to the VIP reception room. The visitors preferred to wait and personally clear their baggage dispensing with the usual protocol. On being whisked away to their hotel room, VIPs would normally not demur about allowing the baggage to follow. Arvind found this preference to stay on as a bit odd and untypical. Then, over a cup of tea, Arvind noticed that the English spoken by the visitors was strange even allowing for the unusual diction of the 'Austraylians'. And soon enough, Arvind discovered that they were an elderly Polish couple on a sight seeing visit and had nothing to do with Australia or its parliament! A perplexed district magistrate and his minions left their guests behind, and scrambled to the baggage area where this time the guest was identified correctly as he was struggling to lift his bag from the baggage belt. Ten pairs of hands suddenly gave him assistance to handle this task; profuse apologies were tendered to the Australian speaker, even though he was not quite clear as to what the fuss was all about.

And then what about the Polish tourists, I asked? Were they dumped unceremoniously and left to their own devices in the VIP reception room? Did they perhaps fear that all this was a ploy to pilfer their baggage? Arvind replied that he remembered in the nick of time and gave hurried instructions as his car sped away that the forlorn Polish couple be gracefully escorted to their hotel rooms. They must have thought India to be a stranger country than they had imagined!

Eastern Uttar Pradesh, bordering on Nepal, is the hallowed land where Lord Buddha lived and preached for most of his lifetime. Kapilavastu, where he was born and Kushi Nagar where he passed on, are both near Gorakhpur. Sarnath near Varanasi played an important role in the Buddha's life. There is a belief, though not widely known, that the Buddha spent eighteen successive *chaturmasyas*, the sacred period during the rainy season between mid-June and mid-October, at a place called Sravasthi, in Bahraich District. This is in northeast Uttar Pradesh. Recent excavations in Sravasthi have unearthed the ruins of the palace where Buddha is believed to have spent those *chaturmasya* periods, where his ideas and teachings were crystallised. In the palace grounds, there is a large open area and legend has it that Buddha used to pace up and down these grounds everyday, composing his thoughts, and preparing for his writings. At Sravasthi, foreign pilgrims, particularly Japanese, clad in underwear and with bare torsos would traverse the grounds prostrate, rolling round and round so that their body could come into contact with the sacred soil: somewhat like the *angapradakshan* done by devotees at Hindu shrines.

The apocryphal legend of a rich trader is meant to illustrate how sacred the land is. Reputed to be the richest man in the world, he wanted to buy some land in the area so that he could acquire a part of the holy turf. He soon discovered that the cost of each square inch of this land was more than what he could earn in a lifetime. He was chastened, as he realised his folly in thinking that he could own a share of this divine property. He burst into tears, prostrated on that land, asked the Buddha for forgiveness for his pride, and became a monk.

There is also a wonderful small shrine at Sankitsa near Farrukhabad where there is a temple dedicated to the Buddha. In one of the stories associated with the Buddha, he recalled his dead mother briefly back to life on earth, prostrated before her and apologised to her for not teaching her the eternal truth during her lifetime, and then proceeded to give her the eternal wisdom. The shrine to Buddha's mother, commemorating this event is located there. The place is in ruins but excavations have yielded remarkable evidence of past events. Carbon dating of rice found in the site established that it was at least 2,000 years old.

When I was chief secretary in Uttar Pradesh, I had invited the then resident representative in India of UNDP with his wife, for a tour of the important Buddhist sites in the state. This Danish couple had spent most of their working life in the Indian subcontinent. They were students of Eastern history, culture and tradition. On their way out to see the historical sites, they showed me the English translation of a diary originally written in Japanese by a Japanese traveller who had visited this part of India sometime in the ninth or tenth century. This diary listed all the places of Buddhist interest visited by the travellers, giving fine details of the buildings and other features that they observed. For instance, there is the mention of the magnificent reclining Buddha, over thirty feet long, at Kushi Nagar, at the site of his *parinirvana* or passing. The diary mentions the name of the sculptor, who was originally from Mathura. It describes minute details of this work of art and similarly the details of the palaces, and other structures that existed at Kapilavastu. Since then, with the ravages of time, many of these structures have vanished.

The neglect is not recent. There is the story of the ambassador of the Imperial Kingdom of Japan at the London Court, who stopped over in India on a pilgrimage to Sankitsa sometime late in the nineteenth century. He saw the ruins and the utter desolation of the place and fell down on his knees sobbing. With tears streaming from his eyes, he said that this place was once a grander and a more important location than London or Kyoto ever was and see what had befallen this hallowed ground now!

For various historical reasons, the active practice of Buddhism has largely disappeared in India. However, it has left magnificent marks at many places all over the country, including at Ajanta, Ellora, Nalanda, Gaya, and Sarnath. Buddhism is a living religion practically in every Southeast Asian country, right up to Japan as well as in many other countries like Sri Lanka. There are millions of practicing Buddhists who would sacrifice much to undertake a holy pilgrimage to the places where the Buddha walked the land, lived, and preached. But the prospect of travelling in these parts, considered strange and dangerous, is enough to deter most visitors. The lack of simple, even spartan, but clean accommodation and hygienic food and safe passage are not available today in any organised manner to visitors. Even Indians who do not belong to this part of India will find it inconvenient at best, and dangerous at worst, to traverse these areas, and would find it expensive anyway.

The government of Uttar Pradesh did undertake some steps for laying down the basic infrastructure for tourism. Thus, there are air-strips today at Gorakhpur, Kushi Nagar, Sravasthi, and Farrukabad and there are regular airports at Varanasi and Gaya. Reasonably well-maintained roads connect these points. However, it will be an eminently viable proposition to establish a 'Buddhist circuit' with regular conducted tours bringing chartered flights from places like Singapore, Shanghai, Bangkok or Hong Kong to Varanasi. The focus has been on visitors from Japan, but elderly Buddhists from

Southeast Asian countries would also happily come for a well-organised tour – it would be a dream-come-true for many of them. I find it surprising that such a circuit has still not caught on. It requires some enterprise, relatively small investments and of course, co-ordination between the state and Central governments.

8 NEW DELHI: UNION MINISTRY OF COMMERCE

The secretary almost caught me by my ears and dragged me down the corridors of the ministry to a spot near the first floor elevator, and asked me if I could smell anything. I got an unpleasant stench wafting in the area emanating from a leaking sewage pipe. Now, I had no special expertise in vacating foul smells from toilets.

For a senior government official, his view of the Middle East was astonishing. He said: "These are dangerous places, where only barbarians live; no one knows what will happen to us there. It is best to avoid." Small wonder that we lost out in the bonanza offered by that region.

IN THE SUMMER OF 1979, I MOVED FROM UTTAR Pradesh to an assignment as joint secretary in the ministry of commerce, in New Delhi. The shift to work in the central secretariat with its change of pace, style and distinctive nature of work required some settling-in. I had hitherto mostly headed field operations. The new assignment had an advisory role with predominance of file work, in a hierarchical set up. My first assignment placed me in charge of exports of engineering products from India. Each officer was also responsible for an area, and the territory assigned to me was West Asia and North Africa. Later, over the next five and a half years, I had the opportunity to deal with a wide range of products such as chemicals, and agriculture, and also deal with other territories including USA, Western Europe and East Asia. During the final three years of my assignment in the ministry of commerce, I headed the Trade Policy Division, which co-ordinated the Indian interface with international agencies such as GATT.

I was suddenly thrown into the engineering desk without a background on the issues to be tackled. Being successor to K Ramanujam of the Bihar cadre helped matters. His notes on each subject would be so comprehensive that they would run into twenty or thirty pages or even more. Ramanujam would meticulously trace the roots and origin of each issue to be tackled, bring in all relevant details on record, analyse the previous initiatives on that subject, and take three or four pages to 'succinctly' sum up the issues to be addressed. It took one nearly an hour to read each note, and far more time and effort must have gone into its preparation. There were no computers or word processors those days, and so the poor stenographer would have had to crank up the entire note *ab-initio* each time that a fresh note on the issue had to be prepared. These long notes had one virtue. They were self-contained and so it was so easy to understand the complete background of each pending matter by reading the latest note on the subject.

The West Asia region was at that time treated with disdain, by Indian government officials. This was despite the region's political and economic importance for India. I recall visiting Istanbul as part of a delegation headed by the industries minister, to attend a seminar on Small Scale Industries, hosted by the Turkish government. Dr Ram K Vepa, the development commissioner for Small Industries in the Government of India, was the other member of the delegation. We had a wonderful time there, with the hosts pulling out all the stops in looking after the delegates. At the end of the trip, as we were planning our return journey to India, Ram Vepa had a specific demand of the travel agent, namely that the return journey should not touch any point in the Middle East. He wanted no connection through Dubai or Abu Dhabi or Jeddah. Since the ticketing did not permit us to travel westwards to a European city to find a connection to Delhi, we had great difficulty in finding a suitable route. Finally, we located a connecting flight via Cairo, which was inconvenient but met Vepa's specifications. We spent five hours in the international terminal in Cairo airport for our connection, in the middle of the night, not having enough time to check into a hotel and return. It was the time of the Haj and we were rewarded with the sight of the airport handling thousands of Haj pilgrims, mostly from different African, and North African points and chaos was reigning supreme. It was remarkable to see the pilgrims, dressed only in a *dhoti*-like lower garment, with a thin coverage of the torso, even the most affluent pilgrims following the same dress code. Faith is the same everywhere – the scene was not dissimilar to what one can see in Guruvayoor or Tirupati on Janmashtami.

I asked Vepa why we should not touch any point in the Middle East. His answer was simplicity itself, "These are dangerous places, where only barbarians live; no one knows what will happen to us there. It is best to avoid." This astonishing view regarding the Middle East was held in 1979 by a senior government official! As the joint secretary dealing with West Asia and North Africa, I later discovered that no senior political leader or senior bureaucrat from India would visit a West Asian country for promoting Indian business interests, not even the finance secretary or petroleum secretary. The only exception was Romesh Bhandari, who was secretary in the External Affairs Ministry with responsibility for that region. Here was a region on which we very heavily depended for our petroleum supplies. It had potential for project as well as commodity exports. A large number of Indians were employed in the Middle East, sending in significant inward remittances of foreign exchange into India from the region. The region was held as strategically important by major powers. And here was this view, that it was a dangerous place to be in. Small wonder that we lost out on the bonanza offered by that region. Indian consultancy companies and project contractors did slowly make inroads into the large market in the Middle East, overcoming obstacles as they climbed the learning curve. It is just a pity that we were about twenty years late, and had missed all the easy pickings.

During 1980-81, I had many opportunities to travel to Libya, Saudi Arabia, UAE, and Bahrain to pursue our project export interests. Even though we were late in the race and the easy pickings had gone, there were still significant opportunities beckoning. I recall on a visit to Libya, seeing some of the remarkable historic sites in that country. One had to read the "Green Book" – a slim publication outlining the thinking of Gaddafi, to understand why he has continued to be popular in that country for decades. While once leaving Tripoli airport, the official at the customs desk asked me to open my suitcase. I demurred, showing him my red diplomatic passport, claiming immunity. Suddenly a guard nearby raised his carbine, levelled it against me and said, "Open the box". So much for diplomatic immunity! By all accounts, the Indian doctors were the most popular amongst all the doctors there, and had endeared themselves to the local population. I was told that one of our earlier ambassadors, Taleyarkhan, had asked the government to send one thousand doctors to that country. The Indian bureaucracy examined the request and denied it, as they would after all. They had a reason too. They cited the indisputable logic that the per capita availability of doctors in India was quite low. Apparently the ambassador went straight to Indira Gandhi, who immediately ordered that the medical doctors be allowed to go. That step helped build goodwill for India in Libya.

In 1980, I visited Baghdad as part of a delegation headed by Pranab Mukherjee, the then commerce minister. The other members of the delegation were Kant Bhargava of the External Affairs Ministry and myself. The delegation represented the Government of India at the Iraqi celebrations to commemorate the twelfth anniversary of the Ba'ath revolution. Saddam Hussain was firmly in the saddle and this was just before the war with Iran. It was a grand occasion when the entire city was transformed into a celebration mode. Since this was the Ramzan period, the public feasting started around 8 pm everyday on the banks of the river Tigris, with lavish food and entertainment offered gratis by the authorities.

The members of the Indian delegation left one evening by a flight from Delhi to Bombay to connect with an Iraqi Airways flight. On the flight, Kant Bhargava showed the minister a copy of the letter from Prime Minister Indira Gandhi to Saddam Hussain, the original of which was being carried by Pranab Mukherjee for presentation to Saddam. It was a one page letter bare on salutations and frills. It read somewhat as follows:

"*Dear President Saddam Hussain,*

On behalf of the government and the people of India, let me congratulate you and the people of Iraq on the 12th anniversary of the Ba'ath revolution. We send our greetings to you.
India is a major importer of oil from Iraq. The following table will give you our annual requirements and imports. Kindly give us more oil on favourable terms.

Yours truly"

And in the space below this letter, following the signature of our prime minister, there was a small chart giving the details of our oil needs. As I read the copy, I groaned. Pranab Mukherjee asked me why. I told him that in my view this was an absurd way for our prime minister to address the Iraqi president. The letter should have been an effusive one with personal references to Saddam, referring to him as a beloved brother. It could have concluded with a small footnote that our representative would take up some matters regarding oil and would Saddam help? My view over the letter was based on the warm and cordial relations that existed between Indira Gandhi and Saddam Hussain. Anyway, it was too late to change that letter. We arrived at Baghdad around three in the morning and were received at the airport by the Iraqi oil minister. When a reference was made that Pranab Mukherjee would like to deliver personally a letter from Indira Gandhi to Saddam Hussain, the oil minister readily agreed to organise a meeting. As per normal protocol, a copy of the message that Pranab Mukherjee was to deliver to Saddam was handed over to the Iraq authorities. That was the last we heard about the matter and no wonder. My apprehensions were not unfounded as subsequent events during that trip were to show. The mission failed but there was comic relief.

We had with us a 'B' team, which in fact fared better than we did. Apparently, the Iraqis had invited an official and a party delegation each from a large number of countries. In addition to our official delegation, the ruling Congress party was represented by a delegation consisting of S S Mohapatra and Arif Mohammad Khan. Mohapatra who is now no more, was about sixty years old at that time, and was the president of the 'Youth Wing' of the Indian Congress! Khan was then a Congress MP. On the morning after our arrival, Mohapatra mentioned to us that he had lost his baggage in transit from Delhi. Even though it was technically irregular, I gave him US $ 200 from the delegation's contingency account to buy some clothing and other essentials. Mohapatra used that money not to buy clothing, but spent it on some electronic goods and other exotica. His baggage did not arrive at least for the next three days and so Mohapatra continued to wear his rough woollen *khadi bandh-gala* suit throughout the visit. Now, this suit was brightly coloured, with loud unseemly checks. What made it further interesting was that the checks of the trousers did not match those of the jacket, thus producing a garish effect. Mohapatra would drop in daily at my hotel room late every evening for a drink. He would then be clad only in a towel, while leaving his only suit to air-dry. I came to find out fairly intimate details about his personal wear. Thus Mohapatra would through the day be wearing his loud check *bandh-gala* suit and as I know for a fact, nothing else.

Over the next three days, we were anxiously waiting for the call for Pranab Mukherjee to meet Saddam. We could see Saddam on the television from morning till night, continuously meeting school children, local citizens and hosting endless foreign delegations. Pranab was getting edgier by the moment. He would ask Peter Sinai, the Indian ambassador every hour or so, "Have you reminded the Iraq authorities? – I am waiting to meet Saddam." Peter would politely say, "Sir, I am doing my level best. They know very well that you are waiting to see Saddam. I expect the call to come any time now." Once Pranab even asked Peter, "Have you told the Iraqi authorities that I am the second most important person in India, after Indira Gandhi"? Sinai diplomatically replied, "Sir, they know it very well". On the third day, around six in the evening, as we were watching televison, we were startled to see Mohapatra and Arif Khan facing us on the television screen. There they were, standing in a line close to Saddam. And then their turn came. They were introduced to Saddam who gave a huge hug to Mohapatra and had a long chat with him. Pranab suddenly got up and asked for the television to be shut off and told Sinai gruffly, "Find us the first flight back to India." Later that night, we found ourselves on the plane for the return journey. I still have before me this image of the hug Saddam gave to Mohapatra and his plaid check suit!

During the entire period of over five years that I was in the commerce ministry, I held the charge of joint secretary, administration responsible for all internal administrative arrangements in the ministry as also in the attached offices in India and abroad. This was a thankless assignment. One morning after attending a conference of the engineering industry, I hastened back to my room for a sandwich lunch. I learnt that the commerce secretary had been looking for me the whole morning and was getting agitated at my absence from the ministry. As soon as the secretary returned from his lunch, I went across to his room. His ill humour had not blown over. He almost caught me by my ears and dragged me down the corridors to a spot near the first floor elevator, and asked me if I could smell anything. I got the unpleasant stench of urine wafting in the area emanating from a leaking sewage pipe. Apparently that morning, the commerce secretary had escorted a senior delegation from Denmark, which included the Danish trade minister, and had felt embarrassed. He ordered me to get rid of the foul smell within twenty-four hours; or else there would be serious consequences. Now as things went, the matter was not in my hands. I had no special expertise in vacating foul smells from toilets. Even though I was in-charge of administration in the commerce ministry, the maintenance of Udyog Bhawan was with the industry ministry, who also occupied the building. In panic, I spoke to my counterpart in the Industry ministry, but rather than seeing the urgent need for action, he found the situation strangely humorous. He casually told me that this matter was not in his hands either. The maintenance of

Udyog Bhawan was under the purview of the Central Public Works Department (CPWD). He did kindly agree that he would soon write a letter to the concerned executive engineer to look into the matter of the leaking urinals. I then jumped levels and went straight to his boss, who invoked the powers that be for some urgent action. That did not help. It took the next three months till the repairs were done and the pipes replaced. All we could do till then was to supplant the stench of urine with doses of bleaching powder. I discovered that none in the government found it necessary to respond quickly to others' woes, even if the sufferer was another government servant.

On another occasion, there was a meeting going on in the conference room of the ministry at which the then Commerce Minister Shivraj Patil was present. Sometime around 1 pm, the noise of slogan shouting wafted into the room. I checked it out and found that the noise was emanating from a group of employees of the commerce and industry ministries, making certain demands as part of an agitation organised by some unions of secretariat employees. As the slogan shouting continued, Shivraj Patil was getting irritated. He looked at me and asked, "Why are you not going to see what the problem is and to find the solution for it?" I mentioned to him that indeed I had checked out and that it was not uncommon for employees to express demands through slogans. After a while, he practically ordered me to go and sort the problem out, at which I had to tell him that there would be no difficulty in my going and talking to them immediately. However, they would demand some assurance to be given to them on the spot, which I was not in a position to give. This would rapidly escalate into the minister having to go himself who himself was in no position to give any assurance on the employees' service matters. This infuriated the minister, even though I do not know if this was due to the logic of what I said, or because he was powerless to act!

As in-charge of administration, I was frequently embarrassed by my colleagues coming to me and pleading for an immediate shift of one or the other of their subordinates with whom they were unable to get along. One of my colleagues used to periodically descend on my room, lock the door from within, burst into tears, and ask for the immediate removal or transfer of one or the other deputy secretary, working in her division. I would mollify her and promise to do whatever I could; and as she left the room, I would look at my watch. On cue, within ten minutes the concerned deputy secretary would charge into my room nearly in tears asking for his transfer from the joint secretary's division and saying that he would not suffer that hell even for one more moment. All in a day's work!

In the course of a bilateral trade meeting with Afghanistan, we found that the trade balance was heavily to India's advantage. We were seeking ways to improve Afghanistan's exports to India. Now Afghanistan had dry fruits to export but we were not able to selectively allow imports of almonds only from this country in view of GATT rules. So we found a device to classify Afghan almonds by size and allowing those that were smaller in size, easier access to Indian markets. This was done, of course, without mentioning Afghanistan by name. Such duplicity is standard practice all over the world. There was an immediate and unforeseen reaction from USA. The export of Californian almonds to India were hit adversely they said. In the context of trade with USA or as part of total US exports, Californian almond exports to India were quite insignificant. However, the California Almond Growers Exchange, an American almond growers lobby, took up the matter strongly to restore parity in treatment between almonds coming from the US and Afghanisthan. A trivial matter it would seem for the US, but one could see how lobbies are so important.

President Reagan, who hailed from California, was said to be personally involved in pursuing the case. We received memoranda from the US embassy to restore the original definition of almonds. Signals started pouring in from different quarters to give in on this matter. It dawned on us that a lever to negotiate with had unexpectedly fallen into our lap. We did not let it go. And so, while we restored the parity in respect of almonds, we were able to get valuable concessions in our on-going negotiations with USA in the field of textiles and other export items from India. So actually the USA lost more than it gained. It would seem that the democratic process in the USA has some similarity with that of India in serving public interest.

There would also be regular bilateral meetings of the Indo-Iraq trade committee that used to meet every year, alternately in Delhi and in Baghdad. As joint secretary in charge of West Asia, I led the Indian delegation at these meetings. My counterpart was the director general in the Trade Ministry of Iraq. Prior to the first round held in Delhi, Iraq had, as a gesture from Saddam Hussain to Indira Gandhi, allowed concessional export of Iraqi oil to India. This was at a time when we were in need. Then, in the bilateral negotiations at Delhi, we had about twenty relatively minor requests to make of the Iraqi side. The Iraqis had a similar number of requests to make to India. As I would raise each of our items of interest with the Iraqi delegation, the Iraqi chairman would summarily reject it saying that it was not Iraqi policy. However, Iraq pressed each of their requests relentlessly and would not give up on even one. In view of the brief to be cooperative during the negotiations with the Iraqis, I tried to be as accommodative as possible on the requests that I could really agree to. The Iraqis, however, did not give up on the other demands; all the while summarily rejecting every one of our requests. In exasperation, I went to the then Commerce Secretary Rao Sahib, and asked him for advice, mentioning that the Iraqis were summarily rejecting even a mention of our requests, while stubbornly asking for acceptance of every one of theirs. Rao Sahib advised me to listen to their requests as sympathetically as possible, but gave me a free hand to tell the Iraqis when they could get off, if they were too unreasonable. I also had the mandate to be rude if I wished. "The arrogance of oil" was the judgement pronounced by him.

During those negotiations, I got quite friendly with one of the delegates, who had studied in Delhi during his younger years. The Iraqi delegation was about thirty strong. The following year the negotiations took place in Baghdad, and I found that most of the Iraqi delegates had changed from the previous year but my old friend was there. I asked him as to why there was this extensive change in the composition of the delegation. Initially his responses were guarded, but over a drink the next evening, he confided in me. He said that Saddam had doubted the loyalties of five of the members of his Cabinet, whom he suspected of hatching a plot for a coup against him. So, one day as the Revolutionary Command Council met, Saddam lined up those five members, whipped out his revolver and shot them in the head, one by one. As they lay dead on the floor, the other remaining members of the Cabinet pumped a bullet into each dead body lying on the floor, turn by turn, as a sign of loyalty. I do not know how much truth there was in this gory story, but it tallied with some of the versions circulating in diplomatic circles at that time, as to how Saddam had dealt with an attempted coup against him. My informant told me that was how major changes of senior staff in many ministries consequently took place. In India too, changes in staff are made in arbitrary ways. But this was something else.

In the autumn of 1982, I got orders posting me as the Indian ambassador to GATT to replace B L Das. I was preparing to leave for Geneva. I had completed my security briefing and also got an advance of the princely sum of Rs.5,000 to prepare for the foreign assignment – which I used mainly for getting a suit stitched and buying a pair of shoes. However, in November, the commerce secretary asked me to stay on for a few more months and assist him in the preparations for the meeting of heads of states of the Non Aligned Movement (NAM) being held in February 1983. My departure to Geneva was thus postponed by about four months. On 31st of December, I got an urgent summons from Vijay Shankar Tripathi, a colleague who joined the service along with me in the same batch. Tripathi, who had by then resigned from the IAS and joined the political bandwagon of Indira Gandhi, was functioning in the post of additional secretary in the prime minister's secretariat. As I walked into his room in the PMO, he was going through voluminous papers. When I asked him what he was up to, he told me that he was perusing the judgements written by a number of judges in the various high courts of India, in order to identify a select group whose opinions and inclinations were acceptable to the current powers in India. He would then prepare a short list for promotion to the post of chief justice of the high courts and elevation to the Supreme Court. This was typical of a US type presidential form of government, where the ruling party packs the courts with persons having acceptable political inclinations. Clearly, India was moving in this direction.

Tripathi kept his papers away and quickly came to the point. He said in his own way, "Partner, leave for Geneva immediately and take charge there; don't wait for one more day; and don't ask me anything more. I am giving you good advice." I rushed back to my office and made my bookings to leave for Geneva that night. I then asked Abid Hussain, the then commerce secretary for permission to hand over charge in the commerce ministry and leave that night. Abid Sahib readily gave me approval, asking me to proceed. And then with a quizzical expression on his face he gave me this piece of advice, "Don't run for anything in life; if you have to get something, it will come searching for you. Nothing is worthwhile for you to give up your composure, that you must hanker after it." I returned to my room, shut the door behind me, and calmly thought about the advice I had received. Then I cancelled my air bookings for that night.

Two days later I understood Tripathi's cryptic advice to me. Indira Gandhi announced policy changes as part of what were called administrative reforms that made me ineligible for the posting. There was petty politics behind these 'major' policy initiatives. One was to enforce tenure rules strictly. Without contesting the validity of these measures, I saw that the immediate purpose was merely opportunistic. One other administrative reform that was announced, and this hurt, was that no one should be sent on a foreign deputation, if he had less than two years' tenure left with the Government of India. The merit of this reform is dubious though at first glance, it would seem virtuous. At any rate, the immediate interpretation of the personnel department was that I was ineligible to go for the ambassador's assignment, as I had less than two years' tenure left as on 1st January 1983. The wording of the pronouncement of the PMO specifically referred to future processing of foreign postings and ought to have affected only prospective cases – it did not cover my case as it already had the approval of the prime minister. Nobody had the courage to take up the matter for clarification with the PMO. Thus, the system ruled that I was ineligible for the posting as India's ambassador to GATT.

There was a comical sequel to this. Six months later, when I had the dubious status of ex-ambassador-designate, I received a notice from the book-keepers in the ministry, asking me to return the advance that I had received for the Geneva posting, as it was still outstanding in their books. I looked at the previous papers carefully, and gave a certificate to the finance division that "I certify that I had utilised the advance for the purpose for which it was given." The finance controller was aghast at this 'false' certification by me. He summoned me to his room and asked me to withdraw the paper quickly before it entered the records, as there could be proceedings against me for false certification. At that point, I showed him the wording of the purpose for which the advance was given namely "to prepare for the assignment in Geneva". I told him that I had done the preparation as required, and that under no circumstances would I refund the money, small as the amount was. I added that I had no objection to delivering the well-worn suit and the used pair of shoes purchased through the advance, to be deposited in the government treasury. The controller laughed out aloud, as he saw the point in what I said. He closed the advance as having been utilised. But true to style, he added a rider. If I were posted again to a government assignment abroad within five years, I would not be eligible for a further preparation advance!

One day in early 1983, after my posting as ambassador to GATT fell through, V P Singh, the commerce minister, called me and asked me to process urgently the posting of K S Bains as ambassador to GATT. He said that Rajiv Gandhi desired this. Apparently Bains, a competent officer, had worked on developing Delhi's road infrastructure and other arrangements in connection with the just concluded Asian Games. Rajiv Gandhi, who was in charge of those games, saw the excellent work done by Bains in this regard and sought to 'reward' him with the posting to Geneva. When I demurred that Bains had no experience in multilateral commercial diplomacy, he told me that these were orders directly from Rajiv, which brooked no opposition. I should make the formal move the same day. At that time, Rajiv was the rising star and even though he had no official position, his word was law. I went to my room and prepared a three-page note on the subject but not on the lines the minister expected. I explained that the ambassador's post to GATT was a key position for our trade interests. India was a kind of leader to represent the point of view of developing countries and was held in high esteem in trade negotiating circles. Any incumbent, however brilliant, could not get to know the technical requirements of the job while on the job and therefore, advance preparation was necessary. I added that Bains had no experience or exposure whatsoever to the commerce ministry or trade negotiations, not even to any trade related matters; and it would be against the national interest to send him to that post. When I gave him the note, V P Singh gave me a quizzical look and reluctantly took the note from me. Four days later, he returned the paper back to me saying, "You are very lucky. He read it and saw your point. It could easily have gone the other way, with consequences for you." I have seen more than once that a principled stand carries the day, if only one would take it.

It was nearly a daily occurrence for a minister, senior bureaucrat or a politician to talk to me recommending the induction of one official or the other into the ministry, and requesting me to commence the necessary paper work for the same. A posting in the commerce ministry was a coveted one. It carried the possibility of the ultimate prize of a foreign posting, the dream of every Indian bureaucrat. Usually I would listen to the *sifarish* politely, and do nothing about it. My theory was that anyone trying to bring political pressure usually lacked intrinsic merit, which needed to be covered up through recommendations. In fact, I would take into account the potential vacancies well in advance. By a very careful search, I would locate suitable officers of requisite seniority and ability, and move the paper work well in advance to secure their services. Many officers may not even have known that their names were being processed for a posting in the ministry or in its attached offices. Contrast this with the current situation, with the massive deterioration of standards in this regard during the past twenty years.

No one can now aspire to a posting in any ministry in Delhi, unless his or her name is vigorously sponsored. Ministers ask for specific officers, whom they know from before, for postings in the ministry, even at junior levels. The merest wish of an official of the PMO becomes a command to the system. The personnel department at the Centre has become helpless in enforcing the existing regulations. Even the Cabinet secretariat has been overwhelmed, unable to stem the rot in recent years The system has sent strong messages to entire cadres of aspiring civil servants that hard work and performance are irrelevant: the path is to gain effective access to one or more in power. Of course, there is a price to pay for the shortcut. The carefully built up structure for identifying suitable officers for posting in Delhi has by now been demolished.

Traditionally, the secretary in a ministry has been the minister's adviser, much as the Cabinet secretary used to be the prime minister's administrative adviser. This system has been seriously subverted since the 1980s by the staff officer to the minister eclipsing the legitimate role of the secretary and emerging as a rival power centre within the ministry. This is akin to the decimation by the PMO, also taking place, of the essential role of the Cabinet secretariat. It is no surprise that staff officers, at some stage or the other, ask their obliging political masters for the reward of a foreign posting. The officers thus selected have no experience to discharge their functions. Besides, such choices distort the value system among the administrators, by rubbing in the lesson that proximity to a minister, not merit, is the sole criterion for a foreign posting. As Cabinet secretary, I had persuaded I K Gujral, then the prime minister, to agree with me that the personal secretaries and staff officers to ministers should not be considered for foreign postings. Selection should be done only from those officers available for central tenure under normal procedure taking into account the experience, background and suitability. Formal orders on these lines were then issued. Sure enough, these orders could not stand the onslaught of the political forces, as ministers felt that their personal privileges were being affected. As soon as the Vajpayee government came to power in 1998, these principles were given the go-by. No wonder. One of the first persons to be sent on an assignment to Washington was the staff officer of Vajpayee himself!

There is another anomaly in the filling of some senior positions abroad such as director in the International Monetary Fund (IMF) or the World Bank at Washington or in Asian Development Bank (ADB) at Manila. Most countries send nominees who are much younger and with a stake in the future financial management of their countries – generally the equivalent of a joint secretary in our government. Thus, a person who is earmarked at middle management levels as a potential finance secretary is seconded to these posts to garner international experience in that field, obtain a global perspective on financial matters, as also to develop valuable personal contacts which would help him on return to his home country. The foreign posting is seen as a necessary preparation for later responsibilities.

In India, as one would expect, the objectives are different. Service officers who have finished their careers in India, are seconded to these postings as a 'reward' for the work done in India. It can be easily seen that the minister expects these senior officials to play ball so long as they are in the ministry, toe the line and not have too independent a mind. They are then eligible for the reward at the end of their services. This is yet one more weapon in the armory of politicians.

Contrast this with K K Dass, who had been chief secretary of Uttar Pradesh in the 1960s, and retired from service sometime in the '70s. When he served as secretary to the Union Ministry of Information and Broadcasting, his minister was the late Uma Shankar Dikshit. Dikshit soon thereafter became the home minister of India, and his staff officer Rajgopal, a dear friend of mine, showed me a file with exchange of correspondence between Dikshit and K K Dass. On his retirement, Dass had written a polite letter thanking Dikshit for all the courtesies extended to him and formally bidding farewell to him. The next letter in the file was the copy of an acknowledgment from the home minister to Dass, with a paragraph added, asking whether Dass would be available for a gubernatorial assignment. It is the home minister who usually initiates proposals for the post of governor in the various states; and it was not a casual offer. Dikshit had made a mention on the file that he had discussed the matter with prime minister. In his reply, which is on record, Dass said that he was flattered and overwhelmed by the kindness shown by the home minister. Then he went on to add, "I have served the government of India for nearly forty years. During this time, I have neglected the two true loves of my life – my wife and my rose garden. Could the home minister excuse me and allow me to spend the few remaining years of my life in the company of my wife and the roses".

9 INDIA'S TRADE POLICY

*I was hovering around in the corridors and I got to
see that as much was going on outside the meeting
hall, as was going on within. There was a field
scrambler telephone system hidden in a corner outside
the meeting room. Off and on, an American officer
would come to the scrambler phone and speak,
doubtless as part of a move to soften a delegation
that was non-cooperative or recalcitrant.*

*The joke making the rounds in Paris was that since
0.2% finance flows was the target, Bangladesh had
sent 0.2% of its population as delegates for the Paris
conference! Every hotel and plaza in Paris seemed to
be full of Bangladeshis. Every room in the conference
facility was half full with Bangladeshis.*

I SPENT MORE THAN FIVE YEARS IN THE
commerce ministry. During this time, I had the privilege of working under
four successive secretaries. Each one of them has left a mark on our
administrative system. All of them were wonderful human beings, with a
large heart. They represented the best in our civil services. So, this was a
unique experience for me. My close interaction with them, right in the
middle of my own career must have left its imprint on me. During that
time, I worked under five commerce ministers. This was my first real
exposure to ministers at the Union Cabinet level. I have narrated some of
my experiences with them in the previous chapter, which also covers the
commerce ministry.

For more than three years, in the later part of my tenure as the joint secretary in the commerce ministry, I was in charge of the trade policy division. Those days, the division backstopped the Indian presence in international trade and development organisations, and in particular the GATT, now known as the World Trade Organisation (WTO). This was a coveted assignment in the ministry and the division had an extensive interface with a number of ministries in the government. The post gave me an excellent overview of India's economic relations with the outside world. I could see the impact of our international obligations on domestic policy and economy. I could also get an insight into the inter-relationship between economics and politics in the international arena. Part of the job was to get briefs prepared for international negotiations in consultation with other ministries, as well as trade and industry organisations. The work also meant participating in the negotiation meetings and in other conferences from time to time. Then, it was necessary to actively keep track of the outcome of these negotiations and discussions. When there was a major international event, the Indian delegation would be led by the commerce minister or the secretary. At other events, I would head the Indian delegation comprising representatives from other ministries and sometimes from outside the government. The trade policy arena was an enthralling field to work in. I felt greatly honoured by the opportunity to wear the national colours, so to speak, at so many significant international events. Of course, there were occasions for rejoicing at the success achieved; and at other times one had to suffer the pain of defeat.

Ever since the creation of GATT from the 1950s onwards, India had played a prominent role in its affairs. In the wake of their independence, triggered by India's freedom movement, a large number of developing countries looked upon India as their natural leader. Nehru played an important role in the post-Independence era and Indira Gandhi had an international stature. The Indian representatives to international fora for the period up to the 1980s had been selected with great care and represented the country ably. They had an excellent reputation, were generally admired and sometimes feared, in every conference across the world. This status was earned from mastery over the subject, meticulous preparation and hard work with long hours put in. The preparation gave them the mental energy to pursue their brief. During the early 1980s, when I had occasion to participate regularly in events in Geneva, and elsewhere, the pre-eminent position of India as a force to reckon with was palpable. It used to be jocularly said those days that the brief given to the representatives of many developing countries, particularly from Asia and Africa by their national governments essentially, was to "carefully follow and toe the line taken by the Indian delegate; if you disagree totally with that line, come back to us for clarification; if the official brief from headquarters contradicts the line taken by India, come back to us for a re-assessment; whenever in doubt, take the advice of Indian delegation". With this support, India was able to participate in debates on key issues on equal terms with the more powerful western countries. If the Indian voice were heard on significant issues, it was because India was not speaking only for itself, it also represented the collective thinking and the common denominator of the developing countries' interests. The 'Morges group' meetings where India was an invitee, illustrate the standing that India then enjoyed. This unofficial gathering consisted of developed countries along with India and a few other developing countries. The group would meet for an informal dinner on a fixed day every week in a village called Morges near Lausanne. This was the sounding board for new ideas and initiatives to be introduced at the GATT, for discussion and informal negotiation to test if new positions would fly. India played a major role in moderating the new proposals, ensuring that they were not unduly inimical to developing countries' interests, and frequently persuading the western powers not to overreach themselves.

Alas, the important position held by India withered away by the late 1980s. India become just one more member and not a particularly significant one among the hundred-odd members of the WTO. India's voice was given no more weight than that of, say, Senegal or Chile. This sad decline in India's role in international economic diplomacy has come about through a combination of several factors. These relate partly, but not only, to our own standing on the world stage. The posture we adopted has also affected our standing. To start with, India's relative position in the international economic scene declined as many other developing countries made significant advances. India's share in world trade had declined steadily in the decades after Independence. Countries like South Korea, Malaysia, Singapore, China, which were insignificant in the 1960s, made rapid economic advances. The effect of the relative advance of a large number of developing countries coupled with India's stagnation, muffled our voice in the international economic forum. This is the reality, which most Indians do not realise, misguided by the drum-beating stance adopted by our political leaders playing up our own achievements for the domestic constituency.

Perhaps as a consequence of India's declining importance in the world stage or perhaps due to poor leadership, I cannot say, there has been a sad decline in India's own ability to sustain its negotiating position, and maintain its standards in the quality of its representation. I was witness to the collapse in India's standing as an opinion builder and leader of the developing countries, dating from the Uruguay Round negotiations during the late 1980s, which concluded in the early '90s. Our negotiations were defensive battles, with the objective of damage control. Rather than to strike a bargain, the chosen position was not to have the negotiations at all. India took an aggressive, all or nothing, posture, and was isolated and routed in the final negotiating arena. I attribute this to extremely poor representation characterised by a rabid, dogmatic, and impractical approach. Represented implacably by our Ambassador Shukla, we took an extreme position. With none in Delhi capable of keeping Shukla under check, we ignored all moderate opinion. Not one other country was left at the end to defend our position. After all, what is a leader without a follower? We had boxed ourselves into a corner and were completely isolated. We lost our relevance not only in the context of the Uruguay Round, but in terms of our capability to participate effectively in future events. This has been a major loss, and the surrender of a position of vantage, held since Independence. We had hitherto also taken extreme positions, fought the battle hard, but at the right moment, brokered a compromise settlement, eliciting the goodwill of both developing and developed countries. Hereafter, India was to become just another voice with hardly anyone listening. With such a rigid stance, it was no surprise that our style had turned abrasive. When I was once chatting with some ambassadors at a cocktail party in Geneva, one of them recalled a session at the Montreal negotiations of the Uruguay Round where he came across an Indian representative whose name he could not recall, but whom he described as a 'bull in a china shop'. The other ambassador identified the negotiator as Ambassador Dubey, and added that the description was perfectly correct. In fact, Ambassador Dubey carried his own china shop to every negotiating session, he said. Can this be the profile of a successful negotiator?

India's declining role also had to do with the decision, mainly taken by the USA, to marginalise and enfeeble all developing countries. The Reagan era changed the nature of international economic negotiations. Reagan ruthlessly countermanded the deference hitherto shown to the developing countries and concessions granted to them. He declared in unequivocal terms that there was no charity in the international economic order. Each country, he said, should look out for itself and compete on equal terms, with no quarter given. Actually the competition on 'equal terms' translates into a situation, where the developed countries retain their enormous economic clout in the international negotiations which consequently are on completely unequal terms. Whereas the early Kennedy Round and the Tokyo Round, dating from a liberal post-Second World War era, supported principles such as 'special and differential treatment' for developing countries and formalised significant concessions to them, the Reagan era repudiated these concessions and enforced new negotiations from a platform of economic dominance. Blown away at one stroke were the codified agreements on tariff concessions, ability to maintain import quotas, right to protect domestic agriculture, and differential and preferential treatment in respect of all trade issues. In the new order of the day, focus shifted to negotiations on freedom of finance flows, labour standards, patents and copyrights, and trade in services – all new concepts brought in to formalise the advantages of the industrialised countries. The developed countries gave short shrift to the point of view of the developing countries and India no longer mattered.

It was only to be expected that there would be a new negotiating posture to go with the shift in direction. The strategy adopted by the US in particular was to use bilateralism and systematically break the unity of developing countries in every key area of international negotiations. Thus, the US merrily entered into a number of bilateral and group arrangements, sponsored its own new economic relations with individual developing countries, made major inroads into the diplomatic space of Latin America, and in general, adopted an extremely aggressive divide-and-rule policy in international economic diplomacy.

But the multilateral fora could not be wished away. Here a tactical approach was adopted by the US with a precision more often associated with warfare. The American negotiation techniques displayed a certain mastery of persuasive skill, though of dubious merit and surely not worthy of emulation. In every developing country, the Americans had developed point men among locals in key positions who would generate internal support for the American position at the appropriate time. They had also developed the ability to divide the domestic opinion in a developing country, through selective intervention. I observed that the US adopted several techniques for this end. One was to have small international groups that would meet under American leadership with participation restricted to key individuals from developing countries, by invitation only. This was aimed to subtly bring about an endorsement of the preferred view-point among opinion makers in various countries.

Thus, for example, if the topic was whether 'Trade in Services' should be an agenda item in the GATT, a subject on which much debate had taken place in developing countries, America would call a meeting at Washington for a contact seminar. The invitees would be handpicked ministers from say, fifteen developing countries, to be chaired by the American minister concerned. The composition would include representation from all the continents. Of say, fifteen invitees, thirteen would be highly articulate American educated quislings, who owed their political existence in their representative countries directly to American support. The two other ministers would be carefully identified from the dissenting group, from independent minded countries. The seminar itself would be in a small room, with all aides blocked out, except an official to help the American minister with the facts. After a gruelling one-day session, where one quisling after another would outline the benefits to accrue to developing countries by having an international agreement on trade in services, the two dissenting ministers would be boxed into a corner; and made to feel embarrassed for holding obscurantist views inimical to their own interests. And then, suddenly in the evening, there would be a high powered press conference, with the American minister showering high praise on the two identified targets and announcing that there was unanimity on the imperative need for having on agreement in trade in services, in the overall interests of the world community! The embarrassed target would capitulate, rather than fight the tide.

I accompanied V P Singh for one such event held in Washington, hosted by Bill Brock, the US trade representative, a member of Reagan's Cabinet. I had briefed V P Singh on what to expect in the closed room, from which all aides were blocked out, except the deputy USTR, an official equivalent to the level of a secretary in the Indian government. At the end of the meeting, as we were driving back to the hotel, V P Singh recounted to me the high voltage attention applied on him in the pressure-cooker atmosphere. As a result, his opposition could be articulated only in muted terms. Predictably, his implied acquiescence was announced and broadcast to the world as full support for the American position.

I came across more than one such American tactic in the run up to the announcement of the new Round of negotiations, which later came to be christened as the Uruguay Round. One day in 1980, the commerce secretary showed me a classified message from our permanent representative at Geneva, A P Venkateshwaran. The message basically said that he had been invited to a lunch hosted by the American ambassador. Over lunch, the idea had been proposed that, as the Tokyo Round had been concluded, a new Round of negotiations should commence the following year. This new Round would include subjects such as trade in services, which were of great benefit to developing countries, as well as new subjects such as agriculture, investment protection, minimum labour standards and others. Venkateshwaran proudly added in the message that he felt that the Round would be in India's interest, and he had signified India's support for the new round.

A S Gill, the commerce secretary was livid at the message. The usual American chicanery had been practiced, namely to invite Ambassador Venkateshwaran for the important luncheon excluding our ambassador to GATT, whose subject in fact was under discussion and who ought to have been present. Clearly our representative was flattered by the invitation. Knowing little on the subject, and anyway not having any mandate to take a view on the issues raised, nor even to participate in the discussions, he had felt pleased to express India's preliminary 'no-objection' to the new Round. The stunned commerce secretary sent a response as rough and virulent as I had ever seen, squarely berating Venkateshwaran for participating in the meeting and expressing a view on behalf of India. He bluntly told Venkateshwaran to withdraw any concurrence he had given and to say that he had referred the matter to Delhi. He was also directed to desist totally from going anywhere near the new Round. Gill, in anger, circulated a copy of this message to the top echelons in Delhi, including the prime minister, foreign minister, commerce minister, the Cabinet secretary and the foreign secretary.

By this time, I was beginning to read the American game. So I soon saw through the next gambit, this time played on home ground. We were invited to a luncheon given by the US ambassador in Delhi, in honor of Mike Smith, the deputy USTR who was passing through Delhi. By that time, Abid Hussain had become the commerce secretary. As Abid Sahib and I reached the ambassador's house, we saw L K Jha, a retired bureaucrat, who had been the governor of the RBI as well as India's ambassador to USA. With him were R N Malhotra, the then finance and economic affairs secretary, and Romesh Bhandari, the secretary in the External Affairs Ministry dealing with economic matters. From the commerce ministry, we had with us my deputy R L Narayan, a brilliant officer on deputation from the Foreign Ministry. As soon as the first gin was served in the luscious lawns of Roosevelt house, the ambassador briskly made the surprise announcement that it was time to start the working session, and shepherded us straightaway to the large dining table, where all the ten or so invitees were promptly seated. Without any ado, the ambassador thanked us for our presence and without the courtesy of an apology for conversion of the social occasion into a semi-formal meeting, introduced Ambassador Smith and asked him to take over the meeting from there on.

Mike Smith was on a whirlwind swing of some key developing country capitals, and repeated the opening spiel that he quite obviously used at each stop on the tour. He provided a fifteen-minute summary of the events leading up to the proposal for the new Round and outlined the benefits that developing countries would receive, especially such an important country as India. He said that he was making a worldwide tour of about ten key developing countries to drum up support for the new Round. As part of the pressure tactic, he added that practically every developing country he visited, saw benefit in the new Round and had informally signified acceptance. As if we did not know our own interests, he went on to state that the subjects like trade in services, investment protection agreement, free finance flows, intellectual property rights and negotiations on agriculture would be to India's benefit. In passing, he gratuitously praised the high level of awareness and ability of all the invitees at the meeting. Summing up, he felt sure that India would agree to support the new Round, and asked for the valued comments of the participants. The first to speak was 'Governor' Jha who was quite flattered to have been remembered and to have been invited to this 'critical' meeting. He said that he saw great value in negotiating the new issues and felt that India should welcome the new negotiations with open arms. Bhandari and Malhotra then chipped in to say that they felt that the idea was a very useful one and that India should enthusiastically join in the new Round. I looked pointedly and imploringly at Abid Hussain to intervene. After all, the subject was of the commerce ministry and the other Indians present did not know the nuances of the issues raised and also had no mandate to talk about them. They were jumping in blithely into territory that required cautious treading. Being short in height, I could not reach out my leg to kick Abid Sahib in the shin across the table, asking him to break the trend of the discussions. I found that his silence was continuing and was worried that the chairman of the meeting was very soon going to declare a consensus. And who could say whether any press attaché was lurking in the shadows? So I broke protocol and spoke sharply for about five minutes. I chided my senior colleagues for talking casually on subjects that had not been carefully studied or examined within our system and for expressing an ad hoc opinion without proper briefing or mandate. I reminded them that the issues raised were of magnitude, with implications for all the developing countries and to India in particular. I thanked Ambassador Smith for raising the issues and making the proposal and concluded that we would study the matter carefully and come back in due course with a proper response at Geneva. There was a stunned silence at the table. I felt that my senior colleagues were quite chastened by being told off for being casual and irresponsible. The working lunch concluded shortly thereafter.

Mike Smith, not one to give up, had his target lined up. He invited me for dinner that night at the American Club, where we discussed the matter over drinks, till he left for the airport at midnight. As he asked me why I was objecting to the new Round, he held out the threat that America would proceed on a bilateral route, and have bilateral deals with practically all developing countries if their efforts were thwarted. I asked Smith a rhetorical question, "Give me one valid reason why I should support the new Round? Already the provisions of the Tokyo Round give developing countries the right for preferential treatment, the dispensation to have their own tariff levels and the right to have quantitative restrictions. The principle of special and differential treatment was fully accepted in the GATT. So, why should any developing country willingly ask for reopening the package, give up all the negotiated advantages and take additional burden and restrictions on new uncharted territory, all of which are to the advantage of the developed countries? You want me to welcome you and ask you to whip me; and say that I am unreasonable if I don't invite you to do that?" I told Smith to give me just one area where India would benefit. I would then immediately see the point for new negotiations. Of course, he knew that what I was saying was true. The usual American technique of bulldozing opposition, dividing developing countries, and finally reaching their destination was under way. And it carried the threat that if forced, America was powerful enough to jettison multilateralism and embrace the bilateral route. In early 2003, the US followed the same familiar route in respect of Iraq, threatening to bypass the United Nations, if full endorsement of its desired course of action was not forthcoming. Similarly, the WTO will continue to be a respectable, hallowed body so long as it meets the US interests. The US will have no compunction in destroying the WTO overnight, if at any stage its perceived national interest, or presidential interest so demands.

The build-up to the new Round, then led to the GATT ministerial conference held in Geneva late in 1982, for evolving a consensus on the issue. Many developing countries expressed reservations on the new Round and India was still at that stage considered as a leader and opinion maker for the developing countries. At one stage, the US resorted to its by now familiar technique, organising a closed door meeting of ministers without aides, and handpicking the delegations and the delegates. This meeting was held at the Hilton Hotel in Geneva, chaired by Bill Brock who had, on another occasion, worked his charm on V P Singh. Some thirty delegations were invited, with seats arranged for only two persons per delegation. Shivraj Patil, then commerce minister and Abid Hussain were invited into the closed room. In my anxiety, I was hovering around in the corridors and as the meeting proceeded I got to see that as much was going on outside the chamber as within. I noticed the remarkable infrastructure organised by the American authorities. There was a field scrambler telephone system temporarily created in a hidden corner outside the meeting room, and I believe that this was a line connecting to a desk in Washington. Off and on, an American officer would come to the scrambler phone and speak to someone, doubtless to soften a delegation that was non-cooperative or recalcitrant. One can sensibly guess that the coordinator at Washington would, in turn, speak to their high level point man in the concerned country's capital; typically a senior minister or a powerful politician, sometimes even the president. Within half-an-hour, that country's delegate from inside the closed room would receive a call from his capital. He would be summoned out of the closed room to listen briefly to a pointed message.

He would then return to the closed room, presumably with his opposition extinguished. I saw this drama repeated at least six times during the five hours duration of the closed room meeting. When the meeting broke up and the participants came out, I had a quick look at the final operative paragraphs that Abid Sahib was carrying. I gave him a cold stare and told him that what had been agreed to in the closed room would never be subscribed to in the full group of developing countries. And so it was. The agreed draft was discussed in the full developing country group that evening. It was torn into pieces and the closed-door delegations were blasted for surrendering their position so meekly. It was thus, that the agreement in the closed room was repudiated and no consensus could be announced at the ministerial meeting. Incidentally my curiosity, as to whether the American point man network included India or not was clarified later that very day. The commerce minister mentioned that he received a phone call from a senior politician in Delhi who had nothing to do with the negotiations, directing him not to hold on to a stiff position. The potent American network had tentacles reaching deep into the Indian system too!

Looking back, it was fun furtively observing the Americans with their scrambler phones. International conferences do have their lighter moments. One day, I was at a conference, listening to the debate in one of the large conference halls in the grand United Nations Conference on Trade and Development (UNCTAD) headquarters building in Geneva – Hall No. IXX, if I recall rightly. We all had our ear-pieces on, and these could be switched from position to position, to hear the translation in any of the six standard UN languages that were available. Sitting next to me was Ajit Seth, the first secretary commercial in the Indian mission. The desultory speeches were rambling on and on and then one speaker came to the podium and started speaking in English. My earpiece was already turned on to the 'English' position and I needed no translation. Suddenly, as the speech was proceeding, a series of high-pitched disturbances intervened, garbling the speech and this continued for a while. We started fiddling with our ear-pieces, wondering about this unusual defect in the audio system.

Ajit who was sitting next to me suddenly got up from his chair, and walked up the aisle to the exit. Since he did not announce his departure to me, I curiously turned back, and saw him as he strode swiftly to the exit. Thereafter, he started sprinting. In another ten seconds or so, the audio interference of the speech terminated, and the speaker could be heard with clarity. A few minutes after this Ajit returned, and heaving a huge sigh of relief slumped down on his chair. He told me what had happened. His wife was in the main corridor, as part of a group of visitors being shown around the facilities. His daughter Priyadarshini, about two years old, was part of the group. As they passed hall No.IXX, she slipped unnoticed into an open door, and started babbling in front of an open microphone. That was the English language translator's booth. The girl there must have left her booth unattended, perhaps to powder her nose, noting that the speaker was anyway speaking in English. Young Priyadarshini thus addressed the august UN gathering for a short while – surely the youngest person to do so! That evening at a cocktail party, I recounted the inside story to an ambassador who had also been present in hall No. IXX. He laughed and said that he had been listening to speeches in UN for many years, and Priyadarshini's contribution was definitely not any inferior in content.

Some conferences were desultory, more froth than substance, with little to recall except an anecdote or two. There was the UN conference on the Least Developed Countries (LDC), conducted under the aegis of UNCTAD. This was held in Paris over a two-week period. Being the host, the French minister for development presided over the conference. Mitterrand had just come to power as president and the French did not wish to miss this opportunity to display support and solidarity with the developing countries, especially the least developed countries from the African region, with whom France had a special relationship. From our own region, Bangladesh, Maldives, Bhutan and Nepal were among the thirty-odd least developed countries represented in Paris. We did not belong to this category. So, even though we were formal participants, our role was really that of observer.

The focal point of the conference was the demand for a 'pledge' from the developed countries to set apart 0.2% of the Gross Domestic Product (GDP) of each country for the benefit of the development of the least developed. The backdrop to this was a previous commitment of the developed countries, made during the 1960s and '70s to set apart 0.7% of their respective GDP to the developing countries. These generous commitments had been made in the earlier days of euphoria in the wake of the independence granted to over a hundred colonies. There was the illusion, sponsored by liberals like John Kennedy that with injection of funds, the newly independent countries would be able to rapidly stand on their own feet and wipe out poverty from their midst. This expectation failed on many counts. Firstly, the amounts actually spared by the developed countries fell far short of the 0.7%. While a few countries were near this figure, most developed countries would not make any contribution at all. Secondly, whatever money was earmarked as 'development aid' was used cynically for the benefit of the donor country. Thus, aid would be given to sweeten the package of an armaments deal or to swing a large project contract under competitive bidding conditions, much like the American motor car salesman dangles a 'cash-back' to his customers. Thirdly, a sizeable part of the aid was routed through multilateral agencies, mostly based in Washington, New York, Geneva or Vienna. A good part of this money went on payroll and administration costs of the clerical staff and consultants of these agencies, who were mostly seconded by western governments, as well as for supporting the airlines, mostly under western ownership. And of course, there was also the inability of many developing countries to make good use of whatever aid finally trickled down, due to factors such as domestic corruption and mal-administration. We have seen in a separate context the failure of World Bank funds to serve their purpose – in fact, many of the projects have had a counterproductive influence on our economy. So the proposed 0.2% had more gimmickry than substance.

There is another significant element that explains the tardy flow of international development aid to developing countries, especially in recent years. There used to be a sanguine belief that progressive elements in developed countries, would in their own interest, in an increasingly interdependent global economy, come to the rescue of the governments and people of developing countries. This touching faith in the goodness of the western man persisted in many innocent and ingenuous minds in the developing world. Events of the last twenty years have exploded whatever faith one may have left in this belief. Reagan's declaration that all countries were equal and that there would be equal give and take, actually meant that the poor shall give and the strong will take. We cannot be surprised at this, as it is practically what we do within our own country in a different context. In fact, the theme of this book is that might and self-interest will prevail. Much later, Bill Clinton had at least mouthed some concerns for a more equitable world order and argued for taking steps in favour of the developing world, even though this too was in the context of the enlightened self-interest of the West. Bush has, in very recent years, reasserted the Reagan doctrine, which is simplicity itself: No quarter shall be given anywhere. If a developing country wags its tail, cut it off; and if it persists, slit its throat. This chapter was first written before the attack on Iraq and the articulation of the doctrine of 'right to regime-change'. The further events only buttress my point of view.

Anyway, at the time of the conference of the least developed countries in Paris in 1983, there was the sanguine belief among the LDCs, that manna would fall from the heavens and funds from the western nations would be set aside for converting the least developed countries into developed countries! The self appointed leader of LDCs was Bangladesh, which had sent a large delegation for the Paris conference. The joke making the rounds in Paris was that since 0.2% finance flows was the target, Bangladesh had sent 0.2% of its population as delegates for the Paris conference! Every hotel and plaza in Paris seemed to be full of Bangladeshis – every room in the conference facility was half full with Bangladeshis.

The Indian delegation led by me had been briefed by the finance ministry that we could welcome the flow of funds from developed countries to LDCs provided it was an 'additionality'. Our position was that this was not to be carved out of the 0.7% of the GDP, already promised to developing countries. This was the brief carried by Govindarajan, then a director in the Finance Ministry and a member of the Indian delegation. No matter that the 0.7% number had no real value or no basis, as the so-called aid flows were not even approximating one-tenth of this number. No matter also, that many developed countries were already weary of giving away aid and the additional aid had an even less chance of realisation than the sun rising in the west. In addition to the brief, Govindarajan carried the threat from the finance secretary that if the word 'additionality' was not there in the final document, he may then have no place to come back to in Delhi! So, with this single-point agenda, Govindarajan led us in chanting the word 'additionality' continually much like Valmiki would chant 'Ram, Ram'. We will later see a similar obsession of a Saudi delegate, this time insisting that the term 'oil' should not feature anywhere in the final document.

The developed countries had their own fun, as they would. At the early stages of the conference, they pointedly asked the delegates from developing countries as to what would happen if the aid to LDCs were not given 'additionally'. This was typical of the games played by the developed countries. It was thus, that at a stormy meeting of the developing countries, of which the LDCs were a sub-group, there was open warfare between the LDCs and the other developing countries. The Bangladeshis fought strongly, invoking the sentiment that in the spirit of the brotherhood of all developing countries, the other developing countries should not insist on additionality of aid over the existing figure. But the LDCs could not hold their ground, and the developing countries passed a resolution that 'additional' resources should flow from the developed countries to the LDCs – as if they owned the money being given away!

The main negotiations on the finance issues took place early in the second week. Govindarajan sat next to me tightly clutching my thigh in his tension, to make sure that the word 'additionality' appeared in the final draft. Not that the developed countries had any intention of giving away any money, but they found it awkward to have to go on record as offering an 'additional' amount to that already committed. It suited them better to keep this as a part of the overall commitment already made earlier. The developing countries would have none of it and made this a make or break issue. So, there were stormy negotiations. As host, France could not afford a failure of this important conference. So, finally it was agreed to insert the word 'additionality' in the draft declaration. As soon as the session ended, Govindarajan kept on thanking me and exulted in getting his mandate executed.

The story did not end here. A comic or perhaps diabolic twist followed. The next morning, the group met to review the final draft and to formally approve the draft negotiated the previous day. Evidently some employees in the secretariat were having their own fun or playing their own games. The draft presented for final approval did not contain the word 'additionality'! Govindarajan was apoplectic. He feared the worst, that the western powers had prevailed upon the UNCTAD secretariat in the late night to effect clandestine changes in the agreement reached the previous day. As the meeting started, the French chairman, who probably well knew about this mischief, indicated with a straight face that a negotiated draft had been circulated, reflecting the results of the previous day's negotiations. He took it that there were no comments. He lifted his gavel with a gesture, and paused a moment for comments. Govindarajan, sitting next to me, was under great stress as I took the floor to say that the negotiations had gone on late the previous night and perhaps the UNCTAD staff were tired and inadvertently had left out the insertion of the word 'additionality'. I then quoted its correct position in the page and line earmarked for its inclusion. There was a brief supportive applause from other delegates. The chairman could not but agree that this was an error, and the missing word was inserted. Govindarajan could safely return to India, to continue his distinguished career in Andhra Pradesh and the central secretariat.

As the LDC conference was drawing to a close, we had the strange experience of an 'intruder' at one of the sessions. This was at a routine meeting to adopt a bland text on trade, slotted at 11 pm as an after dinner session, and expected to last not more than thirty minutes. Though this was not the forum to discus multi-lateral trade matters, it was decided to insert a small segment on trade in the final declaration of the conference. In the assembled room, Ambassador Karim from Bangladesh was requested to take the chair, and it was the turn of the spokesman of the developed countries to present the first draft for the negotiation. Sitting next to the

Indian delegation was the Brazilian delegation. A senior delegate from Brazil, a friend of mine, must have indulged himself during dinner, expecting a tame session ahead. He took one look at the paper and quickly got into a rage. He asked for the floor and in an uncharacteristic outburst chastised the developed countries, accusing them of double standards and chicanery. What made him lose his temper was the apparently innocuous usage of words in the draft, which started with: "The conference agreed that there should be greater rollback of protectionist measures by developed countries…." The Brazilian, under the post-prandial influence of cognac, argued that the term *greater* in the draft implied that there was already some rollback of protectionist measures by the developed countries, which was a falsehood. If anything, protectionism was on the increase. While his point was valid, the temper and tone used by the Brazilian raised the hackles of the European delegates. Suddenly, ten angry flags from the western side were up, asking for the floor. I could see that the situation had taken a turn for the worse. In my anxiety to get to bed early, I asked for the floor. I started speaking, and kept on and on hoping tempers would cool. I asked that the opening sentence of the draft be slightly modified, proposed a new opening sentence which blandly asked for rollback of protectionist measures; and this was agreed to without demur. This took all of fifteen minutes. Karim gave me a look of thanks and the draft was taken up for discussion, line by line and the evening should have soon concluded.

The tactic did not work. The western delegates were agitated and decided to be difficult. The developing countries had made their point and had no further interest in the negotiations. The Bangladeshis as leader of the LDCs took up the negotiations on trade. The European delegates started shooting down the draft they themselves had prepared, denying the LDCs any forward movement. It was evident that trade policy was not amongst the expertise areas of the LDC representatives who were present, and they could not match wits with the irate western delegates who were piling on their demands. The discussion dragged on interminably. Karim sent an SOS for replacements for pressing the arguments on behalf of the LDCs. Reinforcements came by way of some Bangladeshi reserves, apparently roused from their beds, all to no purpose. Around two in the morning, a bright young Bangladeshi came to take over the negotiations. He looked like their first secretary. He was clear headed and knowledgeable and carried the negotiations with expertise and aplomb. He tackled the Europeans ably, and could even extract some additional concessions from the western group. The meeting proceeded swiftly and at around 4 am, the draft was finally approved. I walked up to Ambassador Karim, congratulated him and asked him to pass on my felicitations to the young Bangladeshi officer who piloted the negotiations so well on behalf of the LDCs. Ambassador Karim gave me a self-satisfied smile. He said that the lad was no young officer; he was his own son, studying at Princeton, who had come to Paris for a holiday and to be with his father! Just imagine, such a large delegation, and an intruder carried the day.

The Bangladesh delegation had a reputation for bickering amongst themselves. This is not to say that our own representatives fared very much better but at least they were more discreet. In Geneva, our ambassador to GATT, deputed by the commerce ministry, and our ambassador to the UN system in Geneva, seconded by the external affairs ministry, would each be outsmarting the other. But then, while India's internecine warfare was confined to our embassy in Geneva and the corridors of Delhi, it was curious to see the Bangladeshis allowing the differences to spill over in public. At the Paris conference on LDCs, the Bangladesh delegation had two ambassadors – Ambassador Karim and Ambassador Sultan, both based in Geneva. Sure enough, one of them represented Dacca's external affairs ministry in Geneva and the other was from their commerce ministry. Both were constantly at each other's throats. But then, they must have sorted out the problem, since we did not see Ambassador Sultan after the first two days of the conference. At a conference on jute earlier held by UNCTAD at Geneva, a strong delegation from Dacca had come, headed by the secretary in the jute ministry of Bangladesh. As the story goes, the organisers of the meeting thought it wise to make the visiting jute secretary the chairman of the conference, leaving the Bangladeshi ambassador representing the external affairs ministry to be their chief spokesman. As they might have hoped, the meeting went on smoothly for a while. But then, the visiting jute secretary could not contain himself any longer and relinquished the chair temporarily in favour of his vice-chairman to sit at the delegation's table. He declared himself as a delegate and made a strong intervention, totally opposing the earlier comments by the Bangladesh delegation from the floor! The organisers must have been perplexed at this new *avatar* of a chairman.

I was a member of the Indian delegation to the Non-Aligned Summit held in Delhi in the early spring of 1983. It was a grand affair held at Vigyan Bhawan. As is usual during such events, the Indian delegation comprised about 200 people hand-picked by the external affairs ministry: ministers, politicians, MPs, economists, industrialists and officials from the external affairs ministry. The commerce ministry was responsible for negotiating the international trade segment at the summit, and so, grudgingly, the commerce secretary was named to the delegation. When I saw the delegation list, I demurred with the commerce secretary that I, as joint secretary, would actually have to lead the negotiations, but did not find a place in the Indian delegation. The commerce secretary soothed me by saying that it did not matter, and that he would get a pass for me to enter Vigyan Bhawan for the negotiations. I categorically refused and stated that I would not go near Vigyan Bhawan unless formally designated a delegate. Abid Hussain, then commerce secretary, had to conduct major pre-summit negotiations with our own external affairs ministry to include me as a delegate. As I recall, there was only one full delegation meeting. When Indira Gandhi found to her surprise that the full delegation was nearly as large as the Indian parliament, she promptly ordered the constitution of a sub-group of about thirty persons to assist her in the negotiations at the Non-Aligned Summit meetings. This group would meet twice a day and once in the presence of the prime minister to brief her on the day's proceedings and to debate tactical steps that needed to be taken.

The summit discussions went smoothly, though there was a drama that took place on the last day. This was unknown to most delegations and also to most Indian delegates. It had to do with the poor relations between Indira Gandhi and the Sri Lankan president, Jayawardene. The latter had suggested, as part of the overall strategy, that a delegation of heads of states from different non-aligned countries, under the leadership of Indira Gandhi should tour important global capitals like Washington, Tokyo, London, Bonn, and Paris. They would impress upon the western leaders the need for generosity in dealing with developing countries. Reagan had recently come to power in Washington and Jayawardene's proposal was designed to curry favour with the developed countries. I recall that in one of the Indian delegation's sub-group meetings, somebody had mentioned the proposal but no discussions took place. At some time prior to the last day, the Indian officials charged with negotiating the preamble part of the Delhi declaration had included on Jayawardene's insistence, a sentence to the effect that senior leaders from developing countries would call on the western leaders to impress upon them the need for generous finance flows. On the last evening, when Indira Gandhi saw the final draft and saw this sentence, she apparently flew into a rage saying that there was no question of her going to western capitals with a begging bowl, pleading for mercy and generosity! I was witness to the scene from a distance, and though I could not hear every word, I could well follow the events. Purushotham, India's permanent representative at New York, who was in the small team negotiating the draft, later gave me a blow-by-blow version. Indira Gandhi was beside herself in anger – "Do you think we are beggars?" she said. "That man (Reagan) is not fit to polish my shoes – do you think I will go and wait outside his room and beg?" She peremptorily ordered the sentence to be deleted from the draft, after giving a tongue lashing to Purushotham and others who negotiated the draft.

Now there was one major snag. Jayawardene would have none of it. He had negotiated the draft in good faith, and would not agree to any deletion. According to him, he had spoken to most other major heads of states present at the summit and they were agreeable. Who was Indira Gandhi to scuttle this proposal that had such a wide acceptance? These events happened in the evening around 5 pm; the original schedule was to have the final plenary around 6 pm and conclude by dinner time. However, suddenly this deadlock surfaced. At that time, the debate on the ongoing Iraq-Iran war was the only item left to conclude, and discussion was proceeding in the plenary hall. Most speakers had said their piece on the matter of the Iran-Iraq war. It was a delicate subject, dealing with animosity between two NAM members, and there was not much to be said anyway, in that forum. However, as the deadlock between India and Sri Lanka emerged, the floor managers needed an excuse to delay the concluding plenary scheduled for 6 pm. A word was sent to the Indian delegation, to prolong the Iraq-Iran war debate, for as long as possible. The Indian chairman of the session was quietly briefed and the influential members of the Indian delegation worked on some friendly delegates from other countries to extend the debate indefinitely. Suddenly, for the unsuspecting participants in that debate who did not know this background, the discussions took on an interminable shape. Country after country, which had spoken on the subject, got up to make fresh statements. It was thus that the Iran-Iraq war debate concluded only around 11 at night, providing a legitimate reason to postpone the concluding plenary. I am told that some Indian and Sri Lankan delegates shuttled back and forth between an irate Indira Gandhi and a recalcitrant Jayawardene in his hotel suite, trying to find an acceptable wording. Some final formula was found, thus bringing the summit to an end.

The UNCTAD VI Round was scheduled for late summer 1983, at Belgrade in what was then Yugoslavia. A preparatory meeting, one of a series of such meetings, was held in Manila in early 1983. Participation was from about fifteen Asian developing countries. The meeting was presided over by Gamani Correa, secretary general of UNCTAD. The hosts were the Government of the Philippines, with an active role for Brilliantes, the Filipino ambassador in Geneva. He had been there for seventeen years and was the 'doyen' of the diplomatic corps in Geneva. A leading participant was Vicente Valdepenas, the Filipino permanent secretary in the commerce department. B L Das, our Ambassador in Geneva had come, and I went from Delhi. During that time in Manila, India was in the news. An Indian film, *36 Chowringhee Lane* had just won the prize for the best film at the Manila film festival, an important international event in which President

Marcos had taken much interest. We could have long chats with Shashi Kapoor, the producer of the award winning film, who was in Manila.

During the meeting, a courtesy visit was arranged for the participants to call on President Marcos. At the appointed time, we were at Malacanang Palace, in one of the large waiting rooms. There were other similar rooms where other groups were awaiting an audience with Marcos. Soup, snacks and regular food were being rolled out constantly, along the corridors of Malacanang. Anybody could pick up whatever he wanted, during the period of wait for the audience, which was indeterminate. We were told in hushed tones that some groups had to wait six or seven hours for their turn; and that some groups would even have to return without a meeting. On this optimistic note, we kept guzzling soup and snacks. And then suddenly, our group was invited for the audience, after only a two-hour delay. We felt comforted that the UN apparently rated high in the scheme of things. In the audience hall, there was a long table with chairs all around. At the head of the table, there was a high throne and Marcos was sitting atop the throne about a foot higher than the others. He was flanked on one side by his commerce minister, who was seated on a chair at ground level with all the others. Valdepenas, the permanent secretary and Ambassador Brilliantes were allowed only standing room. They spent the entire one hour period of the meeting on their feet next to their minister.

Marcos had the appearance of a tired old man with a weary look, though his eyes were darting sharply back and forth. Gamani Correa briefly summarised the negotiating issues for UNCTAD VI, talked of the need for developing countries to stand together, referred to the trade and finance issues on the negotiating table with developed countries and then paused for Marcos to lead the discussion. Marcos said that his government's full support was available on the position of the developing countries. Suddenly his eyes fell on me and B L Das. He asked "Are you from India?" and straightaway started talking of *36 Chowringhee Lane* in glowing terms. He went on to say how important it was for a country to produce good movies and then asked questions of both of us regarding how movies were produced in India – how was the distribution done, how were films financed, and what was the role of producers, directors and distributors? With our civil service backgrounds, we rose to the occasion: it was quite easy on the trot for Das and me to transform ourselves into experts and elaborate on the intricacies of the Indian film industry. Gamani tried to intervene to resume the debate on international developmental issues. But Marcos was interested only on the theme of movies. He brushed Gamani aside rudely and came back to us for the expert discussion on cinema. If Marcos was not satisfied with our explanations, he did not show it. Could he perhaps have mentioned to Imelda that night about the two film industry specialists he had met?

There would have been a reason for the discussion on the film theme. Was it Marcos' need to revive his popularity with the local masses in the Philippines? Apparently, he had earlier used the medium of television to project himself in the country and to revive his sagging popularity, without much success. He could well have been debating with himself on the alternate medium of cinema. Hence, the reference to the Indian icons MGR and NTR in the discussions, perhaps to see if he could emulate their use of this medium for enhancement of his own image, especially in the rural areas of the country.

I attended another preparatory conference for UNCTAD VI, this time of the Asian group, held in Baghdad in February that year. The Iran-Iraq war was still raging at the time. Saddam had built a magnificent conference centre and with all the newly found riches, he probably fancied for himself a great role on the world stage – his foolish use of force against Iran put paid to those ambitions. We took the opportunity to travel to many parts of Iraq, during the period of the conference. Bodies of dead soldiers, casualties from the front, were being returned to their villages and towns. I was told that the families of dead soldiers received sizeable monetary compensation but subject to some conditions. The caskets would be delivered to the homes of the dead in the middle of the night and the body was to be buried before daybreak. The mourning was to be done quietly and there should be no mourning thereafter. This was a precondition for obtaining the compensatory amount. During that time, I also visited Karbela and Najaf, the most sacred spots for the Shias, and found entry inside the shrines, where 'infidels' are not normally allowed. I found the same devout atmosphere inside Najaf that one associates with the most sacred Hindu temples – after all, people are the same in their hearts and their emotions. I particularly recall, with poignancy, the face of a young girl in her early teens, lost in thought. She was praying devoutly perhaps for the safety, or bemoaning the loss, of her father or brother on the front. Tears were streaming down her face. The image of sadness tinged with hope and prayer will last with me.

A further conference, this time of all the Group of 77 (G-77) developing countries was held in the late spring of 1983, at Buenos Aires in Argentina. I chaired one of the main committees at this conference. It was an occasion to reconcile the positions of developing countries and to produce a commonly agreed draft for presentation to the developed countries. There were no major issues of potential conflict, and the conference went on smoothly. The only noteworthy item was the role played by the category of oil-rich developing countries, whose sole purpose in the meet was to preempt any hint or suggestion of financial help from them to their poorer brethren. Initially, there was the forlorn hope among developing countries that the oil-rich Arab countries would join hands with the industrial countries to help alleviate poverty and to help develop the third world. Slim chance. Very early in the game, Saudi Arabia, United Arab Emirates and other oil-rich countries made it quite clear that not one dollar would be spared by them for any developing country. Thus, there was only a lone Saudi delegate. His single point brief was to ensure that no reference was made in any document to oil-rich Arab countries with even a hint of any assistance from them to other developing countries. It was amusing to see him shuttling from sub-committee to sub-committee, looking in the drafts for words or paragraphs that even hinted obliquely at oil rich countries. He would then vehemently make one-line statements categorically wanting deletion of any reference to oil in the text. Apart from this spectacle, the G-77 meeting went off without event.

When in Buenos Aires, I could see some similarities with Baghdad where I was earlier that year. In Argentina, it was the period of Galtieri, after the Malvinas or Falklands war. Galtieri ran the country like a despot, and many young people all over the country, who opposed the regime just 'disappeared'. It was interesting to see the galloping inflation. On the streets of Buenos Aires, hawkers were there in every corner, willing to buy the US dollar at a huge premium, with the official exchange rate a mere fraction of the street-rate. During the three weeks of my stay in Buenos Aires, the inflation rate continued to gallop at three digit rates, the dollar street rate went through the roof. I heard that soon thereafter, there was demonetisation in Argentina.

It was in this locale in Buenos Aires that I saw, for the first time, the film *Gandhi* made by Richard Attenborough. I had gone with a friend for the night show at 9 pm, and having purchased the tickets, we were waiting in the foyer for the earlier show of the same movie, in the Spanish version, to conclude. As the earlier show ended, we could see the auditorium emptying and the viewers slowly leaving the hall. It was a touching sight to see persons of all ages, openly in tears as he or she left the hall – could a man like Mohandas Karamchand Gandhi have actually lived? Of course, Gandhi is now forgotten in his own homeland, not even a memory.

And finally, the UNCTAD VI conference itself, in Belgrade was a three-week affair. It was held at the large Hilton Hotel complex, next to the Dunav, (the Danube), in picturesque surroundings. Impervious to the glorious weather of that summer of 1983, the negotiations went on in the adjoining conference centre. There were about thirty members in the Indian delegation headed by Commerce Minister V P Singh, with the secretary commerce, as deputy leader. There were at least six people in the delegation senior to me in service, including two current Indian ambassadors to Geneva and an ex-ambassador to Geneva as the representative of the external affairs ministry. There was, as well, the director-general of shipping from the transport ministry. I could not fathom how an officer holding such a key position as the director general of shipping could afford to be away for a full month in Belgrade doing almost nothing. How could his ministry accept his absence for such a long period, especially when the delegate's role was to negotiate one tiny segment of the final draft? I had, in fact, suggested that a junior officer at the level of deputy secretary or a director would do; but no – the boss himself had to be there, since major issues were at stake! Both V P Singh and Abid Hussain came only for the first three days, returned to Delhi, and came back for the concluding week. There were four MPs in the delegation. They had a full month's holiday. Early in the proceedings, I handed over one of the delegation's cars to the MPs, and told them to use it to travel wherever they wanted; they were no trouble at all. I am told they enjoyed themselves hugely by making daily excursions to different spots in Yugoslavia in the wonderful summer weather. Those days, the local food, including sea food was of excellent quality; local wines and fruit brandys, including slivovic, were delicious and abundant and unbelievably inexpensive; anything imported was prohibitively expensive. In fact, V P Singh had to ask them once or twice to make a token appearance at some of the plenary sessions, which they grudgingly did.

In view of the fact there were so many *prima donnas* in the official delegation, the commerce ministry had to clearly indicate that in the absence of the minister and the commerce secretary, the joint secretary in the commerce ministry would coordinate the work of the delegation. Thus, I was the *de facto* leader of the delegation for most of the conference. With a view to exchange information and co-ordinate our position in the large number of committees in which various Indian delegates would be engaged, I had requested that all the members of the delegation would meet for breakfast every morning at 8'o clock in a specified room. The first morning after the departure of the minister, I found that many members of the delegation were present; but the senior members trickled in casually one by one, some a few minutes late and others more than half an hour late. When the following morning it again happened, I waited to make my point till one of the delegates, a junior enough foreign service officer from our New York mission was late by half an hour. I brusquely told her that the meeting was scheduled at 8'o clock in the morning. She responded that she was having a chat till 2 am with the British ambassador, and had got up a little late. I responded that I too was at that party. The following morning too she came in ten minutes late, and I told her acidly that senior officers need to be admonished only once. For the next three weeks, we had no difficulty with regards to punctuality – all the senior officers turned up on schedule. However, despite the long hours put in, the conference itself was a disaster from the developing country point of view. The Reagan approach to international negotiations had come to stay and the western powers were completely inflexible; they were not even willing to listen to the developing countries, not to speak of giving any quarter. The Indian delegation played a key role in holding the developing country group together, amidst the standard US and European attempts to divide the developing countries and water down the proposals.

I recall an earlier visit to Belgrade in 1980, when one US $ was equal to thirteen Yugo dinars. At that time, a debate was raging within Yugoslavia whether to go in for IMF assistance, accepting the restructuring formula prescribed by it. By the time of the UNCTAD in the summer of 1983, the IMF package had been fully adopted, and was already seen to be an utter failure. As I walked into the hotel on the first day, I checked up that the US $ conversion rate had come down to thirty-two Yugo dinars. I went to the hotel teller, and was going to encash my traveller's cheques, so as to pay for the next fifteen days stay. He looked at me in amazement and told me to my face that I was an idiot; I should pay as I was leaving. Sound advice since in those three weeks the Yugo dinar had slid to forty-two. My next visit to Yugoslavia was in 1986, when I came for a consultancy mission from ITC; and by that time, the dollar could buy about 400 dinars. I subsequently learnt that around 1988, the currency had slid to 1000 dinars at which time demonetisation took place. The conventional wisdom in the 1970s and '80s was that the IMF restructuring formula was the unfailing route to economic disaster; this view has since proved itself repeatedly. After all, there is no shortcut in these matters. Merely opening up the economy, without the collateral hard work involved was not going to rescue a country. While the technical ability of IMF to advice a developing country itself is suspect, its motivation is dubious, triggered as it is from the western perspective.

While on the visit to Yugoslavia in 1986, I again met R L Narayan, who had earlier worked with me in the commerce ministry and who was now working as the counsellor in the mission in Belgrade. With prescience, he predicted nearly to the day, the collapse of Yugoslavia and its dismemberment into many states, as well as the explosion of the Kosovo issue – he had accurately read the situation. Yugoslavia was put together from the erstwhile Balkan states, thanks to Tito's patriotism. His dreams survived for two to three decades. Sometimes I wonder about the real reasons for the unity and integrity of India, which I often feel is the greatest and only real achievement in the post-Independence era. Perhaps it has something to do with our syncretic heritage. On a visit to Kedarnath, one can see that a Namboodri priest or Lingayat Rawal officiates, at Nathdwara an Andhra priest, and at Rameshwaram a north Indian priest. Such are the binders that hold India together.

During my tenure in the commerce ministry, I came across a number of economists who had risen to important positions in Indian administration over time. At different times, many of them had worked as economic advisors in the commerce ministry, and some of them were also attached to the finance ministry as well as the planning commission. I discovered that with a few honourable exceptions, most of them were political economists, spelt with a very large 'P' and a nearly invisible 'e'. I would find that economic theories and postulates could always be readjusted to support the political line taken by the minister of the department or the overall administration; and economic advice could be packaged neatly to suit any situation. They were advisors for all seasons, nimble-footed, quick-thinkers, with the ability to adapt a flexible theory to hard realities and to justify any course of action. What was common to all of them, especially those who rose rapidly in the system, was their adaptability, and facility in the use of spoken and written English. The reality of Indian conditions outside Delhi was mostly unknown to them, as they had spent much of their time in the UK or USA studying economic theories as applied to western countries; but they quickly mastered the art of providing props to politicians. Some of them had hidden godfathers. Many of them held long tenures in key positions in major policy-making ministries, for much longer periods than those held by service bureaucrats. As such, they have had an effective hand in the mismanagement of the economy, and have a lot to answer for, in the context of policy failures. Many of them, with charming manners and fluid use of the English language, contributed to terribly flawed policy decisions, and then smoothly glided to coveted assignments in India and abroad. The administration found it convenient to have them around.

While in the commerce ministry, I dealt at close quarters with a variety of top bureaucrats. It is possible to group them into broad categories. One of them, with a brilliant mind, could analyse any situation objectively and dispassionately but fell short on delivery. I would liken him to a centre-forward in hockey, who would take the ball from his own goal mouth and on his own dribble it forward artistically but only to tamely surrender it just outside the opponents 'D'. He would read every file word by word, and it used to be said jocularly that he studied his files much closer than he had ever examined his wife! Another would show results, but he had no finesse to create situations. He was like a player who would just hang around the opponent's 'D' to pounce on a loose ball and shoot it into the opponent's goal. I believe these days the 'off-side' rule has been dispensed with, and all the better for this player. One of them was a person with great dignity who did not get his due, just like a stopper whose role is soon forgotten after a game ends, however stout a defence he put up. Yet another, was a hail-fellow-well-met type, who would backslap one and all, a mid-field player who would be in the fray at all times, however complex and intricate the situation. In the hockey metaphor, he would enter any goal-mouth, and quickly slam a goal. The home goal was found as often as the opponent's! Continuing with this analogy, I sometimes wonder what position might be ascribed to me in the Indian team.

During the UNCTAD in Belgrade, V P Singh saw my work at close quarters and felt that I was the right person to represent our interests, as ambassador in Geneva. Immediately on return, I believe he met Indira Gandhi to revive my posting, which had once fallen through. He told me with genuine regret that his efforts had failed, and he could not understand why. Later, I understood through a source in the PM's office that Indira Gandhi had mistaken me for Manohar Subramanian, another officer with the same name in the UP cadre against whom she had a prejudice, based on wrong information provided to her. On a previous occasion, a similar confusion had worked in my favour, and so that evened out. Anyway, V P Singh took the initiative to write separately to the secretary general of Economic & Social Commission of Asia & the Pacific (ESCAP) based in Bangkok, and to the executive director of the ITC in Geneva, independently recommending an assignment for me in these agencies. I had forgotten all about these letters. However, as a strange coincidence, both the assignments came through on the same day, one day in late 1984. I had a difficult choice to make, whether to go to Bangkok or Geneva, as my tenure in the commerce ministry was ending at that time. Just a few days earlier I was preparing if asked, to go even to Jaunpur – where I would have gone with great happiness. Instead, I found myself in Geneva.

10 GENEVA: THE INTERNATIONAL DEVELOPMENT CIRCUIT

Saab, I was asked to remove the nose ring; but my hands were trembling and I could not unscrew it. Finally, the nurse removed it and gave it to me. You see, she could not even take this small thing with her when she went.

Nobody would actually walk in the corridors of the office: Ever in a great hurry, they were in sprint-mode. Agencies that do not have much to do, camouflage their lack of action through a show of furious activity.

WE LANDED IN GENEVA LATE 1984, JUST BEFORE Christmas when all offices were closed for the holidays. We were at first lodged in a hotel. That winter was a bitter one, and one of the coldest that the locals had experienced. Temperatures often plunged to −20°C even during daytime. We were ill prepared for the cold, and had not yet learnt about the precautions to take while venturing out. On a couple of occasions, the sun was shining brightly during the daytime, and we felt that it must be quite warm outside. And so, on two occasions, we got caught walking in open stretches of the street in freezing cold, without adequate clothing and had to sprint to the nearest MIGROS store for warmth and shelter. But once we settled down in an apartment, and acquired a car, life was easy and comfortable, as smooth as the proverbial Swiss clock. The change from the hectic pace of work in Delhi and the frenetic preparations for the departure contrasted greatly with the easy living conditions in Geneva, and as I found later, the even easier pace of work there. I found it quite easy to fit in as 'senior advisor', Small and Medium Enterprises at the International Trade Centre, ITC for short. It was my job to create a new programme within the ITC to develop this area of activity. I had known and worked with small industry in India and could claim some expertise in this field; at least as high or higher than that of ITC experts in their own field, which is not saying much.

The ITC had a mixed pedigree. It was jointly parented by the UNCTAD, and the erstwhile GATT now renamed as the World Trade Organisation. ITC partook of the character of both its parents but called itself an UN agency and followed the UN rules and regulations. One parent, UNCTAD, a part of the UN system, was a talking shop dominated by developing countries, which provided a forum for them to let off steam and vent their frustrations – the western powers barely tolerated it, treating it as a necessary nuisance. The western countries dominated GATT, the other parent. GATT was a Treaty Organisation, a part of the Bretton Woods legacy. It considered itself a superior body with its nose in the air. Here, the Riot Act would be read periodically to the developing countries. The relatively few developed countries called the shots, though in theory, each of the eighty-odd GATT members had an equal vote. Practically every decision over time was designed to increase the leverage of the developed countries. As far as I know, GATT had never once reached the stage of voting, and what goes by the name 'consensus' was the normal mode of taking decisions. I am sure that as and when even handed decisions start being taken through voting in the WTO, the organisation will be wound up. Elaborate devices had been created to cajole or arm twist the developing countries to accept new rules or procedures, all slanted in favour of the developed countries, and finally to bludgeon into submission the odd developing country which remained defiant till the end. As we read in the previous chapter, India would usually come in the last category.

The ITC was supposed to assist developing countries improve their capacity to export goods, and in recent years, services. The headquarters in Geneva had some 200 personnel, half of whom were so-called 'experts'. There were also a few project officers located in different countries. It took me quite a while to understand what exactly the ITC was doing. Agencies that do not have much to do, camouflage their lack of action through a show of furious activity. Nobody in ITC would actually walk in the corridors of the office: Ever in a great hurry, they were in sprint-mode. I found that most professional advisors working for ITC had little knowledge in their own field of specialisation. They would have had difficulty holding their own in any self-respecting private agency. Many division chiefs had joined the organisation in its infancy as clerks, and with its rapid expansion had risen to senior executive levels without any qualifications or training or merit. Several had been recruited from the diplomatic or administrative services of the member countries, through political patronage. Thus, it was typical that the donor countries such as Sweden, Belgium or Finland would have a large representation in the professional staff, as part of the quid pro quo for contributing to the annual budget of ITC. Perhaps, it made economic sense to jettison unwanted civil servants, as a recompense for their generous contributions to 'projects'. And then some of their funds were being used to support their own citizens.

I discovered much later that the ITC was considered as one of the more 'efficient' organisations in the UN system with something relatively useful to contribute to the developing countries. This is surprising since the ITC did little for developing countries that was of substance and useful. But then, other economic agencies of the UN system had even less to contribute. This may be seen as a severely jaundiced view by outsiders, who do not know the inside story. But most staff members of the UN agencies would know it for a fact, though they might not admit it.

The 'professionals' did an enormous amount of travel, mostly to developing countries for project formulation, project implementation or for holding seminars. Each visit was called a 'mission'. Everyday, at the luxurious cafeteria, one would come across experts who had just returned from a mission somewhere in Africa or Asia or Latin America. The standard greeting would be to ask politely, "How was your mission?" The invariable reply would be "excellent – extremely successful." In all my five and more years at the ITC, I never came across a single 'unsuccessful' mission! If indeed even half of the missions undertaken every year had been so successful, not a single developing country ought to have had difficulty procuring export markets or suffered an adverse balance of payments situation!

Some missions would be almost ludicrous as one example ought to illustrate. A developed country had earmarked $ 100,000 for a project in an African country. The project preparatory expenses were undertaken from the headquarters budget of the ITC. The desk officer dealing with the subject must have had an interest in travelling regularly to that chosen country. So he had made five separate 'project preparatory visits' over six months to that country, each visit costing about $ 14,000. When the document, which he had prepared, was found worthless by all concerned, the management of the ITC asked for a team of two experts to review and re-prepare the document, which meant further field visits and an additional $ 28,000. When the results were still unsatisfactory, I was asked to look into the matter to provide a solution. We had to find ways to bury the matter quietly. At that stage, the institution had already spent $ 100,000 as administrative costs in order to prepare a project of the size of $ 100,000. There were many such cases, though not all were as comical as this.

With all the heavy international travel going on, Kuoni, one of the world's largest travel agencies, had an office located within the ITC premises, to provide exclusive service to the staff. This small office had two computer terminals and was naturally very active through the day – the main business of the ITC being its 'missions'. Bombay and Delhi were important destinations for the ITC personnel, because there were a number of projects in India in association with Indian public sector agencies. Also, Bombay and Delhi were convenient gateways to other destinations. Those days, Air India used to run a tri-weekly service from Geneva to Delhi. Despite this, I did not come across a single ITC staff member who used Air India, given its abysmal record in punctuality. Instances of the scheduled Air India flights to Geneva over-flying or bypassing Geneva were common knowledge. The ITC staff, savvy travellers, ignored or even refused to bring Air India into their travel plans.

With the limited amount of money and technical knowledge at the disposal of these 'expert' bodies, one may wonder how they succeed in dealing with governmental functionaries in various countries and get access to senior government officials. The methods are quite simple. A considerable amount of project expenditure is earmarked for 'training'. This is a cover for providing air passage to personnel in the target ministries and public sector agencies in developing countries, to travel periodically to Geneva or other salubrious destinations, such as Bali or Chengmai, where international seminars or round tables are organised. With such baits, access is obtained to government departments in the target countries. These are then used to cultivate one or two key functionaries in the target ministries of participating countries, with an implicit suggestion of a regular assignment in Geneva. Occasionally of course, such a promise has to be fulfilled. Whatever the project document may promise or actually perform, an imaginative use of such techniques is the hallmark of a good professional. After all, the client needs have to be met.

I saw again what I had noticed when in the commerce ministry. The poorer the country, the swankier the representation, and longer the limousine used by the delegate. This clear principle applied in respect of the representation of various countries in the UN Missions in Geneva and for their delegates visiting from headquarters. It was almost like a law – the poorer African, Asian, and Latin American country delegates would stay in five star hotel suites; delegates from developed countries would stay in single rooms in three or four star hotels, and use taxis or even public transport. India, as behoved a poor country, had an appropriate representation in Geneva. And its delegates had no intention to break the law that had been laid down prescribing the facilities available to them.

Bureaucrats are to be tamed and controlled, for them to be productive and useful; otherwise they are, by nature, like wild untamed horses – arrogant, lazy and self-willed. In the UN system, by its very nature, there are no forces operating to harness the bureaucrats and make them subserve any particular purpose. Remaining in the UN service is itself the only motivation and purpose. All one has to do is to please the donor country, which is not a very difficult job. Evaluations are easily managed, and are invariably positive. Pleasing the client, namely the developing country they are supposed to assist is not considered as a relevant objective and is not even attempted. This is the position in the UN, especially in the so-called economic agencies. The position of national civil servants, especially in the Indian context has many similarities with UN civil servants. The national civil servants also contribute very little, rarely perform any useful function, are arrogant and rude to the general public, and at the same time subservient and sycophantic to seniors and their political masters. A civil servant from either system generally creates and lives in his own make-believe world, unrelated to reality – that is why most of them have a far away look when you see them – they will not meet you in the eye. However, there are also significant differences. The pay in the national service, at least the legitimate component of the remuneration, is meagre. Whereas the UN civil servant serves no one's interests except his own, the national civil servant has to pander to the requirement of his political masters, in addition to looking after his own interests. The reason for this difference is that sovereignty vests within the country, usurped by the political executive to meet its own ends. There is no such sovereignty in the UN, which is essentially a talking shop.

I have little knowledge of the working of the UN system in New York, particularly the political side. As for Geneva, the UN's economic agencies are basically an enterprise for employment, an arrangement for a patron in the home country to comfortably accommodate a protégé. So, the main topic of conversation and the main pre-occupation of UN employees would relate to service conditions, travel and perks as well as holidays and vacation schedules. There are some treaty and technical organisations like the WTO, International Telecommunications Union (ITU) and World Intellectual Property Organisation (WIPO), which to some extent, do have their uses. This cannot be said of most of the UN's economic agencies such as UNCTAD, ITC, United Nations Industrial Development Organisation (UNIDO), ESCAP and a host of other similar agencies. Indeed, the developing world will not miss anything if any or all are wound up straightaway. The developed world does not need them anyway but to create employment for their staff. In their wisdom, the international community has created these havens to accommodate a few fortunate protégé. Who am I to complain? After all, I have been a beneficiary.

For myself, the work to remuneration ratio between Delhi and Geneva was 100:1 – one hundred times more work in Delhi and one hundred times more remuneration in Geneva! My friend, B L Das, who was the Indian ambassador to GATT at that time and rose to the position of chairman of the Contracting Parties in GATT, would say "a posting in the UN in Geneva is a reward for some pure deeds *(punya)* done in one's previous incarnations *(janma)*. It provides rewards and remuneration with little or no work or responsibility".

Our first winter in Geneva was severe. One day in March 1985, I asked Krishnamoorthy, who worked for another UN organisation, the World Meteorological Organisation (WMO) as to what caused this special cold wave in the Geneva region. The UN expert, with his deep insight, said that there was a special combination of circumstances, including a variety of causative factors that had specially combined to produce this most unusual weather. He opined that it was something like the '*ashtagriha*' confluence of planets. It was a rare occurrence, which does not recur so easily. When I asked Krishnamoorthy whether the *ashtagriha* phase was over, he mentioned that these special factors were now gone and that the weather pattern had settled back to normal. This was at around 1'o clock on a Saturday afternoon. It started snowing at 5 pm that day and did not stop for the next three days, completely disrupting all normal life in Geneva. This was followed by an intensely cold spell, which was unusual. In fact, the following week, much of Geneva was closed. Engblom, the director of ITC, a Swede, produced the rare sight in Geneva town by skiing to his office. All in all, it was a very chaotic season, for a town that rarely sees much snow. So much for *ashtagriha*!

Nearing the end of our stay in Geneva, I again had occasion to consult Krishnamoorthy, the UN expert. Along with my family, and the family of B L Das, I had planned to drive to Holland to see the tulips, sometime in end April or early May of 1990. A week prior to that travel, I sought the advice of Krishnamoorthy, as to the likely weather conditions for the trip and the likely situation in Holland. He consulted his colleagues in WMO, as well as the large weather computer located there and came back with the advice that there was likely to be a depression in North Sea and conditions could be disturbed on the Dutch coast. He suggested I call him again later in the week, closer to the date of departure. I called Krishnamoorthy on the Thursday afternoon prior to the planned departure on Friday. He came back with the advice that the depression in the North Sea was pronounced, and that the conditions were disturbed. He even warned that it would be 'dangerous' and advised us to postpone our trip. We had almost given up our plan and were quite disappointed. Suddenly, Lalitha suggested, "Why don't we anyway proceed tomorrow morning, after breaking a coconut for good luck as we do back home in India, before setting out on a travel? If we meet bad weather we can return." So we decided to 'break the coconut', and left the next day. From that morning till the following Tuesday evening, when we returned, we had glorious weather. The sun was shining at Keukenhof and we saw 'thousands of tulips at a glance'. It was only as we neared Geneva on Tuesday evening, that we found a light shower awaiting us– perhaps the computer had misread the depression in Lake Geneva as one in the North Sea!

There was a sizeable Indian community in Geneva, mainly comprising the staff and families of Indians working in the various international organisations in Geneva. It was a fairly well knit group. The community members met frequently to celebrate various Indian festivals, probably with greater enthusiasm and fervour than they would in India. Thus, the fine arts club was an active place, with regular amateur performances. When Indians left their country, they clung even more closely to their traditions, customs and culture.

We rarely change our outlook, even when living for many years abroad. An experience with B Singh, from east UP, made this point. He had come to Geneva some decades earlier, probably as the domestic help of some senior international official, and had stayed on. He was popular in the Indian community, and ever in demand for weekly visits to various homes, for cleaning the toilets and the kitchens; he was also to be seen at Indian parties, serving the drinks and later helping with the dishes. One day I learnt that he had lost his wife, and went to his house to pay my condolences. It was early afternoon; his apartment was a bare one-room flat. A few other Indians were there to share his grief. Singh had just returned after the cremation of his wife, who had died of cancer at the municipal hospital the previous night. He was dry eyed, drained of all emotions, and talking more to himself than to the visitors in his home. He said, "She died late last night. The nurse asked me to come back early this morning. She was being bathed and the nurse asked me to remove her nose ring, before the cremation. Saab, I have never seen her without the nose ring ever since I had known her and married her when she was a ten-year-old. She wore it all the time, in bed, while bathing – it was part of her. I could not bear the thought of separating her from the diamond nose ring. I told the nurse that I don't want it, let it go with her. The nurse said that the metallic item could not be taken into the crematorium. Saab, I tried to remove the nose ring; but my hands were trembling and I could not unscrew it. Finally, the nurse removed it and gave it to me. You see Saab, she could not even take this small thing with her when she went. But, you see people who madly collect houses and money and property – they cannot take it up with them."

In this assignment with the ITC, I discovered an important truth. The little respect that I commanded was due to my continuing linkage with my home government. If one completely cuts off links with his national government service, and becomes dependent on the contract service of the UN organisation, he gets further devalued. Considering that the nature of UN service is shallow and without any content, many who come on a deputation from their country, make the mistake of cutting off the cord from their national system, leaving themselves to the mercy of the UN agency. They are then treated without dignity. I found unfortunate instances of sensitive individuals with intelligence and ability, having to cut off their links with their service in the home country, due to force of circumstance. I could see them palpably suffering, performing the most trivial and meaningless chores day after day. They were whistling in the dark, comforting themselves that they were doing important work to save the economies of the developing countries. How they would give an arm to return to their nation's service, taking a ninety per cent pay cut!

I recall a senior Indian foreign service official working then for the UN system in New York who would visit Geneva for a week every month as an observer in the monthly committee meeting of the International Labour Organisation (ILO). He would fly in first class and then complain about his tiring schedule. During meetings, his routine was to tackle the challenges of the *London Times* crossword, which was tucked away amongst his papers. At the end of his tour of duty, the UN said it was unable to release him in view of his invaluable services to the system. He finally retired from New York. I once asked him about his work and was surprised to find that he actually believed himself to be doing important work, "all in India's interest," he added.

When I was earlier the joint secretary in the commerce ministry in India, G Engblom, who was then the director general of the ITC visited Delhi a couple of times. During one visit, he had at my suggestion visited the Bharatpur bird sanctuary. Apparently, he greatly enjoyed watching the birds. I attribute his invitation to me to join his staff in Geneva partly to that experience in Bharatpur. I sometimes wonder whether the recruitment of other employees was based on equally weighty considerations! When my term got over, Engblom had offered me a ten year contract, a rarity, which would have carried me through till year 2000, three years later than my normal superannuation date with the Government of India. He also added that he would straightaway give me a promotion to higher status and better pay. Despite this, I did not give a moment's thought, before returning to service in India. At that time, I had nothing lined up in Lucknow or Delhi, and no one was asking for my return to India. In fact, Delhi or Lucknow did not care if I resigned from service and stayed with the UN – that would have meant one less contestant in the fight to climb up the ladder. I had no illusions about being welcomed back with open arms and with garlands. I was aware that I would have to fight to hold my ground and if the luck of the draw went against me, I would have been sidelined ruthlessly, condemned to trivial positions. But having received so much from the Indian service, I felt it my duty to show up and take my chance. In the event, my luck held.

With the irrational and undeserved high salary that I received in the UN, I had substantial savings. I could educate my children well and build a nest egg for a rainy day. Thanks to the strength of the savings, I was able to stand up to the politicians and not hanker for the carrots dangled before me. The value of having this buffer, in standing up to politicians cannot be overstated. A government servant, however high he may reach in the system, does not stand much chance to make reasonable savings if he follows the straight and narrow path. One reason why the politician controls the lives of civil servants stems from the government salary structures. There has been no Cornwallis around for a century or so, to guide our administrative apparatus. The Geneva posting helped me in my subsequent assignments back home, in being fearless with regard to politicians.

At the end of over five years, I bid good-bye to Geneva and found myself back in Lucknow. I had travelled widely in Europe and in Africa, America and the Far East, and taken my family for memorable holidays to every country of Europe. I made a number of friends, and at least one lifelong friend. Even now, I am reminded of the wonderful time I had, when, regular as clockwork early every month, I receive the UN pension. The administrative law, "effort put in public service is inversely proportional to rewards received" is eminently valid. I can testify to that.

11 PUBLIC ENTERPRISES AND PRIVATISATION

In Bollywood film style, we sprinted just as it was settling down and scrambled on to the helicopter, which quickly took off again. Gaining height, we could see the protestors break through the main gate and charge in the direction of the airborne helicopter as it flew off towards Mirzapur.

"The privatisation decisions were the only good ones taken by the previous government. Why do you want to undo these?" He replied: "Please note – I am not consulting you on whether we should repossess the cement plant – only on how we can get this done!"

ON MY RETURN FROM GENEVA TO LUCKNOW in 1990, the state chief secretary made me chairman and managing director of Auto Tractors Limited, a state government owned company. The company made tractors, or at least was supposed to. I thought this was a sinecure post but that was not to be. It became my task to privatise the company. This was followed by more assignments that involved privatisation of units owned by the state government. Looking back, the job was challenging and was laced with some personal danger. I came to believe that the privatisation of sick units can be made acceptable to the public, if it is done in response to genuine financial crisis and so long as the retrenched workmen are properly compensated.

The tractor factory was located some one hundred miles from Lucknow near Pratapgarh town. It was established in the 1960s. It was believed at the time that the tractor unit would provide a fillip to the modernisation of agriculture in the state. A technology tie up with a reputed British company helped Auto Tractors run successfully in the first few years. But the unit had since fallen into bad times, and started losing money, a situation not unknown to public sector units.

For the previous five years, till the time I stepped in, substantial plant and machinery spread over a twenty acre complex had remained idle. On the payroll were about 1500 staff in the company including 700 shop-floor workers, 300 engineers and supervisory personnel, and the inevitable complement of office staff and peons. All operations had closed down except for some job work and the only real sign of life every month was the extraction of a 'loan' from government coffers to meet salary expenses. The unit had mounting debts, with defaults in repayment of principal and interest. It had exhausted all its credit limits and had no elbow-room to proceed in any direction. For the first few months, I was able to cajole the state government to give the company further loans for payment of salaries and with great difficulty half the salaries could be paid. The arrears in wage payments were mounting. I explored avenues for reviving the unit, through injection of fresh funds or new technology or through any other means. But, there was just no way to proceed. To add to its woes, a number of private tractor manufacturers had established themselves all over India with excellent marketing reach in Uttar Pradesh, and Auto Tractors just could not compete.

A stage came when the chief secretary and the secretary of the finance department flatly refused to fund payment of salaries saying that the state exchequer was in bad shape and funds had dried up. In desperation, I met the chief minister, Mulayam Singh Yadav and told him that there was no way to pay the staff. He hardly listened and said, "We may have to close down the company then. Do whatever you want, but don't bother me." I went back to the chief secretary and told him that there was no option but to close down the unit. The chief secretary said he would consult the chief minister and let me know. After some days he got back to say that government would have no objection if I closed down the unit, and in any event no more funds would be available.

The board agreed and passed a resolution that the unit may be closed down and the services of all the employees terminated. It is easier to run an idle unit than to close it down, as I found. This could well be why so many units are just not closed down. It took some weeks of hard work, with the covert assistance of a few trusted employees, to prepare for closure. I had arranged for an advance from the state government to pay all the arrears of the staff, as also the statutory compensation on termination of the workers' employment. And I arranged with the manager of the bank to credit the account of each employee with all arrears along with the statutory compensation.

And then, one morning at six when the first shift of employees reached the plant, they found a notice that the factory was closed and that their services were not required. Overnight the services of all the employees, including even the general manager were terminated, except for around ten persons who had worked with me on the administrative arrangements. There was of course an uproar. The furious employees petitioned the chief secretary and the chief minister, who stood firm. They also moved the courts that the termination was illegal, but as we had prepared our case well, this was infructuous. The decision to close the Auto Tractors Limited was indeed a harsh one. But here was a case where the situation over the previous fifteen years or so had been allowed to deteriorate to a stage where 1500 personnel got idle wages. Meanwhile, the costs were mounting with no benefit to anybody but for those employed. The question was whether the tax-payer should pay wages forever to support idle labour. In the event, I bit the bullet.

At the same time, I was exploring alternate end-uses for the factory premises and the plant. In the first place, the factory had been located unimaginatively in an area with no industrial culture and with no ancillary or spare parts suppliers nearby. No one I approached wanted to touch the unit even if given on a platter. As for privatisation of the unit, there were no takers. So, I contacted all the existing tractor manufacturers, including the private and public sector agencies to see if they could take over the assets on nominal terms to keep the employment alive. I also approached the defence ministry and a number of private industrial groups to ascertain if they had any interest in the unit. Meanwhile, I had negotiated with the lender banks and agencies for a substantial waiver of the interest and penal interest on the loans and a write off of the government advances, which a potential buyer would anyway demand.

Finally, we managed to locate a Bangalore based industrialist, who was interested in purchasing the unit, provided it was free from all encumbrances and not saddled with the full complement of labour and personnel who had worked in the company. The Sipani group took over the factory lock, stock and barrel, on the negotiated terms, and at a price settled by the report of an assessor. It was part of the agreement that the buyers would re-employ on new terms, 300 of the terminated workers. But then there was no way the rest could be accommodated. Prior to the Sipani take over, the chief minister had appointed a ministerial committee chaired by the then co-operation minister, Ram Saran Das, a respected gentleman with a clean reputation. We met the committee members over several sessions. Some of them expressed concern that the Sipani group was not a well reputed one and wondered whether they were the right choice to take over the plant. The minister for co-operation explained to them that there was no alternative, since nobody else was interested. To make his point that the buyer and the closed unit were a good match, he recounted the following village story, in his own humorous style: a marriage party (*barat*), accompanying the groom, reached around sundown for the marriage ceremony. The broker of the marriage was keen that the proceedings should be expedited so that the bridegroom could see the girl before nightfall. When pressed as to why the hurry, the broker mentioned in confidence to the bride's father that the bridegroom suffered from night blindness, and that he would not be able to see after night fall. The bride's father asked him not to worry; there was no problem since the bride could not see even during the day! The anecdote carried the day.

I was lucky to come out of this assignment untainted, and physically unscathed though there were some close calls. One morning at around 9, I suddenly found a commotion outside the guesthouse in Lucknow where I was staying. Some 500 laid-off workers from Pratapgarh had reached by the morning Punjab Mail, naturally without tickets. They forcibly stopped the train on the tracks close to the guesthouse. They had surrounded the guesthouse, armed with sticks and shouting slogans. There were only a couple of unarmed watchmen at the gate. While I had received threatening letters and messages, I did not anticipate that a mob would travel a hundred miles by train to get me. I stayed back inside the locked house while the mob tried to beat down the door. It was sheer luck that a truck carrying armed police was passing that way and stopped to see the commotion. They dispersed the mob. I was to encounter this mob yet once again, this time in Pratapgarh.

The closure and sale of Auto Tractors established me as an 'expert' in disinvestment. The chief secretary promptly made me the principal secretary, public enterprises to the government and also gave me the responsibility of chairman, Privatisation Committee, with a mandate to privatise a number of other state units, principally the Dalla-Churk cement plants which were incurring massive losses. Prabhat Kumar, who later succeeded me as Cabinet secretary in Delhi, was then the industry secretary in the state government. The plethora of literature that is now available on this subject had simply not evolved in those days. Terms such as disinvestment, privatisation, equity sales were used interchangeably without attention to their exact meaning. But there was growing awareness that the bleeding of the public exchequer year after year, to protect the interests of a relatively small number of employees could not be construed as 'public interest' and should stop. The idea that divestment of shares in healthy units could be used to raise resources for the state, in order to fund its profligacy, had not come in vogue, as there were no profit-making public sector units to speak of in UP!

One day, along with Prabhat I set off by helicopter to visit the Dalla-Churk cement factory located in Mirzapur District, with a stopover in the Pratapgarh unit now with the Sipani group. We landed at the helipad in Pratapgarh town and with an armed escort, drove into the plant. We found that the factory had recommenced production and there was much activity in the campus. But the new management had taken only some three hundred of the erstwhile workers and other personnel. After spending an hour at the plant, we sat in the jeep for the journey back to the helipad located in the police lines, and reached the exit gate. To our surprise, we found the gate blocked on the outside by about two hundred or so ex-workers along with their wives and children, shouting slogans. Apparently the news of my visit had got around to the residential areas where I had been marked as their principal enemy. We turned back from the gate and quickly drove to the other two exit gates, only to find them also blocked. This time, there were not so many workers, but at each gate about twenty or thirty women, evidently wives of the workers were sprawled on the ground, blocking the exit. This was an impasse. Our escort, the district police officer ordered the jeep driver to run through the obstacles, over the legs and ankles of some of the women. I quickly intervened to stop this extreme measure and we turned back in to the factory.

For half an hour or so, nothing happened as we considered our next move. Meanwhile, the pilot of the helicopter, who had been waiting for us at the helipad got wind about the goings-on. He sized up the situation and decided to take the initiative. In concert with the police officer present with us, and using the police radio network, he arranged for us to reach the main open quadrangle within the complex and for the helicopter to land inside the factory on a mission to 'rescue' us. This was a dangerous manoeuvre as there were power and telephone lines crisscrossing the campus and the pilot was not familiar with the factory layout. Anyway, he took his chance. The helicopter landed with a whir and kept the engine and rotors on. On a pre-arranged signal, Prabhat Kumar and I sprinted to the helicopter just as it was settling down and in Bollywood film sequence style, scrambled on to the helicopter, which quickly took off again. Gaining height, we could see the nonplussed protesters break through the main gate and charge in the direction of the airborne helicopter as it flew off towards Mirzapur. Such was the field review to monitor the result of the first disinvestment in the state.

At the time I took over as principal secretary for public enterprises, the Dalla-Churk cement plants had a total employment of over 9000. The experience with Auto Tractors had not quite prepared me for such over-staffing. But the rest was much the same – the units were heavily in debt to the financing institutions and banks, and kept alive by state loans. Funds were not available for purchase of consumables and fuel, nor for upkeep and maintenance of machinery, not to speak of modernisation or improvement. Excellent limestone reserves were available, providing a good raw material base; the units had potential to make profits but had simply collapsed due to the weight of public sector management. There was just no way these units could flourish in competition with the private sector even in a profitable industry like cement.

A programme for privatisation of the three cement factories at Dalla-Churk in Mirzapur district was drawn up. Two independent assessors, one each from Delhi and Bombay, were appointed to do the valuation of the assets. The privatisation committee made all the necessary preparations to sell off these units. We had established the terms and conditions, one of which was that there should be no retrenchment for a period of five years from the date of take over. This was a fairly crippling condition, but was insisted upon to protect the employees' interests. We invited sealed tenders from all interested cement groups from across the country. The committee held discussions with about eight groups who had shown interest. I recall that Ganguli, the then chairman of ACC and a respected industry personality, had come for the discussions. He bluntly said that taking all factors into account, Re.1 would be a fair price for all the three units, on an 'as is where is' basis, and that too, without any conditions to desist from retrenchment. After detailed discussion with a number of groups, the committee found the bid of a group run by Sanjay Dalmia to be the best from the financial point of view. Moreover, they were willing to accept all the terms and conditions. The committee, which had several members of good standing and integrity, unanimously selected this group. The recommendation was sent for the approval of the state Cabinet. The Dalmia group was the only local bidder from within UP, and they had indicated that they would match the best offer. They were quite keen to take over all the three units. Sanjay Dalmia was also a close friend of Mulayam Singh Yadav, the chief minister, perhaps from their school days, but this had no bearing on the decision taken by the committee. The three cement units in Dalla-Churk were successfully privatised in early 1991, or so we thought then. But then there was a sequel to this.

Politics, inevitably, was to intervene. State elections were due in a few months time. The opposition party, the BJP, thought it opportune to find fault with what in fact had been done in good faith. They cried foul on the privatisation of Auto Tractors Limited and the cement plants, and alleged impropriety by Mulayam personally and by his government. This became a theme of the election campaign, with the BJP vowing to bring the divested units back under state control. As it happened, the BJP came to power, and when Kalyan Singh took over as chief minister, he viewed me with suspicion, as Mulayam Singh's collaborator in what he believed were improper actions. I was by then the agriculture production commissioner for Uttar Pradesh. Kalyan Singh was cool towards me and would not allow me any role in state affairs. But fortunately, he got over his suspicions towards me.

True to the promise made in the election plank, Kalyan Singh ordered a thorough review of the privatisation process. It was put under a microscope, the files taken through a wringer to sniff out suspected foul play. Apparently Kalyan Singh did not find anything amiss and so became satisfied about due process being followed, and the probity of the deals. Besides, he also discovered that the state exchequer was saving an enormous amount of money exceeding Rs.100 crores in a year, as reported to him by the finance department. I was surprised one day when he called me to his chambers and told me frankly, "I had a suspicion about your role in the two privatisation cases. I have made enquiries and found the deals were done correctly and properly and that these have been in the best interests of the government. Feel free to come to me any time with advice or suggestions on any matter. I will welcome it." The above statement from him was unsolicited and unnecessary. Kalyan Singh, as I found him at that time, was active and straightforward, having the state's interest at heart. He was true to his word, and consulted me even in matters outside my area of work, and often took my advice.

And then some weeks later, at about 10 pm, I got a message that the chief minister was returning from Delhi that night by the state plane, and wanted some officers including me to meet him at 11 pm in his chambers. So we assembled in his room: the chief secretary, legal secretary, legislative secretary, secretary home, principal secretary to the chief minister and myself. Without ado, Kalyan Singh stated that he wished to cancel the privatisation of the Dalla-Churk cement plants and asked us for the best way to get it done. We were aghast. The legislative secretary protested, "The only good decisions taken by Mulayam Singh's government were the privatisation ones. Why do you want to undo these?" Kalyan replied, "Please note – I am not consulting you on whether we should repossess the cement plant – only on how we can get this done!"

We came to know later that there had been a stormy meeting of the BJP high command at Delhi that day. Apparently, Vishnu Hari Dalmia, the grandfather of Sanjay Dalmia was under attack on some political grounds, and the cement plant issue got caught in the political cross fire. The BJP's election promise to reverse the cement privatisation was invoked and Kalyan was charged with not implementing an election 'promise'. Kalyan had protested that the deals were in the best interests of the state and that it would be foolish to go back on what had been done – in any case, no one was really bothered by this particular election promise. But all to no avail. His own job as chief minister came on the line, on this issue. However distasteful the decision was to him, his hands were forced by political circumstances, and he had to agree to cancel the cement deal.

After much discussion, a method to 'cancel' the privatisation was devised. I advised the issue of an ordinance, citing certain factors to cancel the agreement with the Dalmia group and repossess the plants. At the end of the meeting at midnight, after the others had left, I told Kalyan Singh that he had taken a very costly decision. Kalyan was sad. He agreed with me and told me that the decision would cost the state exchequer a few hundred crores, but that the state, however, could afford it. I told him, "Sir, I disagree with you. It is not a matter of a few hundred crores; if it were, I may not be as unhappy as I am. The cost will be your credibility and the credibility of the process of governance in Uttar Pradesh. You are going to Delhi tomorrow to meet the industrialists – asking them to invest in Uttar Pradesh. You are also going to tell them about your plans to trifurcate the Electricity Board, to improve its efficiency. Nobody is going to believe you on these things any more." Kalyan Singh had nothing to say.

The saga of my involvement with privatisation in UP will not be complete without a reference to the Greater Noida Power Supply Company. It is a testimony to the clear-headedness and firmness of Mulayam Singh that he gave me a free hand to pursue the privatisation initiatives. In difficult situations, he gave full backing and unlimited support as befits a political administrator of calibre which he undoubtedly is – or at least was, when I saw him in UP and later in Delhi when I was Cabinet secretary.

Proposals had been under discussion for trifurcating the Electricity Board into three separate units for generation, transmission and distribution, making each accountable and performing on commercial terms. Any subsidy for social purposes would be borne explicitly and separately by the state. The view was emerging that private players should be allowed to enter the electricity field, particularly at the distribution end. Tight management was required to reduce the unacceptably high levels of theft and distribution leakages. We identified Noida, Greater Noida and Kanpur as the first areas to usher in private management of power distribution. We made some headway in Greater Noida.

The RPG group, who had experience in handling power distribution in Calcutta, was short-listed and invited for negotiations. The final round of negotiations were to be held in a building in Mira Bai Marg in Lucknow, where some government offices were located. The venue was an oblong hall in the first floor of the building, with a long table, seating about thirty persons, with only one entrance door from the main corridor. I was seated at the head of the table, on the far end, with a number of government and electricity board representatives on one side, and a team of RPG officials from Calcutta on the other. R P Goenka himself was supposed to have been there, but was delayed by a plane connection – his senior representatives had come to negotiate. As we started the meeting, a din could be heard outside with slogans raised by a mob of electricity board workers agitating outside the main gate of the building. There was a cordon of security guards, to keep the crowd at bay. Suddenly, after about an hour, there was a commotion: the mob below had obviously broken the security ring. A hundred angry agitators charged into the room, gesticulating wildly and shouting slogans. They were shouting, "Where is Goenka – we want to kill him," mistakenly thinking that R P Goenka was actually present there. For a few minutes, there was bedlam, with furniture being thrown about violently, and the air full of flying objects. It was almost like one of those scenes when the Assembly is in disarray. There was no escape route from the charging mob, and I feared the worst, as a large ashtray flew past my ear, just grazing it. By then the policemen had recovered their ground, and freely wielding their *lathis* vacated the room of the intruders. We all took a while to recover our breath and composure; had the room cleaned up of the debris, got ourselves a cup of tea, and it was back to business. An agreement was actually struck with the RPG group in respect of Greater Noida. In fact, as of last count, the Greater Noida Power Company was supplying power to that area. By all accounts, the quality of service in that area is far superior to that seen elsewhere in the state, which is not saying much though, given the abysmal service provided by the state government.

For some time during the 1960s and '70s, the public sector units were touted as a panacea for all the ills of under-development. It was believed that government departments, with their file-bound functioning could not deliver results. So, developmental assistance could be better channelled through the medium of public sector corporations. This was based on the erroneous assumption that public sector units would operate efficiently and with more freedom. Hence, the creation of a large number of such agencies, both at the central and at the state level. But their trajectory over the next two decades was indeed disappointing. In 1990 in UP alone, I counted about a hundred public sector agencies, some tiny, some small and a few relatively large. By that time, practically all were defunct, broke and struggling to pay the salaries of their staff.

I recall that in the mid-'70s, there was an agitation in Bundlekhand area, which covered the then division of Jhansi, protesting against the lack of development. And there was a similar agitation in eastern UP. The disturbances went on for some time and the government led by N D Tewari was getting concerned. T N Dhar, the secretary to chief minister offered a solution to the problem of development which the government swallowed: to establish the Bundlekhand Development Corporation and East UP Development Corporation, each with an endowment of Rs. 1 crore and to charge them with the responsibility of assuring development of these regions. The chief minister launched these corporations with great fanfare and everyone fell prey to the illusion that the problem of development had been tackled! I was at Lucknow those days and remember having a bitter argument with Dhar on this issue and asking him several questions. What will the hapless CEO of this new corporation do? What is his mandate? What is the blueprint for these agencies? Where and how are they going to receive their resources? In today's language, is there a 'Business Plan?' These questions were brushed aside. The pressing need was not development, but to take the wind off the sails of the agitators. The government was so pleased with this novel solution to the development issues of East UP and Bundelkhand, that it extended these measures to the rest of UP. Nine more development corporations were announced. At every divisional headquarters, these were inaugurated with great festivity by the chief minister, with the local minister and legislators in tow. Each corporation was given rupees one crore to spend. The 'development' effort never went beyond the employment and perks created in the offices of these corporations.

The arrangement provided openings for a dozen IAS and PCS officials, and offered new berths for other departmental officers. There was room for a complement of clerical staff and peons who could be recruited afresh with the patronage of the local authorities. Thus, for example, one more domestic servant could be attached to the menage of the local divisional commissioner and paid for from the state exchequer, via the new-found route of the corporation. Everybody was happy. It became fashionable to promote development through the device of the 'corporation'. Even service departments in fields such as health and education discovered that their work could be better undertaken through corporations. After all, this would provide the senior government functionaries with air conditioned cars, air conditioners and an additional servant at home, and other perks including expense accounts that were not available to those left behind in the departmental corridors. The officials were the first to get a whiff of this bounty, but the ministers soon caught on and also jumped into the fray. Thus, the public sector corporations became a milch cow.

Nor was anyone surprised ten years later when all these agencies with no activity to perform went bankrupt, stuck with staff surviving on doles from the state. By the early 1990s, it was a sorry sight indeed, with most of the corporations in decrepit condition, while continuing to provide perks to the minister and officials on an unabated scale.

In Delhi, I discovered that the situation was not too different, though the operations were conducted with greater sophistication. The corporation still provided the joint secretary and secretary with the opportunity to obtain vehicles, cell phones and five-star comforts through the public sector route, with the government professing austerity in its budget mostly for consumption by the general public. I am not suggesting that vehicles and cell phones and comfortable travel should not be provided to senior officials; indeed, they are necessary for efficient performance. I am merely referring to the clandestine and intellectually dishonest means by which these ends are accomplished.

The task of dealing with public sector agencies followed me to my next assignment as secretary in the ministry of textiles in the Government of India. Rather than grappling with growth of the industry, I was grappling with the National Textile Corporation (NTC), and its 110 textile mills scattered all over the country. As many as half of these units were in distress, with idle labour of around 90,000. Not an unfamiliar scenario for me, except for the scale of the problem that had increased in geometric proportions starting with the tractor unit, then the cement units and finally textiles.

It is not as if the unviable public sector units in India cannot be closed down. The political dispensation fears that closures would not be popular with the public. At least, that is the common belief, and hence the cold feet that parties of all persuasions develop when faced with an unviable unit.

My own assessment, based on experience is that the general public is willing to accept the closure of unviable units so long as employees are given a generous hand-shake. In fact, if the policies are properly explained to the public, the government in power gets the credit for not frittering away public money. It is the closure that will be seen as being in the interest of the public.

12 AGRICULTURE AND RURAL DEVELOPMENT IN UTTAR PRADESH

It was not clear how one inaugurates a toilet! Should one actually use it, in public view of the villagers? Actually, I was sorely in need of using the toilet but I baulked. Anyway, my visit there has been immortalised with a small plaque in each toilet.

The subsidy would get disbursed each time a truck from Madhya Pradesh entered a bordering district of Uttar Pradesh. The truck carrying the same bags of pesticides would move back and forth between the state boundaries, claiming subsidy repeatedly.

I TOOK OVER THE ASSIGNMENT OF APC, THE agriculture production commissioner, in the winter of 1990. The coordination of a number of government departments, dealing with agriculture, horticulture, rural development, animal husbandry, farmers' cooperatives and some other departments falls within the ambit of this assignment. In a large, predominantly agricultural state, where most of the citizenry lives in rural areas engaged in agricultural or allied activities, this should actually be the most crucial area for government, demanding the highest attention. Indeed, in the Uttar Pradesh government this is believed to be an important assignment. However, as a matter of fact, this is not quite so. In India, logic is turned on its head.

The truth is that agriculture suffers from benign neglect. It is treated as a necessary evil by the states. Uttar Pradesh is no exception. Farmers are not of importance politically and hence, this neglect. The agricultural segment represents the largest private sector activity in the state, but the players are mostly small and fragmented landholders or landless workers. They have no economic power individually and have little collective bargaining powers through farmers' organisations or cooperatives. Political interests would not encourage any power to be given to the players in the agriculture or rural sector. If this group did become politically important, that would unsettle the existing political equations currently organised on caste or communal or 'secular' lines. Charan Singh was the last state leader who saw the potential for organising the *kisans*. Deve Gowda had the vague notion that agriculturists could be mobilised as a national force. But he did not know how to go about it, nor as prime minister did he get enough time to do so. The political leadership in India for the past half a century or so has had a strong vested interest in using and exploiting the weaknesses of the agriculturists for their own benefit. So, the neglect of the agriculture sector in India is neither casual nor accidental. However tenuous such a link might seem at first sight, the rural and agricultural classes are the base from which the middle classes extract their livelihood, and the upper or professional classes along with bureaucrats, industrialists and politicians derive their opulence. This is not the place to enter into a discussion on net transfer of resources, nor on the deliberate oppression of the agricultural and rural classes that makes such transfers possible. Suffice to say that the organisation and orientation of the government of Uttar Pradesh was a clear testimony to the importance, or lack of it, attached to the rural economy.

My first field visit as APC was to a village near Kannauj to see the programmes being implemented there. I took off from Lucknow, the state capital in my official car, with the official flag fluttering proudly. I met the district planning officer and the block development officer in-charge of the local area at a pre-assigned spot on the highway near Kannauj. I asked the planning officer to sit with me in my vehicle and headed for the village, with the block development officer going ahead of us in his jeep to show us the way. We travelled about eight miles on the highway, turned into a metalled rural connectivity road, and after travelling for two miles, turned on to a dirt track, which ran for a mile till we hit the village. A small reception committee, garlands in hand, was waiting. As I alighted from the car, I looked back at the dirt track that we had traversed. Looming on the horizon was a dirt cloud moving towards us, and what seemed like a hundred jeeps charging ahead of the dust storm to reach the village. It was like a scene from a film showing General Rommel's Panzer drive through the African desert, and even more like a scene from the Mauritanian leg of the Paris-Dakar motor race. On asking, I was told that the government officers in the innumerable development departments of the district and block were presenting themselves. Perhaps it was customary to mark presence during the visit of the big chief. Or perhaps the functionaries did not wish to be away at the time, fearing that in their absence there would be none to stand by them, in case any villager levelled criticism against their activity – or inactivity. I immediately asked all the vehicles to turn back, and once back at headquarters, issued a general direction to stop this practice. Only the district planning officer and the head of the local block could be present along with any other officers representing the specific departments whose work I was to inspect. The total number of local vehicles was in no case to exceed three.

In that village, I was shown around some of the work being undertaken by the government. But the main exhibit was the new type of rural toilet designed by the state research unit. These were being installed in that village. The toilets were supposedly easy to construct and relatively inexpensive. The state was promoting this concept as a part of the drive to enhance rural hygiene. The toilets carried a substantial subsidy so that the cost to the villager for each toilet was nominal. There were at least ten such new toilets in that village, and it was evident that these were hastily constructed during the past few days, after my programme had been finalised. After all, there had to be something to show. I was taken to one of them, located near the cottage of the village headman and was asked to 'inaugurate' it. I was taken aback. It was not clear to me how one inaugurates a toilet! Should one actually use it, in public view of about 500 villagers? Actually, I was sorely in need of using the toilet but I baulked. Anyway, if you go to that village, my visit there has been immortalised; you may still see the toilets, each having a small plaque with the lines in Hindi "Inaugurated by Honorable T.S.R.Subramanian, Agriculture Production Commissioner, on _____ December 1990." I would rather not disclose the name of the village, though I have given the clue that it is about ten miles from Kannauj. Almost certainly the plaques are still in existence, and it is equally certain that the toilets are currently not in use!

When I joined as APC, I was told of a regular practice of annual campaign meetings for the *kharif* and *rabi* crops. Twice a year, once in summer for the *kharif* crop season and then in early winter for the *rabi* crop season, meetings were held in each division to review the preparations for the forthcoming sowing season. The *kharif* meetings were held early in June and the *rabi* meetings in November/December. Those days, there were ten divisional headquarters and the practice was that the commissioner, along with his department heads, would travel to each division by overnight train from Lucknow, conduct a day long meeting and return to the headquarters by the following night train. After a break of a few days, the process would be repeated. This process would take up the whole month of June and November. I felt there should be a way of getting these important review meetings done on time, without spending so much effort travelling to and fro. The small six-seater state plane provided an answer. In November 1990, I organised the first series of meetings with this innovation to complete all the divisional meetings on five working days, with alternate intervening days at headquarters. Two divisions were covered each day, with the divisions chosen adjacent to each other. My first meeting covered Agra and Jhansi and the schedule read as follows:

7.30 am departure Lucknow and arrival Agra airport at 8.30 am
9 am to 1 pm: meeting of Agra Division
1.30 – 2.00 pm flight from Agra to Jhansi (packed lunch provided by Agra Commissioner)

2.15 – 5.15 pm: meeting of Jhansi Division
5.30 pm departure Jhansi airfield and arrival Lucknow airport at
6.30 pm.

The next day would be spent on follow-up action on the Agra and Jhansi meetings and preparatory action for the next day's meetings. The following day would be a similar programme, say Gorakhpur, Faizabad and back. The next round would be Varanasi, Allahabad and back. This would be followed by a trip to Moradabad, Bareilly and back. And finally, we would do Nainital, Pauri and back. It was possible to compress the process for each crop season within a ten-day period. The key to this revised arrangement was careful advance preparation and follow-up, no flabby speeches at the meetings and strict adherence to the time schedules. This last was particularly important in winter, when dusk falls early. Departure had to be before nightfall from airports with no night landing, or take-off facilities, such as Jhansi and Faizabad. The innovation worked well and functioned like clockwork – in the three crop seasons, during which I was APC. One episode in the first meeting helped set the pace.

The first meeting was in Agra and the departure was scheduled at 7.30 am from Lucknow airport. Four officers were to accompany me in the plane beside the pilot in the six-seater aircraft. All assembled at the airport on time except the secretary for rural development, a key member of the team. We got into the plane in which one spot was still available. Bhatnagar, my staff officer, who had come to hand over some papers, was invited to join the group. Promptly at 7.30 when the motor of the plane gunned to life, somebody pointed out that the secretary for rural development was approaching the airport in his car at a fast clip in the far distance. This officer was a senior member in the group who subsequently became chief secretary of the state. The pilot turned to me and asked me, "Should I open the door for him?" I said, "No – our departure is scheduled for 7.30 am and it is already 7.32 am. Please take off now." The missing secretary charged towards the plane as it was rolling, gesturing for us to stop and open the door; I asked the pilot to continue on our way. After concluding the first meeting in Agra we went on to Jhansi where the meeting commenced at

2.15 pm as scheduled. Suddenly, at around 3 pm, the secretary for rural development apologetically made an entry. Left high and dry on the tarmac, he had proceeded by road to Jhansi, a good 200-miles stretch. Bhatnagar, my unlucky staff officer, had to return that night by car from Jhansi to Lucknow, after surrendering his place on the return flight. After that episode, every member of the group arrived fifteen minutes in advance of the appointed hour and every meeting was on schedule!

Coming back to the agriculture department in UP state, it satisfied itself essentially by sponsoring three or four agricultural universities and a few research laboratories. One could locate the odd institution of excellence, but most were mediocre. But what these universities did, how they trained successive generations of students to become useful and relevant to the growth of the agricultural sector was of interest to none. So, these institutions became centres of political patronage. The students were unfit for further studies in any good university or to take a lead role in rural development. The preparation was just enough for them to become lower level field functionaries in the various government departments dealing with agriculture. This was just a route for securing government employment.

The other area of activity of the agriculture department was to 'provide inputs' – especially seeds, fertilisers and pesticides to the agricultural community. This was a lucrative business, and in a manner taken quite seriously. While the actual procurement and distribution of these inputs were left to private operators, a significant amount of subsidy was channelled through the agriculture department and its allied agencies. What got distributed were not the inputs but the spoils from the subsidy amounts. There was a conspiracy by the key participants to share the subsidy amounts between the government functionaries, local politicians and some others in ways I had seen before, and have described earlier. The disbursement of subsidy was based on the proof of entry of the product, say, pesticide into the state and a certification of distribution. Thus, for example, a fifty per cent subsidy would get disbursed each time a truck from Madhya Pradesh entered a bordering district of UP. The truck carrying the same bags of pesticides would move back and forth between the state boundaries, claiming subsidy repeatedly and who can say, perhaps at both ends. There would be complicity between the functionaries; and the leakage on such subsidy schemes was very high. It was the same routine, whether it was for seeds, fertilisers, or pesticides – only the actual mode of operation would differ.

I knew from an earlier experience that it is not easy to break this nexus, which must have had patronage at a high level. Much earlier, when I was regional food controller at Gorakhpur, I went on an inspection visit to look at procurement of paddy by the local departmental officials. I uncovered irregularities in which my own deputy was directly involved. These were two malpractices that related to systematic over payment by about twenty per cent through over-weighment and under correction for moisture content. I spent the full day checking and cross checking samples, preparing a detailed report and sealing the exhibit samples in my presence and taking these into custody, along with statements of some of the members of the public present there, including farmers. My deputy, who was hand in glove with the operation, had a quizzical look on his face. In the evening, when my report was done he mentioned to me gently, "Do not try to correct the existing system – it is beyond you." I took his admonition lightly and sent my report with the evidence to government, recommending exemplary action. My deputy won the day. Within two weeks time I found myself transferred to another assignment. I learnt subsequently that a sufficient number of 'discrepancies' were discovered in my report that prevented the department from fixing responsibility on any official. And therefore the matter was closed.

I got away lightly for my honesty, with a mere transfer. There was a strange coincidence here. I have recounted earlier how sharing a name with a colleague cost me a posting as ambassador to GATT. But this was a small price to pay. Manohar Subramanian, my namesake paid a far heavier price for doing his job. Just as I had, he caught his own deputy regional food controller red handed while making overpayments and got him suspended. Manohar, an impeccably honest officer was transferred within a few days just as I had been. As a bonus, his erstwhile deputy engineered a false charge against Manohar. That inquiry dragged on for years; it was politicised in the Assembly, and ultimately Manohar's promotion prospects were wrecked. He resigned from the service an unhappy man. Meanwhile, his erstwhile deputy got himself reinstated in service, and the inquiry against him was quashed. These are lessons handed out in public view to make an example of an honest officer so that he learns to be careful before taking action against his errant subordinates. It is almost, as if the Empire strikes back. I was lucky during my service to get away somewhat though not fully unscathed.

The most important work in the agriculture department related to transfers and postings of the large army of officials working in the department. This was a lucrative and full time job for the minister and true to style, he would be assisted by a hand-picked team comprising a deputy secretary at head-quarters and joint-director level officers in each field formation. The minister had no concern whatsoever with agriculture policy or such trivia. His full energies were devoted to the onerous task of reshuffling the field staff, in season and out. As could well be imagined, there was a premium attached and depending on the location, the 'cost' of manoeuvering a transfer would vary.

Strangely enough, the overstaffing had to do with the several World Bank and other aided projects implemented in the state between the 1960s and the '80s. The conventional wisdom in the conception of those projects stressed the need for the creation of a large base of 'extension workers' for knowledge-transmission and 'farmer education'. It is alien to the genius of Indian babudom to be a transmitter of knowledge – the Indian field official's forte is 'distributing' scarce resources and enforcing 'controls', feathering his nest in the process. In consequence, successive World Bank and other funded projects not only frittered away large sums on supporting unnecessary and indeed counter-productive complements of field staff. Much worse, such projects resulted in a heavy, recurring pay-roll burden going on for decades after project implementation. Compounding this affliction, the projects were loaded with a generous dose of buildings and civil structures. These would include small buildings for storage, office areas, 'extension work' and the like. The donor agencies loved these structures, as they provided readily discernible 'evidence' that could be used to measure the 'success' of project implementation. These were well liked by the local officials and engineers due to the openings they provided for leakage. What better way to siphon out funds than from building construction. After the project period when maintenance funds ran out, these structures would go to seed, and in course of time, one could see these 'ruins' dotted all over the country side. These remain as monuments to the heavy price we have paid for international assistance in the agricultural field.

At least the state agriculture department had some field work to perform, however relevant or otherwise to the farming community. The agricultural ministry at Delhi washes its hands off on all matters relating to assistance to agriculturists, on the specious and convenient ground that agriculture is a 'state subject'. Any credit for the Green Revolution is quickly assumed by the Central government. But all failures, which are palpable and visible wherever one looks, are attributed to the state governments. The Government of India essentially confines itself to the preparation of the national subsidy budget, disbursement of the subsidy to the state governments, estimation of production for each crop and compilation and consolidation of production figures. The Centre does not assume any responsibility for proper implementation of the programmes. It does not seek to verify the correctness of the subsidies distributed at the field level. A 'Certification of Utilisation' furnished by the state is sufficient proof that funds have been applied properly. Similarly, in estimating and compiling the production figures, the main input is from the state government itself. Quite obviously this is over-simplifying, but in essence, shorn of verbiage, this is the reality. The Centre keeps at an arms length distance from agriculture.

I could see that the functioning of the rural development department in the state was in disarray. This department was the focal point for all the programmes undertaken by the state in the rural sector with a direct bearing on the upliftment of the rural areas, in terms of water supply, rural sanitation, connectivity roads, family welfare. One found the same pattern of diffuse thinking and flabby organisation in this key department too as was seen in agriculture. The Government of India, with its penchant for finding 'designer' names, had over time, produced the Nehru Rozgar Yojana, Indira Gandhi Rural Development Programme and others. With each change of government at the Centre, a new nomenclature was devised, but the programmes and the ground realities remained the same. The Government of India confined itself to massive budget allocations and transfer of these funds to the state governments for field utilisation, without closely monitoring the usage. When later I was in the Government of India as Cabinet secretary, it was evident from the postures of the finance and rural development ministry officials that they perceived these large allocations as an unavoidable evil dictated by the political need of the Central government. This was a token gesture to show empathy with rural areas, in the full knowledge that these amounts were largely wasted. No single individual or ministry could actually challenge the ongoing annual ritual.

A case in point is the history of the 'drinking water mission' named after Rajiv Gandhi, started with great fanfare sometime in the 1980s. The stated objective was to 'bring' drinking water to every village in the country within five years. A 'mission' mode was adopted, as the term sounded stylish. The Centre allocated large amounts of money. I recall attending high-level review meetings in Delhi in the early '90s, representing Uttar Pradesh as the APC, nearly five years after the mission started. There was not much progress though much money had been spent. The emphasis had been on surveys to identify sources for the water supply. I participated in a similar review five further years down the road, this time when I was Cabinet secretary. The position was much the same: Large amounts had been spent, and more surveys were required. I recently enquired about the progress and discovered that the programme was starved of funds but it was not politically expedient to terminate it. A brand new programme, with a new name acceptable to the Sangh Parivar has now taken up the work. No surprise, after twenty years and hundreds of crores, the number of villages not connected with water supply remains constant at about twenty per cent and probably fresh surveys are still required. Meanwhile, I occasionally see on the television or in the press the smiling face of a minister inaugurating yet another drinking water project in some village, giving the touch and feel of success.

At the turn of the century, more than fifty years after Independence, some thirty per cent of the population is in abject poverty and half the people are still illiterate. This is enough evidence of the 'success' of our rural development programmes. There are still large pockets without potable drinking water, and rural electrification in most states is a statistical figure that does not reflect realities on the ground. In short, most states have allowed massive leakages to take place in their rural development programmes. These leakages are not casual. They are deliberately engineered by creating systems designed to lubricate official and political functionaries at various echelons in the field, with full political blessings. This is all part of 'governance', as interpreted by independent India. Perhaps I am being overly cynical and there indeed are some bright spots. But it is beyond doubt that much of the rural development effort and resources has resulted in waste. Whatever advances we see are a result of the use of the residual resources that remain, after leakages. There is also the rare and exceptional private or local initiative. And sometimes there is the drive of an energetic district magistrate, who has the courage to resist political pressures. Such creatures are now an endangered species, not easily sighted.

The co-operative movement that was touted in the 1960s as a panacea for all ills in the agricultural and rural sectors has failed. I still recall the trite old slogan, "Cooperation has failed; but cooperation must succeed." It has not succeeded since. In theory, the network of farmers' cooperatives can provide for themselves the required farm inputs, financial credit, and marketing support. In practice, the district co-operative banks at all levels have been hijacked by influential middlemen and political functionaries who usurp the concessional element in the finance for themselves. A purely economic arrangement undertaken for the convenience of the farmers, the private participants, has been totally subverted. It has turned into a government run programme, diametrically opposite of what was intended. The cooperatives are now a political arrangement for the benefit of the middlemen and the functionaries. The farmers continue to rely on usurious money-lenders for their finance. Such aberrant transformation from what was desired or intended, to what it has actually become, is part of the same pattern that emerges in the implementation of so many other policy initiatives.

It is now widely agreed that diversification and expansion of the agro-industrial sector is the clear path for meeting the mounting challenges of rural poverty and unemployment. In theory, the policy responses sponsored by the Centre and the states endorse this course of action, but this is not put into practice. The key failure has been to succumb to the temptation to devise short term cosmetic solutions with an eye on elections. With this political approach, a pattern of intellectual dishonesty and deceit was initiated, which took hold of the planning and implementation machinery. This was embraced heartily by the officials and local politicians as it precisely served their own petty interests as well. This pattern, which has played havoc with our developmental efforts, was set in 1950s and '60s, and the failure is now complete. In a way, the nation decided to fool itself, and succeeded in this ignoble effort at deception. Thus, while devising the 'million wells scheme', policy makers of course knew that the wells would be dug again and again in the same spot and charged for each time; the same rural road would be reconstructed repeatedly and charged for each time; subsidies would be claimed on seeds and pesticides that never reached the farmer; withdrawals of government funds would take place for purchase of non-existent fodder. One can go on. None of this is new to the reader. What could come as a surprise is that the political process in India deliberately provides loopholes, for the corrupt village and district level politicians and the collaborating civil servants, to exploit. It must be admitted that there was a vague unease in the higher echelons of administration about the massive leak that was taking place, but no one had the time or the energy or even the opportunity to dig deep and identify the problems. Then only could one speak of attempting to eliminate the malaise. Thus, any 'strict' district magistrate or other officer who became too nosy would quickly be identified as 'rigid' or labelled as 'anti-development' and shunted out to a quiet corner. The system tolerated and in fact, encouraged flaccidity; no one was given enough time to stay on in any assignment to fully understand the process and to propose coherent solutions.

The hill districts in the Himalayas, in the northern part of UP state, now hived off as a separate state, have a totally different geo-climatic and cultural ambience from the plains. The development needs are distinctly different. Communication, transport and infrastructure facilities are inferior in the hill areas, compared even to what there is in the plains districts. Even though the spread of literacy has been higher in the hill districts, there is also a lack of job opportunities and so, greater poverty. Traditionally, able bodied men from the hills join the armed forces, or fan out into the plains to find secretarial work, or then work for a pittance as domestics: a money-order economy. The women, who stay back in the households in the far-flung villages with no roads or drinking water, bear the brunt of the hardship along with the aged. Despite favourable agro-climatic conditions for horticulture and diversified agriculture, these have not developed.

I recall a visit organised by my friend J C Pant in 1983, to the sacred shrines of Kedarnath and Badrinath in the hills. We were a bus-load of about forty individuals including both our families, with several elderly people in the group. As APC, I did the same trip by road in 1991, and also went to the shrines using the state helicopter, in 1993. Kedarnath, at a height of about 13,000 feet, is a fourteen km trek from Gowrikund, through a difficult, mountainous foot path. The shrine is revered by Hindus across India. Many make the pilgrimage at least once. After my 1993 visit, I had sanctioned an amount of rupees nine crores, to ease the last stretch by building a motorable road from Gowrikund to Rambada, leaving only a seven km trek to reach the shrine. I made the same pilgrimage again in the spring of 2003 and discovered that the road had not been built. This was because of the strong opposition from the local porters and owners of ponies whose incomes were at stake. They feared that the motorable road would deprive them of their livelihood. This is a struggle we have seen from the age of the steam engine, with vested interests trying to stop the use of technology. Evidently, the local political leadership in Gowrikund had exerted enough pressure on the government to stifle the project. What was forgotten is that if the passage to Kedarnath had become easier, the number of pilgrims visiting that area would have multiplied manifold, generating far more jobs in that region: all scuttled due to the myopic but strong local political interests. Facing a similar situation, Jagmohan had eased access to the Vaishno Devi shrine and this resulted in a major fillip to the economy of the entire area in Jammu. The Gowrikund-Rambada road is a small but clear instance of petty local interests prevailing over larger public interest.

In 1991, as I was once driving in the mountains in the course of an official visit, I stopped the car on an impulse, to visit a village which was situated on a ridge well above the highway, involving a steep climb on foot for about two kilometres. As I started walking up, the local block development officer who was accompanying me frantically tried to stop me, giving me various excuses. He finally talked about a heart-condition and I was a bit intrigued about why this functionary was so unwilling. Anyway, leaving him behind, I went ahead, accompanied by my orderly. We found a medium-sized village with perhaps two hundred inhabitants. A primary school was located there: Only one teacher was present. After some questioning, I managed to find out that the school had a regular strength of five teachers. However, by mutual arrangement among the teachers, only one would be present on any day; each of the five would take turns of fifteen days at a time, to attend to their teaching duties and take the rest of the time out to attend to other matters. I also discovered to my dismay that the village had not seen an inspection visit by a single block level officer, even though there were some fifteen officers attached to each block. The block level officers conveniently visited only the roadside villages. The village I visited was not particularly inaccessible. Yet, such was the apathy to the villagers' needs. In a microcosm, we can, at one stroke, understand the failure of development to take hold in the hills. Nearing the end of my visit to the village, I was quite dispirited. But my spirits soared when at an impromptu function in the school building, I could see the bright eyes and the shining intelligence of the young children. Surely the future citizens of India did not deserve the government they were saddled with.

Twelve years after that last visit, I had occasion to travel again in the interior parts of the hill areas in 2003. Superficially, there were signs of progress but in substance there was deterioration. A new state, Uttaranchal, had been carved out of Uttar Pradesh. This meant a new secretariat with a complement of ministers and bureaucrats. The erstwhile eight hill districts had multiplied into thirteen with an explosion in the number of government jobs. Apart from this unproductive contribution to job creation, there was not much to commend. The roadside towns on the highways were choked. The villages were further deprived of able-bodied men, who had descended to the towns in search of government jobs. The region continued to be money-order dependent. The main activity I saw was the hectic campaigning for the *Panchayat Samiti* and town area elections – democracy has clearly provided for the addictive occupation of electioneering in India. Wherever I travelled, retired long since and with no official position, it was pathetic to see unknown persons approaching me, and on the basis of a fleeting acquaintance, asking me to fix them up in a government job anywhere in India. Even graduates told me unabashedly that they were willing to do menial work – could I get them a job? The one abiding memory of the visit came about when our vehicle was stopped on the way to allow free passage for the chief minister's convoy rolling down at high speed. I counted at least thirty cars in the convoy: who can say that the hill areas are poor? Perhaps, I have been uncharitable. Uttaranchal state is still in its infancy and may yet contribute to the welfare of its citizens. But I could not see any tangible beginnings – tourism, agriculture, horticulture, micro-hydel programmes were all creaking along in the same old rutted path. Unless a new dynamics is introduced to tackle these aspects, little will change.

Talking about the hills, there is the chief secretary's cottage in Nainital. This small property, in a splendid location overlooking the lake dates back to the British days, when Nainital was the summer capital of Uttar Pradesh. The entire Lucknow secretariat would move to the cool climate of Nainital for four or five months each summer. The governor's mansion and the cottages of the chief minister and the chief secretary were vestiges of this long terminated annual migration. The chief secretary's cottage was well staffed, and had two suites – both well furnished and maintained to five-star standards. Traditionally, the caretaker would not allow any one except the chief secretary of the day to make use of the main suite. Though I was chief secretary for two years in Lucknow and had easy access to air transportation, I could not manage to spend even one night in the main suite earmarked exclusively for me. On one occasion, I did go to Nainital with the intention of spending three days there; just after lunch on the first day, I had to return to Lucknow on summons from the chief minister. But a number of my friends on my invitation could use the spare suite. Today I would be happy to spend a fortnight there, but would the caretaker let me in through the door?

During my tenure as APC, a programme was devised in Uttar Pradesh to encourage milk production and usher in a 'white' revolution. A replication of the pioneering milk cooperative system introduced in Gujarat by Verghese Kurien, was tried out on a large scale in Uttar Pradesh, with some additional features to suit local conditions. The classic cooperative marketing structure was supplemented with a government run programme for introduction of animal husbandry methods and investment in milk collection and chilling and processing centres. A large programme to upgrade the milch cattle through artificial insemination centres and cross-breeding was undertaken. In several rural pockets, cows yielding one to two kg of milk per day were upgraded, in two or three generations to yield twenty to twenty-five kg per day. When I visited these areas years later, the success was palpable; and one could clearly see the enthusiasm and the energy of the participants. It was evident that the mood of a whole village or an area could be transformed within a few years.

Canals had become a popular mode for providing irrigation in UP even in areas more suited to private pump-set irrigation. This arose partly due to the lack of a unified approach and partly due to vested interests. As APC I tried unsuccessfully to integrate the major and minor irrigation systems in the state, to bring them under a unified command structure. I failed because of the strong vested interests to retain major canal irrigation as a separate department, unconnected to agriculture. The state is blessed with large resources of underground water, arising from the multitude of perennial rivers originating in the Himalayas, flowing through the plains. The Gangetic plain gradually slopes downwards from UP's western border near Delhi, to its eastern border near Bihar. Thus, the water table is relatively low on the western side, but in central and east Uttar Pradesh, the water table is quite high. In the east, water can be struck at less than ten feet depth. While canals are relatively more useful in the west, the central and eastern areas are ideally suited for lift irrigation, through small agricultural field pumps. A drawback of the canal system is that there is considerable seepage of water, which distorts the aquifers and leads to patches of sodic land, through a process of osmosis and evaporation, rendering the land uncultivable. The process of reclaiming sodic land and bringing it back to cultivation is an expensive one, involving heavy use of chemicals and a large dose of watering.

As a result of the excessive reliance on canals, especially in central and east UP, large tracts of hitherto cultivable land have been laid waste, with the canal systems doing violence to the underground water patterns. I have, on more than one occasion gone on low flying helicopters and airplane rides, to follow the routes of canals, and to link these with the ongoing process of land being rendered waste. It is not difficult to understand the reason for this wrong choice. The construction and maintenance of canals was a lucrative proposition. Money finds its own level I found, as easily as does water.

I took several other initiatives. Sunflower cultivation was taken up on a large scale in many parts of the state and steps were taken to promote horticulture. A successful programme for cultivation of tomatoes and green vegetables in Ghazipur district, and new citrus plantations in Jhansi, are just two examples. As described earlier, the system for payment of subsidies was full of leakages, and I did my bit for revamping the system. Time and again, I had noticed a gap between research and the farmer, and in this post I had the opportunity to pilot a mechanism for coordination between agriculture universities to get their research projects in line with field needs. There were several employment-generation and other rural development schemes that I worked on, with an aim to improve the implementation. I also took the lead to encourage NGOs enter the rural sector for delivery of programmes and also for distribution of farm inputs, in direct competition with government agencies. There were some successes, each with their own moments of satisfaction.

Alas, this tenure of only sixteen months was brief. If I had been given an opportunity to continue in that assignment for the next ten years even without any promotion, I would have gladly accepted it and taken up the work as a mission. The results achieved in my tenure led me to believe that miracles are still possible in India and a turnaround can take place in a relatively short term. If carefully selected officers are placed for a minimum of five years' tenure in such key positions, and given the powers of a CEO with no interference, we can expect miracles to take place. This is what Kurien had shown with the milk cooperatives in Anand. But the present organisation of politics in the rural areas and the vested interests of politicians will come in the way of even miracles that can happen.

I had developed the practice of making at least two field visits every week, for a general inspection of all the programmes and one targeted review of a specific programme, at different points all over the state. Roughly half of these visits were with advance notice, to enable adequate local preparations; and others were surprise visits. Usually these were brief visits, covering half a day or at the most one day. The travels were undertaken by air, train or road or a combination of these. With these trips, I became familiar with all parts of this very large state, and visited practically all the sixty-one districts at least once. I heard the other day that the number of districts has gone up to eighty-nine and now that is progress for you!

During my earlier assignment in Geneva, I would come across a regular stream of visitors from India, come to attend one or the other event at the UN. Thus, one was not short of information and gossip about administrative conditions prevailing in India. The officers from India whom

I met were a disappointment. They were from a later crop of entrants, and had grown in seniority with their years of service. It seemed to me that there was a precipitous decline in standards. I also felt that the norms in respect of probity and efficiency had significantly declined as compared with previous times. This was the impression I carried, when I returned to India in 1990.

Later that year, during my field tours of Uttar Pradesh, I found that the assessment I had made in Geneva was completely incorrect. Contrary to the impression I had formed, most of the young officers I met were not mediocre at all. They were of high calibre, bright and enthusiastic, and totally committed. They were knowledgeable and upright, with the ability to stand up to local pressures. I would meet a large number of officers from different departments, especially those belonging to the IAS and the PCS. Many of the district magistrates and most of the chief development officers were bright youngsters from the IAS.

I had to reconcile this curious difference as to how bright and dedicated young officers, could after some years be seen as sub-standard. There can be only one explanation. When the same talented officers I saw on the field, reached headquarters at Lucknow or Delhi they became transformed into supine pen-pushers, losing their enthusiasm and élan, and forgetting that they had a mission to accomplish. The Union Public Service Commission (UPSC) continues to do a creditable job in finding the right youngsters, but the administrative milieu is able to soon transform talented idealists into petty, self-seeking babus. The system is able to bludgeon them into a state of apathy, if not callousness.

Soon after my return from Geneva, I participated in the first 'Service Week' in my home cadre after being away for about twelve years on assignments in Delhi and Geneva. The Service week, which actually lasts for three days is an annual event held at Lucknow. The tradition, which is peculiar to the UP cadre, is that all members of the IAS currently posted in the state get together over an extended weekend. Conferences are scheduled in the various departments, thus enabling the field officers to assemble at Lucknow. A service dinner is organised, at which it is mandatory for the junior as well as the senior most officer in service to make a speech. Other events include a cricket match and a reception for the chiefs of other civil services and invitees. There is usually an internal meeting of service members to discuss service matters followed by an invitation to the chief minister of the day to address the service members. The chief minister hosts a lunch and usually the governor hosts a dinner, at which there is a skit when the junior officers take the opportunity to make a dig at some of the more senior members of the service, including the chief secretary. All in all, it is an excellent occasion to get to know one another.

That year, Mulayam Singh as the chief minister was the chief guest and he addressed the 200-odd IAS officers who had gathered at the meeting. What he had to say made me sit up indeed. He spoke on these lines: "You all have such excellent minds and education; some of you are scholars; some of you have Nobel-prize minds; you will all succeed in any walk of life, wherever you turn your attention to; you have good jobs; you can educate your children well; and you are all respected by society; – (and then, the clincher, raising his voice) – *Why do you come and touch my feet? Why do you come and lick my shoes? Why do you come to me for personal favours? When you do so, I will do as you desire and then extract my price from you.*" It was an amazing statement because it succinctly summed up the situation and pin-pointed the reason for the collapse of the steel frame!

13 NEW DELHI: UNION MINISTRY OF TEXTILES

The Maharashtra government's cotton procurement scheme is the closest one can get to the absurdity perpetrated by Milo Minderbinder in Catch 22. *The state arranges for the purchase of the entire annual crop. It is a policy where the cotton is purchased dear and sold cheap.*

One would expect that the evaluation mission would try to pick holes in the project implementation leaving the executing agency to defend itself. Here the roles were reversed and the evaluation mission was defending the project. Naturally, the World Bank was keen to show that the silk project was a success. By definition, no project it funded could be a failure.

I WORKED AS SECRETARY IN THE MINISTRY OF textiles in two different spells, the first one for six months in 1992, and then again for nearly two years between 1994-1996. The textile sector is the largest segment of economic activity in the country after agriculture. Its importance can be seen in terms of contribution to GDP, employment creation, and exports. The largest industrial segment in India, as well as its largest export product, textiles directly or indirectly employ some fifty million people in India. Till the 1970s, the ministry was part of the commerce ministry; but then it was carved out as a separate department.

I had thought that the ministry would be engaged in promoting the growth of the industry, but discovered soon enough that preoccupation was with the nursing of the sick state owned units coming under the purview of the ministry. The affairs of the NTC occupied centre-stage. The corporation had eight subsidiaries on regional basis, each covering some ten or twelve textile mills. The corporation was in financial distress. But for the operations in Tamil Nadu and Karnataka, all the others had exhausted their credit limits and had no chance of raising the funds required for operations from the market.

During my first stint in 1992, I commissioned a survey of all the textile mills, and following this a restructuring plan was prepared. This provided for the closure of around twenty unviable mills, and revival of the others with an investment for modernisation of about Rs.500 crores. The key element of the package was to halve the staff strength from the then existing 190,000 to around 95,000 workers. An attractive Voluntary Retirement Scheme (VRS) was drawn up which provided for a golden handshake on terms superior to those which would have been provided through compulsory retrenchment. I had discussions with all concerned financial agencies and got a commitment from the government for provision of funds to pay off the workmen. The programme was launched with the whole-hearted support of Textile Minister Ashok Gehlot. Initially, the workers were somewhat reluctant to accept the package that was offered. After all, why should anyone leave with a golden handshake, when he can sit it out till the end of his career on a feather bed? A carrot and stick policy was adopted. A message was sent down the line that in those units not falling in line by a scheduled date, there would be compulsory retrenchment. The management of the corporation was also brought to heel and tight time schedules were handed over. Once it became clear that the top management was serious, the scheme started to work in a trickle to start with, and then soon gathered much pace. Savvy local mill managers helped in the process by eliciting cooperation of the local union leaders in the concerned mills. These leaders were offered a 'labour welfare payment' of an additional Rs. 2000 per worker who signed on. This incentive was at the disposal of the labour leader ostensibly for the welfare of the employee, and acted as a catalyst in triggering the large-scale utilisation of the VRS. The whole programme started in 1992 around September and by end

November, the 40,000 mark had been reached. We were hopeful that by January 1993, the slimming process would have been completed. And then the recovery process of the NTC could start. Final negotiations had begun with some financing agencies and banks. When they saw the earnestness with which the scheme was proceeding, signals came in that the money for the modernisation would be forthcoming. But then events took their own course.

Early in December 1992, I was suddenly asked to return to Uttar Pradesh to take over as chief secretary, two days after the demolition of the Babri Masjid. Soon after, the minister Ashok Gehlot left the ministry. The new minister who took over was G Venkataswamy, a politician who fancied that his political base was founded on his backing for the interests of labour. The day he took charge as minister for textiles, even before he could set foot in the ministry to understand the state of affairs, he met the press. He made a categorical statement that he was a labour leader, he understood the labour perspectives and therefore not one single worker would be retrenched. This statement was given publicity on television that night and was carried prominently in all the newspapers. All pending applications for voluntary retirement were immediately withdrawn in all the mills. Why should anyone leave after all when there is no threat of retrenchment? The process came to a grinding halt. The banks terminated negotiations. We were back to square-one. That one statement by the minister saw the end of the carefully drawn up restructuring process.

In 1994, I again came back to the textile ministry when Venkataswamy was still continuing as textile minister. By that time, the textile corporation had sunk into a coma and had to be given regular monthly cash injections from the government to meet expenses. There was a need again for a restructuring process. A committee of experts was appointed to assess the new situation. By this time, the proposed rescue package had, naturally, grown in size. Now the experts recommended that at least 60 of the 110 mills had become terminally ill and had to be closed down and fresh funds to the tune of about Rs.3,000 crores had to be injected. This was the escalated cost of the failure to go through with the earlier package, a lot of money for one statement made by a minister. There was a definite possibility that if no action were taken soon, nearly all the mills would have become irreversibly sick. In every state, I had negotiated a deal that we would keep alive one or two units, while closing the others and providing compensation to the workers who stepped down. A programme was prepared and I was anxious to commence with the first phase of the revival process, by closure of some fifty unviable units and payment of voluntary retirement compensation to the affected employees.

The mills were sitting on valuable real estate, particularly in Bombay city where some nine mills were located in prime locations. Venkataswamy felt that the funds for the revival package could be raised by sale of the mill properties. This was not in theory infeasible, since the land was the property of the government, and under its control. But the idea bristled with practical problems – whether the state government would permit the sale of such valuable property and whether they would allow the proceeds from that sale to be ploughed back for resurrection of units located in other states. Besides, the transactions relating to sale of land were sensitive and cumbersome. Those who actually handled the process had to tackle land mafias in Bombay, and were vulnerable to allegations and investigations.

We held a series of discussions with the concerned authorities in each state that had sick mills. They came to see that it was futile to keep pumping money into idle units and pay out salaries to the workers month after month. The sick units were a drain on the better off units. Rather than ploughing the money back for running the healthy mills, the surplus funds were diverted to sick units. I recall having discussions on the issue with the leaders from West Bengal including Gurudas Das Gupta and Somnath Chatterjee. I tried persuading them not to make too much noise if some of the units in West Bengal were closed down so long as one unit of their choice was kept alive. The logic of the proposal appealed to them and they agreed that the government would do what had to be done. I thought I had their cooperation. Of course, they would have to raise the matter in parliament, with the implication that they would make only proforma protests, not the virulent kind. The matter was brought to the final stage of consideration and all ministries had agreed.

I was astonished that at a meeting at the very last stage, the then finance minister refused to give concurrence for the closures. This came as a surprise since he was a known champion of reforms. And now, he would rather agree to continue the monthly dole for meeting the payroll. There was a hint that this had to do with the next elections. Whatever the reason, the textile corporation continued to proceed irreversibly on a downhill path. Some years later when I was Cabinet secretary, I heard that the latest proposal was to close down 90 of the 110 units. A far cry from the twenty sick units we had identified for closure in 1992! Such a needless situation could be reached since taxpayers are generous indeed, forking out some Rs 700 crores each year to pay wages to idle labour.

Under the ministry's purview was also the National Jute Manufactures Corporation, managing a number of sick jute mills in the eastern part of India. The story of jute mills in Calcutta was not much different from that of textiles. Now and then, one reads in the papers about one or the other of these mills being privatised or sold or closed down, but the easiest course of action remains to indefinitely foot the wage bill of the idle workers.

The ministry had also the privilege of being the sole shareholder of another jewel, the Jute Corporation of India. This corporation was supposed to manage the 'support price' operations for jute. This meant that on the years when the price of jute in the market fell below the minimum price established by Government of India for the year, particularly at the time of the jute harvesting season, the company would step in as buyer. In theory, the corporation was supposed to cater to the market on commercially viable terms by purchase of jute from the farmers at the support price. It would hold the jute in its warehouses and sell when the market prices went up later in the season. The Cotton Corporation of India did much the same kind of operations, but did it well and generally managed its affairs those days with a profit, because of the sound management provided by its chief executive, M B Lal. On the other hand, the jute corporation was saddled with a huge number of employees, who were exercised with work only for a couple of months during the harvesting season, and that too only during the years when the market price of raw-jute fell below the support price. The rest of the time, this massive work force sat twiddling its thumbs. Though the support operations were necessary and had to be performed by the state, this work ought to have been organised much better, using commission agents for purchase, renting storage where necessary, with a minimal staff of around 400 persons, not 4000 as was the case. The bloated staff ensured that the corporation was doomed to failure right from the beginning.

The massive initial recruitment was the largesse of ministers who had earlier held the commerce portfolio in the Government of India, and who had interest in Bengal politics. With short-sight, they thought that by providing rural employment on a large scale in the jute corporation, they could buy the political loyalty of the employees. This would help create a local cadre of political workers for the future. In the event, these idling staff had no loyalty to their original patrons, and were more aligned to their current rulers, particularly given the complexion of the state politics. This comment is not confined to the Jute Corporation of India. The same happens practically in every public sector agency in one state or other. Such massive political recruitments are irreversible and deal a body blow to the viability of the public sector agencies, and can be counted as one of the prime reasons for the resultant non-viability of public sector units.

It is in this context that we may see the urge of the government to 'disinvest', and the ongoing debate on the disinvestment policy of the government. The current debate is mainly about raising resources by selling out the profitable agencies, especially to meet the government's rising, infructuous, administrative expenditures. I have not recently seen any debate regarding how to handle the sick units. I presume there is now a political consensus to continue massive injection of funds by the Government of India, year after year, to pay the salaries and keep afloat a large number of public sector units, which have no chance of revival. Perhaps an economist somewhere had found a Keynesian reason to buttress this consensus, and could justify that keeping employees on dole is good for the revival of the economy.

Despite the importance of the textile sector to the national economy, the annual budget of the textile ministry was only about Rs.900 crores, itself a small figure. And of this, Rs.750 crores was spent annually on meeting the payroll deficits of the NTC and the National Jute Manufacture Corporation and protecting the interest of its workers. The balance, a princely sum of Rs.150 crores was available every year for other purposes including the promotion and development of the industry. This is an indication of our priorities and the way the system functions. In a labour-intensive sector, which could generate millions of additional jobs annually, seed money available was a pittance, and five times that amount was spent to keep government employees idling! Suitable strategic investment by government in the textile infrastructure, testing facilities, marketing and technology assistance could have generated hundreds of times more new employment than those protected through the injection of funds to the public sector units – not to mention taking Indian textiles to world class. How much more absurd can public policy be?

The textile industry also suffered due to erratic policies on raw materials. Cotton itself, a basic raw material, came under the purview of the agriculture ministry. As we saw in another context, the main role played by this ministry was to compile statistics and publish data; on the convenient plea that agriculture was a state subject. The states in turn of course, took the convenient position that agriculture was the private business of the farmer, and so nothing substantial could be done about it. This left the poor farmer to his own devices. So it should come as no surprise that the productivity of cotton in India is among the lowest in the world, on an average about one-fifth of the American yield per hectare. With focused effort, there is no reason why the quality of cotton, as well as the yield cannot increase dramatically. The agriculture ministry had sponsored a large number of research projects for creating new varieties of cotton suitable for different agro climatic conditions. The researchers were keen to get new varieties released every year. As a result, small farmers would be confused, with multiple varieties of cotton competing for their attention at any given time.

There was little coordination between agriculture and research, with the farmers and the researchers living in their own separate worlds. Thus, different varieties were sown in contiguous areas in relatively small farms. This resulted in a genetic mix-up, emaciating the virility of successive generations. To compound the problem, neither cotton cultivation nor agricultural research had any relationship whatsoever with the user of cotton, that is the spinning mills. Again the different ministries would guard their turf fiercely. The segment of the agriculture ministry, which considered itself the sole authority on agricultural research matters, would not allow the textile industry to make any kind of demands on cotton agriculture. We may contrast this situation with the American Cotton Council, a trade body, which has representation from cotton agriculturists, spinners and weavers: such interrelationship results in the overall benefit of the textile sector. Sounds obvious, but not so easy to achieve.

In India, the different segments of the textile sector could not really be said to be at loggerheads, since they were not even on talking terms! As textile secretary, I had mooted the idea of a cotton textile mission, to increase productivity and link agriculture with industry's needs. A mission has since been established. However, consistent with our traditions, the turf interests of various ministries prevailed over good sense. The mission was split into two separate parts: one coordinated by the agriculture ministry and the other by the textile ministry. Rarely did they meet. The cotton ginning industry was also a similar casualty: all energy was expended on the question of whether cotton ginning was a textile activity or part of the industry ministry. Quite typical, that we tackle policy issues with the interests of the competing government departments prevailing at the cost of all other participants.

The other major raw material for the textile industry is polyester. All over the world, the average ratio of cotton to polyester in the composition of textiles is of the order of forty to sixty. Synthetics form the main raw material and cotton is the additive. As could be expected from our policy regime, the situation has been the reverse in India. In the late 1990s, the cotton to polyester ratio was about seventy to thirty though this might have changed slightly since then. In India, polyester has been treated as a rare substance, to be made available to the public at a premium. This was ensured by a carefully constructed excise cum import duty structure, designed to protect the interests of a few polyester manufacturers – in fact, probably only one major player. All over the world, polyester is the cheap raw material, and cotton the luxury item. The reverse applied in India. The larger political interest of protecting one polyester manufacturer was supreme, at great cost to the manufacturers of synthetic textiles and the end consumers. This is a bit surprising since it is the widespread cotton farming lobby which should have attracted political support to keep the return to cotton farmers high relative to polyester.

It has not been by chance that in every major economic policy measure taken in India, the main objective has been to protect the commercial interests of a few manufacturers of the basic inputs, at the cost of a large number of processors and converters. Ultimately, it is the consumer, the ordinary Indian citizen who pays. Whereas in a democracy, the citizen ought to be the cornerstone of every major decision, every thing in India is done in his name, while lining the pockets of a few primary manufacturers, who have a quid pro-quo relationship with policy makers. In a country with a large number of nimble-footed small entrepreneurs, people blessed with great skills, we find a consistent pattern of raw materials and basic inputs being priced high, knocking out the potential for efficient processing, and rendering uneconomic the manufacture of a competitive, quality end product. Then we lament that Indian products are uncompetitive in world markets, in terms of quality and price. All this is no accident but the result of carefully conceived policy conspiracies.

It is thus that polyester and synthetics were treated as luxury items in India. One can still recall the craze for polyester based textiles that used to come to India from Dubai, and through the Nepal border. The controls over the polyester sector, including the price and duty structure for these raw materials, were again not with the textile ministry – they were vested in yet another department. The excise and import duty structure for textile products was under the finance ministry. The finances at the disposal of the textile ministry were limited. With all this, the role of the ministry was quite circumscribed. Typical of government, with the levers of control vested elsewhere, and the responsibility for performance with the ministry.

Within the textile sector itself, leave aside cotton ginning, there was a fragmented view. The spinning, weaving, processing and garmenting activities were seen as distinct compartments. Their sequential relationship and compatibility of interests were generally not recognised. In fact, there was a conflict of interest in the interfaces between these components. Thus, separate policies were devised for the spinning sector, the handloom and power-loom segments and for the processing sector, as well as for garments. The total picture was not kept in view. Opportunities for populist measures in this field abounded, with ad hoc assistance provided to one segment, negating the benefits conferred to another. Excise loopholes, only now being plugged, were at that time deliberately created to benefit the power-loom sector and the processors. This made the duty structure unbalanced. The primary focus of the weaving activity was to evade government duties, not to improve quality or inject new technology. The infamous hank-yarn exemption, ostensibly designed as a populist measure to help the handloom sector, was in fact meant to divert duty free yarn to the power-loom sector. These policy loopholes led to rapid growth of *benami* fly-by-night power-looms. In fact, the origins of the Reliance empire stemmed from a power-loom base.

The handloom and hand processing traditions in India have an astonishing variety, and enduring beauty. However, the sad truth is that handloom is a dying segment. There is no way that a handloom can compete with a power-loom for meeting the ordinary needs of clothing the nation – it is like the horse drawn stage coach competing with the steam engine or the motor car. Everyday sarees and dhotis are more cheaply woven on power-looms and not handlooms. This inherent weakness of handlooms cannot be covered by doles and subsidies. The strength of handloom lies in its resplendent beauty. It is this that should form the basis for a strategy. The old adage that give man fish, you give him one day's meal; teach a man to fish, you give him a meal everyday, holds true in the case of handlooms. The need was to identify specific handloom areas with special features, and unique weaving styles, and encourage them to manufacture quality products to meet demand in niche markets. Unfortunately, the actual policy followed was to provide subsidy sops to the handloom sector, while clandestinely encouraging the power-loom sector, through deliberate duty evasion opportunities.

In Joseph Heller's *Catch-22*, an enterprising trader buys up the entire Egyptian cotton crop, with hilarious consequences. I never imagined that I would live to see a similar situation in real life. The Maharashtra government's monopoly cotton procurement scheme is the closest one can get to Milo Minderbinder's absurdity. Maharashtra is the largest producer of cotton in the country. The state government, as a policy and by law, arranges for the purchase of the entire annual crop, produced in Maharashtra. One can imagine the leakages and the lining of pockets by the officials and functionaries at all levels, with enormous opportunities for false weighments, payment at higher slab rates for lower quality and siphoning of stocks. Further, I have seen the appalling storage conditions in many warehouses with the cotton exposed to dust, rain and contamination. Successive governments in Maharashtra of different political colour, either cannot or will not walk out of the scheme; despite the heavy economic and financial loss to the state through a policy where the produce is purchased dear and sold cheap. The system is ostensibly meant to meet the needs of farmers, who are paid for their produce but in fact, the main purpose is presumably to grease the political hierarchy. Where is the incentive to produce higher quality – when the lowest quality will elicit premium prices? State governments, whatever the political colour, are unable to retract from such a catastrophic policy that drains their finances. So, they provide free or heavily subsidised tariffs for power to the farming sector. Urea prices are enhanced in every central budget announcement with reduction in the subsidy, and then rolled back. Examples galore can be found of absurd policy measures, entered into in a frenzy of populism from which successive governments cannot resile.

Similar issues came up in the silk industry as well. I recall the visit of a team of experts to evaluate the implementation of a World Bank project for development of the silk industry in India. The project was nearing conclusion after six years from start. The purpose of the review was to sum up the benefits of the Rs.600 crores or so that had been spent. The project had started well before I joined the ministry. But I had a feel for what was going on. In the course of my travels, I had made it a point to visit some of the centres covered under the project. I chaired the review meeting. One would normally expect that the ministry, being the executing agency, would defend the implementation and claim success, while the evaluation team would try to pick holes in the implementation of the project. Here the roles were reversed and the evaluation mission was defending the project.

I blasted the implementation of the project, noting that while six hundred crores of rupees had been spent, no ongoing benefits to the silk industry in India were in sight. There was not even a spin-off benefit for the Indian economy. The objective was to upgrade the Indian silk industry, in its totality. In reality, the project had been converted into a silkworm research programme, with hardly any linkages with the downstream silk industry. Nearly all the money had been spent on silkworm research. The aim was to develop new varieties of silkworm, suitable for different climatic conditions in different parts of India. Much as the agricultural institutes fiercely generate an endless number of new crop varieties every year; the silkworm institute had generated innumerable new varieties through endless research. The project team had not thought of the further steps in the chain. The focus was on one component, and the objectives of the project had been forgotten. The need in fact was for the silkworms to be commercially reared, the silk reeled, processed and dyed, and then taken up for weaving. And finally, marketing structures had to be created. That the silkworms were to be reared for processing marketable silk was lost sight of. The net result was there were no takers for commercial rearing of the new varieties of silkworms.

I have, in general, held a liberal view in freely making available imported raw materials to encourage value-addition in domestic processing. Silk was one area where I felt that an exception had to be made, in view of the large employment potential in the rearing and reeling sectors. So, from a policy perspective I had taken the position when in the commerce ministry, that the import of raw silk should be carefully regulated. In the event, the failure of the project to see beyond its research nose meant that the linkages were not established, despite heavy expenditure. Not only that, an army of young scientists had been recruited for the silkworm research, whose salaries would be a charge on the central exchequer long after the project's closure. All they would do is to merrily continue to create new silkworm varieties for the next thirty years until they retired. The same malaise has been observed in the context of the CLRI, as well as the agricultural research institutes. Government sponsored research in India is unable to connect with the practical users of the research. It is evident that this is something of a national characteristic.

Naturally, the World Bank evaluation mission was keen to show that the Indian silk project was a success. By definition, no World Bank project can be shown to have been a failure. After all, the members of the evaluation mission would wish to be invited to the next mission in another country! I saw the same phenomenon in the ITC: to show that no mission by the ITC ever failed, and that each one was a success. After all, how can any activity by an international agency funded by western money ever be a failure?

When I was textile secretary, the National Institute of Fashion Technology (NIFT), had already been established. I became the chairman of this organisation in its formative years. Fortunately, it was then possible to insist on and locate talented persons at the chief executive level. They were given longish tenures. This resulted in the establishment of a first-rate institution that valued merit as the criterion. Raw new entrants were shaped into good designers. The alumni were in demand in India and abroad. Some even branched out on their own, some going on to become world-class designers. Excellent traditions were built up and a key reason for this was the close association with the textiles and garment sectors. This helped retain relevance and realism in the curriculum. The entrance to the institute, originally located in Delhi, was on merit basis through competition. I then worked for a limited expansion of NIFT in four additional centers in India, retaining the system of merit-based admissions on the pattern of admission tests to the IITs and IIMs.

In the initial stages, we had to withstand political pressure. I recall a clash with my minister, who wanted a small admission quota to be reserved for the ministry. I flatly refused as this would be the thin end of the wedge. The minister insisted, saying that he was under pressure from his colleagues in other ministries. He said that the textile ministry seeks many favours from other ministries and so it had to reciprocate. He also felt the need to have some avenues for obliging senior ministers and bureaucrats. He even offered a quota to the chairman, to buy his support. I adamantly refused saying that any dilution would open the floodgates and the reputation built up so far would soon vanish. He then called in the executive director of the institute separately and asked him that the admission procedures provide for a small discretionary quota. P K Laheri, to his credit, told the minister that the faculty consisted of proud and motivated people. Any intervention in the admission process would mean that practically the entire faculty would resign. It is not easy to build a quality institution. It takes years of hard work by a group of dedicated and motivated people, with the ability to resist political pressures. Alas, years of hard work can be destroyed rapidly, one weak chief executive or chairman or an interfering minister can nullify years of hard work within a short period of time.

The Crafts Museum in Delhi, which comes under the textile ministry is not such a well known place but well worth a visit. It is a treasure house of Indian handicraft and Indian textile tradition. I recall that when Hillary Clinton visited Delhi, she had scheduled a half-an-hour morning visit to the museum. She found it so fascinating, that she cancelled all her engagements for the day, and was there till late evening. Jyotindra Jain was the dedicated curator of that museum, who showed great acumen and passion in collecting and maintaining the exhibits. I learnt later with no surprise, that he had left. The system cannot for long tolerate dedicated people with ideas.

I worked with four ministers during that period. I have referred to Gehlot, whom I found to be an upright politician with keen interest in doing the right thing. He subsequently became chief minister of Rajasthan. G Venkataswamy, an old Congressman from Andhra Pradesh, was full of old-world charm. Kamal Nath represented the new breed of active political leaders. And finally, Jalappa, from Karnataka was a fine gentleman, with whom I worked for a few days, before I moved on as Cabinet secretary.

Nearly every village in India has a textile tradition. One could see the linkages between our textiles, unique in their variety and our rich cultural and religious tradition. It was indeed a very happy and enjoyable period that I spent in the ministry.

14 PRESIDENT'S RULE IN UTTAR PRADESH: CHIEF SECRETARY AFTER BABRI MASJID

When his staff discovered that they had forgotten to pack his pyjamas, they found it easier for the plane to make a trip to Lucknow and back to fetch the pyjamas. It worked out cheaper than visiting the nearby market in Delhi.

By declaring drought wherever he went, without a formal declaration by the state government, the governor had placed the government in an anomalous position. Amidst all this confusion, the heavens opened up with incessant rains pouring down all over the state.

THE BABRI MASJID WAS DEMOLISHED ON 6 December 1992. At that time, I was working as textile secretary in the Government of India and did not imagine that December would turn out to be such a hectic month for me. Two days later, on the 8th, at around 8 pm, I got a call from the principal secretary to the prime minister, asking about my convenience to go to Lucknow, and take over as chief secretary of Uttar Pradesh. I told him that I had just come from UP and would prefer to stay on in Delhi. A N Varma replied that he was not asking me; he was telling me that I was to go to Lucknow. At 8 am the next morning, the Border Security Force (BSF) plane would be ready at Delhi airport and I should take charge at 9 am immediately on arrival.

On December 6th itself President's Rule had been promulgated by the Congress led Union government. The BJP led state government was removed. Article 356 of the Constitution was invoked. The state of Uttar Pradesh came under the direct administration of the Centre in Delhi. The state's chief secretary, director general of police, as well as the commissioner and the district magistrate of Faizabad division had all been asked to vacate their posts. Satya Narayana Reddy was the governor of UP at that time.

In the aftermath of the demolition of Babri Masjid, which was located at Ayodhya in Faizabad Division, riots had broken out in a number of districts in the state, and conditions were still highly unsettled. In early December, killings of Hindus in Muslim areas and Muslims in Hindu localities were continuing in at least twelve districts. And of these, in at least five districts the riot situation was in an acute phase.

My first task was to meet the new director general of police and the home department officials, to review the situation. I then telephoned all the commissioners and the district magistrates of the disturbed districts to ascertain the position. That afternoon, I called and spoke to the district magistrates and superintendents of police, in the towns where rioting was continuing. I gave them my instructions. The situation must be brought under control within twenty-four hours. All politicians in their districts were to be totally ignored, be they from the Congress, BJP or Samajwadi parties. They were not to differentiate between Hindus and Muslims. I gave a free hand to the district administration to do what they wanted and assured them of full support. But the killings must stop and peace must return instantly. Complete peace was quickly restored. All concerned put in dedicated and vigorous efforts to make this happen. Prakash Singh, director general of police, a very competent officer had an exemplary role to play. Though the official number as reported was only about 190, the final death toll in the aftermath was probably closer to 450. I believe that if prompt and effective measures had not been taken at that time, the disturbances could have escalated and would have spread to other states. Indeed, it could have been worse than what was to come in the Gujarat riots of 2002.

I recall that two days after I took over as chief secretary, Governor Reddy telephoned me at around 9 pm and he gave me a list of changes to be made in several senior positions, including home secretary, finance secretary, planning secretary, and some others. He directed that the orders should be issued the same night. The 'directions' had come from Jitendra Prasad in the PMO and of course, he in turn had got them cleared from the prime minister himself, for immediate implementation. I told the governor that I could meet him the next morning to discuss the matter. However, he insisted that the orders be issued the same night. I then told him point blank that no orders would be issued that night. If any were to be issued, he would first have to issue my transfer orders from the post of chief secretary, and then do whatever he desired.

I called on the governor early the next morning. He was quite upset by my intransigence. I told him that he was responsible for the administration of Uttar Pradesh and that he should not allow anybody to dictate terms by remote control from Delhi: that would leave the governor and the chief secretary holding the sack when something went wrong. In any case, this remote control needed checking out. I went to Delhi the following week and called on Prime Minister Narsimha Rao. I asked him whether indeed he had approved lists of various officers for the different posts in Uttar Pradesh. As anticipated, he knew nothing about any postings in the state. I told the prime minister that a number of people were invoking his name and trying to meddle in the state's affairs. As a seasoned politician, he immediately understood. On being asked, he readily gave me the mandate for a free hand to run the administration in Uttar Pradesh. If anything went wrong, he would surely blame me; but at least I got enough indication that all the busybodies who were meddling in the state's affairs could be shown their place.

The Union Home Minister, S B Chavan and his central team visited Lucknow to review the law and order situation. The highly publicised meeting was held in the governor's house. Chavan expounded on the havoc wrought by the Sangh Parivar and the BJP led Kalyan Singh administration, and asked for the governor's report on the events leading to the demolition of the Babri Masjid. The governor promised such a report, and indicated that it would be prepared within a fortnight. I intervened to say that the home ministry officials had taken the relevant documents away on 7th December itself. Moreover, the Liberhan Commission had already been established by the Government of India to look into the matter of the demolition of the Babri Masjid. We could await this report first. I sensed that all the home minister wanted was a report emanating from the state administration blaming the Kalyan Singh government for the Babri Masjid demolition for political use by the Centre. I expounded, perhaps needlessly and gratuitously, that Uttar Pradesh has nearly 100,000 villages, where Hindus and Muslims have lived amicably for hundreds of years. After the healing of the trauma and wounds of Partition, the recent Hindu-Muslim animosity was a creation of the past few decades purely for electoral purposes. All political parties in India were guilty of fomenting a divide between Hindus and Muslims to garner electoral advantage. The home minister was livid. That is how I earned the displeasure of the home minister who was unhappy with me through his full tenure as minister. Much later, he showed his petulance. By then, peace and normalcy had been restored. But, on the grounds that the situation in Uttar Pradesh was volatile, he refused to give me permission to attend a seminar overseas sponsored by the ITC. The chief secretary could not be spared even for one day, not to mention one week!

In India, commissions of enquiry obfuscate more than they reveal, and they go on and on without any end in sight. The Liberhan Commission to enquire into the demolition of Babri Masjid was appointed in the first week of January 1993 with a mandate to give its findings within two months. It was to commence hearings immediately. When Justice Liberhan visited Lucknow for a day, he told me of the great urgency of commencing hearings as the whole nation was waiting with bated breath for the pronouncements by the commission on the Babri Masjid demolition. I promised him all support. The secretary of the commission, an IAS officer of the Union Territories Cadre called on me to discuss alternate venues for holding the commission's hearing. Every venue I proposed was rejected on grounds of security. The commission's secretary said that so much responsibility had been vested in the commission and tempers ran so high, that the safety of the commission and the security of its work could not be assured unless a proper place for the hearings was established. The commissioner's courtroom, then a wing in the high court complex, and further a whole building of the cooperative department in an isolated location were all rejected. At one stage, I told the commission's secretary that the security of the commission was the job of the state government and I would personally ensure it. However, nothing was secure enough for the commission, at least in Lucknow. It appeared that the ejection of the governor from Raj Bhawan and holding of the hearings in the governor's office was the only safe location left in Uttar Pradesh! Even this might have been rejected on security grounds. In the event, the commission finally held its first hearing in New Delhi, at Vigyan Bhawan. Delhi was safer than Lucknow. As I write this, ten years later in 2003, the commission is still, doubtless with the same urgency conducting its hearings. And periodically, the government is pleased to extend the validity period of the commission. This goes on interminably, the cost borne by the public.

In civil societies, commissions of enquiry are used for quickly getting to the bottom of complex matters and coming out with the basic contours of the event that occurred, analyse its causal factors and propose medium term and long-term action. Commissions ought to be used for proposing and implementing correctives to the system. In India, commissions are used as a device to delay examination of a matter, to bury its basic contours in the sands of time, allow the main actors of a drama to fade away from the scene and ultimately to postpone the need for corrective action. Their use is to allow the parties to escape from the scene. Commissions are used cynically and precisely contrary to the ostensible purposes for which they are created. Any number of examples can be given. In the context of the Babri dispute, I recall the history of at least three commissions established by the Uttar Pradesh government, which delayed their recommendations interminably and were wound up, without producing a report. Much later as Cabinet secretary, I saw the functioning of the commission inquiring into the assassination, in 1991, of the former prime minister, Rajiv Gandhi. I could observe closely the various tactics and dilatory positions adopted by the commission, which finally published its report in the autumn of 1997.

Thus, the numerous commissions of enquiry which have gone into the causes of railway and other accidents usually have no bearing on systemic changes, but end up blaming some low level employee for carelessness. Every administrator uses the device of resorting to a commission of enquiry to postpone the need to do anything. It is even better if the enquiry is entrusted to a retired judge; one can forget the issues for the next decade or two.

During my career, I have been wary, perhaps overly so, of politicians rushing to trouble spots, as this incident will illustrate. Sometime in early January 1993, there was a minor incident in Aligarh town, a communally sensitive area. One night, a university student while walking inside the campus was accidentally run over by a truck and killed. The student was a Muslim and the truck driver happened to be a Hindu. In the communally charged atmosphere at that time, the news spread quickly in the town and a mob congregated in the night to protest the incident. The district magistrate reached the spot, some force was used to quell the riot and peace was restored. One person died in police firing. When the information reached me early the next morning, I convened a meeting of all concerned, and had a telephonic discussion with the district magistrate and the commissioner of the area. In the evening, we reviewed the situation and came to the conclusion that nothing further needed to be done. As parliament was in session at Delhi, we expected some echoes there. So, as a measure of abundant precaution and to defuse the situation, I also ordered an enquiry headed by a retired judge of the high court. We all thought the matter was closed.

The next morning around 8.30 am, the governor summoned me. He said that he had received a phone call from Rajesh Pilot, the minister of state for internal security in the home ministry at Delhi, who was at that time in Mussoorie. Pilot intended to reach Aligarh by helicopter around 10'o clock in the morning and he wanted the governor and me to join him there, so that we could make an on the spot study of the situation. The governor told me that the state plane was ready; could we leave in the next few minutes, to be in Aligarh in time to receive Pilot? I replied that in the light of recent events in the state and the communal riots which had taken place in Aligarh just the previous day, it was better that no political colour be given to the incident. A visit by the Union minister could become counterproductive. I told the governor that he might speak to the minister and suggest that the visit be postponed by three or four days. A visit that very day might aggravate the tension and could lead to new events. The governor appeared convinced, and asked his aide to connect him to Pilot at Mussoorie. Pilot came on the line. Imagine my surprise when the governor straightaway told the minister that the chief secretary wanted to speak to him and without ado handed over the phone to me. The conversation with Pilot started amicably with greetings and then proceeded as follows:

Minister: said he intended coming to Aligarh and could I meet him there.

Chief Secretary: had reviewed the Aligarh incident as late as 10 pm the previous night, the situation was peaceful, and under control and we should let the situation heal for three or four days before a ministerial visit.

Minister: insistent about his visit Aligarh: this would help him gather facts to make a *suo motto* statement in Parliament.

Chief Secretary: conveyed assurances that all relevant material for the statement, including materials for supplementary questions, would await him by the time he reached Delhi and that he need not go to Aligarh for that purpose – a judicial inquiry had been ordered and this would help defuse the discussion in Parliament.

Minister: still insistent on going to Aligarh

Chief Secretary: kept on demurring, satisfied that it would be a political visit, to meet local politicians, which would only exacerbate an already tense situation.

Minister: tone changed, as he said, "Mr.Chief Secretary, I am going to Aligarh now, and I am ordering you to come to Aligarh immediately to meet me there."

Chief Secretary: "I will take my orders only from my governor."

Minister: "Don't you realise that Uttar Pradesh is under President's Rule – under the control of Government of India; the Home Ministry is administering the central rule."

Chief Secretary: "Any orders from the Government of India may come to the state government formally and will be implemented; if it is a directive, it should be backed by a Cabinet decision."

Minister: by now livid – "I am going to Aligarh anyway whether you come or not."

Chief Secretary: "If you go there in your capacity as a Union minister, you will not be received; and the district magistrate will have instructions not to receive you, nor to give a police escort."

Minister: bangs the phone down.

There was silence in the governor's chambers, with his secretary and aides looking on in disbelief at this exchange. I have recounted the incident, as accurately as I could. In retrospect, I still feel I had taken the correct stand. I was afraid that any political intervention could irritate and exacerbate the delicate communal balance, and revive the riots. Aligarh was a highly sensitive town. The stakes were too high for any chances to be taken. Those were not ordinary times, and in the supercharged communal atmosphere in the state, any small irritant could have lit up a conflagration. Some may argue, probably rightly, that this was going too far. The Union minister for internal security after all had every right to visit a trouble spot, during President's Rule. The chief secretary having expressed his views, had done his duty, but he need not have stuck to his guns till the bitter end. But let the counter point be made: If riots had revived in Aligarh and spread to other parts of UP, who would have been blamed? Would it be the Central minister or the state administration? And, who would have to put the fire out again?

Be it as it may, if I was right or wrong, there is a larger point here. Politicians wish to visit trouble spots at the drop of a hat, when they are not needed nor even invited. This gives them media exposure and an apparent image of caring for the public in times of distress. If there is an earthquake or floods or other crises, prime ministers, chief ministers and ministers all rush to the spot. I think this is a harmful practice, in the immediate aftermath of a disaster. The urgent need is to mobilise immediate relief and coordinate the state and the central machinery. Local authorities should be allowed to concentrate on mobilising the resources. At the height of a crisis, a succession of VIP visits diverts the attention of local officials from relief work. It also puts local officials in a quandary. If the district magistrate concentrates on relief, the visiting VIP would feel slighted and he would draw adverse conclusions about the local machinery. If the district magistrate accompanies the visiting VIP and spends time with him, he may earn a good chit from the visitor but in fact, would be neglecting his duty towards the afflicted people. The correct time to visit is after a few days, when the immediate crisis is over. That is when an assessment can be made about the quality of immediate relief works.

I recall that when a typhoon hit the Miami coast in Florida, and there was heavy devastation, Vice President Al Gore wanted to fly down immediately to the spot and offer federal relief. The mayor of Miami refused permission to Gore to visit Miami, saying that he and his staff were fully engaged in disaster relief. The vice-president was welcome to pay a visit after four or five days. One also recalls the events of September 11 in New York, when Mayor Giuliani was handling the disaster relief. President Bush visited the site only after four or five days. Imagine a similar situation in India. The defence minister, George Fernandes would probably have visited the site five times by then. Over the years, we have come to give primacy to image over substance. This has become an unstated theme in our national governance. Urgent action lies in visits by leaders. It does not matter what advance or remedial action is actually taken on the ground.

During those troubled days, in January 1993, the English cricket team was due to visit India. As it happened, their first official match was scheduled at Lucknow. At a meeting to consider the request made for law and order arrangements at the match venue, the police authorities held the view that the attention of police personnel could not be diverted towards security for a mere cricket match and recommended that the match be cancelled. I overruled this view, and asked that full security protection be ensured for the match. This was not merely because I am an inveterate cricket fan. I believed that in the gloomy and communally tense post-Babri atmosphere the cricket match would be a diversion. It was a confidence building measure. Anyway, the match passed off peacefully. There was also a distinct change in the overall atmosphere in the state. Even the infamous Bombay riots in late January could not find an echo in Uttar Pradesh. I believe that this calm prevailed not only because tight precautions were in place. The immediate after-affects of Babri Masjid had been dissipated in the state by a number of measures that were taken, other than on the cricket grounds. The month following the Babri Masjid demolition we had a cricket fixture in Lucknow. Could this have been done in Ahmedabad after the riots?

During summer that year, Chandraswami planned to hold a major *yagna* in Ayodhya at a spot fairly close to the disputed site, where the Babri Masjid existed. The *yagna* was supposed to be for propitiating the gods and for bringing welfare and prosperity to mankind in general, and to the people of UP in particular. Some wags said that the *yagna* was for the benefit of just one person, the then Prime Minister Narasimha Rao. While ostensibly religious in nature, it was clearly a political gambit, a riposte to the Sangh Parivar to attract Hindu votes in the run-up to the elections which were to follow. Chandraswami's cohorts started preparations for the yagna. Chandraswami made helicopter trips all over India to recruit eminent *pundits* to conduct the *yagna*. It was said that three thousand priests would congregate at Ayodhya to appease the gods. When the information reached me, I had mentioned to the governor, Motilal Vora, who had by then replaced Reddy, that the administration could not allow any religious event to take place near the disputed area. But suddenly I was under pressure, not only to permit the *yagna* but to make law and order and the security arrangements for it. A number of politicians from Delhi telephoned, alternately in supplicating and threatening tones, asking me to permit the *yagna* at the identified spot. Even Chandraswami telephoned a couple of times, offering his benedictions, and enquiring as to why I had not come to meet him personally to receive his blessings. He hinted that my continuance as chief secretary was dependent on his goodwill.

Ayodhya at that time was an armed camp. We took the principled position that Ayodhya had been going through turmoil, lives had been lost, and damage had been done. It would be a blunder to allow any religious activity to take place in the immediate vicinity of the disputed area. There was a stormy meeting with the governor when V P Kapur, director general of police and Arvind Varma, the commissioner of the Faizabad Division were also present. Kapur, like Prakash Singh earlier, was a strong and clear-headed officer. Arvind Varma, soft spoken but strong and principled would not buckle down under threat – I was later to see him stand up and speak his mind to the Cabinet in his capacity as personnel secretary at the Centre. That day, in the Governor's Chambers, the three of us explained to him why it was imprudent and against all administrative canons to permit the *yagna* at the desired spot. Having barred entry to all citizens, it would be indefensible that we should permit there a large group of priests to chant *mantras*. I had suggested that another spot be chosen in Ayodhya, across the bridge on the river Sarayu, where we would provide the required support. The governor was adamant. He told us that he had approved the site and that formal orders of the state government may now be issued. I told the governor that I would then leave the post of chief secretary with immediate effect, and he could then talk to the next chief secretary and get whatever orders he wanted issued. Instantly, the director general of police and the commissioner of Faizabad Division announced that they would follow suit. The governor was dumbstruck. He had to withdraw his position and that was how the Chandraswami *yagna* was shifted out to a more distant location.

There was a similar incident when SAHMAT, the Safdar Hashmi Trust, wanted to hold an exhibition in Ayodhya during that troubled period. It was originally projected as a secular exhibition with no religious connotations. In the routine course of enquiry it turned out that the exhibition was, *inter-alia*, portraying the life of Lord Rama, as seen in the various versions of Ramayana, from different parts of India and from other countries. Among the versions portrayed was one that shows Rama and Sita as siblings and many other similar or more bizarre variants, alien to the standard versions in India composed by Valmiki or Tulsidas. While it could be argued that the exhibition merely described the various personalities and events in the Ramayana as depicted in different versions of the epic, I had felt that this was not the opportune time to raise the temperature at Ayodhya. Personally, I had no opinion on the *bona fides* of the exhibition or on the artistic merit of portrayal of the characters of Ramayana in different cultures. I felt though that such artistic works could first be exhibited in galleries in Delhi and Bombay or even in New York or Paris before coming to Ayodhya. Again pressure was exerted on me by the governor and by a number of political personalities to permit the exhibition to be held in Ayodhya. Arjun Singh spoke to me at least twice, asking me to permit the exhibition. I was not concerned about the likely objectives of the sponsors of the exhibition, even giving them the benefit of the doubt, that their motives were apolitical. I was concerned at the potential for flare up of communal tensions. The commissioner of Faizabad division had given an unequivocal written opinion that the exhibition at that juncture in Ayodhya could result in a flare up and renewal of tensions, with potential for resumption of riots. His opinion was that the exhibition should be banned. If the sponsors went to court to assert their right to hold their exhibition, the government should oppose the same firmly. It was thus that the proposed SAHMAT exhibition was called off. Without passing any judgement on the exhibition, I later heard with interest, that the exhibition had to be hastily and prematurely withdrawn after opening in a number of other centres, including one in Canada. Many Indian viewers had objected to it as in poor taste.

In April 1993, Motilal Vora, an old Congress warhorse was appointed as the new governor, replacing Satya Narayana Reddy. Apparently, in the judgment of the Centre, Reddy did not have it in him to swing the state in favour of the Congress. With elections due in a few months, there was a need for a politician with capacity to deliver the state to the Congress. By the current standards of Indian governance, the need during President's Rule is only for a politician who can deliver political results, not for a sound administrator. Governors, with role of neutral observers and impartial umpires under the Constitution are now required to play a partisan game. Vora was quite brazen in playing this role.

A politician of the old school, he started his innings quietly, even though the mandate that he was carrying – to deliver the state to the Congress – was apparent enough. He spent the first month familiarising himself with the large sprawling state and most of his trips out of Lucknow were to the sacred temples, that abound in Uttar Pradesh. On some of his visits to places like Varanasi, Naimisaranya, Chitrakoot, Vindhyachal, I was invited to join him in the helicopter or the state plane, whichever he took. I went along as a keen and devout temple visitor. But then, Vora's travels soon became semi-campaign visits to one district or another. He started his tours, following in the trail blazed by Bahuguna, chief minister in the 1970s, who used to make whirlwind political tours to district after district every day, launching himself from a helipad constructed next to the chief minister's bungalow. The then Prime Minister Indira Gandhi got so scared of the popularity generated by Bahuguna's campaigns, that he was cut down to size, and forced to relinquish his post.

In every district headquarter or town Vora visited, he would announce one local scheme or the other: a new sewage system or a new link road, or a new drinking water scheme and so on. Each announcement was made on the spot, in the style of an emperor announcing a grant during a field visit. To start with, each 'ghoshna' had a relatively small price tag of some two or three crores rupees. In the beginning, I had passed on the daily ghoshnas to the concerned departments for being fitted into the departmental schemes, for implementation. However, with time, as the announcements started becoming bigger and were being trundled out with greater frequency, there was no way to find the funds. At first, politely and subsequently with firmness, I requested the governor to stop these ad hoc announcements. The governor was replacing the entire planning set up and departmental functions through casual announcements of dubious value. I also told him that this kind of cheap popularity might not yield the desired political dividends anyway. These exhortations fell on deaf ears. The governor would fully agree with me, and the very next day he would visit some district headquarters to make more ghoshnas. I had sent explicit notes to the governor to desist. At one stage, the then finance secretary sent a note, bordering on the impolite, refusing to implement the governor's directions. When the governor complained to me about the tone and content of this note, I had to tell him bluntly that I felt the same way as the secretary.

Any pretext for populist measures would do. As the monsoon season approached in 1993, the expected rains would not come on time. Towards the end of June, on return from his visits, the governor would anxiously talk to me about the drought conditions that he had seen. Early in July, he announced at a public speech in one of the districts, that the state was 'drought-stricken'. That evening I mentioned to him that we had not formally declared drought in the whole state or in any part, and would he kindly desist from mentioning the existence of drought? As was his wont, the governor agreed with me wholeheartedly and on his next day's visit he again declared that another district was drought stricken. No formal decision had yet been taken by the Governor's Advisory Council that drought was to be declared in any part of the state. The advisory council technically functioned as an interim Cabinet to aid and advise the governor in the discharge of his duties. However, as is usual with such advisory councils these were toothless, but the formality remained. The declaration of drought would have meant immediate budgetary allocation and opening of 'test works' – an old method instituted by the British to gauge the severity of drought by opening temporarily civil works, paying labour at absolutely minimal rates or by giving food grains in lieu of cash payment. Along with that, a declaration of drought meant remission of land revenue, postponement of recovery of cooperative and other dues and a number of other relief measures. The district magistrates started clamouring for release of funds for test works and for the formal orders remitting the loans. The revenue department and the finance department would not oblige and release funds or issue orders in the absence of a formal declaration of drought by the Governor's Council. I wanted a little while more to make up our minds before approaching the council for declaration of drought. By declaring drought wherever he went, without a formal declaration by the state government, the governor had placed the government in an anomalous position. This abnormal and ludicrous situation continued for a while. Amidst all this confusion, the heavens opened up by the third week of July, with incessant rains pouring down all over the state. Now after his return from each tour, the governor would ask that a paper be brought up for declaring the state as flood-affected! In district after district, he would announce the local area to be 'flood-affected'. Again, we were bombarded with requests from the district magistrates, clamouring for remission of land revenue and formal orders cancelling the short-term loans from recovery. Flood relief measures were taken, including supply of boats and helicopter rescue missions as well as distribution of snakebite serum. In any case, at the end of September, when I presented the annual report to the Governor's Council reviewing the agricultural year, the first sentence of the report read "The year saw the 'wettest drought' experienced in Uttar Pradesh for a very long time without a formal declaration of drought or floods." That report would still be on record somewhere in the state archives!

Aside from illustrating the governor's campaign methods, which were not so subtle, there is a point this episode raises. Little systemic action is taken to prevent calamities, be they earthquake or flood or drought. The floods routinely affected certain parts of the state as an annual phenomenon. To tackle the recurrence of floods, action on a systemic basis in each basin was required and no one had the vision or the time to work out such long term plans, not to speak of even attempting implementation. The easiest route was to declare drought or floods and remit all loans. In this scheme of governance the matter is then forgotten till the next year.

Those summer days, I used to go for a nine-hole round of golf at 5.15 am, get home by about 7.30 am, reach the office by 8.15 am, with breakfast on the short ride from my residence to my office. The days were long and hectic, crowded with the multifarious work of the chief secretary's table; many days I could return home only after 9 pm after a non-stop stint in the office. The early morning golf, in the ozone filled air, and in the midst of the therapeutic greens, was the only relaxation in the day, permitting me some time to be in communion with myself. One morning, this quiet was disturbed.

At 6.30 in the morning, I got a summons through the police radio network – cell phones were not yet in vogue – to go to the governor's mansion urgently. I was in shorts and wearing golf shoes with metal studs – the ban on metal spikes had not been brought into effect those days. As I reached Raj Bhawan, I checked up with his Aide-de-Camp (ADC) to find that nothing was amiss, as far as he knew. Irritated at being disturbed from my golf game, as also concerned about my foothold using the metal sprigs, I walked up the wide ornate stairway, constructed of teakwood, which led up to the governor's residential quarters. As I walked up, my shoes with the metal studs made a huge clatter, which I deliberately accentuated by thumping my foot from stair to stair. The racket shook up the entire Raj Bhawan; and as I reached the top of the staircase, the entire household of the governor was there to greet me with a startled look. When the governor asked me if there was some thing amiss, I responded that I had merely responded to an urgent summons. The governor apologised and said that the urgency had been injected by his assistants. Some months later when we invited the governor to be the chief guest at the annual golf club function, he mentioned in his speech, tongue-in-cheek that even if there were a major catastrophe, he had decided not to disrupt the chief secretary's golf. He wanted that the ancient and ornate stairway in the Raj Bhawan be protected from damage!

Much the same scenario was repeated a year later almost to the day, when Mulayam Singh was chief minister and I was again summoned urgently. Wearing my golf shoes I entered his drawing room, at his residence adjoining the golf course, with a huge clatter. A startled Mulayam told his personal assistant that the chief secretary was not to be disturbed from his golf except in an emergency. Mulayam was a genuine sports lover – and possibly as a gesture of atonement – sanctioned rupees ten lakhs from his discretionary fund for improvement of the golf course. This money the club used to convert hole numbers 1, 8 and 9 from 'browns' to 'greens', with installation of a sprinkler system. Since then, all the nine holes have been converted to well maintained greens.

The Uttar Pradesh government had an advanced Civil Aviation Department, with a number of planes and helicopters at its disposal. As one of the least developed states in India, this was to be expected. Around that time, there were at least seven full time pilots operating the planes and the helicopters, which were used liberally by the governor, chief minister, the chief secretary and other officials. Shashank Shekar Singh was the boss of the airline system and he ran an efficient airline. Those days, the joke was that the airline department in the Uttar Pradesh government was the only department that worked. The airline had a proud record of reliability, with aircraft availability at a moment's notice. Shashank juggled the stables, which included four planes and three helicopters so efficiently that any one with influence who wanted a flight would get it with no difficulty; Shashank also was able to oblige and build enormous goodwill with senior officials and politicians. There were at least two trips to Delhi and back everyday. Every morning a flight would leave for Delhi and in the evening a flight would return from Delhi. Many officers, whose children were studying or working in Delhi, would have them over for the weekends or even on weekday nights, courtesy Uttar Pradesh airways. Officers would say, "Use of the state plane works out cheaper" – naturally, since it cost nothing at all to the officer. I once heard the story of a state plane that took the then chief minister to Delhi in the evening. When his staff discovered that they had forgotten to pack his pyjamas in his suitcase, they found it easier for the plane to make a trip to Lucknow and back to Delhi to fetch the pyjamas than buying it in the nearby market at Delhi. For them, it worked out cheaper! After all, the pyjamas could not have been claimed as eligible travel expenditure.

Some of the pilots were also daredevils – not averse to taking risks. They were impervious to commercial pilot regulations that banned drinking on the night previous to a flying day. It was a relaxed, jovial, obliging group, ready to take any risk to please the clientele. I once heard of the state helicopter returning from Delhi to Lucknow late one night with the chief minister, in violation of the curfew on night flight of helicopters. They flew at treetop height, barely skimming the trees and avoiding the telegraph poles in order to be invisible to the radars located at the Bareilly airforce base. When I chided the pilot for the risk taken endangering the chief minister's life, he cheerfully told me that there was enough visibility, as it was close to full moon! In retrospect, I am surprised at the miracle of their safety record.

With such a service at his call, the governor discovered the joys and benefits of regular air travel to various parts of Uttar Pradesh. He would make at least one outstation trip a day and sometimes two, using the plane or the helicopter or a combination of the two. And soon enough, the governor started taking the state plane all over India, mainly for visiting temples. Thus, a quick visit to Tirupati or to Vaishno Devi in the state plane was in the public interest, and paid for, naturally, by the public exchequer. On a couple of these visits, I was invited and joined happily with my family. After all, due to some *punya* done in the previous *janmas*, state planes were made available for visiting temples. If there is one thing in my conscience about abusing the government's facilities given to me in the public interest, it was the occasional trip on the state plane for private purposes. A large state like Uttar Pradesh does need facilities for rapid transit; nobody could question that. However, the reckless use of these facilities by politicians or bureaucrats for personal reasons was surely undesirable. There is certainly a case for cutting down the fleet drastically. Unfortunately, over time, the success of Uttar Pradesh in running an efficient 'private' airline has been duplicated by a number of other state governments, which are now running relatively large fleets, for use of ministers and senior bureaucrats, all in the 'public interest'.

Officials can sometimes be swayed by local interests, at a cost to law and order and even going against the spirit of Court orders, as this incident shows. One afternoon in May 1993, I got a call from the district magistrate of Ferozabad, a town on the main Kanpur – Delhi Grand Trunk highway. He sounded frantic, and told me that there was *chukka jam* or a blockade on the G.T. Road, at the spot where it passes through the main Ferozabad bazaar; traffic was blocked up on both sides for about half a mile, increasing by the minute. Apparently, the Supreme Court of India had earlier issued directions for the removal of about five hundred heavily polluting small-scale industrial units to other locations and for the installation of antipollution devices in each unit. This was to protect the Taj Mahal, which was located nearby. The protest in Ferozabad was organised by the small-scale units, who wanted the state government to announce publicly that it would appeal against this order, and postpone compliance. The district magistrate said that the situation was getting out of hand. He said he had no means to disperse the jam and the use of force would result in casualties. Would the chief secretary kindly authorise him to make a public announcement that the state would appeal the Supreme Court's orders, and not enforce it immediately? The superintendent of police who was with him was equally emphatic that the situation was going out of control. I got the district magistrate back on line and told him that nobody had a right to block a public road, whatever the provocation. Besides, this was a national highway from Calcutta to Delhi and most sufferers in the *chukka jam* had nothing to do with the local issues in Ferozabad. I would hold a meeting to hear their grievances, but the *chukka jam* had to be vacated immediately. The district magistrate told me that all this had been tried and that the sponsors of the agitation were adamant. I thought for a minute, and gave him instructions: "Hold the fort in the best possible manner for an hour. I am arranging for a new district magistrate and a new superintendent of police to replace you both. They will reach there within an hour and you may both hand over to them immediately". I put down the phone, and spoke to the commissioner at Agra division and identified a civil service officer and a senior police officer to rush to Ferozabad from Agra to take over as district magistrate and superintendent of police respectively. I also spoke to the director general of police to arrange for reinforcements. Suddenly, within fifteen minutes or so I got a call from the district magistrate of Ferozabad. Hey presto! The blockage had been removed, traffic had started flowing and within half an hour, the jam would be cleared fully. I countermanded the change of guard at Ferozabad; while making a mental note to reflect this event in the district magistrate's annual evaluation report.

The elections for the state assembly were announced, scheduled for the early winter of 1993. I convened a one-day conference of all district magistrates and commissioners to discuss various matters, but primarily to give them one simple and straight message. They should be impartial and not on any circumstance come under political influence. They could be fearless, independent and strong. Mistakes would be accepted and I would own these as my own. However, any hint of partiality would be dealt with severely and ruthlessly, and the officer's career would be at stake. These instructions were complied with, and I obtained an unexpected endorsement, narrated in the next chapter.

Coming back to the meeting, the governor too wished to participate. I told him politely but firmly that the meeting was convened only to finalise the operational details of the elections. In the context of the elections, it was not desirable that he participated in the meeting. This was a tricky and apparently anomalous situation – the governor was the constitutional authority heading the state. The chief secretary had no constitutional role except as a servant of the government of the day. However, everyone knew in Uttar Pradesh at that time that the governor was a Congressman at heart and in deed. I was anxious to convey the message of impartiality to the district magistrates, but that would sound hollow and ridiculous in the presence of the governor, a known partisan. I struck a deal with the governor. He would be present for the formal inauguration of the conference, and then leave the scene. After this, I would preside over the meeting. In the event, the elections passed off peacefully. As against a very large number of disturbances with high fatalities in the conduct of the previous assembly elections held three years earlier, the elections of 1993 were very peaceful. As I recall it, only one election-related death was reported. And that was due to the accidental firing from the gun of the personal guard of a candidate.

Despite the differences with Governor Vora, I found him an extremely courteous gentleman, full of old-world charm. There were many tense moments that we shared, but there was not one occasion for him or me to be impolite or aggressive, or make a cutting remark. He recognised that I was doing my job. He had been sent by high command to do his, a political job. But there was no need to inject bitterness in the personal relationship.

15 LUCKNOW: CHIEF SECRETARY, AFTER THE ELECTIONS

The office of the appointments secretary was like a busy railway platform. MLAs and petty politicians from various districts were milling around, practically gheraoing her, to press for the transfer of one official or the other.

At Cabinet meetings, he would sit at the head of an oblong table with the thirty or so ministers sitting along the two sides. He wanted no lip from any member of the Cabinet. No minister would ever express an opinion.

WHEN I TOOK OVER AS CHIEF SECRETARY OF Uttar Pradesh soon after demolition of Babri masjid, President's Rule had just been imposed. The communally charged situation in UP, indeed all over the country, coloured the first year of my tenure. The dynamics changed when President's Rule was lifted and Mulayam Singh was sworn in as chief minister, nearly one year to the day after the fall of Babri masjid. It was perhaps quite appropriate, that the swearing in ceremony should have taken place in the K D Singh Babu Sports Stadium. After all, politics has evolved into the number one spectator sport.

After Mulayam had been formally invited by the governor to form the government, I asked for time to call on him. It was fixed for 8 am on the morning of the swearing in. Word came to me to bring along the planning and finance secretaries. When we met Mulayam at his residence that morning, he gave me a list of twenty or so 'announcements' that he proposed to make, as chief minister, at the press conference immediately after the swearing in. All of these were populist measures, and had been part of his campaign promises. As we went down the list one by one, I objected to nearly all of them. Mulayam was quite adamant. The most innocuous of the announcements was to declare Ambedkar's birthday as a government holiday. I told Mulayam that we already had too many state holidays and that we may instead announce cancellation of a few of the existing holidays. In fact, the public would appreciate that more. Another item in the list was that the women municipal staff engaged by the municipal corporations in the state for street cleaning purposes should start work at 9 am every morning instead of at 5 am as was the current practice. The rationale was that they belonged to the weakest communities, and with the women going to work at 5 am in the morning, the children were neglected and could not be readied for school, thus endangering the future of this class of people. I argued that by 9'o clock the streets become busy and that cleaning would not be possible. Why not ask them to start work at midnight instead and complete their cleaning work by 6 in the morning, in time to get their children ready for school? Mulayam's reply was that at midnight, their personal safety could not be ensured. He added that, in any case, even starting at 5 am they hardly put in any work! Why not let them start at 9'o clock – nothing would change – and this with a twinkle in his eyes. The agenda proceeded in a similar vein and included the regularisation and confirmation of the employment of a number of primary teachers who had been appointed on a temporary basis through dubious selection procedures – a matter pending in the courts. I objected to practically all the items. As a compromise, it was agreed that four of these would be announced formally, another five stated loosely in a garbled form, to be examined later, and the others given up.

After the others had left, I mentioned to the chief minister that it was his privilege to select his chief secretary and as and when he wanted my departure, could he possibly give me a week's notice so that I could try to get another assignment in Delhi, and not be summarily left in the cold. Mulayam looked surprised. He said, there was no question of his asking me to leave – didn't I know that he owed his post of chief minister entirely to me? I pleaded that I did not understand this, having done nothing to help him. Mulayam said that that was not true. I had organised a tight, efficient and impartial election process. For the first time, under-privileged people, minorities and the old, who had hitherto been afraid to come anywhere near the polling booths, could come, and did come, to vote. Mulayam said his analysis of the voting pattern showed that the clean and safe elections conducted that year were mainly responsible for his coming to power. There was no question of asking me to vacate the post of chief secretary. But he agreed that he would give adequate notice in the unlikely event of his asking me to leave.

I found that Mulayam as an administrator was firm, decisive and amenable to reason unless there were compelling political circumstances. We had a working rapport and he encouraged me to express my views. There were many occasions when I would express disagreement with him in my personal meetings. He would not mind it, and would take my point of view into account. On most occasions, he would in fact, be guided by my advice. However, when his political interest was strong, he would not heed any contrary advice.

At Cabinet meetings, he would sit at the head of an oblong table with the thirty or so Cabinet ministers sitting along the two sides. Accompanied by the law secretary and finance secretary, I would sit close behind him on one side with the planning secretary and the official reporter sitting on the other side. Mulayam wanted no lip from any member of the Cabinet; he would have preferred a thirty-item agenda meeting to finish in five minutes. No minister would ever express an opinion when Mulayam introduced an item and the chief secretary would be the only person who would speak, sometimes expressing a contrary view. On many items, I would stand up and explain why the proposed measure was improper or not in public interest and why it should not be approved. After hearing me out, Mulayam would say, "We have heard the chief secretary; I feel it would be useful to get this item approved: any comments?" Pausing for a few seconds, he would announce that the item was approved. Sometimes I would mention before the Cabinet that the decision would be reversed by the courts, and that an immediate stay order would be forthcoming. Mulayam would tell the Cabinet that the chief secretary was perfectly correct, "We will take this course of action – let the court take the blame for shooting it down." On occasion the law secretary, A K Srivastava, who subsequently became a judge in the Delhi High Court would tug me by the side of my trouser pocket, indicating that I was going too far in opposing the proposals and it was time to shut up. One day, during the course of a private discussion, Mulayam asked me why I found it necessary to oppose him so often in front of the Cabinet. He added, "You have already opposed the measure on file. You have spoken to me also privately before the item came on the agenda. Why did you find it necessary to repeat your points at the Cabinet meeting, in full hearing of all the ministers? They would get the impression that we are not getting on together." I replied to him that even though I had opposed the matter on file, I found it necessary to express my views in the full Cabinet, as that was the formal decision making forum – the members present should know the other point of view. It was then up to them to take a decision.

Many policy decisions are taken cynically with a populist motive, knowing these are not sustainable when tested by the law of the land. I found this phenomenon in Delhi too during my stint as Cabinet secretary. The government of the day would champion various populist measures, leaving it to the court to intervene and take the odium of blocking these measures. There is a double standard here, with the administration sometimes complaining about court interference and at other times, abdicating its responsibility to the courts.

Though I could do little to resist the plethora of populist measures introduced by Mulayam, I had a better measure of success in resisting political interference in the matter of arbitrary transfers and postings. Right on the first day, I had sought an agreement with Mulayam that he would not unilaterally shift officials. Despite pressures on him to shift senior administrative and police officials from their posts, Mulayam would usually leave the final decision on postings and transfers to the chief secretary. All transfers and postings of district magistrates, superintendents of police, commissioners, heads of departments, were done after consulting me, and the proposals were invariably initiated by me. But Mulayam would periodically rock the boat, perhaps to gauge my resolve.

So one morning, early in February 1994, when I reached my desk at nine, I was surprised to see a note from the appointments secretary saying that he had been called for a meeting with the chief minister and his principal secretary late the previous night, and that the chief minister had desired certain transfers. These orders were now placed on the accompanying file, along with a note from the principal secretary to the chief minister listing the desired changes. Could the chief secretary approve, to enable the transfer orders to issue immediately! I was taken aback to see this departure from usual practice. As soon as I learnt that he had arrived, I went up to the chief minister's office on the fifth floor. He was cloistered with his principal secretary. Rather rudely, I asked the principal secretary to leave since I wanted to have a word with the chief minister alone. I then told Mulayam that the new procedure for transfers was contrary to what we had agreed earlier and that all proposals relating to transfers were first to be discussed with me, before I initiated the proposals. He feigned ignorance, and asked if we had not discussed these proposals recently, while travelling in the car somewhere? I said those related to some other cases and in any case, the current proposals were not initiated by me. Whereupon, Mulayam summoned his principal secretary, ceremoniously tore away the note signed by him and told me that no transfers would take place without prior consultation. Orders would be issued only after receiving the chief secretary's formal proposals.

Imagine my surprise, when a month later, I walked into my room to the same scenario. The appointments secretary was there, with a file mentioning a meeting with the chief minister and his principal secretary the previous night. There was a note from the principal secretary indicating that the chief minister desired a list of changes that may be implemented immediately. The formal orders of the transfer were placed on the file. Would the chief secretary approve before issue? I was aghast, and then quickly recovering, asked the appointments secretary to leave the papers and await orders. I then wrote a short note to the chief minister that for personal reasons, I desired forty-five days leave and could he kindly approve? I had the note sent up to the chief minister's office to await his arrival, and then came back to my house, locked all the doors and told my personal staff that I should not be disturbed by any phone calls whatsoever. I was not in the habit of drinking on working day afternoons, but that day I poured myself a couple of gins and went to sleep. At 4'o clock in the afternoon, when I checked if there had been any phone calls, I was informed that the chief minister's office had called several times and that he urgently wanted to see me. At 5'o clock, I went to his office and met him alone. He solicitously asked me why I was upset, and I bluntly told him that I had thought he was a man of his word and that I was disappointed. I had no pleasure in working with him any more; and could I be allowed to go? The same scenario was repeated. The principal secretary was summoned and admonished as to why the agreed procedure was not followed. The chief minister solemnly stated that this would not recur and that I should resume work immediately. This time, he did not renege. To be fair to him, every transfer and posting thereafter was done after consultation with me and on proposals made by me, and he overruled me only when he had significant political compulsions.

The political interference I encountered in the matter of transfers and postings is by no means unique to Uttar Pradesh. In many states, by all accounts, the chief secretary has by now given up the ghost. Many do not even pretend that they participate in postings and transfers of senior officials in the state. The show is run entirely by the chief minister, assisted by cronies located in his personal secretariat, who respond to demands for transfer from political sources. In some cases, financial deals are linked to such transfers. The sordid position prevails in state after state. It is no longer relevant that good administration is linked to reasonably long tenures.

The power to transfer civil servants is the most important weapon held by the chief minister and other ministers. Politicians expect district officials to function at their bidding and not exercise independent judgement. Frequent and random transfers, especially in field postings are the bane of administration. Coalition governments and unstable chief ministers are the order of the day. With this, the ability of political leaders at headquarters to resist pressures from field politicians has all but gone. In fact, the only work some chief ministers do is to comply with requests for transfers and postings of officials. All it requires is for two prominent politicians of the district to come to headquarters and demand a transfer; and it is done. In 1990, when I returned to the state from Geneva, I went to the office of the appointments secretary to intimate my arrival and mention my availability for a posting. Her room was like a busy railway platform. MLAs and petty politicians from various districts were milling around, practically *gheraoing* her to press for the transfer of one official or the other. Contrast this with the old story about Morarji Desai when he was chief minister. He received a complaint from a MP that a superintendent of police in his constituency would not listen to him, and so should be transferred away. Morarji bluntly responded that his officers were not supposed to listen to the local politicians: "He is my representative; not yours; I would be upset if he had taken directions from you. He will be transferred if he takes instructions from you." This is a far cry from the current practice.

Normally one need not shed tears if officers are frequently transferred. After all, they are all public servants. If the chief minister, who carries the public mandate, transfers a public servant, what is wrong with that? But public servants are in fact, instruments for implementing the mandate given to the executive. How can an officer in the field perform his functions effectively, if he is not given the time to get familiar with the special features of the place where he is posted? And how can a person in a desk job in the secretariat be effective if he is not given the time to understand his desk? Why would those in charge of public affairs disable their own instruments by shifting them around? The very fact that senior officers get shunted around at rapid intervals is a clear sign that the government of the day has its own agenda, unconnected with efficiency. Shifting a district magistrate once in a few months, as has recently become the practice, is tantamount to saying that the post is no more required. We might as well abolish the post and save the expense. A citizen cannot expect any benefit from such a government. It is almost axiomatic now that when there is a clash between the self-interest of a few and public interest, the former shall always prevail. Transfers of officials are made in India based on this law.

Though still not as bad as in most states, the situation has also deteriorated in the Central government. The Civil Service Board still functions and there is some security of tenure. However, promotions and postings are victim to political intervention, especially from the PMO. Earlier there used to be a system for identifying and empanelling officers from the state government, for assignments to posts of deputy secretary and joint secretary in a ministry at the centre. But now, increasingly, ministers choose their own favourite officers to work with them.

Aside from impeding good governance, arbitrary transfers do harm in deeper ways. In the scramble to safeguard their tenures against arbitrary transfers, officers become pliant and unprincipled. A field official, not being sure of his tenure, is compelled to dance to the tune of the local political boss of the day, in order to survive in his post. Many civil servants in their younger days are able to display independence and perform the functions allotted to them impartially without fear or favour; but not for long. As they get buffeted around, and as their family grows in size, the pain and trauma of an untimely transfer becomes unbearable. Schooling of children, inability to find accommodation at the new place of posting, disruption in medical attention to parents and the sheer physical and financial cost of frequent moves become unbearable. At some stage, the wife of an officer asks him, "Do you think you are Mahatma Gandhi? Why should my children and I suffer for your principles? Why don't you learn to get on with people?" The officer learns soon enough after two or three shifts from one end of the state to the other. He becomes pliant, obedient to the local political master of the day, and his principles are set aside. Soon he discovers that he not only can live with ease but the quality of his life improves. He discovers that a government assignment, with all the power and the position it bestows, is also lucrative. The transition from a public servant to a private servant is complete.

In our society today, such aberrations are not just accepted, but are becoming the ideal. I recall the story of my friend Ramakrishnan, also from the IAS, who was with me in Harvard, from where he returned to the state of Gujarat after obtaining his doctorate. He was soon made the finance secretary of the state, but was unhappy with his surroundings and wanted to get back to the academic life of Harvard. He mentioned his plans to the finance minister. The minister was quite surprised on hearing this. He said, "Why do you want to go, when you now have so much opportunity to make real money, good enough for generations: If you have any difficulties, I will arrange the deals for you." I have recounted earlier, in the course of the narrative about my early days, about my wife observing a group of women in a marriage party gloating over the bridegroom's illicit income. Much the same now, but spoken by a minister!

An even worse affliction than corruption, if such a scale exists, is the widespread cancer of auctioning transfers, postings and recruitment for private gain. It is an open secret that senior positions are auctioned, the incumbents having to pay an entry fee as well as monthly instalments to hold on to their assignments. How can one otherwise explain five changes in the position of chief executive officer in Noida in the course of the second half of 2002? Once upon a time during my early years, the posts of station officers of certain lucrative police stations carried a price tag. But now we have progressed – the price tag is set for positions of district magistrate, superintendent of police as well as for some appointments in the secretariat.

If the government is downsizing in certain areas, there are growth areas for recruitment which provide ample scope for raising cash. Security has become one such sunrise industry. New employment opportunities abound in the fields relating to internal security, anti-terrorism and the various special forces. Thus, in some states, the chief minister's office directly controls recruitment to the police force. A special recruitment cell is constituted with a handpicked inspector general of police and a chosen medical officer. The paper work is done carefully to ensure that all is in order in the unlikely event an enquiry takes place. It is all an open secret. When a candidate is selected through such a system, after all the tests are completed, a hefty 'entry fee' has to be deposited before the appointment orders are forthcoming. The other day I learnt that in a state neighbouring Delhi, the entry fee to become a police constable was Rs.2 lacs. One can imagine a poor boy from a rural background trying to raise two or three lacs, an astronomical sum for him, to enter government service. He has to borrow from family, friends and relatives, at usurious rates of interest. As soon as his training period is over, and his first field assignment commences, there is a pressing need to raise money and repay the loans drawn for paying the bribe.

Such a person has no option but to raise illegal resources in the first year or two of his service to repay the bribe amount. He has tasted blood, and his thirst will be ever increasing. Instead of being a guardian, he will be a menace to society, a punishment imposed on society for the duration of his thirty-five years of 'service'. The officials recruited by dishonest means, in course of time will reach senior positions in the administration. Not only will they be blood suckers, a dishonest senior officer will not allow an honest employee to flourish under him. The potential for destruction of the administrative machinery is frightening. Reports of underhand dealings and shady recruitments in a number of public service commissions in different states, such as those recently unearthed in the Punjab Public Service Commission are cause for serious concern. Recruitment commissions are amongst the most sacrosanct institutions in a democratic society. If the evil of corruption, backed by political patronage has reached these bodies, then that is the death knell to our public services. That is the enormity of the offence.

Once upon a time, in the period soon after Independence, it was quite understandable for the courts to hold the view that transfers and postings were the prerogative of the political executive. So, no regulatory procedures under law were needed and challenges to transfer orders were not entertained. There has been a sea change in the situation since those days. Public interest has suffered in the face of frequent, irrational and whimsical political transfers. I am surprised that the courts, in particular the apex court, has not stepped in to demand rational procedures to be set in place, not so much to protect the interest of officials, but for the very large public interest involved. I will come to this point in a later chapter, but I believe that a review of the system of transfers and postings and promotions is a basic first step towards administrative reform in India. This is a fundamental aspect of our administration and not a procedural appendage. Till these changes occur, the downhill slide in the quality of administration will continue.

In the course of a visit to Lucknow, the British high commissioner made a courtesy call on me. He enquired as to why people in such posts as chief secretary wish to leave the state, and why the passion to go to the central secretariat in Delhi? It was a perceptive question. After all, in the state administrative apparatus, the chief secretary is the one person wielding the maximum authority, after the chief minister. He has a ringside view of events, and is in a position to make a significant contribution. Yet, many officers wish to move to Delhi. Over decades, I have seen that officers posted in districts gravitate to Lucknow; officers based in Lucknow hanker after assignments in Delhi; while those in Delhi are manoeuvering for postings in international organisations. How does one explain this phenomenon when the level of satisfaction in getting things accomplished is highest in a district, much less at the state headquarters; and one is merely a cog in the wheel in Delhi; and completely insignificant in an international organisation.

This centripetal tendency among bureaucrats has something to do with the quality of job satisfaction one gets in posts dealing with public affairs. In British times, field officers used to refuse postings to Lucknow or to Delhi; since they had the satisfaction of getting things done on the field. There was one collector who was based in Mirzapur for eighteen years and refused to move, even on promotion. During the nineteenth century, the Kumaon and Garhwal regions, which had hitherto been part of Nepal were annexed to the British Empire, and were centrally administered by the British through the first half of the century. During this period of half a century, there were only two commissioners in charge of this territory. One commissioner was in charge for twenty-two years and his successor for all of twenty-eight years – practically a whole career. Such people could build a rapport with the territory, devoting themselves to the region. In the 1990s in UP, the average tenure of a collector in a district was nine months. I was to see, as Cabinet secretary, that the average tenure of a collector all over india was about thirteen months and that of a superintendent of police was some two months less. One can safely wager that the average tenure of a district magistrate in UP would become less than six months and that of a chief secretary about the same. In circumstances that are not conducive for the pride of satisfaction in work, how can one expect meaningful results? No wonder we have reached the state in which we are in today.

In another context, I had mentioned that in the early 1990s, if I had been allowed to continue as APC without promise of any further promotions, and given ten years tenure in that post, I would have grabbed that opportunity. One talks of the high quality of administration in a country like Singapore; no doubt driven by the genius of Lee Kuan Yew. In the administrative structure he established, officers are selected with great care, on merit alone. Then, when in their early forties, they are hand-picked for high responsibilities. The chosen officers are given a ten-year run in one position to develop strategies and implement them. At the end of the period, the less successful ones are discarded and the successful ones are picked up for even higher responsibilities. In our corrupt and highly political administrative milieu, all of this may sound utopian. But, at the very least, it is imperative to provide a minimum tenure of three to five years in any assignment.

In the current state of affairs, few officers have the thought of contributing anything. An officer merely wishes to extract as much as he can for himself and his family in each successive assignment. So when the British high commissioner told me that he was puzzled as to why senior officers from the state wish to go to Delhi, I had a wry smile and tongue-in-cheek said, that perhaps they feel they have a greater chance to contribute to policy in Delhi than in the state headquarters.

One major event during that period in UP was the threatened strike by the UP Electricity Board. The board had the monopoly position on power throughout the state. It was a corruption ridden organisation setting the national benchmark for inefficiency; not that the performance of similar boards in other states was too different. The plant load factor in most of the generating units, a measure of the utilisation of capacity, was close to the worst in India. Transmission and distribution losses were also high. The immediate provocation for the strike threat was the talk in the air about a proposal to trifurcate the board into three separate agencies – for generation, transmission, and distribution – in order to improve efficiency and to fix responsibility on each agency for its operations. The word spread that Mulayam, a strong chief minister, was likely to push for such a move. The employees of the board saw this as a potential threat and hence the preemptive step of a total strike. Combined strike notices from twenty-eight of the twenty-nine unions were received, giving about ten days to the government to settle their 'grievances'.

In the course of a strategy meeting within a small group, the chief minister expressed a desire to handle the strike with a strong hand, but was afraid to do so, because of the monopoly power enjoyed by the board and its employees. I had done my quick homework. I advised him that I would handle the strike totally, with an iron hand and take full responsibility for the same. Mulayam readily agreed and asked me what I would like him to do. I advised him to criss-cross the state and address a number of public meetings in agricultural areas. He should create an awareness among the farming community about the impending strike, prepare them for a three-four week period of hardship, and explain the need for fortitude. This would also condition the public mood against the striking staff of the electricity board. But he should not at any stage negotiate with the striking workers or their representatives, nor allow any move by any party to inject politics into the strike. Mulayam agreed, and he was true to his word. Flying from place to place, he made fifteen public speeches in different parts of the state within three days. And we rushed about with our plans.

In Delhi, I contacted the Cabinet secretary and the defence and power secretaries. Arrangements were made to fly in some five hundred engineers from different agencies, including the Central Electricity Authority, state electricity boards and defence establishments, on a pre-assigned date. B K Chaturvedi, the secretary of the Power Department, and G B Singh, chairman of the board were both honest and competent professionals, and this was fortuitous. In retrospect, it was to the credit of Mulayam that he allowed such people to stay on in critical posts – the tendency of weak chief ministers would be to hand-pick feeble, pliant officials in key posts. In consultation with them as well as with the director general of police, another upright officer, we planned a surprise take-over of the key generating plants and other vital installations.

This was done swiftly and effectively, in a sudden move one morning. The engineers from out of the state, some of whom had come from as far away as Pondicherry, were quickly given charge of vital installations with the assurance that their personal security would be fully taken care of. They were given absolute authority to do what they wished within their domain. Instructions had gone to all superintendents of police and para-military forces, to specially provide security to the outstation engineers, with the added threat that if there was even a minor assault on any visiting engineer, the concerned superintendent would pay for it with his career. The few loyal staff available was given police protection and full encouragement. Voluntary forces were organised in villages to patrol the transmission lines and preempt sabotage. The cause was helped when somewhere near Bulandshahr, a transmission line was sabotaged by the electricity board workers, who were thrashed to within an inch of their lives by the local villagers. The hapless workers had to prevail on their superiors to get the damaged lines repaired within three hours. As soon as I heard of this incident, we publicised it through newspapers, television and radio. This publicity might well have helped, since no further sabotage took place.

As the day of the strike approached, the wind had been knocked out of the sails of the employees. They sent feelers for a face saving formula. I asked first for an unconditional withdrawal of the strike, with media publicity. Just before midnight when the strike was to start, Mulayam called me to say that the strike leaders were with him and they would make a statement of withdrawal of strike notice, provided he assured them that their demands would be examined sympathetically. I chided Mulayam for breaking his promise to me that he would not negotiate or make any promises; and advised him that the strikers should first call off their strike unconditionally and then seek an appointment with him. That was how the strike was unconditionally called off an hour before it was scheduled to start. I understood later that the affairs in the electricity board had drifted back to their normal state, within a few months. There was another strike threat a number of years later by the board, and this time the government capitulated.

Much later, as Cabinet secretary in 1997, I saw again the threat of a strike, this time nationwide, by the Central government employees, in the context of the implementation of the Fifth Pay Commission awards. The government buckled under the pressure. The saga of processing of the recommendations of the Pay Commission, headed by Justice Pandian, is an unsavoury one, not reported in the required detail, by the media. A more detailed account is given later.

In Uttar Pradesh, the Bahujan Samaj Party (BSP) was actively building up its base all through the period of the late 1980s and early '90s. Kanshi Ram was quite active and Mayawati was his lieutenant in charge of UP at that time; with both extensively touring the state to drum up support and organise chapters in each district. During 1993, local party workers in many districts embarked on a venture to appropriate public land for their own purposes. They adopted an interesting technique. Overnight, an Ambedkar statue would be established in a prominent public area. The following morning, it would be garlanded and a small public meeting held in that area to celebrate the occupation of the piece of land. Thereafter, any attempt to remove the statue, or to vacate the occupation would be fraught with opposition from party followers, causing embarrassment to the local administration. Having thus occupied a public area, small temporary structures would then appear, to consolidate the occupation. It was soon evident that this was part of a statewide strategy to grab land. As chief secretary, I issued directions that no statue of any sort, of any political or religious leader should be allowed in any public land without going through a formal process of approval by the relevant district authorities. I also indicated that I would hold district magistrates personally responsible for any slackness in this regard, if they allowed statues to emerge overnight.

By the early 1990s, many officials were getting identified personally with political parties and caste-based movements, and some officers were inclined to provide open support to such land grabbing. So, I had to ensure that the local intelligence machinery should remain active, and that any attempt to occupy land should be nipped in the bud. Informal instructions were that if the statue was being established in the middle of the night, it was okay to have it forcibly vacated, using strong-arm methods if necessary, provided this was done before day break. After that, any such strong action would be difficult, as large crowds would gather. Following my instructions, a number of attempts to grab land through this technique were thwarted. I became *persona non grata* in certain quarters, and demands started for my removal from the post.

Throughout my service in UP, I had been seen as a south Indian, unconnected with local political and caste considerations. But suddenly, there was a move to label me as a 'Brahmin Chief Secretary', and to colour my actions from a caste perspective. At a press conference, some reporters asked me regarding these allegations. I replied, "Public servants belong to no caste in the exercise of their functions. My caste is administration and my Bible or Gita is the Constitution of India. Much like electricity or roads are caste-neutral – they serve all even-handedly, an administrator in the public domain is totally caste-less – he is an instrument of society."

The Mulayam Singh government in 1993 was based on a sort of tie-up with the BSP. The exact nature of the arrangement between Mulayam and Kanshi Ram was not clear, but there were suggestions of a *quid pro quo* for political support extended by the BSP to Mulayam's government. There were also rumours about the Samajwadi Party (SP) trying to buy over legislators belonging to the BSP to rid itself of this dependency. Be that as it may, I got a first hand account of a meeting between Mulayam and Kanshi Ram, just the day previous to one of my visits to Allahabad. The events were described by an official of the collectorate, who was attending on Mulayam Singh.

The scene was the circuit house where Kanshi Ram was camping and where I had stayed the next day. As the chief minister arrived, Kanshi Ram was in confabulation with his political cronies in the living room of the

VIP suite in which he was staying. Mulayam was ushered into the adjoining outer visitor's room of the suite, and asked to sit there till Kanshi Ram was free to meet him. The meeting went on for two hours, with the chief minister cooling his heels in the outer reception room. When the visitors left after a couple of hours, the chief minister thought he would be ushered in next. No such thing happened. After an hour or so, he inquired as to what was happening. He was told that after having his shave and bath, Kanshi Ram was currently having his lunch! Mulayam continued to wait till Kanshi Ram had a short nap; and finally came to the outer reception room to see him, after making the chief minister wait for four hours. My informant said that even he felt humiliated by the treatment meted out to the chief executive of the state, and that too in his own terrain. What transpired at that meeting is not known, but as Mulayam emerged from the room, his face was red. Kanshi Ram did not even show the courtesy of walking with the chief minister and escorting him to his car. I told myself that the price to pay for holding on to power is very high indeed.

About the Allahabad circuit house, there is more than one story to tell. Dr Verma, then the director of the Central Drug Research Institute (CDRI), narrated this one to me. It throws light on the pomposity displayed by senior bureaucrats. One morning, in the late 1960s, waiting for breakfast to be laid, Verma was sitting in the drawing room of the Allahabad circuit house. A gentleman walked in, looking gruff and stiff, sat down in the nearby chair, and carefully ignoring Verma started reading the newspapers. After a few minutes, he lowered the newspaper and asked Verma, "What is your name?" The reply was, "I am Verma, director of the Central Drug Research Institute." Without further ado, the questioner grunted and went back to his newspaper. After a couple of minutes, Verma in turn asked him politely, "What is your name?" The barked answer came, "I am commissioner, Allahabad Division." Verma told me he could not contain himself, as he spontaneously exclaimed, "What a funny name!" He also told me that he later discovered that the commissioner in question was J D Shukla of the ICS.

That visit of mine to Allahabad was to meet the chief justice of the high court in connection with misbehaviour by some lawyers in the

Allahabad courts. Lawyers of the high court were agitating for some reason, and they threatened to cripple the functioning of the high court, by blocking the entries of judges. Chief Justice Sodhi, who had just come from the Punjab High Court had the reputation of being a no-nonsense person. He had telephoned me asking for support. I gave instructions to the local district authorities and the inspector general of police based in Allahabad, to give full support to the high court and do as necessary to meet the situation. The agitating lawyers were prevented from disrupting the normal functioning of the courts. I had followed up a few days later with a personal visit to meet the chief justice and to assure him of full and continued assistance. Strangely, in India, the judges are afraid of none but the lawyer community. One would have expected it to be the other way around!

At one stage in the early 1990s, there was the menace of the neelgai, overrunning the farming areas of Uttar Pradesh districts. The neelgai is an antelope, and even though its Hindi intonation suggests a bovine origin, it is in fact a species of deer. The neelgai has a voracious appetite, can travel long distances and procreates quickly – a deadly combination. Initially, its presence and activities was reported in the farmlands of east UP, but it slowly managed to move westwards to cover a large number of central districts in the state. Reports started pouring in, of the major crop damage caused by neelgai sprinting across vegetable patches and other farm fields. One day, I learnt that the neelgai, sprinting across the airstrip in Varanasi, nearly brought down an aircraft on the runway. I asked the district authorities to hunt them down from the vicinity of the airport.

The Hindu villagers were reluctant to have the animal shot down, as it was seen to be of bovine origin, or so its name sounded. Besides, as the law then stood, it was a protected species and could not be hunted. Very soon, reports of the damage caused by large herds came multiplying. We decided to issue a notification amending the Forest Act, providing general license for the neelgai to be shot in the plain areas of the state. Secondly, the animal was renamed as *vanrose* and a campaign was undertaken to publicise the fact that it belonged to the deer family and was not of bovine origin. I also discreetly asked the district magistrates to arrange only for Hindu *shikaris*, to organise hunts and exterminate those animals roaming the fields freely. The *shikari* who bagged the animal could keep the skin and the meat as his prize.

During my tour of the districts, I always felt embarrassed by the elaborate security arrangements that were made for my visits. As I would go from the airport or the railway station, on the route to the city, there would be a policeman posted every fifty yards or so. He would shoo the pedestrian or the cycle traffic away from the road, to give my escort vehicle and my car a clear path, however ineffectively. I have seen unsuspecting cyclists on the road ahead in a crowded bazaar street lifted bodily, cycle and all, and unceremoniously thrown on the pavement. I wondered what that poor fellow's opinion would be about the unidentified VIP! In the districts, there would be a sub-inspector in elaborate uniform manning a motorcycle, with blaring siren and flashing red lights, acting as the pilot vehicle. One or two jeeps full of armed policemen would be trailing my car. The lack of coordination between the pilot and the driver of my vehicle was comical: The pilot would not be clearly told the destination, whereas the driver of my car would know it. The pilot thus would make a particular turn; while the driver of my vehicle, with a knowing smile, would take a turn in the other direction, muttering to himself about the ignorance of the police pilots. On occasion, the pilot knew the destination for the trip but not the route, whereas the driver knew the way but did not know the precise venue. Communication and coordination is generally unknown at that level.

In Lucknow, I tried to reduce the level of security provided to VIPs on tour and inhibit the practice of senior officials flashing red lights with a siren. The ministers would have none of it. For them, the red light and the siren was a symbol of their position. Even district judges, not even of the grade of high court judges, became devoted to the fashion of having red lights and a siren. For the life of me, I cannot understand why a judge would want to advertise his travel. Such obscene pomp is a way of life in our officialdom. It is a strange sight, VVIPs gallivanting all over, escorted by highly visible sten-gun toting Black Cats. Imagine a solemn marriage ceremony in a small town; with a couple of politicians fully surrounded by gun waving escorts, prominently stomping up and down the scene. The more such politicians come, the happier the host is, as it enhances his standing in the community.

As Cabinet secretary in the Government of India, I found the scenario much the same. When the prime minister or the president would land or take off from any Indian airport, extraordinary security requirements kept the skies clear around them for a long period. The airport would be closed for civilian national and international air traffic. I did my best to reduce the level of security to a number of Z and Y rated politicians and bureaucrats, with only limited success. The prime ministers I worked with – Deve Gowda and I K Gujral – fully agreed about the need to rationalise and reduce the level of security, and some reductions were made. For movement of the prime minister or the president within Delhi, a new security regimen was introduced, reducing disruption to city traffic. The practice of the prime minister using the helicopter within the city, and for travel to the airport was increasingly resorted to.

As noted earlier, provision of security is a sunrise industry, and innovative new methods are found to harass the citizen. There has to be a basic realisation – if you reach certain posts, your risk levels go up and these are occupational hazards. One should also then curtail one's movements and regulate them in a manner as to provide least disruption to the public. However, for politicians, this requirement is a contradiction in terms – they need vastly increased visibility, with each higher level of responsibility. I am not arguing against provision of security, but there has to be some rationality and a balance between the level of risk and public convenience.

As chief secretary, I continued to visit field areas regularly. I used to allocate half a day once a week for district tours, and travel to remote areas, to keep in touch with the people in the field and get a feel for their thinking and reactions to current issues. During these visits, some of which were with advance notice and some with little notice, I had a chance to meet the local politicians at the block or sub divisional level. It also helped me to keep informed on the responses to the instructions issued periodically from headquarters. I kept apart a couple of hours everyday to meet visitors, particularly from out of town and my staff was instructed to give priority appointment to them.

I had very good working relations with Governor Reddy and then Vora during President's Rule and later with Chief Minister Mulayam Singh. So I never felt the strain of the long hours or the heavy burden of the post. Mulayam was an excellent chief minister, with sound administrative acumen, decisive, and generally sure of his position.

16 CABINET SECRETARY: REFORMS IN INFRASTRUCTURE

"My sons and my relatives will want to exploit my position to their advantage. They will use their proximity to me, through open and subtle ways, to put pressure on you and influence you. I want you to be completely fair and impartial and not oblige them."

The officer from the ministry was worth a billion dollars. He saw it as a game to constantly throw a spanner in the works, to impede any forward movement in power projects. The government would have been better off paying him a billion dollars and retiring him from service.

ON THE LAST DAY OF JULY 1996, I GOT THE NEWS that I was to take over as Cabinet secretary, on the retirement of Surendra Singh the next day. The Deve Gowda coalition government had already been in power for about three weeks. I had not had a chance to meet Deve Gowda before that date. I had made a courtesy call on his principal secretary, Satish Chandran, whom also I had not known before. This was a brief call lasting about ten minutes. I believe the invitation had come based on my service record, and surely the prime minister and his secretary must have made inquiries about my reputation. I held the post of Cabinet secretary for nearly two years. My elevation to this post, the highest in the bureaucracy may seem a contradiction of all that has been said. The repeated assertion has been that honest, bold and independent officers are filtered out of the system. The reader could well wonder if I am as lily white after all. Anyway, all I can say is that the government's decision had something to do with the coalition politics of that particular period. Perhaps my being apolitical with no patron, helped in that coalition situation. The new prime minister was not steeped in the Delhi system. He had no vested interest or axe to grind, not during this period at any rate. He had a principal secretary who was straightforward, not prone to playing games. So, it was a quirk of circumstance. I mean this as no slight on so many of my illustrious predecessors some of whom I revere. But in these times, my selection indeed was a bit of an oddity.

After assuming this post, I often used to wonder about the criteria for selection – the desired experience and background – aside of course from the issues of seniority, and acceptability at the highest levels of government. I recall that in the state, it used to be said that a minimum stint of two years as a district magistrate was an essential part of the training of an officer in his formative years. The rough and tumble of events in a district that he confronts, gives him a solid exposure to the administrative realities in India. Thus, in the past, an officer was generally not considered for a central deputation, in the level of joint secretary and above, unless he had 'done a district'. When the districts used to be large as was the case in early days, and with the district magistrates each having longer tenures, it was difficult for young officers to find openings as district magistrate. Nowadays, there is a multiplication in the number of districts, in general elevating each tehsil to the level of a district. These are but populist moves to name the new district after one local noteworthy or the other, to please this or that caste or community. Coupled with the shorter tenures of district magistrates in the game of musical chairs, it is now easier for officers to find openings in districts. Anyway, it is still considered an asset for an officer to have held a district in his early years. After all, a file is not merely a collection of papers – it represents a real life situation, on the ground; and the way it is settled has an impact on the life of real people. Many secretariat officers treat the noting on the files as a sterile intellectual exercise as if it were a crossword puzzle. They also look for the best way to deflect a file, to send it down or up or sideways and get it out of the way. This attitude, ingrained in most secretariat officials, is based on a lack of perception of the direct linkage between files and real life. Field contact with citizens provides such an exposure, and hence the importance of a district posting in the early stages of one's service.

The same can be said about the need for prior experience in administering a state as an important criterion for taking up the post of Cabinet secretary. But in the past few decades, B G Deshmukh, Naresh Chandra and I were the only ones to have first been the chief secretary in their states. Earlier, some other too were in that category. I do not recall any other such instance. The post of chief secretary provides an insight into all aspects of management in a state, be it in the fiscal, economic, infrastructure, environmental, regulatory, internal security or social fields. Handling a state at the level of chief secretary is a good preparation for taking up the post of Cabinet secretary. In a sense, each road would have been travelled before, though perhaps in only a regional context. There are of course more dimensions to the job in Delhi relating largely to external relations and some other areas. But still, it appears a bit odd to me that only the three of us who reached the position of Cabinet secretary had prior experience in managing a state. I know of some Cabinet secretaries who were handicapped in this regard.

Extending this analogy further, those prime ministers who have had a stint as chief ministers would tend to have a much better grip over the administrative machinery. The example of Narasimha Rao, arguably one of the more effective prime ministers we have had, comes to mind. Deve Gowda was in this category too, and brought tremendous politico-administrative acumen to his work as prime minister, for the short while that he was there. It is my belief that in a short period, he made a major impact on Indian administration. It is true though that his achievements have not been recognised. This was due to the fact that he was heading a coalition government and did not have the aura of leading one or the other major national parties. Morarji Desai and Charan Singh had also become prime ministers after serving as chief minister. Perhaps Morarji lends support to my thesis. Any rule needs to have an exception, and in this case it was Charan Singh.

The converse is also generally true. Those who do not have experience of state politics and administration, especially at the chief minister level, would rarely be effective as prime minister. Gujral and Vajpayee come in this category. The failure of Rajiv was due to inexperience at both the state and central levels. But then, Indira, seemingly an exception, was quite effective. This was because of her long association with state politics in the shadow of Nehru's political career.

I had the good fortune of working with Deve Gowda and I K Gujral, who were prime ministers during my tenure. I would rate Deve Gowda very high indeed, for his administrative ability and quick understanding. It is a pity indeed that he did not have a much longer innings, as he would have had a significant impact on India's future. Deve Gowda was much misunderstood – in conferences and seminars, he would be portrayed as yawning prodigiously, and ever pictured in the midst of forty winks. Having been with him on so many occasions, I can vouch for the fact that he was fully alert and alive to the issues under discussion. He proudly described himself as a farmer and as a farmer's representative. He had a shrewd political mind and given adequate time, he would have created a strong national farmers' front. Incidentally, I too feel that a strong farmers' front is essential for ushering in rural development in India and for eradication of poverty. I recall a couple of occasions when he would go out of the way to parade his rural, unsophisticated manners. Once, we were at lunch with a very small group at his residence, which included Wolfensohn, the president of the World Bank. As we were discussing the efficiency of bank-aided agricultural projects in India, I saw Deve Gowda assiduously scraping the insides of his bulbous nose with his fingers; proclaiming to his visiting foreign dignitary that he was of rustic, peasant stock. Likewise, on another occasion, we were again at lunch for a very small group in his residence, this time including Camdessus, the chief of IMF. I saw Deve Gowda, while still at the dining table at the conclusion of the meal, take a mouthful of water, and gargle it loudly and ostentatiously, and then swallow it; again designed to indicate to the visitors that he was a true son of the soil. Why he sent these signals only he would know but I can say that it was deliberate. For all these eccentricities, Deve Gowda had an extraordinarily shrewd mind, and his thinking was positive. He was also action oriented. Presiding over a fractious coalition, representing many different points of view, he had the ability to provide support to push through major reforms. I will list some of these measures later. It is a pity that the Vajpayee government that followed could not effectively follow through on these measures and consummate them. I do not think that Vajpayee, or more pertinently his closest advisers, genuinely understood the significance of these measures. They churlishly denied the existence of these initiatives and started groping for new steps in a futile manner.

I called on Deve Gowda on the day I took over charge as Cabinet secretary. He was busy that day, and asked me to see him the following evening at his residence, where he spent half an hour alone with me, discussing the things he wanted to accomplish and asking me to help him execute his plans. What he then said impressed me greatly and I am quoting as well as I can remember. "I have spent many years in state politics, seen a lot of things. I have enough money for my lifetime. God has given me the opportunity, unexpectedly, to serve the country as the prime minister. I will be completely honest, straightforward and will keep all politics out when national interest is involved. I want you and Satish Chandran to help me with my plans. My sons and my relatives will want to exploit my present position to their pecuniary advantage. They will use their proximity to me, through open and subtle ways, to influence you, and to put pressure on you. I want you to be completely fair and impartial and not oblige them. Sometimes they may speak to you in my presence, giving the impression of my full agreement. I may not at that time be in a position to contradict them, because of my close relationship. Even then you should ignore them totally. If I need anything from you, I will ask you privately – but that will be very rare." Deve Gowda was true to his word. He never asked me to go out of the way in any matter, except on one trivial instance, when he explained the reason why he wanted me to stretch a point.

Deve Gowda had full trust in Satish Chandran, his principal secretary. Chandran had been chief secretary in Karnataka much earlier, when Deve Gowda was the chief minister. Some years earlier, he had also held the post of secretary to Government of India. The reader can well ask again how the system allowed such able persons to reach the top. Blessed with transparent honesty and highly intelligent, he is one of the most morally upright persons I have come across. Chandran probably represented the ideal civil servant. His analysis was brilliant based on a sound command of his facts, and he could, in any forum, express his views calmly and cogently, without fear or favour. His stint as chief secretary in Karnataka, had obviously given him an insight into Indian administration. As the principal secretary, he had enough confidence in his own position and himself that he did not have to score brownie points against the Cabinet secretary. Though he had not held that position himself, he wished to sustain and strengthen the institution of Cabinet secretary – an extraordinary position to take for an officer in the PMO. On any issue, where both of us agreed, Deve Gowda would concur instantly without a second thought. In the rare instance when Chandran and I disagreed, Deve Gowda would apply his own mind and if he were undecided, he would side with his principal secretary. Where Deve Gowda had to disagree with both of us due to political compulsions, he would apologetically overrule us, and then gently explain to us that he had no choice. The tendency of most of the earlier secretaries to prime ministers had been to use their close proximity to undermine the Cabinet secretary and ensure that he did not get too close to the prime minister. Narasimha Rao for instance, knew this game being played between his principal secretary and the Cabinet secretaries of the time. He would enjoy supporting one or the other turn-by-turn, playing one against the other.

Gujral was a sophisticated, scholarly politician who commanded respect for his intellectual abilities. However, he had little experience of the rush and tumble of national politics. I believe he himself was personally honest and had faith in the goodness of all around him. N N Vohra, an experienced and able civil servant was his principal secretary. Vohra had worked in the defence and home ministries, and had an impressive command over regulatory and security issues. Chandran and I functioned as administrative advisers to the prime minister, and would rarely give Deve Gowda any political advice. I believe Vora was also in that category.

Contrast this with the Vajpayee government. I believe that the principal secretary has fully overshadowed the role of the Cabinet secretary and has become the dominant power centre in India. He is not averse to give political advice to the prime minister. I do not have first hand experience of this period, but I go by the accounts of a number of people who had worked with me, and have intimate familiarity with events of the past few years. Brajesh Mishra's own domestic administrative experience in India is scanty. With his diplomatic background, his main policy experience has been with the United Nations in New York. There is one important contrast between New Delhi and New York in that 'sovereignty' vests in the Government of India and final decisions on key issues concerning the country need to be taken at New Delhi. However, the UN represents an association of governments, and no sovereignty vests in New York. The UN, as we saw, is a forum for interplay of independent countries, large and small. The work of the policy makers at UN headquarters is to manipulate the various forces and interests represented by the different countries, and maintain a peaceful balance. A comfortable *status quo* is the need of the hour. There is no need to decisively proceed forward. Contrast this with New Delhi, where to deal with the innumerable problems of an under developed illiterate country, the pressing need is to shake the *status quo* and proceed boldly forward with administrative, social and economic reforms. Besides, India's problems are complex. They are almost entirely indigenous, oriented to the domestic situation. Issues concerning our external interface have a relatively limited relevance. Thus, it would have been better if the main advisor to the prime minister had experience in domestic affairs, rather than specialisation in external politics. This is perhaps just as well and perhaps even a deliberate decision. With the kind of coalition represented by the ruling alliance, it would seem that Vajpayee has set himself a *status quo* objective – how to proceed for five years showing a lot of activity with no real action. Probably, and cynically, this was the hidden governance objective that dictated the choice of his advisor!

It is significant that Brajesh Mishra got himself designated as national security advisor. Without going into the merits of this appointment, there is one relevant aspect that has been overlooked by all analysts. In a country with a nuclear and missile capability, the ultimate decision maker in times of real emergency or crisis in security matters is the prime minister. He obviously deserves the best possible advice, rendered in a dispassionate manner, to help him to take that right decision in a crisis. His principal secretary, particularly one who also renders political advice would subconsciously carry the prime minister's political interest while formulating his advice on crucial security matters. In times of real crisis, there could be a potential conflict between the national interest and the prime minister's public image. It would therefore be a sound practice to have a national security advisor who is far enough removed from the prime minister's personal and political circle to be in a position to render dispassionate and independent advice of high technical merit.

Vajpayee took over as prime minister in the middle of March 1998. I was his Cabinet secretary for a fortnight, till I laid down my office on the last day of that month. I had occasion to participate in two or three Cabinet meetings, as well as a number of other smaller meetings chaired by Vajpayee to discuss specific issues. As I was about to step down, there was the hope that the pace of change would be sustained. And there was the expectation that a government, fresh from electoral successes, would bring into action a strong tone of governance. But the trends that I saw during that fortnight were worrisome. For example, at a meeting to fix the pricing formula for certain types of fertiliser involving heavy subsidies, I had felt that the government would set the right tone by giving a signal that they would keep under check the fiscal deficit by scaling down subsidies. I instead found, a generous finance minister who was more than willing to declare a heavy new dose of fertiliser subsidy, not to speak of a cut or a roll back. He was encouraged by the prime minister, on the grounds that 'farmers interests' were involved, and that they could not afford to be too strict. I had pointed out in that instance that it was a question not so much of farmers' interest but more of subjugation to the large private fertiliser manufacturers, and that there were powerful vested interests working to keep the level of subsidies high. At this, the prime minister, in a now familiar gesture, shut his eyes, and with a shake of the head declared solemnly that "we will not tolerate vested interests; we will root out all vested interests" – after which proclamation he proceeded to approve the increase in subsidies. I told myself at that time that the finances of this government were in for a run. The drastic increase in the fiscal deficit in the past four years is a matter of record. There were a few more such instances that gave me the indication that serious governance was not going to be on top of this government's agenda. In the event, the quality of governance in the past few years is there for all to see.

During the period of the Deve Gowda government, and to a lesser extent in the Gujral government, a number of measures of far-reaching significance were initiated. The Finance Minister P Chidambaram and industry minister the late Murasoli Maran, despite coming from opposing political formations, were capable and reform minded. Jairam Ramesh, a brilliant economist with genuine interest in reforms was the advisor to the finance minister. With the prime minister lending active support, and with Satish Chandran and I in a position to push through the reforms, and give them a formal shape, I believe that those two years saw a number of significant initiatives. After the initial reforms ushered in by Narasimha Rao and Manmohan Singh in the early 1990s, mainly in the field of finance, investment and banking, the new wave of reforms covered a wide spectrum, significantly in the area of infrastructure development.

The opening up of the telecom sector was accomplished with telling effect. The concept of an independent Regulatory Authority was ushered in. This was based on a model successfully followed by USA. Thus, the Telecom Regulatory Authority of India (TRAI) was established, through legislation, to provide for a non-political and neutral umpire in the field of telecom. Unfortunately, the Vajpayee government could not suffer an independent authority to regulate on key matters. This emaciated the ministry, depriving it of its clout. The opportunity for meddling for private gain was curtailed. The telecom regulatory body was cut to size and a rival appellate body was created to lock up the two in internecine battles. As we have seen, this is a simple expedient the government follows when it wants to turn the clock back.

The issues relating to convergence between information technology, telecom, and broadcasting were well recognised at that time. The Indian communication and broadcasting scene continued to be curiously regulated by the Indian Telegraph Act, which the British had enacted over a hundred years earlier. A new Broadcasting Act of India was drafted, taking into account all relevant interests, and implicitly acknowledging the interrelationship between broadcasting, telecom and information technology. The draft Act was cleared by the Cabinet in quick time, and almost certainly would have become law had it not it become a casualty of the change in government. The finally approved legislation, much later, took this draft as the basis, but made a number of important changes to meet different kinds of concerns.

The monopoly of Videsh Sanchar Nigam Limited (VSNL) and Mahanagar Telephone Nigam Limited (MTNL) was greatly curtailed; in fact a successful disinvestment exercise of VSNL was undertaken during that time. I chaired the technical committee that processed the disinvestment exercise, including supervision of the bidding and fixing of the final price. Again during this period, the Internet monopoly of the government agencies was broken and the public use of Internet became widespread. A massive multiplication of rural telephone offices, public call offices, as well as Internet cafés followed these decisions. This period saw the launch of the extensive development of communication facilities, in all parts of the country. A major fillip was also given to investment in broad band connectivity between important centers in India; as well as to connect these centers with international trunk routes. The results are being seen now. Telecom reforms, with the steps taken in those two years, yielded major results. But there is so much more to be done.

The critical nature of physical infrastructure, and the need to encourage private participation were recognised during the period of my tenure.

Hitherto, it had been the popular belief in India that roads, bridges, ports, airports, mining, power – all these were the responsibility of the government or the public sector. The need for massive new investments in these areas was recognised then for the first time by government. It can be said that perhaps this realisation has not seeped into public awareness even today. The massive investments required in these sectors were no longer within the capability of the central and the state governments, heading as they are towards bankruptcy. In fact, the scale of funding required is not even within the capacity of the Indian private sector, which anyway depends on public finances for their private investments. The amounts needed for investment in power and infrastructure projects are staggering by Indian standards. Despite this mismatch between requirement and availability of resources, very few decision makers appear to be genuinely worried about raising the necessary resources for infrastructure, to meet tomorrow's needs of the economy.

I have found successive power ministers speak blithely about adequate steps being taken to improve the power situation; that the state owned agencies would undertake the necessary investment to meet our future power needs. Those in metropolitan areas, the decision makers in India, do not understand the current shortage of power in the smaller towns and rural areas, particularly in north India; in many areas, so-called electrified villages frequently have to do with two or three hours of power a day. And there is no recognition as yet of the looming crisis that would engulf our metropolitan areas, as early as five years from now.

Some initiatives were taken to reform electricity pricing and make this remunerative for the producers. The pricing and tariff system in the power sector all over India has been riddled with politics and corruption. No ruling party in any state, of whatever complexion, could do without subsidies on agricultural power. Deve Gowda, himself a self-proclaimed champion of the farmer, openly talked of the hypocrisy in all the states in so far as agricultural power was concerned. He was able to get the unanimous commitment of all the state governments to take politics out of this field by having an independent electricity regulatory authority in each state, to fix power tariffs. Satish Chandran and I pursued the idea of having a national system for fixing an equitable power tariff, through a central regulatory authority. A central authority was established through an act of parliament, along with the provision for a state regulatory authority. This could have had a far-reaching effect on improving the management of the power sector in India. Unfortunately, the Vajpayee government did not go along with this move, taking it lightly. The Centre allowed the state governments to play politics with these regulatory agencies. An important reform with far-reaching potential was ingloriously nipped in the bud.

I got involved in the complexities of clearances for power projects. All my experience and abilities had not prepared me for the labyrinths I had to enter. As is known, to establish a large thermal power plant there has to be coordination among a number of agencies. There are countless agencies that need to 'bless' a project. If I have not left out some, at central level these are the Central Electricity Authority, power ministry, environment ministry, finance ministry, coal ministry, railway ministry. Others such as the CBI would come in, but a bit later. At the state level too, there are a number of agencies that need to bless a project. This goes right down to the local district authorities. When the project promoter is one of the domestic public sector agencies, these clearances could be taken for granted as routine. Time consuming but the approvals would come. However, when a private investor, Indian or foreign enters the scene, the whole process turns into a circus. Each of these important agencies mentioned above thinks that it can hold the country to ransom.

The problem is further aggravated when a tripartite agreement was required; say one between the power producer, the public sector coal mining company and the railways. The latter two agencies will not budge an inch, and give anything away from their kingdom to reach an agreement. That the project would add electric power to the system is lost sight of. The power department or the finance department at the Centre, which is supposed to coordinate the various agencies will hold its nose high in the air, and have a hands off policy. To some extent, this is understandable, as any official who takes an interest in coordinating a forward movement could quickly be accused of having a personal interest in the success of the project. Thereafter, intervention of the vigilance department or the CBI would only be a short distance away.

The independent power producer has to tackle these hurdles, and then wend his way through the obstacles created at the level of the state government. At the same time, the power producer has to carry his main financing agencies, whose patience is not unlimited. And for us in the government, the concept is alien, even anathema that time costs money. So, the financiers are led on a merry-go-round. International financiers are used to financing power projects in different countries of the world and have standard norms, uniform terminology and certain patterns for funding. There would be a clash in terminology between those used by financiers and those used by the Indian agencies, and reconciliation would be near impossible. Thus, for example, the *force majeure* clause would have a certain definition for the Swiss banker, differing from the interpretation of the term, say, by the Indian railways. The Swiss banker would not alter his definition, as it would impact his various projects in different countries. The railways would argue that they have had a certain interpretation of the term for over one hundred years and had no intention to change it just because the definition does not suit some Swiss banker. If we assume that no investigations or court cases have intervened, all these above steps would have taken three or four years or more. By that time, one or more elements in the objective situation on the ground would have altered, requiring recasting of some project parameters. A junior officer in the power or finance ministry, clever by half would point this out, on record. One or more rounds of elaborate new negotiations would be required. Meanwhile, fresh assessments by a series of international consultants deployed on the project would be obtained. Invariably, the opinion of the different experts would vary in one detail or the other. All these would provide new opportunities to any number of junior bureaucrats to write their elbows off, pointing out various anomalies. Like a story foretold, they would jump to an adverse conclusion on the viability of the projects, and in passing take some pot-shots casting aspersions on the motives of the investor.

After all, it is so much easier to sip tea, sitting in a comfortable chair and say why something will not work. One can stand vindicated if and when the project actually fails for whatever reason; one then even has a vested interest in making it fail. It is so much more difficult to come to a constructive agreement that takes a project forward. The senior bureaucrats in the concerned ministries, some celebrated as able administrators, would not dare to overrule their subordinates on the file, for fear of incriminating themselves in a possible subsequent enquiry. The problem is that no department or agency sees itself as a part of the overall system, one of whose tasks is to facilitate the implementation of a project in the national interest.

On occasion, even the Cabinet secretary had to join the fray to cajole, tempt, woo and persuade the fractious parties to sort out the matters. In the eight or nine so called fast track projects, which were initiated around 1993, and which were still under discussion in 1996 when I took over as Cabinet secretary, I tried hard to coordinate the forward movement; by bringing the various agencies and parties together, and coaxing them to find mutually accepted positions. Despite the endless hours that were spent, I could not make much headway. Various junior officials including those from the finance ministry, saw it as a game to constantly throw a spanner in the works, to impede any forward movement. They would demonstrate authority without accountability. Written objections from a peeved department would follow after a meeting, demanding the appointment of yet another international consultant to look into one aspect or another. There used to be one officer whom on first sight at a coordination meeting, I valued as worth a billion dollars. The Indian nation would have been better off paying him a billion dollars and retiring him from its services. Towards the end of my tenure, I found that he was in fact worth five billion dollars!

Looking to the reasons why none of the so-called 'fast track' projects ever took off, the blame rests on our implacable government agencies. From what I could see, the power producers and their financing agencies were quite willing to water down their terms and conditions, to reach a reasonable compromise. But it was the unspoken position of some of the government departments that they would not allow the projects to come up on any terms and conditions, indeed under any circumstances. I am sad to say that many young officers took great delight and got a perverse pleasure in slowing down and in ensuring that no investment took place at any price. Not knowing the power and joy of positive action, they assumed the mantle of destroyer. How deep must be their frustration. To my astonishment, I found their superiors, even at the level of secretary, unwilling to overrule them as perhaps this may have put their careers in jeopardy.

There is an attitudinal block in the approach of the departments to new business initiatives and ventures. Unless an atmosphere is created where the bureaucracy encourages and fosters new investment, the future of infrastructure sectors is bleak indeed. It has not helped the image of the foreign investors that Enron in India has also come a cropper, thanks to the massive fraud perpetrated by the Enron headquarters in USA. The net result of these has been that in the past five years, there have been no initiatives for any significant new investment in the power sector. The future of electric power, which is a basic requirement of all progress in India, is bleak indeed. Nearly every other country, including the underdeveloped, is able to attract investment in the power sector, on reasonable terms. India indeed is unique in not being able to put its act together. We saw how Indian entrepreneurs were handicapped in moving to world class manufacturing by policies that affected the availability of raw materials at fair prices. Similarly, the millions of farmers in India are the ultimate sufferers of the mishandling of the power sector.

In some other sectors, the results were not quite so dismal, though again in case of mining, the initiatives failed. India has large mining reserves but due to the lack of financial resources and technical knowledge, the exploitation has been limited. So, the mining sector was opened up for international private investment. However, in mining, the state governments have a major role to play. They have not been forward looking. Besides, they have a limited understanding of broader national issues. Short-term local political interests came in the way of a constructive approach. I understand that this initiative has not met with much success.

In infrastructure, significant reforms were legislated in the fields of ports, airports, mining as well as in new highway construction. The policy to encourage private investment in minor ports was announced. I believe significant progress has been made in a number of states in the east and west coasts. Investment opportunities were also opened up for private sources to come into the major ports through construction of jetties and berthing facilities. The national highway sector got a major impetus during this period. Projects for linking cities through highways and a programme for construction of by-passes, around the major towns and cities were given concrete shape. A major advance was made when a sum of Re.1 per litre of diesel was levied to create a special fund, to finance highway projects. I believe this significant step has triggered sizeable activity in private investment to enter in highway construction. I was amused to read the other day that the credit for ordering a national grid of highways was claimed by the Vajpayee government amidst much fanfare. Some one should look at the decisions and the steps taken during the period of the coalition government.

I was equally amused to read the other day, at the time of inauguration of Delhi Metro, that the Congress government of Delhi state and the central BJP alliance were vying with each other to claim credit for Delhi's metro. As a matter of fact, this project was finalised in 1997, in a series of hard negotiating sessions, and the contract signed in quick order, for completion of the project in five years time. The genesis of the five year period came about as follows: when I was posted in Geneva, I used to go to Singapore every year, around November, for an international seminar conducted by me, with the participation of senior officials from the Far East and the subcontinent. The first year I was in Singapore, I went for dinner to the house of a close friend, who mentioned to me that Singapore was examining the construction of an underground rail system. The second year, he told me that the project for the metro system had been finalised and that there was severe competition between the Japanese and the Koreans in the bidding for the construction. The third year he mentioned that the work had started and was continuing apace. The fourth year he told me that the metro work was proceeding at a brisk pace. The fifth year, after dinner, he told me that instead of driving me to my hotel in his car, he would take me by the newly opened metro railway – which is what we did. This was a contrast to the memories of my college days in Calcutta where the underground system, from the point of planning to final execution and commencement of operation, took all of thirty years. This caused great inconvenience to Calcutta's citizens, aside from the huge cost escalation.

I insisted that at all costs the Metro Railway system, at least the first phase must be completed within five years. In one furious week of negotiations, I had the warring factions, representing different government departments locked up in my committee room with the injunction that they would not be allowed passage to the outside world till they came up with an agreed solution on all outstanding issues – I did not care what the solution was, so long as it was viable. The project was finally approved and the formal agreement of the Government of India and the state government of Delhi obtained, and the documents with the Japanese aid agency consummated speedily. After some months when one day I checked up as to the progress, I learnt to my horror that there was no forward movement, as there was no agreement on the appointment of a managing director for the project. The railways wanted a serving railway officer for the post, the Government of India wanted an IAS officer as its nominee and the state government was proposing its own person for the job. As usual, every agency wanted a hand in the till. At that time, I had heard of Sreedharan's work in completing the Konkan railway project on time in the face of seemingly insurmountable obstacles. I had never seen him before, nor have I met him till today and nor had we even spoken on the phone. Yet, I sponsored Sreedharan for the post, after making enquiries and learning that he was a no-nonsense man and would not brook any intervention from anyone, even the highest placed politicians. As events have proved, he was the ideal choice for the Metro of such a highly political place as Delhi. When I sponsored his name, there was an objection that he was over-age and as per government rules he could not be appointed. I requested the lieutenant governor of Delhi to come for a meeting and got him to agree to Sreedharan's nomination. That was how he became the first managing director of Delhi Metro. That was also how, contrary to the traditions and normal experience of Indian projects, the first Metro rail rolled out, just short of five years to the day after the project was approved. True to form, the Congressmen from Delhi government and the senior

BJP leaders have competed in claiming all the credit for the project. The only credit they can actually claim is for not interfering with the progress of the project. Even this perhaps was not for want of trying – Sreedharan, I guess gave them short shrift!

In 1961, when I had returned from London, the development of new underground routes was an ongoing process. The first underground railway system had been laid way back early in the twentieth century. I have since been to so many cities which have an elaborate network of lines – Paris, Moscow – and even small cities like Barcelona or Madrid or Taegu. In the 1960s, the Ring Road in Delhi was far and away the outermost point of Delhi city. But Delhi was furiously expanding inside the Ring Road, and new colonies were being planned outside the Ring Road perimeter. I had asked a senior railway officer at that time as to why some advance planning could not be done by our railway system, to have a circular railway abutting the Ring Road, and have say twelve spokes, originating in Connaught Place, reaching out to Ring road and spanning the entire city. These corridors could preempt the need for constructing an underground railway system much later, at a vastly multiplied cost. The answer was simplicity itself. He told me that it would be costly; and that the public would resent paying a high price for local transit. He was obviously thinking in terms of the financials of the railway department, not of the national economy. An excellent intra-city railway system in Delhi could have been established at a fraction of the cost in real terms that we have incurred today. It was the typical response of an Indian bureaucrat with a myopic departmental view. Any urban transit facility anywhere in the world would have to be appropriately subsidised – the benefits, savings in terms of pollution and other externalities are great indeed. Thus, in the case of Singapore metro, I understand that the entire capital cost of construction, including the cost of the initial set of rolling stock has been fully absorbed by the government, and the system has been handed over to a private party for free, to run it efficiently and charge a tariff to cover only operation, maintenance and upgradation costs.

I had also wondered for a long time as to why there has been no super highway constructed from Santa Cruz/Bandra area to the Fort area in

Mumbai, a highway on the bay, by-passing most areas of Mumbai. I am sure there would be no shortage of bureaucrats objecting to this proposal, raising innumerable hurdles. With the peculiar geography of Mumbai city, such a highway would probably pay for itself in pure financial terms, even ignoring the side benefits in terms of improved quality of life in parts of Mumbai city. If Mumbai had been in any other country in similar circumstances, I am certain that such an auto-route over the sea would have been a reality by the 1960s. In fact, a bridge between Alibag and Gateway of India might even have been in place. I recently heard of plans for a road link from Bandra to Worli. I will believe it when I see it.

In May of 1997, I led a team of officials to meet business leaders in USA, to explain to them the investor-friendly policies being ushered in, and inviting them to come to India for investing there, especially in the infrastructure sector. Our team visited New York, Washington, Los Angeles and San Francisco. We were received cordially by the business community. They were fully alive to the changes in the Indian economic and investment climate and showed genuine interest. The team had excellent meetings everywhere, and I believe a lot of enthusiasm was generated. They were sharing in the general euphoria about business prospects in India.

It could not be said then at that forum, but it is regrettable that the Indian system cannot be changed so easily. It requires persistent and sustained action over time, by all agencies and authorities concerned, so that the overall climate can be improved. I liken the Indian situation to a visitor being welcomed into a house with a red carpet. As soon as he enters through the main door, the door is locked from inside, and he is chased from room to room, flogged all the time. After some time, the poor visitor does not know which way to run, and he falls down exhausted. The welcome nominally advertised before the foreign investor is not transferred into actual practice by the various agencies and authorities in India. At some stage, the investor is in distress and he wants to run away. But he is too deeply involved by then to find his way out of the labyrinth. We must ponder over how to usher in the much needed attitudinal change, before we are really serious to welcome investment from abroad. I am not suggesting that whatever the foreign investor wants should be freely given to him without question. We should make up our minds what we can do and what we cannot do taking our overall interests into account; and publicise this. But then, we must fulfill what we promise.

As part of the US tour, I was invited to a meeting in the Silicon Valley near San Francisco with an organisation called The Indus Entrepreneurs (TIE). This is a group of Indian entrepreneurs, who have done pioneering work in information technology and have recorded remarkable achievements for themselves amidst the US business community. Many became millionaires and there were quite a few billionaires. As is the case with newly rich people, they were an arrogant lot, and thought no end of themselves – each one thought he personally owned India. I understand that the recent market crash has sobered them up. At any rate, prior to my trip to Santa Clara, Finance Minister Chidambaram had warned me that the TIE meeting could be quite brutal and suggested I take care. In the event, at the meeting, there were about forty members, who were extremely rude and impolite and they were blaming me for all the perceived ills of India. I found that we were going nowhere with abuses being hurled freely. I put my hand up to stop the discussion, and told them bluntly, "This meeting reminds me of a meeting of small businessmen in a district in UP more than twenty years back. The level of discussion is about the same. I came here because I was invited but I find that you have nothing to tell me except that Taiwan is a good place to do business – please go ahead and do business in Taiwan; I have nothing further to tell you or to hear from you!"

There was an uneasy silence and then someone asked, "What do you propose?" I said, "I have come in good faith to listen to your suggestions; if I feel something can be done and if it is in my capability, I will promise to initiate the necessary steps, as soon as I return. Do you have some constructive suggestions?" Suddenly the meeting changed in tone and two concrete suggestions emerged. The first was about Internet becoming a major international force. In India, Internet operations had remained fully under government control, and access to Internet was only through a government monopoly. This greatly restrained the flow of information and expansion of business in India. The second problem related to delays in clearance of import cargos at main seaports, as also the airports of India, leading to unnecessarily high inventory levels of electronic components, which seriously inhibited the growth of the information technology sector. The meeting ended with my promise to do whatever I could do in both these areas. That was the genesis of the break up of the VSNL monopoly over Internet in India, and the opening up of the Internet field for a large number of private players. I believe we have seen a sea change in this segment of activity over the past few years, all stemming from one meeting at Santa Clara. I also took strenuous steps to streamline the clearance of import cargo at major airports and at seaports, particularly in respect of electronic components. I believe I was partially successful. I do not know what the current situation is in this regard. There are so many vested interests at work to inject complexity into simple processes.

In February 1998, I led the official Indian delegation to the economic conference at Davos in Switzerland. In the previous years, our delegation had been led either by the prime minister or the finance minister. No politician would join the delegation due to the election season. I led a small delegation, which included Montek Ahluwalia, the then finance secretary as well as a number of Indian business leaders. I found that the conference was an occasion designed to facilitate the global businessmen to rub shoulders with international statesmen, politicians, and heads of international financial agencies. It was basically a snob club, and an occasion for R & R – rest and recreation – for businessmen. It was a jamboree of very rich people basically going there on the principle, "every one who should be here, is here". It was also an occasion to sit in the same room and have dinner with presidents and prime ministers and directors of international agencies, so one could talk about it back home.

There is one daily event during the three days of the conference that is not publicised; it does not even find a mention in the daily diary published by the organizers. This is the informal meeting of heads of delegations, in a post dinner session, starting every night around 10 pm and going on till midnight. I attended the informal meetings on the two nights I was there, along with the thirty or so other heads of country delegations – mainly presidents and prime ministers and senior ministers, with some dictators thrown in. Also present were the president of World Bank, managing director of IMF and the secretary general of the United Nations. One evening, the organisers broke us up into three informal groups, and gave each group one hour to work on an after dinner exercise: Each group should list the main international issues likely to engage the world in the first half of the twenty-first century. Each group was chosen carefully, to have a mixture of dignitaries from the various continents, as well as representatives from different types of economies. I could add that the group was at that time meeting in the backdrop of the Asian financial crisis, with the market crashes in. Asia, part of recent memory. The sub groups worked in their separate corners and the leader of each group was asked to present the conclusions. It was noteworthy to find that the lists, independently compiled by the three groups, were astonishingly similar. International terrorism was the first or second issue in all the three lists, and this was well before 9/11. Rapid inter border finance flows and information flows across nations was another subject that was in each list. Information technology and Convergence was the third topic, which was common. Acute international water shortages and potentiality for wars therefrom was yet another item on the three lists. Since they were quite close on the first three, I wonder about the last.

As Cabinet secretary, in the midst of my busy schedule with pressing matters, there were some interludes. One morning, I got a call from the prime minister requesting me to attend a small meeting called by the president. Gujral did not provide any further details but only suggested that I might help sort out a minor problem. The Cabinet secretariat is located in the Rashtrapati Bhawan. It was only a few minutes walk to reach the president's office. I had no time to find out what the meeting was about. As I walked into President K R Narayanan's office, I found the Foreign Secretary Raghunath and the Civil Aviation Secretary M K Kaw with the president, in addition to his secretary. The meeting had begun. I could make out that it involved the question of providing Air India planes for foreign tours scheduled by the president in the summer of 1997. The president was to visit some Latin American countries for about two weeks, and then after a gap of a fortnight to visit a few European countries for another period of time. Security requirements were that the main plane for use of the president and the back up plane had to be taken out of the Air India fleet and delivered and reserved for the president's use a few weeks prior to the visit to Latin America. Thus in all, the two planes would not be available for Air India's normal services for nearly two months. The secretary for civil aviation was explaining his difficulty in getting the planes detached from the fleet, in view of the severe disruption to the heavy summer commercial schedule of Air India flights.

The background to his objections stemmed from an earlier discussion in the Cabinet about the airlifting of Haj pilgrims from Jeddah to Delhi and Mumbai the previous winter. At that time, one Air India aircraft and two Indian Airlines planes were pulled out of their normal schedules, to meet the emergency to clear the Haj backlog. At the Cabinet meeting, I had strongly objected to such an action disrupting the commercial schedules of Air India and Indian Airlines flights. I had raised the issue that the concerned authorities should have planned the requirement in advance as the post-Haj traffic jam was an annual feature. I referred to the foul reputation enjoyed by Air India, due to the cumulative impact of such ad hoc disruption in its schedules. For the Haj traffic, planning should have been done to hire aircraft from the open market, to clear the traffic backlog. After discussion, the Cabinet had taken a decision that in future, planes shall not be pulled out on an ad hoc basis from Indian Airlines and Air India, and that they should lease in the open market to meet any special needs. This was to build a good commercial reputation for Air India in the international market. The Cabinet decision was duly conveyed to the civil aviation department. This was the background, based on which Kaw was expressing his inability to provide the aircraft for use by the president.

At the meeting, a dogfight started between the foreign secretary and civil aviation secretary. The foreign secretary said that traditionally Air India aircraft had been used for presidential travel and he had merely followed past practice. Kaw replied very politely that the foreign secretary had never contacted him in this matter and that he was unable to spare the planes in view of the Cabinet directive. There was an impasse. The president looked at me. I confirmed that the Cabinet direction did exist. The president then asked Kaw to go to the Cabinet and get the decision reversed. Very politely, Kaw replied that it would be appropriate if the president himself took up the matter with the prime minister. At this, the president flared up and angrily asked Kaw, "Do you think a presidential visit to Latin America and Europe is not important? Will this not get a lot of goodwill for India?" To his credit, Kaw was unfazed, as he replied calmly and in an even tone, "I am not competent to give an opinion on the subject." There was complete silence in the room. The president asked me then to speak to the prime minister, to direct that two Air India Boeing 747s be released. I explained to the president very politely that it was on my initiative that the decision was taken and that surely the civil aviation ministry would be able to arrange suitable sized planes leased out for the presidential visit. I also added gratuitously and totally needlessly, that in many countries the prime minister or the president travelled by commercial aircraft. Perhaps for the day of the president's flights, we could book the entire First Class for the use of the president and his family, and as I understood it this was done when the Queen of England visited Africa sometime earlier. More silence, and then a phone conversation between the president and the prime minister who apparently agreed to spare the planes, Cabinet decision or no Cabinet decision. The president looked at Kaw and mentioned that a particular 747 aircraft that had been acquired most recently by Air India should be kept at his disposal. Kaw was again unfazed. He said that the particular aircraft was in a very heavy density sector; and he would pull out another smaller aircraft for the use of the president. The president then referred to the high safety standards that required the latest aircraft to be provided to him; at which Kaw blurted out, "Sir, is the safety and security of 350 passengers not equally important?" That was how the two identified planes were placed at the disposal of Rashtrapati Bhawan, in the public interest. That was how also, I was never invited thereafter to any Rashtrapati Bhawan function; I did not check with Kaw if he ever was.

As Cabinet secretary, I was witness in 1997 to the threat by the central government employees' unions for a nationwide strike in the context of the implementation of the Fifth Pay Commission award. The saga of processing of the recommendations of the pay commission, headed by Justice Pandian, is an unsavoury one, not previously reported in detail, in the media. Perhaps, Pandian had been relatively generous to the government employees in recommending higher scales of pay, without extracting commensurate sacrifices and promise of greater efficiency from the bureaucratic machinery. Perhaps, his recommendations for downsizing government were too nebulous and insignificant. However, he had still tried to balance the proposed higher scales with some minor sacrifices on behalf of the staff such as reduced number of holidays and increased working hours.

Many impartial observers have considered the final decisions taken by the government on the Fifth Pay Commission as one of the great tragedies in Indian administrative history, comparable to the Mandal edict issued by V P Singh. The Central government is still reeling from the effects of the implementation of the pay commission report as the cascading effects on the finances of the state governments are still in the process of working themselves out, en route to financial bankruptcy of many states. The combined fiscal deficit in the year 2002-03 is quite high, a far cry from the 0% deficit target, mouthed by the first finance minister in the NDA government of 1998.

When the report came up for discussion for first time at the time of the Gujral government, there was a general feeling that there was no option but to implement the recommendations made by Justice Pandian. At that time, the defence minister jumped in, referring to some anomalies in respect of certain categories of jawans, and wanted these redressed, along with more cash and additional sops like increased high altitude allowance and some additional benefits for junior commissioned army officers – evidently he had been briefed by the interested groups from the defence forces, who wanted to sweeten the pie further for themselves. When he heard this, the then home minister, Indrajit Gupta did not want to be left out. He wanted some further sops to certain categories of para-military forces. The prime minister jumped in himself – his darlings were the Indian scientists, who were not given adequate recognition or compensation for the brilliant inventions and research papers they come up with. At a stormy meeting, I firmly opposed all of these, even going somewhat out of my way, and argued that it would be foolish and dangerous to selectively amend any element in the package proposed by the pay commission. Every segment of bureaucracy could come up with its own real and imagined grievances, and demand instant redressal. Despite Finance Minister Chidambaram's strong argument that the measures proposed by the pay commission were already outrageously expensive, and that he would not be in a position to add one paisa to the Pandian package, and despite my strong plea for not touching the pay commission's package, it was decided to concede some further benefits to the armed forces, the policemen and the scientists. It was an uneasy political coalition that was considering the recommendations, and ministers were not shy of championing the causes of the segment of bureaucracy they presided over, especially as it cost them nothing. Despite my suggestion that all we needed to do was to make a one-line announcement accepting the pay commission's report with effect from a date to be specified, the proposed amendments were accepted. I could not muster support for my proposal that the additional sops could be considered later at the time of submissions to the 'Anomalies Committee'. No sooner was this done, than it was the turn of Beni Prasad Varma to bring out the special needs of the postal and telegraph workers as well as the telecom staff. Ram Vilas Paswan was also forced to defend his constituency, and seek justice for the railway men. Now the postal, telegraph and telecom and the railway staff formed the bulk of central government employees – the additional effect would be enormous. Anyway, the package was further revised and finalised, and I was to announce it formally one Monday morning in early August.

The previous Friday I received a strike notice from the confederation of Central government's employees unions, who had met that week at Mount Abu and decided that the revised 'improved' package was not adequate. Also Pandian had proposed some sacrifices on the part of the staff; these required the employees to work more and this burden was unacceptable. A list containing twenty-six demands was forwarded for further examination by the government. That Saturday morning, I met the prime minister at Parliament house, on another matter, when I told him about the strike notice received from the central staff and proposed that we might discuss the matter in the normally scheduled Tuesday morning meeting and pending that, did I have the prime minister's concurrence to withhold the announcement of the 'revised' pay commission package? Home Minister Indrajit Gupta, a fine human being and a thorough gentleman, eminently suited to the Opposition benches, but highly unfit to manage such a complex ministry as Home, was also present at that time. The prime minister agreed with me that we could discuss the matter at the forthcoming Tuesday meeting. As I left his chambers, I was confronted by the usual complement of TV cameras outside the parliament building. In reply to a question as to when the revised pay commission package would be announced, I mentioned that the matter was being discussed on Tuesday, and that we would see the position after the date. That was the headline news for the day – every TV channel made the announcement "Government defers announcement of Pay Commission's decisions". That Saturday evening I got a call from Chidambaram from Chennai inquiring as to what had happened – I was to announce the final decision on Monday morning. I explained to him about the strike-notice, the discussions with prime minister and that we would review the matter on Tuesday; Chidambaram was fully satisfied and told me that I had done the correct thing.

That Monday morning in parliament, pandemonium broke loose. Question hour could not start. Members from the government benches as well as Opposition were on their feet demanding why the decisions on the pay commission had been deferred. Great anger was displayed at this injustice perpetrated on the civil servants. It is so anomalous and ludicrous that ministers and parliamentarians who day in and day out criticise the flabby, bloated, over paid, inefficient and corrupt bureaucracy – all of it true – were in one loud voice the champions of the rights of this deprived class. The prime minister was summoned to the House and the finance minister made an immediate statement that the government's decision on the pay commission would be definitely announced the next day – Tuesday morning. Around 1'o clock, I had an irate prime minister on the phone, berating me for being irresponsible and for defying orders of the government in not announcing the decision on schedule. When I reminded him gently that we had discussed the matter on Saturday and also that he did not object to the Saturday evening news on TV or the Sunday morning headlines, he berated me for insubordination. I remembered the advice given to me in Moradabad thirty-five years earlier, that decision makers should never give finality to their views. Gujral who belonged to the old school, clearly knew this!

On Tuesday, some ministers aggressively asked me as to why the previous decisions of the government were not implemented. I stood up and in explicit terms mentioned that I was fully responsible and was ready for all consequences. I thought it was necessary to bring the strike notice to the attention of the government so that our position did not get further diluted. I also argued we should not announce a new pay package in the face of a strike threat. We should either face the strike or we announce a negotiated settlement. I added that if the political will were there, I would handle the strike totally; and that at the end of the day, not only would we settle the matter efficiently, but we would also carry public support in this matter.

Clearly political will is not there in any reasonable quantum, at the best of times. In a coalition government, with poor leadership, there is no question of taking any principled stand, when public interest is involved. This has been clearly established, repeatedly reinforced through many episodes in the subsequent NDA government. It was decided to first announce the revised package that day and then to start a dialogue with the representatives of the employees union, on their further demands. I declared that I personally would not participate in the dialogue with government employees, and later stuck to my word. The finance minister declared he would not agree to one rupee extra to the revised package, and that he also would not participate in any dialogue with the unions. In the event, a committee consisting of Madhu Dandavate, Ram Vilas Paswan, Jaipal Reddy and others negotiated the issues with the civil servants. Those present at these discussions told me that the dialogue went on smoothly, peacefully and 'successfully' – the Committee agreed to nearly every one of the fifteen additional demands. At the end of discussions, one member actually asked if there were any further demands! In due course, the recommendations of the negotiating committee to concede whatever was asked for came up for consideration and these were approved unanimously, while the finance minister feigned not to hear them. This is the brief history of the unsavoury saga of the Fifth Pay Commission, with final results that will have a catastrophic long-term impact on the finances of the Central government and even more so on the state governments.

I enjoyed my tenure as Cabinet secretary immensely. I did not feel the strain, because of the goodwill and trust placed on me by Deve Gowda and Gujral. In the event, it was unfortunate that Deve Gowda, perhaps unwisely provided political support to Sitaram Kesri and was forced out of office. And then Gujral had to submit his resignation, under peculiar political circumstances following the release of the Jain Commission Report on the assassination of Rajiv Gandhi. I left my office happily by the end of March 1998, and since then, for the last five years and more, have not had occasion to set foot in any office of the Government of India.

17 CABINET SECRETARY: ADMINISTRATIVE REFORMS

My informant laughed sarcastically. It was very simple, he said. If cases were not registered, there were no cases. So the target is not the reduction in the number of crimes committed, but in reducing the number of crimes registered.

The MPs argued that anyway they come under the citizens' scrutiny once in five years, as part of the election process. In a democracy the citizen is supreme, and hence, what need was there for any other authority to scrutinise their conduct? In mathematical terms, this could be deemed to be a fallacy of political absurdity.

WHEN I TOOK CHARGE AS CABINET SECRETARY, I had felt that the two key issues to work on were infrastructure and administrative reform. As I have recounted in the previous chapter, there was a measure of success in the infrastructure sector. I cannot say the same of administrative reforms. I could contribute little to stem the downslide in governance. Some steps towards administrative reform were taken. But important measures taken up by me fell by the wayside. Quite often, there was general agreement about the need for reform, and even agreement on the specific problem areas, but in tune with the hypocrisy practiced by those supposedly in the service of the public, the actual moves would be scuttled. Perhaps it was foolish of me to have believed that I could tinker with the system.

A position paper providing a direction for administrative reforms was prepared, based on which awareness seminars were conducted all over the country. Two conferences of chief ministers, one chaired by Deve Gowda and another by Gujral, were convened in Delhi. The background paper circulated was candid, referring to corruption among politicians and bureaucrats as well as the nexus between politicians and criminals. All chief ministers unanimously and wholeheartedly agreed that there was a crying need for reforms in administration. But there was a catch. While all chief ministers agreed with this analysis, they would have none of it when it came to specific reform measures. Thus, the idea of a Civil Services board to regulate transfers and postings of officials was shot down summarily. If the politicians surrendered this right, then what remained? We had reached an impasse: The disease had been identified, but the cure was not acceptable.

One of the reform measures proposed during this period was to pare down the Official Secrets Act, and usher in an era of transparency and open administration. A draft incorporating major changes in the Official Secrets Act was approved, but subsequently got lost somewhere in the legislative process. I had requested a group led by H D Shourie, the noted crusader for administrative reforms, to propose the first draft of a Right to Information bill. The first draft was in fact approved by the Cabinet but again could not be pushed through. The government had fallen by that time; and this too got lost. The right of every citizen to information in the public domain is in fact a basic right, but in reality much of administration is conducted far away from public scrutiny. It is a matter of inconvenience particularly to the politicians, if a search-light based on full information is turned on them. Thus, it is not at all surprising that politicians of all colours, even those who belong to radically opposed groups, have got together to deny the voter the basic information on the criminal antecedents, educational qualifications and financial worth of candidates who stand for election to the state assembly or to the national parliament – and we call this a working democracy! It is in fact, a conspiracy to keep the electorate permanently in the dark. It is a pity that the citizens of India cannot rise up in one voice to demand this information from those who claim to represent them. This drama is not yet played out, as the courts have meanwhile taken a constitutional position.

Yet another dramatic demonstration of abuse of the right to information is the Tehelka tapes episode. Indeed I do not know if these tapes were in fact doctored and this is a subject of investigation. However, no primary actor has denied the very basis of these scenes, that they did not take place at all. In any self-respecting democracy, the journalists would have got the equivalent of the Pulitzer Prize for their exposure of the brazen corruption in the system, including the indelible image of a senior leader of the ruling party accepting a wad of bank notes with consummate insouciance. Indeed he did resign, as if mere resignation is expiation for the sins. Incredible as it sounds, the minutiae of defence purchases were discussed with dubious characters, and with a lady in close proximity to the defence minister, right inside his residence. In any self-respecting system, such characters ought to have withdrawn permanently from the public eye. But what do we see? The minister is back in business making his near daily visits to Siachen as if nothing has transpired. The journalists are the guilty ones! The recent episode of the so-called Mayawati tapes brought to surface by the Samajwadi Party in UP is also noteworthy for its concealment. As far as I know, these video materials have not been shown to the public. We are given to understand that the explanation given by Mayawati cannot be disclosed to the public; presumably because it casts aspersions on MPs. It would almost seem that in a secular democracy the Members of Parliament are beyond reproach, placed on a pedestal higher even than god. Every allegation of mischief can be obfuscated with impunity. This is the country where I had inanely thought that the mere passage of a bill on right to information would cleanse the system!

An infructuous effort was also made during my tenure to resolve the Lok Pal Bill issue, enabling the creation of an Ombudsman to keep an eye on the political leadership of the country. Despite the sporting offer by both Deve Gowda and Gujral to include the PMO within the purview of the Lok Pal, the very thought of coming under any one's scrutiny was not acceptable to the MPs. The draft bill was scuttled on one flimsy ground or the other and would not see the light of the day. The MPs would argue that they anyway come under the citizens' scrutiny once in five years, as part of the election process. In a democracy, the citizen is supreme, and hence, what need is there for any other authority to scrutinise the conduct of politicians? In mathematical terms, this could be deemed to be a fallacy of political absurdity.

During that time, the chief justice of the Supreme Court commented upon the CBI. He in effect opined that it should be made a fully independent body. Formally, the CBI has been under the administrative purview of the personnel department. However, no CBI director in recent times, has cared a fig for that department. He usually found an informal nexus with the prime minister of the day. The CBI is, in fact, a footloose department, beyond supervision. Thus, successive directors have been a law unto themselves, only amenable to the prime minister's direct influence. In recent years, the CBI has increasingly started resorting to framing false cases, with a shrewd eye on the political who's who. But the reality is that it is a government agency, paid for by the government. Its integrity can be trusted only to the same extent that we can trust the probity and the sense of fair play of its political masters. It was but natural that the lower functionaries of the CBI could find and exploit lucrative routes while pursuing their various investigations. Over the years, I have come across many frivolous and deliberately framed cases. Whenever I now read in the newspapers about a charge against one senior functionary or the other, my first thought is that here is an innocent man being framed. This is not to suggest that all senior functionaries and politicians are lily white. On the contrary, the reality is that one would be hard put to identify even one honest politician and one would increasingly hesitate to certify with complete certainly the probity of any senior official. But such politicians and officers have the savvy to get away from the scrutiny of the watch-dogs. More often than not, the innocent and the honest find themselves trapped in the web of a departmental or a criminal investigation. Such has been the fall in standards.

The 'Single Directive' as it is called, came up for scrutiny during my time. This is a practice that has come down from the British days with the aim to protect senior officials from frivolous charges. The Single Directive provided for prior permission of the Central government before launching investigations into the acts of public servants undertaken in the discharge of their duty. This applied to officers of the level of joint secretary and above in the government, and officials of equivalent seniority in government undertakings. The mechanism was supposed to ensure that *bona fide* official decisions taken in good faith would not be questioned. With the intervention of the Supreme Court, the directive was withdrawn, on the grounds presumably that senior civil servants alone did not require an extra layer of protection, when similar protection was not afforded to junior functionaries of the government. From the court's perspective, this was a discriminatory measure.

In a system where the process of decision making was already slow, the withdrawal of the Single Directive wreaked further havoc. It has opened the floodgates for frivolous enquiries and witch-hunts. After all, the state gives no award to a senior bureaucrat for quick and effective decision-making; but if he makes even one mistake he can be pilloried through an enquiry. Withdrawal of protection to upright officers has been the net result of the roll back of the Single Directive. It is noteworthy that though they are also public servants, the judiciary itself retains immunity from investigation. Likewise, the armed forces would not allow any civilian authority to investigate any officer's conduct, undertaken in the course of duty. It is also idle to argue that such protection should be available even-handedly even to the lowest functionary when the original intention was to protect the decision makers at senior levels in government from frivolous investigation. The distinction needs to be made that lower functionaries do not have discretionary or executive powers. They can be faulted mainly for procedural lapses. This is not the case with senior officers, where judgement comes into play. When I had joined the services, I had been told that collectors were behaving like tehsildars. The system has now reduced them to that status.

Some of the significant reforms undertaken by the government during the period I was Cabinet secretary included the revamping of the Foreign Exchange Regulations Act. Likewise, thanks to the initiatives of Minister Chidambaram, several changes in the Companies Act to make it more business friendly were undertaken. Another reform was attempted, to put an end to the Board of Industrial and Financial Reconstruction (BIFR). The BIFR Act had come into being a number of years earlier, essentially to provide a forum for restructuring sick industrial undertakings. While the concept was good, as the BIFR act was enacted, two fatal clauses were injected in the last minute. Whereas it was originally envisaged that the rehabilitation package should be pushed through with a strict time limit, this clause was amended at the last moment, making the process open-ended. Secondly, the financial agencies that provided the consultancy and crafted the restructuring package were not compelled to back their own recommendations with their funds. As a result, the BIFR's only purpose was to delay action. For canny businessmen it came in handy, to postpone doomsday and indefinitely stave off creditors. This is not quite the same as what Chapter 11 has achieved in the US. In the event, the BIFR, and its appellate version became comfortable berths for retired senior bureaucrats to find refuge. Other than this, they served no useful purpose. It was best to have these agencies wound up; and the recommendations for this were well advanced by the time I left my assignment.

Another body badly in need of overhaul was the administrative tribunal at the state and Central levels. I perhaps paid a price, amounting to one day of service really, for trying to disband these tribunals. Originally, it was envisaged that these agencies would have the powers of the high court, so that disputes related to government service and grievances of government servants could be settled finally at this forum. Rulings by the judiciary whittled down these powers to make the tribunals subordinate courts to the respective high courts. Again the tribunals became happy hunting grounds for retired bureaucrats and members of the judiciary. As Cabinet secretary, I conducted a review and made a proposal to do away with these tribunals. They were functioning almost on the same lines as the courts, with their elaborate, expensive and time consuming procedures. The disputes related to adverse entries in service rolls, denial of promotion, wrongful findings on departmental enquiries and other similar service matters relating to government servants. For resolving such disputes, it was quite enough to replace the tribunals with an informal dispute settlement mechanism at the level of each ministry or department. The proposed mechanism would consist of a senior retired official, who would arbitrate on the disputes between the aggrieved employees and the department. The arbitrator, without fanfare, would look at the relevant records and give his summary findings. If the employee was aggrieved with the finding, he had the full right and opportunity to appeal at the level of the high court. However, if the decision went against the department, it was bound to accept the findings – this asymmetry was introduced to reduce mindless litigation by the government. I thought this was a neat approach but again, there was no time to push this reform through by the time I left my office. It is not easy to implement simple solutions.

There was a fall out, a pin-prick really, possibly arising out of this proposal to disband these tribunals, but this pretty much bore out my own assessment of these tribunals. On the 31st of December 1997, I was to retire. However, by that time the Gujral government had fallen, and was continuing in office pending fresh general elections in February 1998, with the new prime minister scheduled to take over by mid-March 1998. Apparently, Gujral must have felt that the incoming prime minister should not be saddled with a Cabinet secretary not of his choice, and should have the opportunity to choose for himself. Hence, he refrained from naming my successor; and instead gave me an ad hoc extension of three months, as a sort of caretaker till end March 1998. This was a correct decision by Gujral in the circumstances, but I had nothing to do with it. As a matter of fact, I had given him my suggestions well in advance, in November 1997, as to who my possible successor could be, providing him with a small panel of names to select from. Imagine my surprise, when on the evening of 31st December, as I was returning home, I heard of an order passed by the Central Administrative Tribunal (CAT) in Delhi, ruling that the three months extension given to me was illegal and that I ceased to be Cabinet secretary as of 31st December 1997. I learnt later of someone's interest that had worked to get the post vacated quickly, so that he had a chance of taking over the post the next day. This is to indicate how our system is tainted even at the top levels. In the event, the personnel department decided to move the high court against the patently absurd order that was bad in law. That evening, I got a call from Ashok Desai, the attorney general, saying that he had spoken to Soli Sorabjee, the eminent lawyer who had agreed to take up the matter in the CAT next morning. On the evening of 31st December, Sorabjee called me at my residence around 8.30 pm, asking me to come to his house the next morning at 9, so that he could have a further briefing from me, prior to the matter being taken up in the court. I politely refused saying quite accurately that the order quashed by the CAT was that of the Government of India. Technically, I was not working for government at that moment and had no *locus standi* to brief him! He laughed, and told me to enjoy the freedom for a little while more. The 'dismissal' of the Cabinet secretary by CAT was well publicised in the TV and in the newspapers. The high court, later, apparently took only two minutes to set aside the order by the CAT and I was Cabinet secretary again soon. On the day of the verdict, I had a leisurely lunch, followed by a nap and when I reached the office at 3'o clock, I was surprised to see a battery of media photographers waiting to greet the new Cabinet secretary. I could not understand why, since I had been out of work just about a couple of days.

During my tenure, I again observed a significant fact which I had seen as chief secretary in Uttar Pradesh – very few, if any of the ministers had any interest in developmental matters or in economic or social transformation of India. Genuine alleviation of poverty, and upliftment of the rural masses was the last thing in their mind. I had occasion to move closely with so many ministers in the course of my career, and each one seemed to have a tunnel vision. Their interest was only in their own future in public life aside from feathering the nest. I had occasion to openly oppose the then railway minister, Ram Vilas Paswan, who blithely promoted a large number of new railway lines all over India, mostly in Bihar. He had come up with proposals for approving the construction of these lines. I pointed out that in the past twenty years, so many new railway lines had been promised that at the rate at which annual financial allocations were taking place, it would take 150 years for all the lines to be constructed! I had suggested that before new lines were proposed, the railway ministry should review and cancel the proposed routes announced earlier, so that we could come up with a practical and reasonable working list. While many other ministers silently agreed with me, this did not make me popular with Paswan. He insisted that token funds should be allocated, to enable him to make populist announcements at the various locations, promising manna from the heavens. The prime minister found a face-saving formula for him.

There was also the case of one minister who was bluntly overruling his department, to distribute favours, certainly for his own personal advantage. Even going by our low standards, I was aghast. Using an obscure provision of the rules of business, the Cabinet secretary summoned the file from the department, and wrote a note for the prime minister requesting him to formally overrule the minister, in the ministry's own file. This was a rare event indeed, and I do not know of any precedent. There were so many other episodes that had led me to wonder if the parliamentary form of democracy, in the manner that we practice it today, is resulting in the greatest good for the greatest number of people in this country. But then, what is the alternative?

There was once an administrative system in place to control crime. Politicians have injected new forces to disrupt and nearly demolish this system in the district, moffusil and village areas. There is by now a direct linkage between the ruling party in the state, local political henchmen and the police and revenue department. This has had a catastrophic effect on the management of crime and criminal administration at the sub-district level. The Government of India from Delhi may argue that law and order and criminal administration is a 'state' subject and that the states are responsible for management of these areas. This is typical of the abdication by the Centre of its duty to take responsibility for matters directly affecting the welfare of the citizen. We have seen earlier, in the case of primary education or public health or in the field of agriculture, that the Centre has washed its hands off and not taken responsibility for national failures in these areas. Law and order, and local criminal administration, constitute another such failure on the part of the Centre.

I heard with amusement the other day that the chief minister of Uttar Pradesh had stated at an internal security conference held by the home minister in Delhi that the crime rate in UP had dropped by fifty per cent in the month of December 2002. I was curious as to what magic wand was waved by the chief minister to produce these astounding results. I called the state's home secretary, in early March 2003 to find out how this astonishing success was achieved. He told me that the performance for January 2003 was even better; the crime rate had dropped by seventy per cent! When I interjected that at this rate, all crime would disappear from Uttar Pradesh, my informant laughed sarcastically. The device was very simple. If cases were not registered, there were no cases – as simple as that. So the target is not the reduction in the number of crimes committed, but in reducing the number of crimes registered. There is much to learn here about how the crime rate can be controlled.

It is said that the wheels of justice grind slowly but they grind well. Is that really so in India? It is a safe bet that in all cases where public personalities are involved, or even when no public personality is involved, the final word on the case will be delivered when most principal players and witnesses have reached heaven or hell, as the case may be. Sometime in the early 1990s, one heard that Laloo Prasad Yadav, the then chief minister of Bihar had misappropriated hundreds of crores of rupees in the fodder-scam. Nearly ten years down the road, I have not heard of any court that has pronounced him guilty. It is not as if the necessary evidence in the case has to be procured from Switzerland or Sweden or Italy or Malaysia; all the necessary evidence is presumably available in the districts of Bihar and Jharkhand. If for ten years, a man cannot be found guilty surely there should be some presumption of innocence. Jayalalitha continues as chief minister with the trials and appeals going on. I can only presume that she is innocent till proven guilty – that is the right of every citizen. But do the people not have a right to know during her tenure if the chief minister of their state is a dirty criminal or a blooming innocent rose? Why should the country be deprived of this critical information? We have reached a level of depravity where even conviction is no disgrace. Sukh Ram was found with crores of rupees stacked up in his house. True he has been convicted, and sentenced with rigorous imprisonment but then his appeals are being heard. Meanwhile, he is back on his beat, a thriving leader, jumping nimbly from one political party to another, and bringing glory to our political process.

Elected representatives say they are accountable only to the people and they will be judged at election time. They can break the law, if the purpose is 'political'. Even misappropriation is done for the benefit of the 'party'. Then, why not have a system that dispenses with the long process of criminal litigation in respect of politicians? As in the days of yore, they can merely go through the *agni pariksha* of a popular election. They will be deemed guilty if they fail to get elected and they will be declared innocent if they win. After all, India is a democracy, where the will of the people is supreme. Extending the argument further, why not have every accused tried by a committee of parliament or the state legislature. This might sound like fantasy but it is not quite so. This method may be much cheaper and may reflect the 'will' of the people accurately. Already to a large extent, this process is under implementation. The investigation phases starting from the FIR stage, are already firmly under political control. Since acquittal of the guilty in most cases is a foregone conclusion, we may as well spare the time consuming legal processes by declaring the person's innocence at the investigative phase itself, through a political trial!

I recall that when I was Cabinet secretary, I was watching the shenanigans of Biswas, a CBI officer, who was then investigating the fodder-scam. He behaved abominably, openly defied orders from his superiors in Delhi and appeared keen to grab publicity in the TV and other media. He also showed himself as the darling of the judiciary by being the 'great investigator', who was keen to get to the bottom of the truth instantly, and bring nemesis to the guilty. At that time, the high court ordered that Biswas should not be transferred even on promotion, as he was pursuing a very important investigation. If that yardstick were indeed to be applied to all investigations, no officer of CBI or any other investigating agency can ever be transferred, as he would be investigating at any time at least one 'important' case. In the event, Biswas could not dig deep enough to find the truth – after all, he was looking into a bottomless pit.

It is fashionable in India to denigrate the US legal system, based on the fact that the members of the judiciary have to declare their political affiliations. However, it cannot be said of the US that justice is denied, or that it is slow. The person accused of killing a Sikh in Arizona, in a fit of rage following the 9/11 incident was convicted in a short time. As for speed, I could refer to the litigation in the USA, in the last two months of 2000, following the casting of ballots in the presidential contest between George Bush and Al Gore, leading to declaration of the former as the winner. There were many allegations and counter allegations relating to malpractices, 'hanging chads', non-uniform procedures, and a multitude of other relevant and irrelevant issues. I happened to be in the US during that period, and followed the events closely in the media. I believe that in all there were over 300 legal actions instituted by interested parties, at different times during that period. It merely needed one day's cursory examination by the Florida Supreme Court to club all the related cases, and tackle them in one set of hearings. It was interesting to see that cases were heard on different issues at different county courts. This was a form of parallel processing. During a total period of less than one month, the matter in its different facets came up for hearing in numerous courts, and was then taken up for hearing at least twice in the Florida Supreme Court. The issues also went up to the US Supreme Court at least twice for regular arguments and for final and conclusive orders. Surely the issues and facts involved were at least as complicated as those relating to the fodder case in India. How did the US judicial system manage to tackle such a vast mass of material, issues, points of view, witnesses, and other minutiae relating to a potentially explosive subject, in such a short time? Many in India dismiss the US legal system as partisan and biased, premising their opinion essentially on the fact that judges to the state and national Supreme Courts are appointed though the political process and those at the lower courts are elected on party tickets. This is a fact, as all bureaucrats and public servants including the members of the judiciary in the US declare their political affiliations in advance. It does not naturally follow that their political leanings will influence their findings in every matter pending before them.

Even before the courts intervene in election matters, there is a mechanism in place. It was in this scenario that the various county courts, the Florida Supreme Court and the US Supreme Court heard the various issues in a time bound manner to produce remarkably effective findings in a limited time. I found out, when tracing this presidential contest that in every county in the US, which can be compared to an Indian district, there is a three-man standing committee. Going by Indian equivalents, this is chaired by the district judge, with the district collector and the district election officer being the other two members. This committee meets regularly in an open forum, and their meetings are held in public, with access to all. The clerk publicly announces every matter placed before the committee. The committee takes a majority decision. We may note that all members of the committee are registered as members of one or the other political party. However, I found that in many matters brought up to the group, the majority view did not necessarily have any relationship with the political disposition of the membership. Each member voted, based on his or her appreciation of the facts of each matter brought before the committee. Any member of the public could raise any issue with the committee, which had to be taken up in public. Those disagreeing with the committee's decision in the various counties could agitate the matter in the courts.

At the next stage, in various courts, the practice followed was simple, straightforward and effective. Whenever an action was instituted, the court clerk would give publicity to the matter through the local media, including the newspapers and on television. Then a telephonic notice would be given to the parties concerned, fixing a time period of about twenty four hours to ask that they produce their written submissions and arguments, a brief summary of the evidence and a list of persons who could provide oral testimony. Thus, if a matter was agitated before the Florida Supreme Court at noon time, say on a Wednesday, the court clerk would issue notices that the written submissions and arguments, in thirty copies, were to be submitted to the court, say by 4 pm, the next day i.e., Thursday. Presumably, the written briefs would have been circulated that very evening to the members of the bench hearing the case. The hearing would be fixed for the following day, Friday morning at 8 am. The hearing would start promptly at 8 am on Friday and conclude at 11 am. No long and dramatic speeches were permitted for the attorneys. Each party was given thirty to forty minutes to present its case, and a subsequent fifteen minutes each to make additional points or for rebuttal. The same day, immediately after the hearing concluded, the Bench would meet among themselves and a brief verdict pronounced the same evening by 4 pm, with the detailed written judgements to follow the next day. One could see that despite the declared political affiliation of the various judges, each one took an independent view on each matter, not necessarily on a partisan basis. No excuses were accepted about non-availability of witnesses or that the attorney was busy elsewhere. At the hearing itself, sharp pointed queries were asked to elicit responses on the various nuances. The complex set of issues were all taken up; witnesses heard, clarifications asked and given, arguments pressed up and down – and astonishingly, a final verdict reached on a complex, emotive, sensitive and vital matter on schedule.

One footnote to the Bush-Gore legal episode. After the verdict, I never saw public demonstrations or agitations or riots in USA, despite the fact that the issue was highly emotive and sensitive and divided the country, with sharply differing opinions. The American public knew that the final verdict of the Supreme Court was the end of the matter. There could be no argument or dispute thereafter. No greater testimony to the rule of law prevailing in the USA is required, than a recapitulation of the Gore-Bush court battles of the year 2000. It is another matter that many people feel that the courts allowed the wrong man to win! Imagine if a similar circumstance arose in India!

I believe that the concept of contempt of court as applied in India, needs to be reviewed. While frivolous and trivial charges against the courts cannot be countenanced, one ought to have the right to disagree with the findings of the judicial process. It is in this context that one could refer to the stand taken by Arundhati Roy in the case of the contempt charge against her. Frankly, I do not care much for her writings nor of her award-winning book, nor even approve of the social cause she espoused in a manner that elicited the wrath of the Supreme Court. But I did appreciate the stand she took in the Supreme Court and her right to say what she did. We will fool ourselves if we wish to protect the judiciary from all criticism, treating it with kid gloves. Truth should be adequate and valid defence in any matter relating to contempt of court, and the people's right to express themselves.

Authors of Indian origin writing in English, have to be discovered in New York or London – a Booker stamp of approval is essential before the author can get a foothold in India. This is well in keeping with the Indian tradition of recognising indigenous quality only after the stamp of approval is available from abroad. Thus, we needed a Max Muller to unlock our own cultural and literary treasures in India. It needed a Curzon to point out to us the grandeur of our architectural traditions. Ramana Maharishi had to be discovered by Paul Brunton. In fact, it required a psuedo-intellectual rendering of the Gita by Dr. Radhakrishnan, for this immortal work to be fully recognised in India by the intelligentsia. I recall that in the '70s, I made several efforts to get hold of Sant Gyaneshwar's rendering of the Gita, in the English language. After searching many bookshops in India, I finally located a copy in Bombay and discovered that UNESCO sponsored it! Incidentally, with great delight and the thrill of discovery, I recently went through the Tamil version of Gyaneshwari – sponsored of course by a group of people from Singapore – to enjoy its great spiritual and literary quality. The wonderful creation of Gyaneshwar was originally in the Marathi language – I envy those who can follow the language well. I have digressed in making my point that we need to revisit the concept of contempt of court.

The dichotomy between precept and practice in our public affairs – is it accidental? Is the deviation between what is said and the real purpose just a coincidence? I was once willing to give the benefit of doubt. No more do

I hold this view. Having seen the working of governmental processes from inside, I know that we in government have become pathologically unable to speak the truth as we see it, but need to put a spin on every event or every occurrence. On countless occasions, I have seen efforts by the ministers in response to even starred parliamentary questions to hide the essentials of any situation, disclose only whatever is absolute minimally acceptable, deny any wrong doing of any sort, and generally make sure that the true picture does not emerge. The way the government of the day has never accepted in parliament any failure, however trivial, would suggest that we have had, over the past fifty years, the most successful administration anywhere in the world. We are hiding from ourselves.

Again, public servants have been ever willing to turn themselves to become private servants. Increasingly, the attitude of new entrants to various public services is to see what they can extract from the system – not what they can contribute. Many of our leaders who got us freedom belonged to a category of eminent lawyers and doctors who deliberately left their lucrative vocations and came into public life, with a sense of purpose. Till the 1970s, a number of entrants to the public services were bright young men from universities who entered the civil services with genuine intentions to contribute, coupled with expectations of a reasonably good standard of living. Those days are long gone by. In my four decades of public service, I have come across thousands of politicians, small and large, operating at the district or village or state or national level. I have worked closely with hundreds of them in one context or another. I am saddened to say that I have come across only a handful of honest politicians. Politicians in power seek out corrupt officers and ask them to be collaborators, for mutual benefit. That many corrupt officers exist is also in no doubt. This tribe is increasing alarmingly in strength. In the UP of the 1980s, one could think of say five rotten eggs, in an IAS cadre of 400. Today, that number has increased by tragic proportions, though it is a bit better still than the condition in many other class I services. If the malignancy in the IAS is yet at a primary stage, it has reached the secondary stage in some other services.

Even if the vast proportion of civil servants in the higher civil services are not corrupt in the financial sense, several have exhibited intellectual dishonesty of a high order. Whenever they sniff a tainted request or issue, they quickly withdraw and sideline themselves, allowing the operators to have their own way. I recall that one of our ministers would quickly find a way to travel out, when given notice of a difficult issue soon to come up before the Cabinet. He wished to avoid being part of a controversial decision. I recall with amusement the plight of his personal staff, desperately trying to locate a destination abroad where he could be officially received at short notice. Metaphorically, most civil servants follow this route, when confronted with any issue of importance. They find ways of not tackling the matter or not having to express an opinion on the subject, and find avenues for avoiding agreement or disagreement with any proposed action. The brighter amongst these usually rise to the top, and find cushy berths in the upper reaches of the central administration. Their ultimate aim is to find an international assignment, and leave the country for good.

Officers who are not corrupt, often go out of their way to endear themselves to their minister. Civil servants collaborate with their political masters to curry favour with them. The relationship is not at arm's length. Officials wish to be in the good books of ministers, with an eye on a good annual entry or a prestigious posting in India, or abroad. They can also ask for petty favours. Shrewd as he is, what the minister does is to gradually break in the pliant official, taking him through his paces. There is a steady increase in the number of obligations sought by the minister and the intensity of departure from the norms. The official is fully exploited. Then, after the official has been fully used, he is suddenly dropped. He is no longer in favour as other officials are found to do the biddings. I have watched innumerable officials compromise themselves and bend over backwards to oblige their political master, only to be unceremoniously cast aside. I have seen it a hundred times. I could even predict, to the day, when the minister would suddenly not even recognise the official, who had hitherto sold his soul to enable the minister get his way. It is usually a pathetic sight.

It is not as if the category of honest and forthright civil servant does not exist, but they are being side-lined. Some officers do not hesitate to stand upright and express their views without fear or favour, never mind that a few untimely transfers or even some enquiries come their way. There was a time when some of the abler and brighter ones in this category would get the opportunity for promotion in the state and also at the Centre. In today's administrative conditions, my judgement is that such types no longer stand even a slim a chance to climb the administrative ladder. The rot has set in and has become irreversible: the steel frame is corroded, and is in danger of collapse.

This could leave the impression that most members of the civil service are indolent, indifferent, unmotivated, and are mere passengers. But I need to correct that impression and stop short of such a sweeping generalisation. At all levels of administration, one does find brilliant and outstanding young people; motivated, dedicated, and imbued with a spirit of service. I have had the chance to work with many such people. The civil services can be proud of officers such as Rajeeva Kumar, who was my staff officer when I was chief secretary in UP, B P Sharma who was my deputy secretary in the Cabinet secretariat and thousands of such people, who are dedicated to their work, self-effacing and not seeking the limelight. What contribution the Indian administration might have made is indeed thanks to such people. These are the best available anywhere in the world, in public or private service. Indeed, many are not allowed to perform and this is a failure of the system and no fault of such officers themselves.

Another systemic failure is the undue importance given to postings in the economic ministries. The impression has gained ground that these are more important desks and thus such postings are coveted. This is wrong, since in the government, all departments serve the public and so are of equal importance. The present culture is that civil servants are obsessed with the need to have postings of their choice and they are willing to go to any extent in search of these. Further, Delhi is a draw. An unseemly glamour is attached to certain posts in the economic ministries in Delhi, unrelated to the contribution that the officer can make to policy formulation and implementation. There are similar positions of equal importance in the state governments. Officers get a false sense of importance when industrialists and the business community fall at their feet to extract concessions, and this leads to a false sense of values. Several examples illustrate this point.

In the early 1990s, a colleague of mine almost broke down when he was posted as secretary, in the statistics department in Delhi. My comment that this was a major opportunity to revamp the systems and bring in modern technologies to upgrade the quality of data available in India was no consolation. However, a year later I found that he was delighted with his assignment. He told me gleefully that he was busy with so many international conferences and seminars that he was able to go abroad nearly all the time, merely visiting home to get his laundry done. As Cabinet secretary, I assigned a bright officer to a post at the secretary level in Delhi to deal with NGOs. With the increasing role sought for NGOs in the development process, this was an excellent opportunity to revamp the entire structure. The role of good domestic and foreign NGOs could be enhanced with the bad eggs – the superficial NGOs functioning largely for the social climbing of their founders – weeded out. I expected him to make an important contribution but when I met him after a couple of months, I was distressed to see that he was treating his assignment with contempt. He was bitterly disappointed not to be fitted in any 'economic' ministry. Recently, I came across a bright officer who was posted as the secretary in the ministry for culture in the Government of India. India and China, as the oldest civilizations are treasure houses of ancient culture and wisdom, manifested in every conceivable art form – architecture, music, literature, and fine arts. There is a need to protect, publicise, broadcast, and display our culture, our heritage. The opportunity to preserve, interpret, and to disseminate our ancient wisdom from this post is unlimited. India offers unlimited scope to encourage our scholars, authors and publishers to rediscover our past, to bring new perspectives to our present and share these ancient treasures with the whole world. As I have said earlier, it is in fact the foreigners who have assumed this role to a large extent. I thought a civil servant would have considered this opportunity at the end of his career as a gift from the heavens. I was astounded to see him grumbling disconsolately about his luck that he had been ignored for a posting in an economic ministry. Has 'something happened' to our civil servants, though seemingly normal, that they have lost their sense of balance?

The average civil servant looks at a file as a piece of paper, on which he has to write and express his views, without compromising his own position. It is of little concern to the civil servant, whether issues raised in the file get settled or not and if so, in what time frame. He sees no immediacy. Key concerns that engage his attention relate to his transfers and promotions. However, the minister sees the file from an entirely different perspective. For him, each file represents a potential gold mine: the file has to be nursed carefully, and brought up to a position where it can yield maximum benefits. For him also, time is not of the essence. However, timing is important as the yields from the file will depend on how and when the decision is timed. The games that are played have infinite variety, great ingenuity and are lucrative. In such a scenario, how can public interest be served?

Ministers take lightly their oath of office. I have been present at a number of occasions to witness the swearing-in of ministers. Not many would have noticed that the oath taken by the minister is in two parts – the first part refers to his allegiance to the Constitution. It is the second part of the oath that requires attention. This oath affirms that on each official matter the minister will not share any information received by him in the course of his official work with anyone not directly concerned, nor will he disclose any official information unless such sharing or disclosure of information is essential for the discharge of the official work he is entrusted with. I wish to be given one rupee, each time this oath is violated by a minister. I would soon be the richest man in India. I have repeatedly seen ministers disclose details of official matters even on sensitive issues, to their benefactors. Many ministers routinely show the noting of the secretariat or the secretary, opposing a particular proposal to the private party directly concerned. It is amazing how private businessmen get to know of what the secretariat and the secretary himself have written, to the minutest detail. And then, it would come as no surprise to see the minister's rebuttal note, obligingly drafted by the interested party. Even a cursory glance at the papers would reveal this. The extent of detail, finesse in argument and command over the technical aspects evidenced in the minister's orders would be startlingly high, with no loopholes to pick.

The rule of law is of no value unless every citizen is aware of his rights and obligations. In most rural areas, we are indeed ruled by the greasy hand of the local politician, local policeman and the patwari in tow. In urban areas, most people with money think that they are above the law. As I travel in my car from my residence to the Golf Club in central Delhi, a drive that takes twenty minutes, I keep looking out for violations of traffic laws. These are mostly minor in nature. The offenders appear well educated, from the middle and upper middle class. They have scant regard for traffic laws. We have seen that no politician feels that the law applies to him, and as long as he is in power, he is immune from the reach of the law. One of my golfing colleagues, a businessman, is quite bemused at the occasional anger displayed by me at the spread of corruption in India. He does not understand how an even-tempered person like me can get worked up on a simple matter like a bribe. He says with conviction that the person who pays the bribe gets his work done, and the receiver of the bribe is satisfied; why should it bother anyone else? Why should anyone unnecessarily get worked up over something that makes things move in India? After all, the bribe keeps the economy moving efficiently. To paraphrase in an economist's language, corruption is merely a transfer payment, not affecting a nation's wealth or GDP and so we may summarily dismiss it as an issue not of great importance. I cannot bring myself to explain to my golfing friend or the economist the complex linkages between corruption, political thuggery, mal-administration and lack of governance, illiteracy, and poverty. The common thread is a notion called the 'rule of law'.

Finally, if one were to summarise the essence of all that I have seen in the course of my career, it is ironic that these could take shape in the form of four laws that govern public affairs in India. Indeed, it might well be that these are timeless and universal laws of public administration. The laws are as follows:

1 *Administration is conducted for the benefit of the administrators.*

2 *In a conflict between private interest and public interest, the former shall prevail.*

3 *The country belongs to the haves and the have nots do not exist.*

4 *A public servant's work output and rewards are inversely related.*

EPILOGUE

AND THEN, ONE DAY, HE TOOK OVER THE REINS of administration. He threw away his false whiskers and at last, the country was blessed with a genuine leader. He started a drastic overhaul of the existing order. With vision and acumen he started ringing the changes in, and soon enough every part of this great country was humming with activity. He made it clear that politicians had no part to play in day-to-day administration; politicians from village level to national level were told that they had no authority to meddle in administration.

Half of the government budget was diverted to programmes designed to bring sustained benefits to the poorest half of the population. A quarter of the budget was focused on physical infrastructure. International funds started pouring in to support Indian infrastructure, on terms that provided reasonable returns to investors while safeguarding the country's basic interests. Money was available to meet all genuine developmental needs.

Bureaucracy was cut down to one third of its present size. Fifty key positions were identified in the Central government and talented young men and women were identified to fill in these slots. They were given ten year contracts, with the mandate to conceive, plan, implement and show success on the ground, in their identified fields. They were assured of resources, freedom of action, with no interference in the discharge of their duties. Gradually, all government servants were made accountable for results. A system of punishment and rewards spurred the official class into right action. A new meaning emerged for the expression 'Rule of Law'. Education and employment generation became key areas of attention. Education up to high school became a reality for all. Higher education also became free at all levels but was permitted only on merit.

Indian entrepreneurs found new avenues to expand their energies; at the same time, violation of laws and regulations resulted in punishment. The country's energies had been released. In ten years, there was a dramatic transformation of the country, under the leader – who achieved all these within the framework of democracy, with the full backing of the people. By 2020, India had become a developed country!

...Just at that time, the setting rays of the evening sun slanted into my bedroom, through the curtains. I woke up with a start...

LIST OF ACRONYMS

G-77	–	Group of 77
ADB	–	Asian Development Bank
APC	–	Agriculture Production Commissioner
BIFR	–	Board of Industrial and Financial Reconstruction
BJP	–	Bharatiya Janata Party
BSP	–	Bahujan Samaj Party
CAT	–	Central Administrative Tribunal
CBI	–	Central Bureau of Investigation
CDRI	–	Central Drug Research Institute
CFTRI	–	Central Food Technology Research Institute
CSTRI	–	Central Silk Technological Research Institute
CID	–	Criminal Investigation Department
CLRI	–	Central Leather Research Institute
COFEPOSA	–	Conservation of Foreign Exchange and Prevention of Smuggling Activities Act 1974
CPWD	–	Central Public Works Department
DGTD	–	Director General of Trade and Development
DIG	–	Deputy Inspector General
EIA	–	Export Inspection Agency
ESCAP	–	Economic and Social Commission of Asia and the Pacific

FERA   – Foreign Exchange Regulations Act

GATT   – General Agreement on Tariffs and Trade
GDP   – Gross Domestic Product
GTR   – Grand Trunk Road

IAS   – Indian Administrative Service
ICS   – Indian Civil Service
IIFT   – Indian Institute of Foreign Trade
ILO   – International Labour Organisation
IMF   – International Monetary Fund
ISI   – Indian Standards Institution
ITC   – International Trade Centre
ITU   – International Telecommunications Union

LIFMA   – Leather Importers Factors' Merchants Association
LC   – Letter of Credit
LDC   – Least Developed Countries

MISA   – Maintenance of Internal Security Act, 1971
MLA   – Member of Legislative Assembly
MP   – Member of Parliament
MTNL   – Mahanagar Telephone Limited

NAM   – Non-Aligned Movement
NGO   – Non-Governmental Organisation
NIFT   – National Institute of Fashion Technology
NTC   – National Textile Corporation

PCS   – Provincial Civil Service
PMO   – Prime Minister's Office
POTO   – Prevention of Terrorism Ordinance
PWD   – Public Works Department

RBI   – Reserve Bank of India

SP   – Samajwadi Party
STC   – State Trading Corporation

TADA   – Terrorist and Disruptive Activities (Prevention) Act
TIE   – The Indus Entrepreneurs
TRAI   – Telecom Regulatory Authority of India

UN   – United Nations
UNCTAD   – United Nations Conference on Trade and Development
UNDP   – United Nations Development Programme
UNIDO   – United Nations Industrial Development Organisation
UPSC   – Union Public Service Commission
USTR   – US Trade Representative

VSNL   – Videsh Sanchar Nigam Limited
VRS   – Voluntary Retirement Scheme

WIPO   – World Intellectual Property Organisation
WTO   – World Trade Organisation

INDEX